A·N·N·U·A·L E·D·I·T·I·O·N·S

World History Volume I

Sixth Edition

Prehistory to 1500

EDITOR

David McComb
Colorado State University

David McComb received his Ph.D. from the University of Texas at Austin and is currently a professor of history at Colorado State University. Dr. McComb has written 8 books and over 100 articles and book reviews, and he teaches courses in the history of the United States, sports, and the world. He has traveled twice around the world as a Semester at Sea faculty member of the University of Pittsburgh, and he has spent additional time in India and Mexico. Currently, he is a member of the executive council of the World History Association.

Dushkin/McGraw-Hill
Sluice Dock, Guilford, Connecticut 06437

Visit us on the Internet
http://www.dushkin.com/annualeditions/

Credits

1. Natural History and the Spread of Humankind
Overview photo—© 1999 PhotoDisc, Inc. 8-9—*Scientific American* graphic by David Starwood. 10-11—*Scientific American* graphic by Patricia J. Wynne. 24—Map by Nenad Jakesevic © 1998 by Discover magazine.

2. The Beginnings of Culture, Agriculture, and Cities
Overview photo—WHO photo. 52-53—Illustration by Laszlo Kubinyi.

3. The Early Civilizations to 500 B.C.E.
Overview photo—United Nations photo #88320.

4. The Later Civiliations to 500 C.E.
Overview photo—United Nations photo #134459.

5. The Great Religions
Overview photo—Courtesy of Brian Spykerman. 119—Illustration from The Metropolitan Museum of Art, Gift of Alexander Smith Cochran, 1913. 120—Illustration from The Metropolitan Museum of Art, Rogers Fund, 1938. 123—Illustration courtesy of the Arthur M. Sackler Gallery, Smithsonian Institution, Washington, DC. Iran painting from ca. 1550, double-page Illuminated frontispiece from a Koran. 124—Illustration courtesy of the Arthur M. Sackler Gallery, Smithsonian Institutiion, Washington, DC. Iraq painting from a copy of the *Materia medica* of Pedanius Dioscorides, A.H. Rajab 621. 125—Illustration from The Metropolitan Museum of Art, The Theodore M. Davis Collection, Bequest of Theodore M. Davis, 1915.

6. The World of the Middle Ages, 500–1500
Overview photo—WHO photo. 171—The British Library. 184—Illustration from *The Cyclopaedia of Arts, Sciences, and Literature* by Abraham Rees, London, 1920. 185-186—Illustrations courtesy of Bodleian Library Film Strip Service, Oxford. 187—Illustration courtesy of Biliotheque Nationale, Lisbon. 189—Mansell Collection Library.

7. 1500: The Era of Global Explorations
Overview photo—Courtesy of the Library of Congress. 201, 204—Illustrations from the Granger Collection, New York. 205—Reproductions from the collection of the Library of Congress.

Cataloging in Publication Data
Main entry under title: Annual Editions: World history, vol. I: Prehistory to 1500. 6/E.
    1. World history—Periodicals. 2. Civilization, Modern—Periodicals. 3. Social problems—Periodicals. I. McComb, David, *comp.* II. Title: World history, vol. I: Prehistory to 1500.
905   ISBN 0–07–233948–9   90–656260   ISSN 1054–2779

© 2000 by Dushkin/McGraw-Hill, Guilford, CT 06437, A Division of The McGraw-Hill Companies.

Sixth Edition

Cover: Statues of Ramses II in front of the main temple of Abu Simbel on the Nile River in Egypt. © 1999 PhotoDisc, Inc.

Printed in the United States of America   1234567890BAHBAH543210   Printed on Recycled Paper

iii

In publishing ANNUAL EDITIONS we recognize the enormous role played by the magazines, newspapers, and journals of the public press in providing current, first-rate educational information in a broad spectrum of interest areas. Many of these articles are appropriate for students, researchers, and professionals seeking accurate, current material to help bridge the gap between principles and theories and the real world. These articles, however, become more useful for study when those of lasting value are carefully collected, organized, indexed, and reproduced in a low-cost format, which provides easy and permanent access when the material is needed. That is the role played by ANNUAL EDITIONS.

New to ANNUAL EDITIONS is the inclusion of related World Wide Web sites. These sites have been selected by our editorial staff to represent some of the best resources found on the World Wide Web today. Through our carefully developed topic guide, we have linked these Web resources to the articles covered in this ANNUAL EDITIONS reader. We think that you will find this volume useful, and we hope that you will take a moment to visit us on the Web at **http://www.dushkin.com** to tell us what you think.

International events crowd the front pages of modern newspapers and television news broadcasts. Increasingly, the U.S. government and its citizens are caught up in a daily vortex of concerns such as exported terrorism, peacekeeping missions, nuclear proliferation, outbreaks of viral disease, illegal immigration, and environmental degradation. It has become impossible to comprehend even local newspapers without a knowledge of the world, and responsible citizenship now requires broad knowledge in order to act and vote intelligently for the welfare of the individual, the nation, and the planet. Educators, in recognition of the importance of global events, have responded by making world history courses, along with United States history classes, a central curriculum feature in the secondary schools. In addition, since the early 1980s world history courses have spread through higher education, and the first generation of world history scholars has emerged. The *Journal of World History,* a marking point of academic interest in the field, is now 10 years old.

The organizational problems in world history include the traditional difficulties of scope and relevance. What should be included and what may be left out? How can diverse material be arranged to make sense of the past? In all history courses, choices must be made, particularly in the surveys. No one learns all about each country of Europe (in a survey of Western Civilization) or all about each state (in a survey of the United States) with the hope that such details add up to a comprehensible story. Instead, there is an emphasis upon ideas, technology, turning points, significant people, movements, and chronology. Efforts are made by historians and teachers to place events in perspective in order to demonstrate cause and effect, and to focus upon what is important.

World history is no exception but the range of choices is greater. There are simply more people, places, and events in the history of the world. There is more material, and thus world history courses demand the broadest level of abstraction from teachers and students. A few historians have even enlarged their scope to teach "big history," a one-semester course that covers the beginning of the universe to the present time on Earth. World historians, however, generally focus upon civilizations, cultures, global economic systems, and international relationships. Often they attempt cross-cultural comparisons and struggle with particular historiographical problems.

Probably the most difficult question involves periodization—how to subdivide history into meaningful time spans. In Western Civilization courses the division of ancient, medieval, and modern works nicely. In world history, however, this division does not fit so neatly because civilizations have evolved at different rates. The development of medieval Europe makes little sense for Asia, the Middle East, Africa, or the Americas. World historians, however, have reached some grumbling consensus about the following: the two most important technological events in human history are the invention of agriculture and the industrial revolution; the thousand years before Columbus are significant because of the rise of Islam, the development of Eurasian trading routes, the evolution of civilizations in the Western Hemisphere, and the power of China; and 1500 C.E. is a practical dividing point for two-semester classes because of European explorations and their global consequences.

In this volume, I use a periodization of early civilizations to 500 B.C.E., later civilizations to 500 C.E., and the world from 500 C.E. to 1500 C.E. This is fairly traditional, but there are additional units on natural history and the spread of humankind, the great religions, and exploration. Within the broad units can be found information about women, technology, the family, historiography, urbanization, sports, and other subjects. Since the development of Western civilization is a part of world history, Western topics are also included. The *topic guide* is a useful index for this varied information. This edition of *Annual Editions: World History, Volume 1* also contains World Wide Web sites that are cross-referenced by number in the topic guide and that can be hot-linked through the *Annual Editions* home page: *http://www.dushkin.com/annualeditions.*

The articles were selected for readability, accuracy, relevance, interest, and freshness. They are meant to supplement a course, to provide depth, and to add spice and spark. The articles do not cover everything; that is, of course, impossible. Sometimes older selections have been included to provide balance when nothing current is available. You may know of other articles that would do a better job. If so, please return the prepaid article rating form at the back of this book with your suggestions. Thank you.

David McComb

David McComb
Editor

Contents

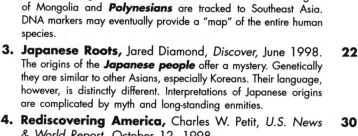

UNIT 1

Natural History and the Spread of Humankind

Four articles discuss how Earth
may have come to be and what
impact the environment had on the
shaping of early human society.

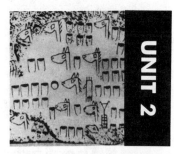

UNIT 2

The Beginnings of Culture, Agriculture, and Cities

Six selections examine early mile-
stones in the history of humankind: the
origin of writing, the beginnings of
agriculture, and urbanization.

The concepts in bold italics are developed in the article. For further expansion please refer to the Topic Guide and the Index.

UNIT 3

The Early Civilizations to 500 B.C.E.

Five articles consider the growing
diversity of human life as civilization
evolved in the ancient world.

The concepts in bold italics are developed in the article. For further expansion please refer to the Topic Guide and the Index.

UNIT 4

The Later Civilizations to 500 C.E.

Five articles discuss some of the dynamics of culture in the New World, Egypt, and Greece.

The concepts in bold italics are developed in the article. For further expansion please refer to the Topic Guide and the Index.

vii

UNIT 5

The Great Religions

Nine articles discuss the beginnings of the world's great religions, including Judaism, Christianity, Islam, Hinduism, and Buddhism.

The concepts in bold italics are developed in the article. For further expansion please refer to the Topic Guide and the Index.

UNIT 6

The World of the Middle Ages, 500–1500

Seven selections examine
the development of world
cultures during this period: in the
Western Hemisphere, flourishing
Mesoamerican cities; in the
West, feudalism and the growth
of the nation-state; in the East, the
golden age of peak development.

The concepts in bold italics are developed in the article. For further expansion please refer to the Topic Guide and the Index.

The concepts in bold italics are developed in the article. For further expansion please refer to the Topic Guide and the Index.

Overview   **192**

UNIT 7

1500: The Era of Global Explorations

Five articles examine the enormous
global impact of the voyages of
discovery, essentially by the Europeans.

The concepts in bold italics are developed in the article. For further expansion please refer to the Topic Guide and the Index.

This topic guide suggests how the selections and World Wide Web sites found in the next section of this book relate to topics of traditional concern to world history students and professionals. It is useful for locating interrelated articles and Web sites for reading and research. The guide is arranged alphabetically according to topic.

The relevant Web sites, which are numbered and annotated on pages 4 and 5, are easily identified by the Web icon (⊙) under the topic articles. By linking the articles and the Web sites by topic, this ANNUAL EDITIONS reader becomes a powerful learning and research tool.

TOPIC AREA	TREATED IN	TOPIC AREA	TREATED IN
Africa	15. Out of Africa		35. Making of Magna Carta
	19. Cleopatra		36. Clocks: Revolution in Time
	34. Islamic Legacy of Timbuktu		37. Images of Earth in the Year 1000
	⊙ **4, 5, 6, 16, 21, 22, 23**		40. Taste of Adventure
Agriculture	5. New Clues Show Where People Made the Great Leap to Agriculture		41. After Dire Straits
			⊙ **1, 2, 3, 4, 9, 10, 14, 20, 21, 24, 25, 31, 34, 35, 36**
	14. Empires in the Dust	**Geography**	1. Evolution of Life on the Earth
	40. Taste of Adventure		2. Mapping the Past
	⊙ **1, 2, 5, 9, 18**		3. Japanese Roots
Americas	4. Rediscovering America		4. Rediscovering America
	8. Tale of Two Cultures		8. Tale of Two Cultures
	9. City of the Gods		37. Images of Earth in the Year 1000
	16. Tiny Sacrifices at 22,000 Feet		38. Columbus and the Labyrinth of History
	30. Cracking the Maya's Code		40. Taste of Adventure
	38. Columbus and the Labyrinth of History		41. After Dire Straits
	39. How Many People Were Here before Columbus?		⊙ **1, 2, 5, 9, 10, 21, 32, 35, 36**
	⊙ **15, 18, 32, 33, 35, 36**		
Asian Civilization	3. Japanese Roots	**Greek Civilization**	17. In Classical Athens
	8. Tale of Two Cultures		18. Old Sports
	22. Buddha in the Round		⊙ **20, 21**
	29. Confucius	**Hinduism**	21. Ancient Jewel
	⊙ **5, 6, 11, 15, 16, 19, 21, 26, 27, 30**		⊙ **30**
Buddhism	21. Ancient Jewel	**Historiography**	23. What Is the Koran?
	22. Buddha in the Round		26. Reason God Tested Abraham
	⊙ **28, 30**		29. Confucius
Christianity	27. 2000 Years of Jesus		38. Columbus and the Labyrinth of History
	28. Live Longer, Healthier, & Better	**Indian Civilization**	11. Indus Valley, Inc.
	⊙ **28, 29**		21. Ancient Jewel
Economics	10. Cradle of Cash		⊙ **6, 21, 30**
	14. Empires in the Dust	**Islamic Civilization**	23. What Is the Koran?
	31. Islamic Legacy of Timbuktu		24. State and Society under Islam
	40. Taste of Adventure		25. Dome of the Rock
	⊙ **9, 21, 34, 35, 36**		31. Islamic Legacy of Timbuktu
Egyptian Civilization	15. Out of Africa		32. Arab Roots of European Medicine
	18. Old Sports		⊙ **21, 27, 28, 30**
	19. Cleopatra	**Judaism**	26. Reason God Tested Abraham
	⊙ **22, 23**		⊙ **29**
Environment	1. Evolution of Life on the Earth	**Middle East**	5. New Clues Show Where People Made the Great Leap to Agriculture
	4. Rediscovering America		
	14. Empires in the Dust		6. New Dig at a 9,000-Year-Old City
	28. Live Longer, Healthier, & Better		7. When No One Read
	39. How Many People Were Here before Columbus?		10. Cradle of Cash
	⊙ **12, 35**		12. Saving Knossos
Europe	17. In Classical Athens		13. Five Ways to Conquer a City
	18. Old Sports		14. Empires in the Dust
	19. Cleopatra		18. Old Sports
	32. Arab Roots of European Medicine		19. Cleopatra
	33. Viking Longship		23. What Is the Koran?
	34. Persistence of Byzantium		

2

◉ AE: World History, Volume I

The following World Wide Web sites have been carefully researched and selected to support the articles found in this reader. If you are interested in learning more about specific topics found in this book, these Web sites are a good place to start. The sites are cross-referenced by number and appear in the topic guide on the previous two pages. Also, you can link to these Web sites through our DUSHKIN ONLINE support site at *http://www.dushkin.com/online/*.

The following sites were available at the time of publication. Visit our Web site—we update DUSHKIN ONLINE regularly to reflect any changes.

General Sites

1. Gateway to World History
http://www.hartford-hwp.com/gateway/index.html
One section of this collection of resources is an organized tree of history-related links to online resources. Another section searches world history archives. The site also includes a search engine.

2. The Historical Text Archive
http://www.geocities.com/Athens/Forum/9061/index.html
This award-winning site contains links to world history, regional or national, and topical history and resources. For speed, use the text version.

3. History of Science, Technology, and Medicine
http://www.asap.unimelb.edu.au/hstm/
A database of information on science, technology, and medicine with alphabetical listing of resources, the site has search features and multiple links.

4. Hyperhistory on Line
http://www.hyperhistory.com
At this Web site, click on "hyperhistory" and navigate through 3,000 years of world history. Links to important historical persons, events, and maps are also here.

5. The History Index
http://www.ukans.edu/history/
Here you'll find an immense collection of links (4,000) to sites devoted to different aspects and periods of history, for example, Prehistory, Ancient Egypt, Ancient Greece, Archaeology, Byzantine Empire, Maritime History, Military History, Women's, Medieval, Renaissance, and many more.

6. International Network Information Systems at University of Texas
http://inic.utexas.edu
This gateway has pointers to international study sites for Africa, India, China, Japan, and many other countries.

7. National Humanities Institute Home Page
http://www.nhumanities.org
This Web site includes philosophical, cultural, and historical worldwide links, including archives, history sites, and an electronic library of full texts and documents, which is useful for research in history and the humanities.

8. WWW Virtual Library—Humanities
http://www.hum.gu.se/w3vl/VL.html
This main subject index leads to many humanities-related research subjects, many of which relate to historical studies.

9. Yahoo's History Search Engine
http://www.yahoo.com/Arts/Humanities/History/
Yahoo's history search engine has links to ancient history, archaeology, the seventeenth through the twentieth centuries, religions, and specific topics such as military and maritime history, economic history, women's history, and much more.

There is a direct link to "Eurodocs: Primary Historical Documents from Western Europe."

Natural History and the Spread of Humankind

10. The Ancient World
http://www.omnibusol.com/ancient.html
The first part of this online book, *The Amazing Ancient World of Western Civilization*, begins with the dinosaurs and moves to Stonehenge.

11. ARCHNET:WWW Virtual Library—Archaeology
http://www.lib.uconn.edu/ArchNet/
This archaeological Web site, with many links to other sites, is reached by geographic region or subject area. The site includes a search mechanism and up-to-date news.

12. The Origin and Evolution of Life
http://cmex-www.arc.nasa.gov/VikingCD/Puzzle/EvoLife.htm
This site contains NASA's Planetary Biology Program, which is chartered to investigate the origin and evolution of life.

13. Talk-Origins
http://www.talkorigins.org
This is the site of a newsgroup devoted to debate on the biological and physical origins of the world. Many articles are archived here and there are links to other Web sites. Be sure to click on "The Origin of Humankind," a comprehensive source for students of human evolution, which has the latest news about new discoveries, a link to an exhibition of human prehistory, and links to many other related sights, including Yahoo's creation/evolution material.

14. WWW-VL Prehistoric Web Index
http://easyweb.easynet.co.uk/~aburnham/database/index.htm
This site is an index to prehistoric, megalithic, and ancient sites in Europe.

Beginnings of Culture, Agriculture, and Cities

15. Ancient World Web
http://www.julen.net/ancient/Language_and_Literature/
Early language is explored at this fascinating Web site, which includes Akkadian, Ogham (Celtic/Irish), Mesoamerican writing systems, ancient Berber script, and even 5500-year-old pottery shards found at Harappa in Pakistan.

16. Assyria-on-Line
http://www.aina.org/aol/
All there is to know about ancient Assyria, including the epic of Gilgamesh and Hammurabi's Code, can be found at this Web site.

17. Diotima: Women and Gender in the Ancient World
http://www.uky.edu/ArtsSciences/Classics/gender.html
Historical information about women in the ancient world is available at this site, which also includes search possibilities.

18. Civilization of the Olmec
http://loki.stockton.edu/~gilmorew/consorti/1bcenso.htm
Robert Knaak is the curator of this complete Olmec site, which includes history and origins, achievements, and archaeological sites of this "hearth culture" of Central America, whose traditions have carried over through the centuries.

19. Oriental Institute
http://www-oi.uchicago.edu/OI/DEPT/RA/ABZU/
Click on "ABZU.htm" in the index of the University of Chicago's Oriental Institute for information about ancient Near East archaeology and a bibliographic reference on women in the areas covered.

The Early Civilizations to 500 B.C.E.

20. Ancient City of Athens
http://www.indiana.edu/~kglowack/Athens/
Look in the Index for images of ancient Athens as well as insights into Greek history and links to other Greek historical sites.

21. Exploring Ancient World Cultures
http://eawc.evansville.edu
Eight ancient world cultures can be explored from this starting point. They include Ancient China, Egypt, India, Greece, Rome, Near East, Early Islam, and Medieval Europe.

22. Reeder's Egypt Page
http://www.sirius.com/~reeder/
Click on the tomb opening to reveal a wealth of historical and archaeological information about Egypt, including a tour of the tombs of Niankhkhnum and Khnumhotep.

The Later Civilizations to 500 C.E.

23. The Institute of Egyptian Art and Archaeology
http://www.memphis.edu/egypt/main.html
This site offers an exhibit of artifacts, a color tour of Egypt, and links to other Web sites about Egypt.

24. ROMARCH—Roman Art and Archaeology
http://www.stanford.edu/~pfoss/2romarch.html
This resource is the original Roman index and link to over 175 sites. It is also an Internet discussion group of over 450 professionals and laypersons worldwide.

25. World of Late Antiquity
http://ccat.sas.upenn.edu/jod/
Click on "World of Late Antiquity" in the left side panel for interesting documents, many concerning military history, about late Roman and early medieval times.

The Great Religions

26. Kong Fu Zi—Confucius
http://www.albany.net/~geenius/kongfuzi/
Here is a major Web site on Confucius, which includes a biography, an overview of Confucius's teachings, a bibliography, and Web links put together by Keith Ammann.

27. Islam Page
http://www.geocities.com/Athens/Aegean/8264/
Features of this page include an introduction for non-Muslims, the Holy Quran, the prophet Mohammad, the fundamental beliefs in Islam, prayer, and other information about Muslim character and culture.

28. Major World Religions
http://www.omsakthi.org/religions.html
Information at this site provides short introductions to the major world religions. There are also links to great books on religion and spirituality.

29. Religion Search Engines: Christianity and Judaism
http://www.suite101.com/article.cfm/search_engines/13501/
Paula Dragutsky's collection of search engines will lead to a wide-ranging directory of Christian Web sites. Shamash is a comprehensive search engine for Jewish information.

30. Religion Search Engines: Islam, Hinduism, Buddhism and Baha'i
http://www.suite101.com/article.cfm/search_engines/14603/
Specialized search engines reviewed on this page can be very helpful in leading to original and interpretive documents that explain the philosophy and practices of Islam, Hinduism, Buddhism, and Baha'i.

The World of the Middle Ages, 500–1500

31. Labyrinth Home Page to Medieval Studies
http://www.georgetown.edu/labyrinth/
Complete information about medieval studies on the Web can be found here. Site also has a search capability.

32. Lords of the Earth: Maya/Aztec/Inca Exchange
http://www.realtime.net/maya/
History, geography, and art about the indigenous inhabitants of the Americas before the arrival of Columbus is available here.

33. The Maya Astronomy Page
http://www.astro.uva.nl/~michielb/maya/astro.html
The focus here is on Mayan civilization, especially astronomy, mathematics, and the Mayan calendar. There are also links to other Maya-related sites. Click on "Maya Astronomy Page."

34. WWW Medieval Resources
http://ebbs.english.vt.edu/medieval/medieval.ebbs.html
This site has links to different resources concerning medieval times.

1500: The Era of Global Explorations

35. The Age of Exploration
http://www.teleport.com/~dleahy/themes/explore.htm
A complete index to the age of exploration is available at this page, which includes a tutorial about the Spanish and Portuguese in the fifteenth and sixteenth centuries. Individual explorers of important sites are available here.

36. Gander Academy's European Explorers Resources on the World Wide Web
http://www.stemnet.nf.ca/CITE/explorer.htm
Access to resources for each of the European explorers of the "New World" is available here, organized by country for which they explored.

We highly recommend that you review our Web site for expanded information and our other product lines. We are continually updating and adding links to our Web site in order to offer you the most usable and useful information that will support and expand the value of your Annual Editions. You can reach us at: *http://www.dushkin.com/annualeditions/.*

Unit Selections

1. **The Evolution of Life on the Earth,** Stephen Jay Gould
2. **Mapping the Past,** Adam Goodheart
3. **Japanese Roots,** Jared Diamond
4. **Rediscovering America,** Charles W. Petit

Key Points to Consider

❖ How did life on Earth begin? What is the evidence? What other theories might be considered?

❖ Why does Stephen Jay Gould say that modern humans might not evolve again?

❖ How did human beings reach the Western Hemisphere? What is the evidence? Is the evidence conclusive? Why or why not?

❖ What scientific tools are used to probe the distant past?

❖ Of what use is DNA testing in population research? What difference does it make to the world about who goes where and when? Use the Japanese and the Native Americans as examples.

 **Links**   **www.dushkin.com/online/**

10. **The Ancient World** *http://www.omnibusol.com/ancient.html*
11. **ARCHNET:WWW Virtual Library—Archaeology** *http://www.lib.uconn.edu/ArchNet/*
12. **The Origin and Evolution of Life**
    http://cmex-www.arc.nasa.gov/VikingCD/Puzzle/EvoLife.htm
13. **Talk-Origins** *http://www.talkorigins.org*
14. **WWW-VL Prehistoric Web Index**
    http://easyweb.easynet.co.uk/~aburnham/database/index.htm

These sites are annotated on pages 4 and 5.

The late astronomer Carl Sagan in his famous book *The Dragons of Eden* (1979) imagined all time compressed into a single year. New Year's Day began with the "Big Bang," a moment when the universe was created in an enormous explosion of compressed matter. Twenty-four days of his imaginary year was equal to a billion years, and thus the universe was fifteen billion years old. The Earth formed in mid-September of his year, and life began near the end of that month. Stephen Jay Gould, a popular science writer, explains in the first article of this section that the evolution of life is haphazard. Human beings are lucky to be here in their present form, and if it were to be done again, evolution might not take the same path. In Sagan's scenario humans do not appear until 10:30 p.m. on December 31. The Akkadian Empire, the first known one, did not form until the last 9 seconds of the year. When thinking in cosmic time, such as this, human existence seems both recent and precarious. It is the human story, nonetheless, that is the main concern of world history.

The migration of human beings across the face of the planet has long been of interest to anthropologists who have used dental patterns, language, and related tools to follow groups. The recent development of DNA analysis has provided an additional powerful means for tracing the movements. Related groups have similar DNA patterns. Adam Goodheart in his article notes the work of these genetic historians in tracking American Indians back to Mongolia and Polynesians to Southeast Asia. Charles W. Petit summarizes the recent ideas about Native American populations. The older thought that a Clovis culture of 15,000 years ago arrived first is now in question. There is speculation about earlier migrations of maritime people along the coastlines. The discovery of Kennewick Man, an 8,000-year-old skeleton, found in 1996 in the state of Washington, also has been disturbing. When reconstructed he looks little like Native Americans and much like the popular actor Patrick Stewart. Current thought is that he may have been part Ainu and part Polynesian. Questions about migrations will continue, however, since there has never been uncovered any but modern *Homo sapiens* in the Western Hemisphere.

Such a discovery as Kennewick Man is upsetting to contemporary native groups who claim to be the first people to occupy the land. The same is true of the Japanese, as Jared Diamond points out. Genetically the Japanese are similar to other Asians, but their language is very different. They may be related to Koreans, but this analysis is complicated by legend and prejudice. Japanese origins remain a mystery. Humankind, nonetheless, has occupied the far corners of the planet. In Carl Sagan's year this has been accomplished in less than a minute.

The Evolution of Life on the Earth

The history of life is not necessarily progressive; it is certainly not predictable. The earth's creatures have evolved through a series of contingent and fortuitous events

Stephen Jay Gould

STEPHEN JAY GOULD teaches biology, geology and the history of science at Harvard University, where he has been on the faculty since 1967. He received an A.B. from Antioch College and a Ph.D. in paleontology from Columbia University. Well known for his popular scientific writings, in particular his monthly column in *Natural History* magazine, he is the author of 13 books.

Some creators announce their inventions with grand éclat. God proclaimed, "Fiat lux," and then flooded his new universe with brightness. Others bring forth great discoveries in a modest guise, as did Charles Darwin in defining his new mechanism of evolutionary causality in 1859: "I have called this principle, by which each slight variation, if useful, is preserved, by the term Natural Selection."

Natural selection is an immensely powerful yet beautifully simple theory that has held up remarkably well, under intense and unrelenting scrutiny and testing, for 135 years. In essence, natural selection locates the mechanism of evolutionary change in a "struggle" among organisms for reproductive suc-cess, leading to improved fit of populations to changing environments. (Struggle is often a metaphorical description and need not be viewed as overt combat, guns blazing. Tactics for reproductive success include a variety of nonmartial activities such as earlier and more frequent mating or better cooperation with partners in raising offspring.) Natural selection is therefore a principle of local

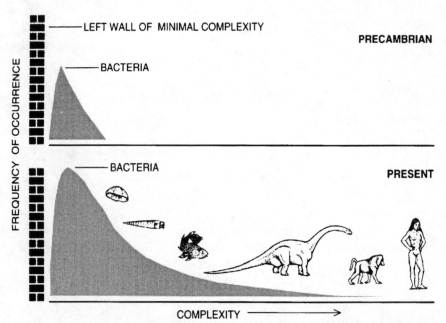

PROGRESS DOES NOT RULE (and is not even a primary thrust of) the evolutionary process. For reasons of chemistry and physics, life arises next to the "left wall" of its simplest conceivable and preservable complexity. This style of life (bacterial) has remained most common and most successful. A few creatures occasionally move to the right, thus extending the right tail in the distribution of complexity. Many always move to the left, but they are absorbed within space already occupied. Note that the bacterial mode has never changed in position, but just grown higher.

adaptation, not of general advance or progress.

Yet, powerful though the principle may be, natural selection is not the only cause of evolutionary change (and may, in many cases, be overshadowed by other forces). This point needs emphasis because the standard misapplication of evolutionary theory assumes that biological explanation may be equated with devising accounts, often speculative and conjectural in practice, about the adaptive value of any given feature in its original environment (human aggression as good for hunting, music and religion as good for tribal cohesion, for example). Darwin himself strongly emphasized the multifactorial nature of evolutionary change and warned against too exclusive a reliance on natural selection, by placing the following statement in a maximally conspicuous place at the very end of his introduction: "I am convinced that Natural Selection has been the most important, but not the exclusive, means of modification."

Natural selection is not fully sufficient to explain evolutionary change for two major reasons. First, many other causes are powerful, particularly at levels of biological organization both above and below the traditional Darwinian focus on organisms and their struggles for reproductive success. At the lowest level of substitution in individual base pairs of DNA, change is often effectively neutral and therefore random. At higher levels, involving entire species or faunas, punctuated equilibrium can produce evolutionary trends by selection of species based on their rates of origin and extirpation, whereas mass extinctions wipe out substantial parts of biotas for reasons unrelated to adaptive struggles of constituent species in "normal" times between such events.

Second, and the focus of this article, no matter how adequate our general theory of evolutionary change, we also yearn to document and understand the actual pathway of life's history. Theory, of course, is relevant to explaining the pathway (nothing about the pathway can be inconsistent with good theory, and theory can predict certain general aspects of life's geologic pattern). But the actual pathway is strongly *underdetermined* by our general theory of life's evolution. This point needs some belaboring as a central yet widely misunderstood aspect of the world's complexity. Webs and chains of historical events are so intricate, so imbued with random and chaotic elements, so unrepeatable in encompassing such a multitude of unique (and uniquely interacting) objects, that standard models of simple prediction and replication do not apply.

History can be explained, with satisfying rigor if evidence be adequate, after a sequence of events unfolds, but it cannot be predicted with any precision beforehand. Pierre-Simon Laplace, echoing the growing and confident determinism of the late 18th century, once said that he could specify all future states if he could know the position and motion of all particles in the cosmos at any moment, but the nature of universal complexity shatters this chimerical dream. History includes too much chaos, or extremely sensitive dependence on minute and unmeasurable differences in initial conditions, leading to massively divergent outcomes based on tiny and unknowable disparities in starting points. And history includes too much contingency, or shaping of present results by long chains of unpredictable antecedent states, rather than immediate determination by timeless laws of nature.

Homo sapiens did not appear on the earth, just a geologic second ago, because evolutionary theory predicts such an outcome based on themes of progress and increasing neural complexity. Humans arose, rather, as a fortuitous and contingent outcome of thousands of linked events, any one of which could have occurred differently and sent history on an alternative pathway that would not have led to consciousness. To cite just four among a multitude: (1) If our inconspicuous and fragile lineage had not been among the few survivors of the initial radiation of multicellular animal life in the Cambrian explosion 530 million years ago, then no vertebrates would have inhabited the earth at all. (Only one member of our chordate phylum, the genus *Pikaia*, has been found among these earliest fossils. This small and simple swimming creature, showing its allegiance to us by possessing a notochord, or dorsal stiffening rod, is among the rarest fossils of the Burgess Shale, our best preserved Cambrian fauna.) (2) If a small and unpromising

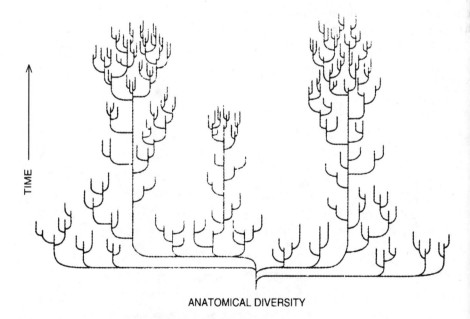

ANATOMICAL DIVERSITY

NEW ICONOGRAPHY OF LIFE'S TREE shows that maximal diversity in anatomical forms (not in number of species) is reached very early in life's multicellular history. Later times feature extinction of most of these initial experiments and enormous success within surviving lines. This success is measured in the proliferation of species but not in the development of new anatomies. Today we have more species than ever before, although they are restricted to fewer basic anatomies.

group of lobe-finned fishes had not evolved fin bones with a strong central axis capable of bearing weight on land, then vertebrates might never have become terrestrial. (3) If a large extraterrestrial body had not struck the earth 65 million years ago, then dinosaurs would still be dominant and mammals insignificant (the situation that had prevailed for 100 million years previously). (4) If a small lineage of primates had not evolved upright posture on the drying African savannas just two to four million years ago, then our ancestry might have ended in a line of apes that, like the chimpanzee and gorilla today, would

have become ecologically marginal and probably doomed to extinction despite their remarkable behavioral complexity.

Therefore, to understand the events and generalities of life's pathway, we must go beyond principles of evolutionary theory to a paleontological examination of the contingent pattern of life's history on our planet—the single actualized version among millions of plausible alternatives that happened not to occur. Such a view of life's history is highly contrary both to conventional deterministic models of Western science and to the deepest social traditions and psychological hopes of Western culture

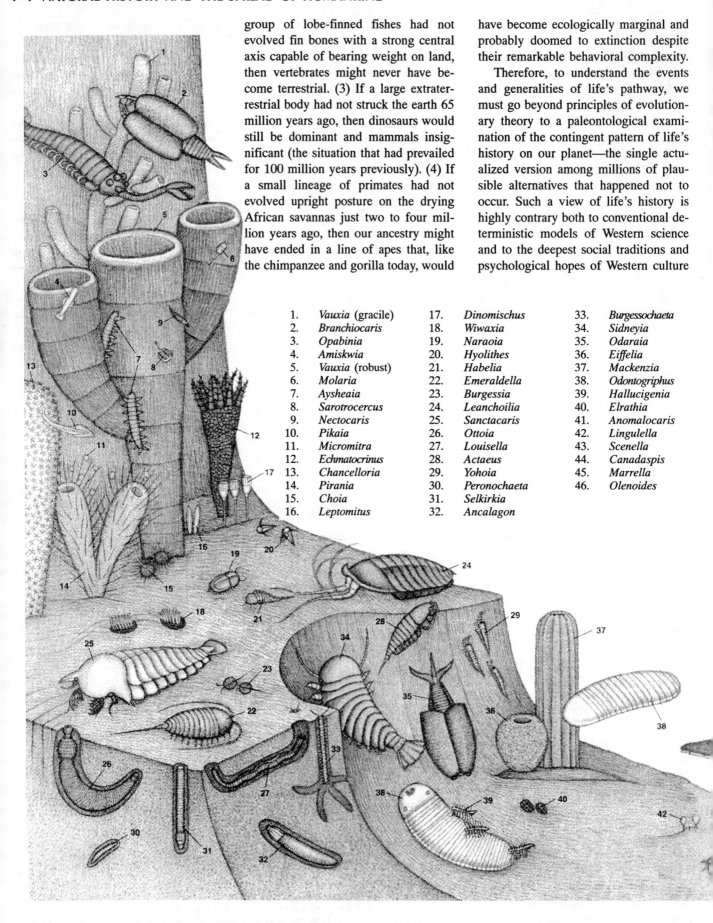

1.	*Vauxia* (gracile)	17.	*Dinomischus*	33.	*Burgessochaeta*
2.	*Branchiocaris*	18.	*Wiwaxia*	34.	*Sidneyia*
3.	*Opabinia*	19.	*Naraoia*	35.	*Odaraia*
4.	*Amiskwia*	20.	*Hyolithes*	36.	*Eiffelia*
5.	*Vauxia* (robust)	21.	*Habelia*	37.	*Mackenzia*
6.	*Molaria*	22.	*Emeraldella*	38.	*Odontogriphus*
7.	*Aysheaia*	23.	*Burgessia*	39.	*Hallucigenia*
8.	*Sarotrocercus*	24.	*Leanchoilia*	40.	*Elrathia*
9.	*Nectocaris*	25.	*Sanctacaris*	41.	*Anomalocaris*
10.	*Pikaia*	26.	*Ottoia*	42.	*Lingulella*
11.	*Micromitra*	27.	*Louisella*	43.	*Scenella*
12.	*Echmatocrinus*	28.	*Actaeus*	44.	*Canadaspis*
13.	*Chancelloria*	29.	*Yohoia*	45.	*Marrella*
14.	*Pirania*	30.	*Peronochaeta*	46.	*Olenoides*
15.	*Choia*	31.	*Selkirkia*		
16.	*Leptomitus*	32.	*Ancalagon*		

for a history culminating in humans as life's highest expression and intended planetary steward.

Science can, and does, strive to grasp nature's factuality, but all science is socially embedded, and all scientists record prevailing "certainties," however hard they may be aiming for pure objectivity. Darwin himself, in the closing lines of *The Origin of Species,* expressed Victorian social preference more than nature's record in writing: "As natural selection works solely by and for the good of each being, all corporeal and mental endowments will tend to progress towards perfection."

Life's pathway certainly includes many features predictable from laws of nature, but these aspects are too broad and general to provide the "rightness" that we seek for validating evolution's particular results—roses, mushrooms, people and so forth. Organisms adapt to, and are constrained by, physical principles. It is, for example, scarcely surprising, given laws of gravity, that the largest vertebrates in the sea (whales) exceed the heaviest animals on land (elephants today, dinosaurs in the past), which, in turn, are far bulkier than the largest vertebrate that ever flew (extinct pterosaurs of the Mesozoic era).

GREAT DIVERSITY quickly evolved at the dawn of multicellular animal life during the Cambrian period (530 million years ago). The creatures shown here are all found in the Middle Cambrian Burgess Shale fauna of Canada. They include some familiar forms (sponges, brachiopods) that have survived. But many creatures (such as the giant *Anomalocaris,* at the lower right, largest of all the Cambrian animals) did not live for long and are so anatomically peculiar (relative to survivors) that we cannot classify them among known phyla.

Predictable ecological rules govern the structuring of communities by principles of energy flow and thermodynamics (more biomass in prey than in predators, for example). Evolutionary trends, once started, may have local predictability ("arms races," in which both predators and prey hone their defenses and weapons, for example—a pattern that Geerat J. Vermeij of the University of California at Davis has called "escalation" and documented in increasing strength of both crab claws and shells of their gastropod prey through time). But laws of nature do not tell us why we have crabs and snails at all, why insects rule the multicellular world and why vertebrates rather than persistent algal mats exist as the most complex forms of life on the earth.

Relative to the conventional view of life's history as an at least broadly predictable process of gradually advancing complexity through time, three features of the paleontological record stand out in opposition and shall therefore serve as organizing themes for the rest of this article: the constancy of modal complexity throughout life's history; the concentration of major events in short bursts interspersed with long periods of relative stability; and the role of external impositions, primarily mass extinctions, in disrupting patterns of "normal" times. These three features, combined with more general themes of chaos and contingency, require a new framework for conceptualizing and drawing life's history, and this article therefore closes with suggestions for a different iconography of evolution.

The primary paleontological fact about life's beginnings points to predictability for the onset and very little for the particular pathways thereafter. The earth is 4.6 billion years old, but the oldest rocks date to about 3.9 billion years because the earth's surface became molten early in its history, a result of bombardment by large amounts of cosmic debris during the solar system's coalescence, and of heat generated by radioactive decay of short-lived isotopes. These oldest rocks are too metamorphosed by subsequent heat and pressure to preserve fossils (though some scientists interpret the proportions of carbon isotopes in these rocks as signs of organic production). The oldest rocks sufficiently unaltered to retain cellular fossils—African and Australian sediments dated to 3.5 billion years old—do preserve prokaryotic cells (bacteria and cyanophytes) and stromatolites (mats of sediment trapped and bound by these cells in shallow marine waters). Thus, life on the earth evolved quickly and is as old as it could be. This fact alone seems to indicate an inevitability, or at least a predictability, for life's origin from the original chemical constituents of atmosphere and ocean.

No one can doubt that more complex creatures arose sequentially after this prokaryotic beginning—first eukaryotic cells, perhaps about two billion years ago, then multicellular animals about 600 million years ago, with a relay of highest complexity among animals passing from invertebrates, to marine vertebrates and, finally (if we wish, albeit parochially, to honor neural architecture as a primary criterion), to reptiles, mammals and humans. This is the conventional sequence represented in the old charts and texts as an "age of invertebrates," followed by an "age of fishes," "age of reptiles," "age of mammals," and "age of man" (to add the old gender bias to all the other prejudices implied by this sequence).

I do not deny the facts of the preceding paragraph but wish to argue that our conventional desire to view history as progressive, and to see humans as predictably dominant, has grossly distorted our interpretation of life's pathway by falsely placing in the center of things a

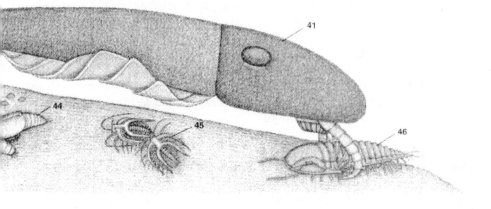

41

44

45

46

relatively minor phenomenon that arises only as a side consequence of a physically constrained starting point. The most salient feature of life has been the stability of its bacterial mode from the beginning of the fossil record until today and, with little doubt, into all future time so long as the earth endures. This is truly the "age of bacteria"—as it was in the beginning, is now and ever shall be.

For reasons related to the chemistry of life's origin and the physics of self-organization, the first living things arose at the lower limit of life's conceivable, preservable complexity. Call this lower limit the "left wall" for an architecture of complexity. Since so little space exists between the left wall and life's initial bacterial mode in the fossil record, only one direction for future increment exists—toward greater complexity at the right. Thus, every once in a while, a more complex creature evolves and extends the range of life's diversity in the only available direction. In technical terms, the distribution of complexity becomes more strongly right skewed through these occasional additions.

But the additions are rare and episodic. They do not even constitute an evolutionary series but form a motley sequence of distantly related taxa, usually depicted as eukaryotic cell, jellyfish, trilobite, nautiloid, eurypterid (a large relative of horseshoe crabs), fish, an amphibian such as *Eryops,* a dinosaur, a mammal and a human being. This sequence cannot be construed as the major thrust or trend of life's history. Think rather of an occasional creature tumbling into the empty right region of complexity's space. Throughout this entire time, the bacterial mode has grown in height and remained constant in position. Bacteria represent the great success story of life's pathway. They occupy a wider domain of environments and span a broader range of biochemistries than any other group. They are adaptable, indestructible and astoundingly diverse. We cannot even imagine how anthropogenic intervention might threaten their extinction, although we worry about our impact on nearly every other form of life. The number of *Escherichia coli* cells in the gut of each human being exceeds the number of humans that has ever lived on this planet.

One might grant that complexification for life as a whole represents a pseudotrend based on constraint at the left wall but still hold that evolution within particular groups differentially favors complexity when the founding lineage begins far enough from the left wall to permit movement in both directions. Empirical tests of this interesting hypothesis are just beginning (as concern for the subject mounts among paleontologists), and we do not yet have enough cases to advance a generality. But the first two studies—by Daniel W. McShea of the University of Michigan on mammalian vertebrae and by George F. Boyajian of the University of Pennsylvania on ammonite suture lines—show no evolutionary tendencies to favor increased complexity.

Moreover, when we consider that for each mode of life involving greater complexity, there probably exists an equally advantageous style based on greater simplicity of form (as often found in parasites, for example), then preferential evolution toward complexity seems unlikely a priori. Our impression that life evolves toward greater complexity is probably only a bias inspired by parochial focus on ourselves, and consequent overattention to complexifying creatures, while we ignore just as many lineages adapting equally well by becoming simpler in form. The morphologically degenerate parasite, safe within its host, has just as much prospect for evolutionary success as its gorgeously elaborate relative coping with the slings and arrows of outrageous fortune in a tough external world.

Even if complexity is only a drift away from a constraining left wall, we might view trends in this direction as more predictable and characteristic of life's pathway as a whole if increments of complexity accrued in a persistent and gradually accumulating manner through time. But nothing about life's history is more peculiar with respect to this common (and false) expectation than the actual pattern of extended stability and rapid episodic movement, as revealed by the fossil record.

Life remained almost exclusively unicellular for the first five sixths of its history—from the first recorded fossils at 3.5 billion years to the first well-documented multicellular animals less than 600 million years ago. (Some simple multicellular algae evolved more than a billion years ago, but these organisms belong to the plant kingdom and have no genealogical connection with animals.) This long period of unicellular life does include, to be sure, the vitally important transition from simple prokaryotic cells without organelles to eukaryotic cells with nuclei, mitochondria and other complexities of intracellular architecture—but no recorded attainment of multicellular animal organization for a full three billion years. If complexity is such a good thing, and multicellularity represents its initial phase in our usual view, then life certainly took its time in making this crucial step. Such delays speak strongly against general progress as the major theme of life's history, even if they can be plausibly explained by lack of sufficient atmospheric oxygen for most of Precambrian time or by failure of unicellular life to achieve some structural threshold acting as a prerequisite to multicellularity.

More curiously, all major stages in organizing animal life's multicellular architecture then occurred in a short period beginning less than 600 million years ago and ending by about 530 million years ago—and the steps within this sequence are also discontinuous and episodic, not gradually accumulative. The first fauna, called Ediacaran to honor the Australian locality of its initial discovery but now known from rocks on all continents, consists of highly flattened fronds, sheets and circlets composed of numerous slender segments quilted together. The nature of the Ediacaran fauna is now a subject of intense discussion. These creatures do not seem to be simple precursors of latter forms. They may constitute a separate and failed experiment in animal life, or they may represent a full range of diploblastic (two-layered) organization, of which the modern phylum Cnidaria (corals, jellyfishes and their allies) remains as a small and much altered remnant.

In any case, they apparently died out well before the Cambrian biota evolved. The Cambrian then began with an assemblage of bits and pieces, frustratingly difficult to interpret, called the "small shelly fauna." The subsequent main pulse, starting about 530 million years ago, constitutes the famous Cambrian explosion, during which all but one modern phylum of animal life made a first appearance in the fossil record. (Geologists had previously allowed up to 40 million years for this event, but an elegant study, published in 1993, clearly restricts this period of phyletic flowing to a mere five million years.) The Bryozoa, a group of sessile and colonial marine organisms, do not arise until the beginning of the subsequent, Ordovician period, but this apparent delay may be an artifact of failure to discover Cambrian representatives.

Although interesting and portentous events have occurred since, from the flowering of dinosaurs to the origin of human consciousness, we do not exaggerate greatly in stating that the subsequent history of animal life amounts to little more than variations on anatomical themes established during the Cambrian explosion within five million years. Three billion years of unicellularity, followed by five million years of intense creativity and then capped by more than 500 million years of variation on set anatomical themes can scarcely be read as a predictable, inexorable or continuous trend toward progress or increasing complexity.

We do not know why the Cambrian explosion could establish all major anatomical designs so quickly. An "external" explanation based on ecology seems attractive: the Cambrian explosion represents an initial filling of the "ecological barrel" of niches for multicellular organisms, and any experiment found a space. The barrel has never emptied since; even the great mass extinctions left a few species in each principal role, and their occupation of ecological space forecloses opportunity for fundamental novelties. But an "internal" explanation based on genetics and development also seems necessary as a complement: the earliest multicellular animals may have maintained a flexibility for genetic change and embryological transformation that became greatly reduced as organisms "locked in" to a set of stable and successful designs.

In any case, this initial period of both internal and external flexibility yielded a range of invertebrate anatomies that may have exceeded (in just a few million years of production) the full scope of animal form in all the earth's environments today (after more than 500 million years of additional time for further expansion). Scientists are divided on this question. Some claim that the anatomical range of this initial explosion exceeded that of modern life, as many early experiments died out and no new phyla have ever arisen. But scientists most strongly opposed to this view allow that Cambrian diversity at least equaled the modern range—so even the most cautious opinion holds that 500 million subsequent years of opportunity have not expanded the Cambrian range, achieved in just five million years. The Cambrian explosion was the most remarkable and puzzling event in the history of life.

Moreover, we do not know why most of the early experiments died, while a few survived to become our modern phyla. It is tempting to say that the victors won by virtue of greater anatomical complexity, better ecological fit or some other predictable feature of conventional Darwinian struggle. But no recognized traits unite the victors, and the radical alternative must be entertained that each early experiment received little more than the equivalent of a ticket in the largest lottery ever played out on our planet—and that each surviving lineage, including our own phylum of vertebrates, inhabits the earth today more by the luck of the draw than by any predictable struggle for existence. The history of multicellular animal life may be more a story of great reduction in initial possibilities, with stabilization of lucky survivors, than a conventional tale of steady ecological expansion and morphological progress in complexity.

Finally, this pattern of long stasis, with change concentrated in rapid episodes that establish new equilibria, may be quite general at several scales of time and magnitude, forming a kind of fractal pattern in self-similarity. According to the punctuated equilibrium model of speciation, trends within lineages occur by accumulated episodes of geological

instantaneous speciation, rather than by gradual change within continuous populations (like climbing a staircase rather than rolling a ball up an inclined plane).

Even if evolutionary theory implied a potential internal direction for life's pathway (although previous facts and arguments in this article cast doubt on such a claim), the occasional imposition of a rapid and substantial, perhaps even truly catastrophic, change in environment would have intervened to stymie the pattern. These environmental changes trigger mass extinction of a high percentage of the earth's species and may so derail any internal direction and so reset the pathway that the net pattern of life's history looks more capricious and concentrated in episodes than steady and directional. Mass extinctions have been recognized since the dawn of paleontology; the major divisions of the geologic time scale were established at boundaries marked by such events. But until the revival of interest that began in the late 1970s, most paleontologists treated mass extinctions only as intensifications of ordinary events, leading (at most) to a speeding up of tendencies that pervaded normal times. In this gradualistic theory of mass extinction, these events really took a few million years to unfold (with the appearance of suddenness interpreted as an artifact of an imperfect fossil record), and they only made the ordinary occur faster (more intense Darwinian competition in tough times, for example, leading to even more efficient replacement of less adapted by superior forms).

The reinterpretation of mass extinctions as central to life's pathway and radically different in effect began with the presentation of data by Luis and Walter Alvarez in 1979, indicating that the impact of a large extraterrestrial object (they suggested an asteroid seven to 10 kilometers in diameter) set off the last great extinction at the Cretaceous-Tertiary boundary 65 million years ago. Although the Alvarez hypothesis initially received very skeptical treatment from scientists (a proper approach to highly unconventional explanations), the case now seems virtually proved by discovery of the "smoking gun," a crater of appropriate size and age located off the Yucatán peninsula in Mexico.

This reawakening of interest also inspired paleontologists to tabulate the data of mass extinction more rigorously. Work by David M. Raup, J. J. Sepkoski, Jr., and David Jablonski of the University of Chicago has established that multicellular animal life experienced five major (end of Ordovician, late Devonian, end of Permian, end of Triassic and end of Cretaceous) and many minor mass extinctions during its 530-million-year history. We have no clear evidence that any but the last of these events was triggered by catastrophic impact, but such careful study leads to the general conclusion that mass extinctions were more frequent, more rapid, more extensive in magnitude and more different in effect than paleontologists had previously realized. These four properties encompass the radical implications of mass extinction for understanding life's pathway as more contingent and chancy than predictable and directional.

Mass extinctions are not random in their impact on life. Some lineages succumb and others survive as sensible outcomes based on presence or absence of evolved features. But especially if the triggering cause of extinction be sudden and catastrophic, the reasons for life or death may be random with respect to the original value of key features when first evolved in Darwinian struggles of normal times. This "different rules" model of mass extinction imparts a quirky and unpredictable character to life's pathway based on the evident claim that lineages cannot anticipate future contingencies of such magnitude and different operation.

To cite two examples from the impact-triggered Cretaceous-Tertiary extinction 65 million years ago: First, an important study published in 1986 noted that diatoms survived the extinction far better than other single-celled plankton (primarily coccoliths and radiolaria). This study found that many diatoms had evolved a strategy of dormancy by encystment, perhaps to survive through seasonal periods of unfavorable conditions (months of darkness in polar species as otherwise fatal to these photosynthesizing cells; sporadic availability of silica needed to construct their skeletons). Other planktonic cells had not evolved any mechanisms for dormancy. If the terminal Cretaceous impact produced a dust cloud that blocked light for several months or longer (one popular idea for a "killing scenario" in the extinction), then diatoms may have survived as a fortuitous result of dormancy mechanisms evolved for the entirely different function of weathering seasonal droughts in ordinary times. Diatoms are not superior to radiolaria or other plankton that succumbed in far greater numbers; they were simply fortunate to possess a favorable feature, evolved for other reasons, that fostered passage through the impact and its sequelae.

Second, we all know that dinosaurs perished in the end Cretaceous event and that mammals therefore rule the vertebrate world today. Most people assume that mammals prevailed in these tough times for some reason of general superiority over dinosaurs. But such a conclusion seems most unlikely. Mammals and dinosaurs had coexisted for 100 million years, and mammals had remained rat-sized or smaller, making no evolutionary "move" to oust dinosaurs. No good argument for mammalian prevalence by general superiority has ever been advanced, and fortuity seems far more likely. As one plausible argument, mammals may have survived partly as a result of their small size (with much larger, and therefore extinction-resistant, populations as a consequence, and less ecological specialization with more places to hide, so to speak). Small size may not have been a positive mammalian adaptation at all, but more a sign of inability ever to penetrate the dominant domain of dinosaurs. Yet this "negative" feature of normal times may be the key reason for mammalian survival and a prerequisite to my writing and your reading this article today.

Sigmund Freud often remarked that great revolutions in the history of science have but one common, and ironic, feature: they knock human arrogance off one pedestal after another of our previous conviction about our own self-importance. In Freud's three examples, Copernicus moved our home from center to periphery; Darwin then relegated us to "descent from an animal world"; and, finally (in one of the least modest statements of intellectual history), Freud himself discovered the unconscious and exploded the myth of a fully rational mind.

In this wise and crucial sense, the Darwinian revolution remains woefully incomplete because, even though thinking humanity accepts the fact of evolution, most of us are still unwilling to abandon the comforting view that evolution means (or at least embodies a central principle of) progress defined to render the appearance of something like human consciousness either virtually inevitable or at least predictable. The pedestal is not smashed until we abandon progress or complexification as a central principle and come to entertain the strong possibility that *H. sapiens* is but a tiny, late-arising twig on life's enormously arborescent bush—a small bud that would almost surely not appear a second time if we could replant the bush from seed and let it grow again.

Primates are visual animals, and the pictures we draw betray our deepest convictions and display our current conceptual limitations. Artists have always painted the history of fossil life as a sequence from invertebrates, to fishes, to early terrestrial amphibians and reptiles, to dinosaurs, to mammals and, finally, to humans. There are no exceptions; all sequences painted since the inception of this genre in the 1850s follow the convention.

Yet we never stop to recognize the almost absurd biases coded into this universal mode. No scene ever shows another invertebrate after fishes evolved, but invertebrates did not go away or stop evolving! After terrestrial reptiles emerge, no subsequent scene ever shows a fish (later oceanic tableaux depict only such returning reptiles as ichthyosaurs and plesiosaurs). But fishes did not stop evolving after one small lineage managed to invade the land. In fact, the major event in the evolution of fishes, the origin and rise to dominance of the teleosts, or modern bony fishes, occurred during the time of the dinosaurs and is therefore never shown at all in any of these sequences—even though teleosts include more than half of all species of vertebrates. Why should humans appear at the end of all sequences? Our order of primates is ancient among mammals, and many other successful lineages arose later than we did.

We will not smash Freud's pedestal and complete Darwin's revolution until we find, grasp and accept another way of drawing life's history. J. B. S. Haldane proclaimed nature "queerer than we can suppose," but these limits may only be socially imposed conceptual locks rather then inherent restrictions of our neurology. New icons might break the locks.

Trees—orrather copiously and luxuriantly branching bushes—rather than ladders and sequences hold the key to this conceptual transition.

We must learn to depict the full range of variation, not just our parochial perception of the tiny right tail of most complex creatures. We must recognize that this tree may have contained a maximal number of branches near the beginning of multicellular life and that subsequent history is for the most part a process of elimination and lucky survivorship of a few, rather than continuous flowering, progress and expansion of a growing multitude. We must understand that little twigs are contingent nubbins, not predictable goals of the massive bush beneath. We must remember the greatest of all Biblical statements about wisdom: "She is a tree of life to them that lay hold upon her; and happy is every one that retaineth her."

FURTHER READING

THE BURGESS SHALE. Henry B. Whittington. Yale University Press, 1985.

EXTINCTION: A SCIENTIFIC AMERICAN BOOK. Steven M. Stanley, W. H. Freeman and Company, 1987.

WONDERFUL LIFE: THE BURGESS SHALE AND THE NATURE OF HISTORY. S. J. Gould, W. W. Norton, 1989.

THE BOOK OF LIFE. Edited by Stephen Jay Gould. W. W. Norton, 1993.

Mapping *the* Past

Adam Goodheart

Adam Goodheart, an associate editor at CIVILIZATION and author of its Lost Arts column, has also written for *The New York Times, The Washington Post* and other publications.

ANCESTORS HAVE ALWAYS been hard to keep track of. We all have them, of course, but most of us can trace our families back only four or five generations. Even the oldest lineages are fairly new on the grand scale of human history; Prince Charles, with his 262,142 recorded ancestors, has a family tree little more than 1,500 years old. (Only one reliable pedigree in the world—that of the Bagratid kings of Georgia—stretches back into classical antiquity, petering out in 326 B.C.) "As each of us looks back into his or her past," wrote E. M. Forster, "doors open upon darkness."

Writing in 1939, Forster was arguing the futility of ever tracing the genetic history of a nation. Indeed, if ancestral accounts are muddled and incomplete at the level of individual families, the genealogies of entire nations and peoples are impossibly confused. Historians who refer to "the Irish" or "the Jews" as though they were well-defined groups have only the vaguest idea of their origins, of how they fit into the family tree of the human race. And when it comes to the origins and fate of long-vanished peoples like the ancient Egyptians, the darkness is almost complete. "A common language, a common religion, a common culture all belong to the present, evidence about them is available, they can be tested," Forster wrote. "But

race belongs to the unknown and unknowable past. It depends upon who went to bed with whom in the year 1400 . . . and what historian will ever discover that?"

Yet scientists are now discovering just that—not just who went to bed with whom in 1400, but an entire family history of our species stretching far into the past. It's in an archive we've been carrying with us all along: the coiled molecules of our DNA. "Everybody alive today is a living fossil who contains their own evolutionary history within themselves," says Steve Jones, head of the genetics department at University College, London. Genetics has recently made headlines with the pronouncements of scientists looking ahead, toward medical breakthroughs and moral dilemmas. A far less publicized group of geneticists is looking backward, using new technology to analyze deoxyribonucleic acid, molecule by molecule—and trace the migrations, conquests, expansions and extinctions of ancient peoples.

Genes are often described as a blueprint. That's only a partial analogy. For besides its role in mapping out the makeup of our bodies (and perhaps our personalities), DNA serves as an internal archive handed down from generation to generation. Every individual's genetic code, though unique, contains sequences that have been passed down from parent to child, not just since the beginning of human history, but reaching back over a billion years of evolution.

Picture the human genome, then, not as a blueprint but as an elaborate medieval coat of arms, perhaps the family crest of some inbred princeling of the Holy Roman Empire. To most people,

such a heraldic device would look like a mass of meaningless symbols: dots, bars and crosshatchings, rampant lions quartered with screaming eagles. But an expert in heraldry could read in it an entire family history, tracing the prince's forebears as they married Hapsburgs, fathered bastards, conquered duchies, far back through time. Similarly, the genome

---

Using new genetic techniques, scientists are solving the ancient mysteries of mankind's origins and migrations

---

looks like gibberish: an endless repetition of four chemicals, represented by the letters A, C, G and T. But geneticists are beginning to recognize sequences that identify specific human lineages, and are using them to reconstruct the family history of the species. Recent technology is also enabling them to unearth fragments of DNA from the remains of our long-dead ancestors. Using these two approaches, one scientist says, researchers are undertaking "the greatest archaeological excavation in history."

EVER SINCE EARLY EXPLORers of the new world announced that they had discovered the lost tribes of Israel, the origin of the Native Americans has been the subject of intense debate. Experts now agree that the Indians' ancestors crossed into Alaska over a land bridge from Siberia. Yet no one knows exactly when or how. Even the vaguest legends of that time have been long forgotten, and the land that the hunters crossed, with whatever faint traces their passage left, is hidden beneath the waters of the North Pacific.

Far to the south, Connie Kolman was following the ancient immigrants' track when she drove out into western Panama in the fall of 1991. A molecular biologist with the Smithsonian Institute,

Genetic historians have begun to read the vast archive in our DNA directly, molecule by molecule

Kolman was conducting a study of the genes of some of the New World's most ancient populations. Archaeologists had known for many years that despite Panama's location on a narrow causeway between two continents, many of the tribes who lived there had been isolated from outsiders for many millenniums—perhaps almost since their hunter-gatherer ancestors arrived.

Kolman's scientific team set up their equipment in the small cinder-block schoolhouse that served an entire community of Ngöbé Indian farmers. Just past dawn, the Ngöbé started to arrive: dozens of them, coming down over the hillsides in single file, the traditional ruffled dresses of the women and girls standing out in vivid reds and purples against the tall grass. As the Indians gathered, the visitors explained their mission and asked for volunteers. A medic collected a small vial of blood from each Indian's arm. Over the next few months, back at their lab in Panama City, Kolman and her colleague Eldredge Bermingham broke down the blood cells in the samples and decoded the ancient historical text that they contained. The text, it turned out, read something like this: TGGGGAGCAC-GCTGGC...

The work that genetic historians like Connie Kolman have started to do—reading the DNA archive directly, molecule by molecule—relies on technology

that is little more than 10 years old, so their conclusions are often controversial. Like medievalists poring over a newly unearthed manuscript, geneticists argue about every fresh interpretation, every cryptic passage and variant reading.

By the mid-1980s, scientists had begun to identify the specific genetic markers common to all Native Americans, which are similar to sequences found in present-day Asians, as one would expect. What was surprising, however, was that American Indians seemed to be divided into three distinct genetic groups. One lineage included most of the native tribes of North and South America, from northern Canada down to Patagonia. Another comprised the Eskimo and Aleut peoples of the far north. The third group included a number of tribes in northwestern Canada, as well as the Navajos and Apaches of the southwestern United States. These genetic lines corresponded with the three major Indian linguistic groups.

Some scientists, particularly a group from Emory University, have suggested that several different waves of migration crossed the Bering land bridge at different times, not the single migration most scientists envisioned. And in order to account for the genetic differences among modern Indians, these researchers maintain, their ancestors must have begun to arrive around 27,000 B.C.—more than twice as long ago as most archaeologists believe. That would mean that humans were living in North America even before the last ice age, in the days when Neanderthals and woolly rhinoceros still roamed the European continent. "Another migration about 9,000 to 10,000 years ago . . . into northwestern North America gave us the Na-Dene speaking peoples, who about 1,000 years ago went down to become the Apaches and the Navajo," says Douglas Wallace, head of the genetics department at Emory. "Finally, there was a recent migration out of Siberia to the northern part of America that gave us the Eskimos and Aleuts."

Could such a radically new version of American history be correct? This is what Kolman hoped to learn from the Ngöbé blood samples. Her research turned up an unanticipated answer: The

same kind of separation that existed among the three major Indian genetic groups also divided the Ngöbé from neighboring tribes in Panama. Yet archaeological evidence showed it was impossible that the Panamanian Indians had come over the land bridge in more than one migration. Therefore, she concluded, the genetic difference between Indian groups is the result of their separation from one another over the centuries after their arrival in the New World. Based on her own research, she says, "there doesn't appear to be any support for three waves of migration." The most likely scenario, Kolman argues, is that all of today's Native Americans, from Canada to Patagonia, are the descendants of one hardy group of prehistoric pioneers. In fact, researchers have pinpointed a region of Mongolia where the genetic patterns are similar to those of all three major Indian groups. Some modern Mongolians, then, appear to be remnants of the same population that settled the New World.

Slowly but surely, researchers like Kolman are rewriting history. In the Pacific, scientists are tracing the genetic trail left by the ancient mariners who settled Polynesia, finding evidence of a journey that began in Southeast Asia nearly 4,000 years ago—and sinking for good the widely publicized theories of Thor Heyerdahl, who sailed the balsa raft *Kon-Tiki* from Peru to the Tuamotu Archipelago to "prove" that American Indians had settled the Pacific. And in disproving Heyerdahl, the geneticists have found evidence of the Polynesians' traditional sagas, which speak of their ancestors' frequent voyages between Hawaii and Tahiti in huge oceangoing canoes. "Archaeologists kept saying it was impossible, that it was just a story people told," says Rebecca Cann, a geneticist at the University of Hawaii. "But by doing a very fine analysis of the DNA, we've seen that there is in fact one very common cosmopolitan lineage that's spread throughout the Pacific, [which] could only have happened if people were in constant physical contact. The idea that these islands were so isolated is really a foreign invention. The Polynesians used the ocean as a superhighway."

THE GREAT ARCHAEOLOGI-cal dig into the human genome began in the villages of northern Italy. In the 1950s, a young Italian geneticist named Luigi Luca Cavalli-Sforza traveled among the towns near Parma, taking blood samples in the sacristies of parish churches after Sunday Mass. He began with the prosperous communities in the river valley, then worked his way up into the smaller towns in the hills until he reached the mountain villages with 100 or fewer inhabitants. As he gathered blood samples, Cavalli-Sforza also began another investigation that, for a geneticist at least, was quite unorthodox: He pored over the parishes' manuscript books of births, marriages and deaths, records dating as far back as the 1500s.

Cavalli-Sforza was investigating the theory of genetic drift, which had never been conclusively proved. Genetic drift proposes that Charles Darwin's law of "survival of the fittest" doesn't suffice to explain all the differences among species, or among peoples. Certain changes just happen naturally over time, independent of the mechanisms of natural section—especially when populations are isolated from one another for many generations. Sometimes the changes can be quite noticeable, as in the case of remote Alpine valleys were many of the inhabitants are albinos. But more typically the effects of genetic drift are neutral and invisible: For instance, the people in an isolated region will have high percentages of an uncommon blood type. Barring extensive marriage with outsiders, every population will develop a distinctive genetic profile. (This is the same phenomenon that Connie Kolman found among the Panamanian Indians.)

In the 1950s, of course, the technology didn't exist that would allow Cavalli-Sforza to read the DNA directly. But he was able to test for blood type, and what he found confirmed the presence of genetic drift. In the large valley towns, where the parish books recorded many marriages with people from different communities, the blood-group profile was typical of that entire region of Italy. But as Cavalli-Sforza moved up into the small, isolated mountain villages, the genetic "distances" between the various settlements increased. The longer a population had been isolated, the more it differed from its neighbors. If the principle worked for villages in Italy, why shouldn't it work for the rest of the world? "My supposition was this: if enough data on a number of different genes are gathered, we may eventually be able to reconstruct the history of the entire human species," Cavalli-Sforza later wrote. And so he embarked on a decades-long project to study thousands of gene markers in hundreds of indigenous peoples around the world.

Of course, scientists had tried before to establish the relationships among the world's populations, often using methods that they claimed were based on strict Darwinian science. They traveled the world with calipers and charts, measuring the bone structure and skin color of the "natives." (One Victorian geneticist even created a "beauty map" of Britain, grading the women of various regions on a scale of 1 to 5. The low point was Aberdeen.) If you trusted such findings, the Australian aborigines, with their dark skin and flat noses, were closely related to sub-Saharan Africans. Cavalli-Sforza didn't believe it. Those visible similarities, he reasoned, might just be the result of similar adaptation to hot climates. To gauge relationships accurately, one had to measure factors that were genetically neutral, immune to the mechanisms of natural selection.

One of the most elegant aspects of Cavalli-Sforza's approach is that there is no need to sample huge numbers of people in each group under examination. Genetically, after all, each of us represents not only ourself but all of our ancestors. (Long before genome mapping, Henry Adams explained this principle quite well. "If we could go back and live again in all of our two hundred and fifty million arithmetical ancestors of the eleventh century," he wrote, speaking of those with Norman blood, "we should find ourselves . . . ploughing most of the fields of the Cotentin and Calvados; going to mass in every parish church in Normandy; [and] rendering military service to every lord, spiritual or temporal, in all this region.")

In 1994, Cavalli-Sforza, along with Paolo Menozzi and Alberto Piazza, published his magnum opus, *The History and Geography of Human Genes*—a sort of combination atlas and family tree. Cavalli-Sforza's genealogy places Africans at the root of the tree, with the Europeans and Asians branching off from them, and American Indians branching off in turn from the Asians. He finds the genetic traces of the Mongol invasions of China, the Bantus' sweep across Africa and the Arabs' spread through the Middle East under the successors of Muhammad.

In his analysis of Europe's genetic landscape, Cavalli-Sforza has shaken the foundations of conventional history. Nine thousand years ago, a technological and cultural revolution swept Europe. From the Balkans to Britain, forests sparsely dotted with the campfires of hunter-gatherers gave way to a patchwork of cultivated fields and burgeoning settlements. In the course of a few thousand years, as the practice of agriculture spread from southeast to northwest, Europeans abandoned the way of life they had led for tens of thousands of years. That much is agreed upon. But Cavalli-Sforza suggests that the agricultural revolution was a genetic revolution as well. It wasn't merely that the Europeans gradually learned about farming from their neighbors to the southeast. Instead, the Middle Eastern farmers actually migrated across Europe, replacing the existing population. This wasn't a case of prehistoric genocide, Cavalli-Sforza emphasizes: The farmers simply multiplied far more rapidly than the hunters, and, as they sought new land to cultivate, they pushed their frontiers to the northwest.

Today's Europeans, Cavalli-Sforza argues, are almost wholly the descendants of these interlopers—with the exception of the Basques, whose gene patterns are so anomalous that he believes they are the last close relatives of the Cro-Magnon hunters. Furthermore, Cavalli-Sforza believes, there was a *second* genetic invasion of Europe around 4000 B.C.—this time from the steppes of Central Asia. His maps show that an important component of the European gene pool spreads out from the area north of the Black Sea like ripples in a pond. Cavalli-Sforza connects this to a controversial archaeological theory: the idea that nomadic herdsmen swept in from the east, bringing with them domesticated horses, bronze weapons and the Indo-European language that would become the basis for all major European tongues.

Cavalli-Sforza's ideas have drawn criticism as well as praise. "All genetic data has a time depth of one generation back from the past," says Erik Trinkaus, an anthropologist at the University of New Mexico: Cavalli-Sforza's maps only prove that present-day Europeans demonstrate genetic divergences that occurred at some point in the past. All the rest is interpretation. Some scholars have argued that these patterns could be explained by more recent migrations, such as the barbarian invasions that toppled the Roman Empire. Even Alberto Piazza, who collaborated with Cavalli-Sforza, admits that "it's important to try to get the dates. If we find that we're talking about 6,000 or 7,000 years ago, as we believe, then it's justifiable to say that we're talking about Indo-Europeans. But if we discover instead that the dates are more recent—2,000 or 3,000 years ago—we could be talking about the Huns."

What was needed, obviously, was a more direct route into the past. As it happened, by the time Cavalli-Sforza's genetic atlas appeared, scientists were already starting to catch glimpses of the DNA in our ancestors' cells.

SINCE THE 19TH CENTURY, scientists have been studying fossils to reconstruct our past. But there was no evidence to tell them definitely whether these represented our direct ancestors or were merely dead branches on the family tree. So scientists did the logical thing: They arranged them with the oldest and most dissimilar hominids first, leading up to the most recent and close-to-human types. It was a convenient time line, familiar from textbook illustrations and museum dioramas. And then came Eve.

She debuted before the world in the winter of 1988: a naked woman holding an apple on the cover of *Newsweek*. The article explained that a team of biochemists at Berkeley had discovered the single female ancestor of the entire human race. The scientists, led by Rebecca Cann, had done so by looking at the DNA found in a specific part of the cell called the mitochondria. Unlike other DNA, mitochondrial DNA isn't a combination of both parents' genes; it is inherited only from the mother. This means that the only changes to the mitochondrial genes, as they pass from generation to generation, are occasional mutations. By calculating the rate of these mutations, and comparing the mitochondrial DNA of people from around the world, the Berkeley researchers had come up with a surprisingly young com-

---

Genetically, each of us represents not only ourself but, in a certain sense, all of our ancestors

---

mon ancestress: Eve, as the scientists dubbed her, was only 200,000 years old. "Genetically speaking," writes James Shreeve in *The Neanderthal Enigma*, "there was not all that much difference between a [modern] New Guinean highlander, a South African !Kung tribeswoman, and a housewife from the Marin County hills. . . . Whatever appearances might suggest, they simply hadn't had time enough to diverge."

The Eve discovery shocked evolutionary historians. It meant the hominids that spread out of Africa 1.2 million years ago were not modern humans' direct ancestors. Instead they and their descendants had been supplanted by a far more recent out-of-Africa migration—perhaps only 100,000 years ago. That would mean that all the old standbys of the museum diorama—Peking Man, Java Man, Neanderthal Man—were evolutionary dead ends.

Not surprisingly, traditional paleontologists have attacked Eve with vigor, arguing that Cann's sample was skewed, her computer program flawed, and that even if all humans share a recent female ancestor, it doesn't mean there weren't other contributions to our gene pool. Eve's partisans counterattacked: A num-

ber of independent researchers have looked at different parts of the DNA and arrived at similar dates for our divergence from a common ancestor. Last fall, a geneticist at the University of Arizona claimed to have found a common male ancestor who lived 188,000 years ago.

Now scientists are tying to resolve the Eve debate by looking in the most logical place of all: ancient DNA. "If we had even one Neanderthal DNA sample we could be sure of, it would quickly emerge how closely related it was to modern *Homo sapiens*," says Sir Walter Bodmer, former president of the Human Genome Organisation. Just a few years ago, the idea of finding a sample of Neanderthal DNA would have seemed about as probable as the idea of finding a live Neanderthal living deep in some cave, since scientists believed that the fragile DNA molecule decayed rapidly after death. But now geneticist are reading DNA recovered from ancient human remains. Despite skepticism from many scientists, their results are winning acceptance.

In 1984, a group of Berkeley scientists announced that they had sequenced the DNA of a quagga, an African animal, similar to the zebra, that was hunted to extinction in the late 19th century. They had accomplished this using the polymerase chain reaction (PCR), a chemical method for amplifying tiny DNA sequences. This is the same technique that scientists like Cann and Kolman use on fresh DNA from blood samples; the Berkeley team simply applied it to a fragment of quagga skin that was preserved in a German museum.

Quickly, other researchers began applying PCR to ancient specimens—and reporting spectacular results. Scientists claimed to have cloned DNA from Egyptian mummies, woolly mammoths, even a 120-million-year-old weevil trapped in amber, à la *Jurassic Park*. There was only one problem: The PCR process is extremely vulnerable to contamination, so nearly all these results turned out to be false—the mammoth's DNA, for instance, was that of a lab technician.

However, a few ancient-DNA laboratories have started to produce credible and verifiable work. Last year, two labs independently sequenced genes from the Ice Man, the Stone Age hunter whose

---

Ancient DNA may allow scientists to establish a continuum from very early times to the present

---

frozen body was found high in the Italian Alps in 1991, and both arrived at the same results. Many of the best samples, oddly enough, have come from bones and teeth. "Now people generally accept that you can get DNA from hard tissues," says Oxford geneticist Bryan Sykes, who is generally considered one of the most careful ancient-DNA researchers. "I suppose the oldest we've ever got to was about 15,000 years—that was for some animal bones from a limestone cave in England. But I think most people wouldn't be too surprised if one were to report recovery of DNA from well-preserved bone up to maybe even 100,000 years ago."

That implies that Neanderthal DNA should be waiting to be discovered in the collections of museums around the world. The treasure hunt is now in full swing. No lab yet claims publicly to have sequenced Neanderthal genes (although Sykes, when asked if he has obtained results, hesitates and replies, "Nothing I could reveal to you"). "It's only a matter of time," says Andrew Merriwether of the University of Pittsburgh, who is looking for Neanderthal DNA in some 35,000-year-old teeth from a Croatian cave. "There are a lot of Neanderthal remains around."

Once the treasure hunters find their quarry, they'll use it to put the Eve hypothesis to a powerful test. And that's not all they'll learn. "One particularly burning question just begs to be answered," writes Walter Bodmer in *The Book of Man*. "Exactly what evolutionary advantage did Homo sapiens have over this hominid competitors, and in particular over our nearest evolutionary brothers and sisters, the Neanderthals? What genetic gifts made Homo sapiens

so special and allowed us to inherit the Earth, while other hominids conspicuously failed?"

In the meantime, scientists are using more recent ancient DNA to answer less profound questions. Scott Woodward of Brigham Young University is working with the royal mummies of Egypt's 18th dynasty, trying to chart the pharaohs' complex family tree. Sykes is using Neolithic bones from Europe to test Cavalli-Sforza's ideas about the spread of agriculture. Merriwether and Kolman are comparing DNA from ancient American specimens with that of modern Indians, hoping to resolve conclusively the history of the peopling of the New World.

Scientists hope that, bit by bit, ancient DNA samples will allow them to interpret more accurately the history encoded in modern genes. "What ancient DNA will allow us to do is establish a continuum from very early times up to the present," says Woodward. "Right now, all we can look at is a single snapshot. If we go back to 500 years ago, 1,000 years ago, 1,500 years ago, it will give us snapshots of the past. And as we fill in the gaps, soon there will be a motion picture and we'll be able to watch history unfold."

SOUTHWEST OF CAIRO, ON the edge of the great Fayum oasis, the desert sand teems with thousands upon thousands of graves. Here ancient Egyptians buried their dead, the bodies wrapped in linen cloth, with only a few possessions—a reed mat, a cup, a loaf of bread—to accompany them into the afterlife. For these were common folk, and although they lived in the shadow of the pyramids, the age of the pharaohs was already past. The Fayum cemetery was in use from the middle of the first millennium B.C. to the middle of the first millennium A.D., during the period of Greek and Roman dominion over Egypt.

Still, Scott Woodward is unearthing treasure from the simple burials: clues to the identity of the Egyptian, and to the spread of Christianity. The cemetery's history spans the time when the Egyptians abandoned paganism for the new faith, and the graves reflect the change. Until late in the first century

a.d., the dead were buried facing west. Then, suddenly, they were oriented facing east—reflecting the Christian belief that the resurrected Christ would return from the east, according to Woodward and his collaborators. Woodward is analyzing the bodies' DNA to find out just who these early Christians were—native converts or immigrants. "We're [also] trying to answer the question of how much sub-Saharan African influence there was in the ancient Egyptians," Woodward says. "Egypt was probably a very cosmopolitan place, as much of a melting pot as the United States is today. . . . My guess is that we'll see African, we'll see Asian, we'll see Caucasian markers." In time, he says, it will be possible to get a genetic picture of the entire population of the cemetery.

So far, Woodward only has results from a half-dozen burials, none of which shows the typically African DNA marker. Even so, his investigation suggests how DNA research can confirm or question disputes over the identity of a particular people, like the modern Coptic Christians, who claim that they are the sole descendants of the ancient Egyptians, or those of sub-Saharan African origin, especially in the United States, who derive ethnic pride from the theory that the pharaohs were black.

Sometimes, such research can turn up unwelcome results. "Judaism is without doubt the most genetic of all religions—it depends on descent," says Steve Jones. "Orthodox Jews are very much of the opinion that Judaism is a huge pedigree of individuals who descend from Abraham." Yet studies of Jewish DNA indicate extensive mixing with outsiders. The Yemenite Jews, Jones notes, who have been accepted without question into Israeli society, appear to be almost entirely the descendants of Arab converts. Meanwhile, members of the black Lemba tribe of South Africa, who claim to be one of the lost tribes of Israel, have never been accepted as Jews. But their genes, Jones says, seem to support their claim: They show patterns typical of Middle Eastern origin.

"The genome pushes us to redefine ourselves," says Howard University immunogeneticist Georgia Dunston. Dunston plans a major genetic study to trace the origins of American blacks back to the lands from which their ancestors were taken. "At this point in the history of African-Americans, we are seeking to make connections to roots that extend beyond slavery," she says.

OUR GENES CANNOT WHOLLY account for our diversity. In fact, the work of genetic historians would be far easier were it not for the fact that the peoples of the world are so similar under the skin. "It is because they are external that ... racial differences strike us so forcibly, and we automatically assume that differences of similar magnitude exist below the surface, in the rest of our genetic makeup," Cavalli-Sforza has written. "This is simply not so: the remainder of our genetic makeup hardly differs at all." Indeed, research has shown that culture usually drives the spread of genes and not vice versa. "In the history of human development," Cavalli-Sforza says, "whenever there has been a major expansion geographically or demographically, it has been because one people has had an increase in food or power or transportation. . . . Whenever I see an expansion, I start looking for the innovation that made it." The invention of agriculture or the wheel makes history; genes only reflect it.

Even so, the story that the genes' tiny gradations tells is altering the way we think about the past. "Genetics changed something fundamental about our view of history," says Jones. "It shows us that history is largely the story of love, not war." The genetic historians suggest that it's time we started asking, with E. M. Forster: Who *did* go to bed with whom in the year 1400? And as we consider the possibilities—a Mongol chieftain and his Chinese bride, say; an Aztec woman and her husband; a fumbling pair of teenagers on a French hillside— it is pleasing to think that those ancient acts of love left their mark somewhere within each of us.

Japanese Roots

*Just who are the Japanese? Where did they come from and when?
The answers are difficult to come by, though not impossible—the
real problem is that the Japanese themselves may not want to know.*

By Jared Diamond

Unearthing the origins of the Japanese is a much harder task than you might guess. Among world powers today, the Japanese are the most distinctive in their culture and environment. The origins of their language are one of the most disputed questions of linguistics. These questions are central to the self-image of the Japanese and to how they are viewed by other peoples. Japan's rising dominance and touchy relations with its neighbors make it more important than ever to strip away myths and find answers.

The search for answers is difficult because the evidence is so conflicting. On the one hand, the Japanese people are biologically undistinctive, being very similar in appearance and genes to other East Asians, especially to Koreans. As the Japanese like to stress, they are culturally and biologically rather homogeneous, with the exception of a distinctive people called the Ainu on Japan's northernmost island of Hokkaido. Taken together, these facts seem to suggest that the Japanese reached Japan only recently from the Asian mainland, too recently to have evolved differences from their mainland cousins, and displaced the Ainu, who represent the original inhabitants. But if that were true, you might expect the Japanese language to show close affinities to some mainland language, just as English is obviously closely related to other Germanic languages (because Anglo-Saxons from the continent conquered England as recently as the sixth century A.D.). How can we resolve this contradiction between Japan's presumably ancient language and the evidence for recent origins?

Archeologists have proposed four conflicting theories. Most popular in Japan is the view that the Japanese gradually evolved from ancient Ice Age people who occupied Japan long before 20,000 B.C. Also widespread in Japan is a theory that the Japanese descended from horse-riding Asian nomads who passed through Korea to conquer Japan in the fourth century, but who were themselves—emphatically—not Koreans. A theory favored by many Western archeologists and Koreans, and unpopular in some circles in Japan, is that the Japanese are descendants of immigrants from Korea who arrived with rice-paddy agriculture around 400 B.C. Finally, the fourth theory holds that the peoples named in the other three theories could have mixed to form the modern Japanese.

According to the earliest recorded Japanese chronicles, the emperors of Japan are descended from the sun goddess Amaterasu. Archaeology, of course, tells a different story.

When similar questions of origins arise about other peoples, they can be discussed dispassionately. That is not so for the Japanese. Until 1946, Japanese schools taught a myth of history based on the earliest recorded Japanese chronicles, which were written in the eighth century. They describe how the sun goddess Amaterasu, born from the left eye of the creator god Izanagi, sent her grandson Ninigi to Earth on the Japanese island of Kyushu to wed an earthly deity. Ninigi's great-grandson Jimmu, aided by a dazzling sacred bird that rendered his enemies helpless, became the first emperor of Japan in 660 B.C. To fill the gap between 660 B.C. and the earliest historically documented Japanese monarchs, the chronicles invented 13 other equally fictitious emperors. Before the end of World War II, when Emperor Hirohito finally announced that he was not of divine descent, Japanese archeologists and historians had to make their interpretations conform to this chronicle account. Unlike American archeologists, who acknowledge that ancient sites in the United States were left by peoples (Native Americans) unrelated to most modern Americans, Japanese archeologists believe all archeological deposits in Japan, no matter how old, were left by ancestors of the modern Japanese. Hence archeology in Japan is supported by astronomical budgets, employs up to 50,000 field-workers each year, and draws public attention to a degree inconceivable anywhere else in the world.

Why do they care so much? Unlike most other non-European countries, Japan preserved its independence and culture while emerging from isolation to create an industrialized society in the late nineteenth century. It was a remarkable achievement. Now the Japanese people are understandably concerned about maintaining their traditions in the face of massive Western cultural influences. They want to believe that their distinctive language and culture required uniquely complex developmental processes. To acknowledge a relationship of the Japanese language to any other language seems to constitute a surrender of cultural identity.

What makes it especially difficult to discuss Japanese archeology dispassionately is that Japanese interpretations of the past affect present behavior. Who among East Asian peoples brought culture to whom? Who has historical claims to whose land? These are not just academic questions. For instance, there is much archeological evidence that people and material objects passed between Japan and Korea in the period A.D. 300 to 700. Japanese interpret this to mean that Japan conquered Korea and brought Korean slaves and artisans to Japan; Koreans believe instead that Korea conquered Japan and that the founders of the Japanese imperial family were Korean.

Thus, when Japan sent troops to Korea and annexed it in 1910, Japanese military leaders celebrated the annexation as "the restoration of the legitimate arrangement of antiquity." For the next 35 years, Japanese occupation forces tried to eradicate Korean culture and to replace the Korean language with Japanese in schools. The effort was a consequence of a centuries-old attitude of disdain. "Nose tombs" in Japan still contain 20,000 noses severed from Koreans and brought home as trophies of a sixteenth-century Japanese invasion. Not surprisingly, many Koreans loathe the Japanese, and their loathing is returned with contempt.

What really was "the legitimate arrangement of antiquity"? Today, Japan and Korea are both economic powerhouses, facing each other across the Korea Strait and viewing each other through colored lenses of false myths and past atrocities. It bodes ill for the future of East Asia if these two great peoples cannot find common ground. To do so, they will need a correct understanding of who the Japanese people really are.

JAPAN'S UNIQUE CULTURE began with its unique geography and environment. It is, for comparison, far more isolated than Britain, which lies only 22 miles from the French coast. Japan lies 110 miles from the closest point of the Asian mainland (South Korea), 190 miles from mainland Russia, and 480 miles from mainland China. Climate, too, sets Japan apart. Its rainfall, up to 120 inches a year, makes it the wettest temperate country in the world. Unlike the winter rains prevailing over much of Europe, Japan's rains are concentrated in the summer growing season, giving it the highest plant productivity of any nation in the temperate zones. While 80 percent of Japan's land consists of mountains unsuitable for agriculture and only 14 percent is farmland, an average square mile of that farmland is so fertile that it supports eight times as many people as does an average square mile of British farmland. Japan's high rainfall also ensures a quickly regenerated forest after logging. Despite thousands of years of dense human occupation, Japan still offers visitors a first impression of greenness because 70 percent of its land is still covered by forest.

Japanese forest composition varies with latitude and altitude: evergreen leafy forest in the south at low altitude, deciduous leafy forest in central Japan, and coniferous forest in the north and high up. For prehistoric humans, the deciduous leafy forest was the most productive, providing abundant edible nuts such as walnuts, chestnuts, horse chestnuts, acorns, and beechnuts. Japanese waters are also outstandingly productive. The lakes, rivers, and surrounding seas teem with salmon, trout, tuna, sardines, mackerel, herring, and cod. Today, Japan is the largest consumer of fish in the world. Japanese waters are also rich in clams, oysters, and other shellfish, crab, shrimp, crayfish, and edible seaweeds. That high productivity was a key to Japan's prehistory.

From southwest to northeast, the four main Japanese islands are Kyushu, Shikoku, Honshu, and Hokkaido. Until the late nineteenth century, Hokkaido and northern Honshu were inhabited mainly by the Ainu, who lived as hunter-gatherers with limited agriculture, while the people we know today as Japanese occupied the rest of the main islands.

In appearance, of course, the Japanese are very similar to other East Asians. As for the Ainu, however, their distinctive appearance has prompted more to be written about their origins and relationships than about any other single people on Earth. Partly because Ainu men have luxuriant beards and the most profuse body hair of any people,

During the ice ages, land bridges (striped areas) connected Japan's main islands to one another and to the mainland, allowing mammals--including humans--to arrive on foot.

guage, its origins are thoroughly in doubt; it may not have any special relationship to Japanese.

After genes and language, a third type of evidence about Japanese origins comes from ancient portraits. The earliest preserved likeness of Japan's inhabitants are statues called haniwa, erected outside tombs around 1,500 years ago. Those statues unmistakably depict East Asians. They do not resemble the heavily bearded Ainu. If the Japanese did replace the Ainu in Japan south of Hokkaido, the replacement must have occurred before A.D. 500.

Our earliest written information about Japan comes from Chinese chronicles, because China developed literacy long before Korea or Japan. In early Chinese accounts of various peoples referred to as "Eastern Barbarians," Japan is described under the name Wa, whose inhabitants were said to be divided into more than a hundred quarreling states. Only a few Korean or Japanese inscriptions before A.D. 700 have been preserved, but extensive chronicles were written in 712 and 720 in Japan and later in Korea. Those reveal massive transmission of culture to Japan from Korea itself, and from China via Korea. The chronicles are also full of accounts of Koreans in Japan and of Japanese in Korea—interpreted by Japanese or Korean historians, respectively, as evidence of Japanese conquest of Korea or the reverse.

The ancestors of the Japanese, then, seem to have reached Japan before they had writing. Their biology suggests a recent arrival, but their language suggests arrival long ago. To resolve this paradox, we must now turn to archeology.

The seas that surround much of Japan and coastal East Asia are shallow enough to have been dry land during the ice ages, when much of the ocean water was locked up in glaciers and sea level lay at about 500 feet below its present measurement. Land bridges connected Japan's main islands to one another, to the Russian mainland, and to South Korea. The mammals walking out to Japan included not only the ancestors of modern Japan's bears and monkeys but also ancient humans, long before boats had been invented. Stone tools indicate hu-

they are often classified as Caucasoids (so-called white people) who somehow migrated east through Eurasia to Japan. In their overall genetic makeup, though, the Ainu are related to other East Asians, including the Japanese and Koreans. The distinctive appearance and hunter-gatherer lifestyle of the Ainu, and the undistinctive appearance and the intensive agricultural lifestyle of the Japanese, are frequently taken to suggest the straightforward interpretation that the Ainu are descended from Japan's original hunter-gatherer inhabitants and the Japanese are more recent invaders from the Asian mainland.

But this view is difficult to reconcile with the distinctiveness of the Japanese language. Everyone agrees that Japanese does not bear a close relation to any other language in the world. Most scholars consider it to be an isolated member of Asia's Altaic language family, which consists of Turkic, Mongolian, and Tun-

gusic languages. Korean is also often considered to be an isolated member of this family, and within the family Japanese and Korean may be more closely related to each other than to other Altaic languages. However, the similarities between Japanese and Korean are confined to general grammatical features and about 15 percent of their basic vocabularies, rather than the detailed shared features of grammar and vocabulary that link, say, French to Spanish; they are more different from each other than Russian is from English.

Since languages change over time, the more similar two languages are, the more recently they must have diverged. By counting common words and features, linguists can estimate how long ago languages diverged, and such estimates suggest that Japanese and Korean parted company at least 4,000 years ago. As for the Ainu lanman arrival as early as half a million years ago.

Around 13,000 years ago, as glaciers melted rapidly all over the world, conditions in Japan changed spectacularly for the better, as far as humans were concerned. Temperature, rainfall, and humidity all increased, raising plant productivity to present high levels. Deciduous leafy forests full of nut trees, which had been confined to southern Japan during the ice ages, expanded northward at the expense of coniferous forest, thereby replacing a forest type that had been rather sterile for humans with a much more productive one. The rise in sea level severed the land bridges, converted Japan from a piece of the Asian continent to a big archipelago, turned what had been a plain into rich shallow seas, and created thousands of miles of productive new coastline with innumerable islands, bays, tidal flats, and estuaries, all teeming with seafood.

That end of the Ice Age was accompanied by the first of the two most decisive changes in Japanese history: the invention of pottery. In the usual experience of archeologists, inventions flow from mainlands to islands, and small peripheral societies aren't supposed to contribute revolutionary advances to the rest of the world. It therefore astonished archeologists to discover that the world's oldest known pottery was made in Japan 12,700 years ago. For the first time in human experience, people had watertight containers readily available in any desired shape. With their new ability to boil or steam food, they gained access to abundant resources that had previously been difficult to use: leafy vegetables, which would burn or dry out if cooked on an open fire; shellfish, which could now be opened easily; and toxic foods like acorns, which could now have their toxins boiled out. Soft-boiled foods could be fed to small children, permitting earlier weaning and more closely spaced babies. Toothless old people, the repositories of information in a preliterate society, could now be fed and live longer. All those momentous consequences of pottery triggered a population explosion, causing Japan's population to climb from an estimated few thousand to a quarter of a million.

The prejudice that islanders are supposed to learn from superior continentals wasn't the sole reason that record-breaking Japanese pottery caused such a shock. In addition, those first Japanese potters were clearly hunter-gatherers, which also violated established views. Usually only sedentary societies own pottery: what nomad wants to carry heavy, fragile pots, as well as weapons and the baby, whenever time comes to shift camp? Most sedentary societies elsewhere in the world arose only with the adoption of agriculture. But the Japanese environment is so productive that people could settle down and make pottery while still living by hunting and gathering. Pottery helped those Japanese hunter-gatherers exploit their environment's rich food resources more than 10,000 years before intensive agriculture reached Japan.

Much ancient Japanese pottery was decorated by rolling or pressing a cord on soft clay. Because the Japanese word for cord marking is *jomon,* the term Jomon is applied to the pottery itself, to the ancient Japanese people who made it, and to that whole period in Japanese prehistory beginning with the invention of pottery and ending only 10,000 years later. The earliest Jomon pottery, of 12,700 years ago, comes from Kyushu, the southernmost Japanese island. Thereafter, pottery spread north, reaching the vicinity of modern Tokyo around 9,500 years ago and the northernmost island of Hokkaido by 7,000 years ago. Pottery's northward spread followed that of deciduous forest rich in nuts, suggesting that the climate-related food explosion was what permitted sedentary living.

How did Jomon people make their living? We have abundant evidence from the garbage they left behind at hundreds of thousands of excavated archeological sites all over Japan. They apparently enjoyed a well-balanced diet, one that modern nutritionists would applaud.

One major food category was nuts, especially chestnuts and walnuts, plus horse chestnuts and acorns leached or boiled free of their bitter poisons. Nuts could be harvested in autumn in prodigious quantities, then stored for the winter in underground pits up to six feet

deep and six feet wide. Other plant foods included berries, fruits, seeds, leaves, shoots, bulbs, and roots. In all, archeologists sifting through Jomon garbage have identified 64 species of edible plants.

Then as now, Japan's inhabitants were among the world's leading consumers of seafood. They harpooned tuna in the open ocean, killed seals on the beaches, and exploited seasonal runs of salmon in the rivers. They drove dolphins into shallow water and clubbed or speared them, just as Japanese hunters do today. They netted diverse fish, captured them in weirs, and caught them on fishhooks carved from deer antlers. They gathered shellfish, crabs, and seaweed in the intertidal zone or dove for them. (Jomon skeletons show a high incidence of abnormal bone growth in the ears, often observed in divers today.) Among land animals hunted, wild boar and deer were the most common prey. They were caught in pit traps, shot with bows and arrows, and run down with dogs.

The most debated question about Jomon subsistence concerns the possible contribution of agriculture. Many Jomon sites contain remains of edible plants that are native to Japan as wild species but also grown as crops today, including the adzuki bean and green gram bean. The remains from Jomon times do not clearly show features distinguishing the crops from their wild ancestors, so we do not know whether these plants were gathered in the wild or grown intentionally. Sites also have debris of edible or useful plant species not native to Japan, such as hemp, which must have been introduced from the Asian mainland. Around 1000 B.C., toward the end of the Jomon period, a few grains of rice, barley, and millet, the staple cereals of East Asia, began to appear. All these tantalizing clues make it likely that Jomon people were starting to practice some slash-and-burn agriculture, but evidently in a casual way that made only a minor contribution to their diet.

Archeologists studying Jomon hunter-gatherers have found not only hard-to-carry pottery (including pieces up to three feet tall) but also heavy stone tools, remains of substantial houses that show signs of repair, big village sites of 50 or more dwellings, and cemeteries—all further evidence that the Jomon people were sedentary rather than nomadic. Their stay-at-home lifestyle was made possible by the diversity of resource-rich habitats available within a short distance of one central site: inland forests, rivers, seashores, bays, and open oceans. Jomon people lived at some of the highest population densities ever estimated for hunter-gatherers, especially in central and northern Japan, with their nut-rich forests, salmon runs, and productive seas. The estimate of the total population of Jomon Japan at its peak is 250,000—trivial, of course, compared with today, but impressive for hunter-gatherers.

With all this stress on what Jomon people did have, we need to be clear as well about what they didn't have. Their lives were very different from those of contemporary societies only a few hundred miles away in mainland China and Korea. Jomon people had no intensive agriculture. Apart from dogs (and perhaps pigs), they had no domestic animals. They had no metal tools, no writing, no weaving, and little social stratification into chiefs and commoners. Regional variation in pottery styles suggests little progress toward political centralization and unification.

Despite its distinctiveness even in East Asia at that time, Jomon Japan was not completely isolated. Pottery, obsidian, and fishhooks testify to some Jomon trade with Korea, Russia, and Okinawa—as does the arrival of Asian mainland crops. Compared with later eras, though, that limited trade with the outside world had little influence on Jomon society. Jomon Japan was a miniature conservative universe that changed surprisingly little over 10,000 years.

To place Jomon Japan in a contemporary perspective, let us remind ourselves of what human societies were like on the Asian mainland in 400 B.C., just as the Jomon lifestyle was about to come to an end. China consisted of kingdoms with rich elites and poor commoners; the people lived in walled towns, and the country was on the verge of political unification and would soon become the world's largest empire. Beginning around 6500 B.C., China had de-

All through human history, centralized states with metal weapons and armies supported by dense agricultural populations have swept away sparser populations of hunter-gatherers. How did Stone Age Japan survive so long?

veloped intensive agriculture based on millet in the north and rice in the south; it had domestic pigs, chickens, and water buffalo. The Chinese had had writing for at least 900 years, metal tools for at least 1,500 years, and had just invented the world's first cast iron. Those developments were also spreading to Korea, which itself had had agriculture for several thousand years (including rice since at least 2100 B.C.) and metal since 1000 B.C.

With all these developments going on for thousands of years just across the Korea Strait from Japan, it might seem astonishing that in 400 B.C. Japan was still occupied by people who had some trade with Korea but remained preliterate stone-tool-using hunter-gatherers. Throughout human history, centralized states with metal weapons and armies supported by dense agricultural populations have consistently swept away sparser populations of hunter-gatherers. How did Jomon Japan survive so long?

To understand the answer to this paradox, we have to remember that until 400 B.C., the Korea Strait separated not rich farmers from poor hunter-gatherers, but poor farmers from rich hunter-gatherers. China itself and Jomon Japan were probably not in direct contact. In-

stead Japan's trade contacts, such as they were, involved Korea. But rice had been domesticated in warm southern China and spread only slowly northward to much cooler Korea, because it took a long time to develop cold-resistant strains of rice. Early rice agriculture in Korea used dry-field methods rather than irrigated paddies and was not particularly productive. Hence early Korean agriculture could not compete with Jomon hunting and gathering. Jomon people themselves would have seen no advantage in adopting Korean agriculture, insofar as they were aware of its existence, and poor Korean farmers had no advantages that would let them force their way into Japan. As we shall see, the advantages finally reversed suddenly and dramatically.

More than 10,000 years after the invention of pottery and the subsequent Jomon population explosion, a second decisive event in Japanese history triggered a second population explosion. Around 400 B.C., a new lifestyle arrived from South Korea. This second transition poses in acute form our question about who the Japanese are. Does the transition mark the replacement of Jomon people with immigrants from Korea, ancestral to the modern Japanese? Or did Japan's original Jomon inhabitants continue to occupy Japan while learning valuable new tricks?

The new mode of living appeared first on the north coast of Japan's southwesternmost island, Kyushu, just across the Korea Strait from South Korea. There we find Japan's first metal tools, of iron, and Japan's first undisputed full-scale agriculture. That agriculture came in the form of irrigated rice fields, complete with canals, dams, banks, paddies, and rice residues revealed by archeological excavations. Archeologists term the new way of living Yayoi, after a district of Tokyo where in 1884 its characteristic pottery was first recognized. Unlike Jomon pottery, Yayoi pottery was very similar to contemporary South Korean pottery in shape. Many other elements of the new Yayoi culture were unmistakably Korean and previously foreign to Japan, including bronze objects, weaving, glass beads, and styles of tools and houses.

While rice was the most important crop, Yayoi farmers introduced 27 new to Japan, as well as unquestionably domesticated pigs. They may have practiced double cropping, with paddies irrigated for rice production in the summer, then drained for dry-land cultivation of millet, barley, and wheat in the winter. Inevitably, this highly productive system of intensive agriculture triggered an immediate population explosion in Kyushu, where archeologists have identified far more Yayoi sites than Jomon sites, even though the Jomon period lasted 14 times longer.

In virtually no time, Yayoi farming jumped from Kyushu to the adjacent main islands of Shikoku and Honshu, reaching the Tokyo area within 200 years, and the cold northern tip of Honshu (1,000 miles from the first Yayoi settlements on Kyushu) in another century. After briefly occupying northern Honshu, Yayoi farmers abandoned that area, presumably because rice farming could not compete with the Jomon hunter-gatherer life. For the next 2,000 years, northern Honshu remained a frontier zone, beyond which the northernmost Japanese island of Hokkaido and its Ainu hunter-gatherers were not even considered part of the Japanese state until their annexation in the nineteenth century.

It took several centuries for Yayoi Japan to show the first signs of social stratification, as reflected especially in cemeteries. After about 100 B.C., separate parts of cemeteries were set aside for the graves of what was evidently an emerging elite class, marked by luxury goods imported from China, such as beautiful jade objects and bronze mirrors. As the Yayoi population explosion continued, and as all the best swamps or irrigable plains suitable for wet rice agriculture began to fill up, the archeological evidence suggests that war became more and more frequent: that evidence includes mass production of arrowheads, defensive moats surrounding villages, and buried skeletons pierced by projectile points. These hallmarks of war in Yayoi Japan corroborate the earliest accounts of Japan in Chinese chronicles, which describe the land of Wa and its hundred little political units fighting one another.

In the period from A.D. 300 to 700, both archeological excavations and frustratingly ambiguous accounts in later chronicles let us glimpse dimly the emergence of a politically unified Japan. Before A.D. 300, elite tombs were small and exhibited a regional diversity of styles. Beginning around A.D. 300, increasingly enormous earth-mound tombs called *kofun,* in the shape of keyholes, were constructed throughout the former Yayoi area from Kyushu to North Honshu. *Kofun* are up to 1,500 feet long and more than 100 feet high, making them possibly the largest earth-mound tombs in the world. The prodigious amount of labor required to build them and the uniformity of their style across Japan imply powerful rulers who commanded a huge, politically unified labor force. Those *kofun* that have been excavated contain lavish burial goods, but excavation of the largest ones is still forbidden because they are believed to contain the ancestors of the Japanese imperial line. The visible evidence of political centralization that the *kofun* provide reinforces the accounts of *kofun*-era Japanese emperors written down much later in Japanese and Korean chronicles. Massive Korean influences on Japan during the *kofun* era—whether through the Korean conquest of Japan (the Korean view) or the Japanese conquest of Korea (the Japanese view)— were responsible for transmitting Buddhism, writing, horseback riding, and new ceramic and metallurgical techniques to Japan from the Asian mainland.

Finally, with the completion of Japan's first chronicle in A.D. 712, Japan emerged into the full light of history. As of 712, the people inhabiting Japan were at last unquestionably Japanese, and their language (termed Old Japanese) was unquestionably ancestral to modern Japanese. Emperor Akihito, who reigns today, is the eighty-second direct descendant of the emperor under whom that first chronicle of A.D. 712 was written. He is traditionally considered the 125th direct descendant of the legendary first emperor, Jimmu, the great-great-great-grandson of the sun goddess Amaterasu.

JAPANESE CULTURE UNDER-went far more radical change in the 700 years of the Yayoi era than in the ten millennia of Jomon times. The contrast between Jomon stability (or conservatism) and radical Yayoi change is the most striking feature of Japanese history. Obviously, something momentous happened at 400 B.C. What was it? Were the ancestors of the modern Japanese the Jomon people, the Yayoi people, or a combination? Japan's population increased by an astonishing factor of 70 during Yayoi times: What caused that change? A passionate debate has raged around three alternative hypotheses.

One theory is that Jomon hunter-gatherers themselves gradually evolved into the modern Japanese. Because they had already been living a settled existence in villages for thousands of years, they may have been preadapted to accepting agriculture. At the Yayoi transition, perhaps nothing more happened than that Jomon society received cold-resistant rice seeds and information about paddy irrigation from Korea, enabling it to produce more food and increase its numbers. This theory appeals to many modern Japanese because it minimizes the unwelcome contribution of Korean genes to the Japanese gene pool while portraying the Japanese people as uniquely Japanese for at least the past 12,000 years.

A second theory, unappealing to those Japanese who prefer the first theory, argues instead that the Yayoi transition represents a massive influx of immigrants from Korea, carrying Korean farming practices, culture, and genes. Kyushu would have seemed a paradise to Korean rice farmers, because it is warmer and swampier than Korea and hence a better place to grow rice. According to one estimate, Yayoi Japan received several million immigrants from Korea, utterly overwhelming the genetic contribution of Jomon people (thought to have numbered around 75,000 just before the Yayoi transition). If so, modern Japanese are descendants of Korean immigrants who developed a modified culture of their own over the last 2,000 years.

The last theory accepts the evidence for immigration from Korea but denies that it was massive. Instead, highly productive agriculture may have enabled a modest number of immigrant rice farmers to reproduce much faster than Jomon hunter-gatherers and eventually to outnumber them. Like the second theory, this theory considers modern Japanese to be slightly modified Koreans but dispenses with the need for large-scale immigration.

By comparison with similar transitions elsewhere in the world, the second or third theory seems to me more plausible than the first theory. Over the last 12,000 years, agriculture arose at not more than nine places on Earth, including China and the Fertile Crescent. Twelve thousand years ago, everybody alive was a hunter-gatherer; now almost all of us are farmers or fed by farmers. Farming spread from those few sites of origin mainly because farmers outbred hunters, developed more potent technology, and then killed the hunters or drove them off lands suitable for agriculture. In the modern times European farmers thereby replaced native Californian hunters, aboriginal Australians, and the San people of South Africa. Farmers who used stone tools similarly replaced hunters prehistorically throughout Europe, Southeast Asia, and Indonesia. Korean farmers of 400 B.C. would have enjoyed a much larger advantage over Jomon hunters because the Koreans already possessed iron tools and a highly developed form of intensive agriculture.

Which of the three theories is correct for Japan? The only direct way to answer this question is to compare Jomon and Yayoi skeletons and genes with those of modern Japanese and Ainu. Measurements have now been made of many skeletons. In addition, within the last three years molecular geneticists have begun to extract DNA from ancient human skeletons and compare the genes of Japan's ancient and modern populations. Jomon and Yayoi skeletons, researchers find, are on the average readily distinguishable. Jomon people tended to be shorter, with relatively longer forearms and lower legs, more wide-set eyes, shorter and wider faces, and much more pronounced facial topography, with strikingly raised browridges, noses, and nose bridges. Yayoi people averaged an inch or two taller, with close-set eyes, high and narrow

faces, and flat browridges and noses. Some skeletons of the Yayoi period were still Jomon-like in appearance, but that is to be expected by almost any theory of the Jomon-Yayoi transition. By the time of the *kofun* period, all Japanese skeletons except those of the Ainu form a homogeneous group, resembling modern Japanese and Koreans.

In all these respects, Jomon skulls differ from those of modern Japanese and are most similar to those of modern Ainu, while Yayoi skulls most resemble those of modern Japanese. Similarly, geneticists attempting to calculate the relative contributions of Korean-like Yayoi genes and Ainu-like Jomon genes to the modern Japanese gene pool have concluded that the Yayoi contribution was generally dominant. Thus, immigrants from Korea really did make a big contribution to the modern Japanese, though we cannot yet say whether that was because of massive immigration or else modest immigration amplified by a high rate of population increase. Genetic studies of the past three years have also at last resolved the controversy about the origins of the Ainu: they are the descendants of Japan's ancient Jomon inhabitants, mixed with Korean genes of Yayoi colonists and of the modern Japanese.

Given the overwhelming advantage that rice agriculture gave Korean farmers, one has to wonder why the farmers achieved victory over Jomon hunters so suddenly, after making little headway in Japan for thousands of years. What finally tipped the balance and triggered the Yayoi transition was probably a combination of four developments: the farmers began raising rice in irrigated fields instead of in less productive dry fields; they developed rice strains that would grow well in a cool climate; their population expanded in Korea, putting pressure on Koreans to emigrate; and they invented iron tools that allowed them to mass-produce the wooden shovels, hoes, and other tools needed for rice-paddy agriculture. That iron and intensive farming reached Japan simultaneously is unlikely to have been a coincidence.

WE HAVE SEEN THAT THE combined evidence of archeology, physical anthropology, and genetics supports the transparent interpretation for how the distinctive-looking Ainu and the undistinctive-looking Japanese came to share Japan: the Ainu are descended from Japan's original inhabitants and the Japanese are descended from more recent arrivals. But that view leaves the problem of language unexplained. If the Japanese really are recent arrivals from Korea, you might expect the Japanese and Korean languages to be very similar. More generally, if the Japanese people arose recently from some mixture, on the island of Kyushu, of original Ainu-like Jomon inhabitants with Yayoi invaders from Korea, the Japanese language might show close affinities to both the Korean and Ainu languages. Instead, Japanese and Ainu have no demonstrable relationship, and the relationship between Japanese and Korean is distant. How could this be so if the mixing occurred a mere 2,400 years ago? I suggest the following resolution of this paradox: the languages of Kyushu's Jomon residents and Yayoi invaders were quite different from the modern Ainu and Korean languages, respectively.

The Ainu language was spoken in recent times by the Ainu on the northern island of Hokkaido, so Hokkaido's Jomon inhabitants probably also spoke an Ainu-like language. The Jomon inhabitants of Kyushu, however, surely did not. From the southern tip of Kyushu to the northern tip of Hokkaido, the Japanese archipelago is nearly 1,500 miles long. In Jomon times it supported great regional diversity of subsistence techniques and of pottery styles and was never unified politically. During the 10,000 years of Jomon occupation, Jomon people would have evolved correspondingly great linguistic diversity. In fact, many Japanese place-names on Hokkaido and northern Honshu include the Ainu words for river, nai or betsu, and for cape, shiri, but such Ainu-like names do not occur farther south in Japan. This suggests not only that Yayoi and Japanese pioneers adopted many Jomon place-names, just as white Americans did Native American names (think of Massachusetts and Mississippi), but also that Ainu was the Jomon language only of northernmost Japan.

That is, the modern Ainu language of Hokkaido is not a model for the ancient Jomon language of Kyushu. By the same token, modern Korean may be a poor model for the ancient Yayoi language of Korean immigrants in 400 B.C. In the centuries before Korea became unified politically in A.D. 676, it consisted of three kingdoms. Modern Korean is derived from the language of the kingdom of Silla, the kingdom that emerged triumphant and unified Korea, but Silla was not the kingdom that had close contact with Japan in the preceding centuries. Early Korean chronicles tell us that the different kingdoms had

different languages. While the languages of the kingdoms defeated by Silla are poorly known, the few preserved words of one of those kingdoms, Koguryo, are much more similar to the corresponding Old Japanese words than are the corresponding modern Korean words. Korean languages may have been even more diverse in 400 B.C., before political unification had reached the stage of three kingdoms. The Korean language that reached Japan in 400 B.C., and that evolved into modern Japanese, I suspect, was quite different from the Silla language that evolved into modern Korean. Hence we should not be surprised that modern Japanese and Korean people resemble each other far more in their

appearance and genes than in their languages.

History gives the Japanese and the Koreans ample grounds for mutual distrust and contempt, so any conclusion confirming their close relationship is likely to be unpopular among both peoples. Like Arabs and Jews, Koreans and Japanese are joined by blood yet locked in traditional enmity. But enmity is mutually destructive, in East Asia as in the Middle East. As reluctant as Japanese and Koreans are to admit it, they are like twin brothers who shared their formative years. The political future of East Asia depends in large part on their success in rediscovering those ancient bonds between them.

Rediscovering America

The New World may be 20,000 years older than experts thought

By Charles W. Petit

Late in the afternoon last May 17, a tired archaeological team neared the end of a 14-hour day winching muck to the deck of a Canadian Coast Guard vessel. It was in water 170 feet deep in Juan Perez Sound, half a mile offshore among British Columbia's Queen Charlotte Islands. For four days, team members had fruitlessly sieved undersea mud and gravel. Then, in the slanting light of sunset, a deckhand drew from the goop a triangular blade of dark basalt. Its sharp edge and flaked surface said this was no ordinary rock. Someone long ago sculpted it into a knife or other cutting tool.

When Daryl Fedje, an archaeologist for Canada's national parks system, saw the 4-inch artifact, his jaw dropped in amazement: "I immediately recognized it as made by humans." For years Fedje has led efforts to find prehistoric evidence of human occupation in the misty, fiord-laced archipelago. This stone meant that people lived at a spot directly under the ship well before the end of the Ice Age, at a time when the sea level was far lower than today.

The bit of basalt is just one stone. But from Alaska to near the tip of South America, bits of just such intriguing evidence are emerging that suggest the standard textbook story—that humans first settled the Americas by pouring down from Alaska about 12,000 years ago—is wrong, perhaps very wrong. People may have gotten here thousands to tens of thousands of years sooner, over a longer period of time, by a wider variety of routes, and with a more diverse ancestry. If this proves true, it will force a rethinking of the whole concept of America: a land whose human history may be three times longer than imagined, and one where Columbus would have been just one of the last of many waves of "discoverers."

"The bottom line is that people could have reached here a long, long time ago," says Dennis Stanford, chairman of the anthropology department at the Smithsonian Institution. Stanford is among a growing number of scientists advancing the still heretical belief that the first North Americans did not walk over in one main migration but came much earlier, and by boat. Under fire is the time-honored "Clovis-first" theory, named after a site in New Mexico where big, stone spear points were found in the 1930s (story, "They came from the north"). The artifacts were left by a mammoth-hunting culture that appeared in North America a little more than 11,000 years ago. The Clovis people were real, but the standard textbook lessons about them may well be wrong. It now appears that they were not the first in the New World. "I think we're in a whole new ballgame of discovery about who the first Americans were and when they got here," Stanford says.

That would spell the end of the heroic saga generations of schoolchildren have learned—of a great invasion of big-game hunters showing up on a virgin landscape. The peopling of the Americas is beginning to look more like a continuation of another, even grander, saga: the human occupation of the Old World that started perhaps 100,000 years ago. The peopling of Europe and Asia was an expansion featuring multiple migrations and an ebb and flow of cultures that, it now appears, may have washed into the Americas in a series of waves starting well before Clovis times, perhaps as early as 30,000 years ago.

Scholarly rejection. Despite the primacy of the Clovis-first tale, some scientists never could quite embrace it. Over the years, hundreds of sites have been touted as older than the 11,200-year-old early Clovis sites, including Calico in San Bernardino County, Calif., endorsed in the 1960s by famed African anthropologist Louis Leakey as possibly more than 200,000 years old. But each time, at Calico and elsewhere, parades of outside experts said the "tools" were

MAMMOTH HUNTERS

They came from the north

The standard explanation of human arrival in the Americas is a stirring tale with mythic overtones, of fur-clad big-game hunters marching out of the far, frozen north to conquer a New World, an Eden whose immense beasts had never before seen human beings. This Clovis-first theory is under assault but has not yet crumbled, as scientists examine scanty evidence to decipher how North and South America were first occupied. The Clovis-first theory, named after an archaeological site near Clovis, N.M., proposes that, perhaps 15,000 years ago, Arctic-adapted peoples moved across a 1,000-mile-wide land bridge where the shallow Bering Strait today separates Alaska from Siberia. After being bottled up for a few thousand years by glaciers south of Beringia—the name given the combined land mass of Alaska and northeastern Siberia—about 12,000 years ago this vanguard moved down into what is now Alberta, travers-

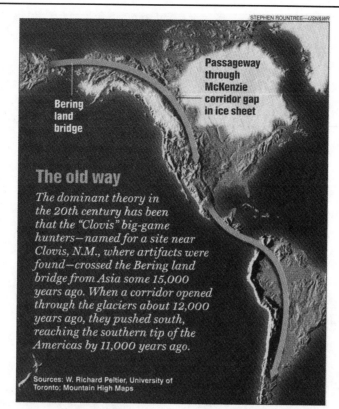

STEPHEN ROUNTREE—USN&WR

Bering land bridge

Passageway through McKenzie corridor gap in ice sheet

The old way

The dominant theory in the 20th century has been that the "Clovis" big-game hunters—named for a site near Clovis, N.M., where artifacts were found—crossed the Bering land bridge from Asia some 15,000 years ago. When a corridor opened through the glaciers about 12,000 years ago, they pushed south, reaching the southern tip of the Americas by 11,000 years ago.

Sources: W. Richard Peltier, University of Toronto; Mountain High Maps

Clovis spear points display distinctive fluting.

ing an ice-free corridor that opened through the glaciers just east of the Canadian Rockies as the Ice Age waned. Splitting into smaller groups and developing new cultures as they went, and bearing large families supported by the vast resources before them, these Paleo-Indians supposedly raced all the way to the tip of South America in 1,000 years or so. And, except for some later-arriving groups, includ-

ing today's Inuits, or Eskimos, these people would have been the ancestors of nearly all of today's Native Americans.

Heavy artillery. Clovis-first arose from discoveries, starting in the 1920s, of chipped and shattered bones of bison and mammoths. These bones were the first proof that people had arrived in time to see, and kill, the last great beasts of the Ice Age, and that hunt-

ing may have contributed to the animals' extinction.

Distinctive long spearheads, called Clovis points after the New Mexico site where they were discovered, have been found with bones of prey dated as much as 11,200 years ago. Hundreds of Clovis sites have been identified throughout North America, implying that wherever the hunters came from, their culture exploded across the landscape with astonishing rapidity. The robust Clovis points bear grooves of "flutes" carved in their bases where they attached to wooden shafts. Propelled with powerful atlatls, or throwing sticks, the stone-tipped spears served as heavy artillery as the newcomers butchered their way across North America's great plains in a virtual blitzkrieg.

—*C.W.P.*

VICTOR BOSWELL—NATIONAL GEOGRAPHIC IMAGE COLLECTION

natural stones, or the dates were wrong, or supposedly human bones weren't human, or the charcoal was from a naturally caused wildfire, not a man-made hearth, or all that and more. The sites "have gotten their 15 minutes of fame, then disappeared into obscurity," said James Adovasio, professor of archaeology at Mercyhurst College in Erie, Pa.

Adovasio has his own tale of scholarly rejection. Since 1973 he has led excavation of the Meadowcroft Rockshelter, a 43-foot-high jutting cliff that provides protection from rain along its base. It looks out on Cross Creek, in rugged country 30 miles southwest of Pittsburgh. The landowner, Albert Miller, whose family

has had the property since 1795 and operates a colonial-era museum there, called archaeologists in the early 1970s to investigate his hunch about Indian traces under the overhang. Miller's instincts were right. "Everybody and his brother stopped here," marvels Adovasio. Using razor blades to peel layers away, his crews have uncovered a rich trove of relics—20,000 stone tools, woven goods, nearly a million animal bones, and 300 fireplaces loaded with charcoal, making it easy for scientists to calculate dates. (Scientists estimate the age of charcoal and other organic material by measuring how much radioactive carbon-14 it contains. Living things ab-

sorb this isotope from the atmosphere; when they die, the radiocarbon begins to decay away. Although new studies suggest that solar variations throw the scale off slightly—11,000 radiocarbon years may be closer to 13,000 actual years, for instance—radiocarbon dating is still the gold standard for archaeological dating.) The cave was on a highway for traders, hunters, and migrants moving to and from the Ohio River Valley to the West. "If you were out camping and saw this place, this is where you'd stop, too," Adovasio says. Every accepted cultural period in Indian history and prehistory is represented: the contemporary Iroquoian Seneca; earlier and

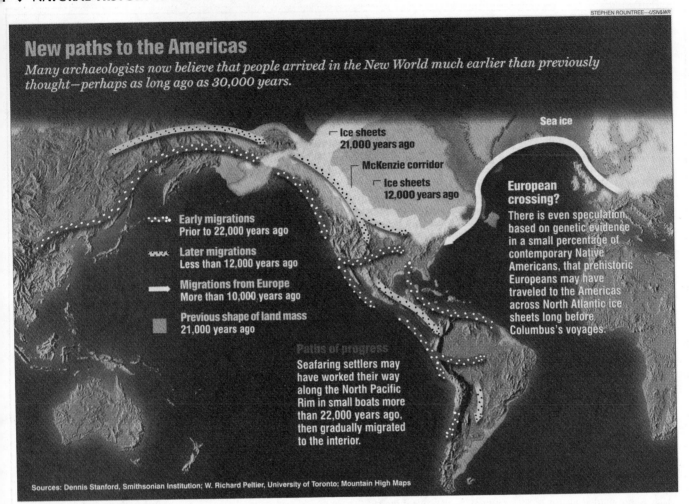

STEPHEN ROUNTREE—*USN&WR*

New paths to the Americas
Many archaeologists now believe that people arrived in the New World much earlier than previously thought—perhaps as long ago as 30,000 years.

Ice sheets
21,000 years ago

McKenzie corridor

Ice sheets
12,000 years ago

Sea ice

European crossing?
There is even speculation, based on genetic evidence in a small percentage of contemporary Native Americans, that prehistoric Europeans may have traveled to the Americas across North Atlantic ice sheets long before Columbus's voyages.

Early migrations
Prior to 22,000 years ago

Later migrations
Less than 12,000 years ago

Migrations from Europe
More than 10,000 years ago

Previous shape of land mass
21,000 years ago

Paths of progress
Seafaring settlers may have worked their way along the North Pacific Rim in small boats more than 22,000 years ago, then gradually migrated to the interior.

Sources: Dennis Stanford, Smithsonian Institution; W. Richard Peltier, University of Toronto; Mountain High Maps

closely related "woodland" societies that reach back 1,000 years; the so-called archaic groups to around 8,500 years ago; and Paleo-Indians, including the Clovis big-game hunters, to about 11,000 years ago.

Trouble came when Adovasio began saying in the late 1970s that charcoal from human-made fire pits deep in the excavated floor of the shelter carried dates going back more than 14,000 years, with some indications approaching 17,000 years. He ran into what he calls the "Clovis curtain" of resistance. Critics told him the charcoal that he presumed came from wood may actually have been contaminated by ancient coal or carbon in the local sediments, which would carbon-date much earlier. Adovasio retorts that what he calls the "Clovis mafia" peculiarly rejects only dates at his site that are older than Clovis but not younger material. Contamination would skew ages for everything, he points out, not just for the finds that run counter to standard theory.

Accumulating evidence. But after years of being almost alone as a challenger of Clovis, Adovasio suddenly has company. Similar deposits are being reported by archaeologists at sites throughout the Americas, including one called Cactus Hill, in coastal Virginia. That project's leader, Joseph McAvoy of the privately supported Nottaway River Survey in Sandston, Va., can't discuss his newest findings because he's under a gag order from the National Geographic Society, which is helping pay for the excavation. But in a 1996 report, McAvoy described his discovery of possible pre-Clovis tools that Adovasio says look a lot like his at Meadowcroft.

Evidence also has shown up in Wisconsin. For 10 years, David Overstreet, director of the Great Lakes Archaeological Research Center in Milwaukee, has excavated two mammoth butchery sites that he says are at least 12,500 years old, and where stone tools lie among giant bones and long, curved ivory tusks. Nearby are bones of two more of the

extinct elephants, 1,000 years older, bearing what appear to be the distinctive cut marks made by people chopping out meat for food. The roughly shaped tools look nothing like the precisely grooved Clovis points. Overstreet figures that by the time any corridor through the glaciers opened, somebody had already been living for a few millenniums along the ice front, hunting the megafauna of the plains south of it.

But the big break that persuaded many to rethink the conventional theory has come thousands of miles from Clovis in Monte Verde, Chile. There, archaeologist Tom Dillehay of the University of Kentucky has, for 20 years, been excavating wood, bone, and stone tools from rolling pasture land. Last year he was joined by a blue-ribbon group of archaeologists, including many who were skeptical of Dillehay's long-controversial assertions that the artifacts probably are at least 12,500 years old. The expert panel viewed the site and wound up agreeing with Dillehay: The tools bore no re-

KENNEWICK MAN

A fight over the origins of ancient bones

The hunt for the first Americans does not go without resistance: Witness the bitter court battle over the mysterious "Kennewick Man."

The central figure is a 9,300-year-old skeleton that has been packed in sealed plastic bags in a government lab for more than two years. Frustrated scientists, hoping desperately to scrutinize its bones and analyze its DNA, are up against an American Indian group that believes the bones belong to an ancestor and should be reburied with no further study.

It is clear that the remains, named after the town near the spot on the Columbia River in southeast Washington where two college students found them in July 1996, are of a slender, middle-aged fellow bearing scars of a very rough life, including multiple fractures, a crushed chest, a withered arm, and a healed skull injury. It is the most complete and among the oldest of skeletons found in North America.

When the bones were found, the Benton County coroner asked James Chatters, a local forensic anthropologist, to examine what looked like a possible homicide victim. Chatters thought the bones were older than that, but he thought they might belong to a 19th-century settler. Then Chatters made what he now says was a big mistake: He labeled some of the man's facial features "Caucasoid," based on the fact that the narrow face, long head, and jutting chin were not an Indian's typically broad face, prominent cheekbones, and round head.

But when Chatters spotted a stone projectile buried in a hip bone, he realized the bones were much older— that type of point disappeared from the region at least 4,500 years ago. A quickly arranged carbon dating test revealed the bones' age, and significance. Word got out, and all hell broke loose. Some people of European ancestry claimed Kennewick Man as a long-lost brother, even though the "Caucasoid" label now looks wrong. Instead, Chatters and physical anthropologists say, Kennewick Man looks more Asian than anything—a bit like the ancient Ainu people of Japan. These bones argue that the people who lived in the New World 9,000 years ago were more physically varied than today's Indians.

Conflict. The legal battle over Kennewick Man was prompted by a 1990 federal law, the Native American Graves Protection and Repatriation Act, under which Indian relics found on U.S. property are to be offered to tribes affiliated with them. The bones were found on Army Corps of Engineers land. After Chatters had studied the bones for two weeks, the corps locked them up and offered them to the local Umatilla Indians, who said they would rebury them without further study. "Our elders have taught us that once a body goes into the ground, it is meant to stay there," said Armand Minthorn, a member of the tribe's board of trustees, who is sure the man is an ancestor. "We do not believe that our people migrated here from another continent, as the scientists do."

Eight scientists, including Chatters and two from the Smithsonian Institution, sued the Corps of Engineers to block reburial, arguing that there is no evidence the bones are related to any living Indians. That is where things stand. A federal judge has ordered the Corps of Engineers and the Department of the Interior to figure out who gets the bones. It may be a year before the dust settles.

Chatters said he has been painted as some "evil person" by Indian leaders. "They say it is their history, but I think when people start to try to control their own history and deny anybody from studying it, that's a mistake." Besides, his wife is partly of Indian ancestry, as are their three children. "It's my family history, too," he said.

—*C.W.P.*

semblance to those of the vanished Clovis culture. Dillehay and his Chilean colleagues now are planning more excavation to explore hints that people were at the site as many as 30,000 years ago.

Some scientists say one needs only to study modern Indians to conclude that their ancestors got here before Clovis time. One hint is in genetic material passed down only from mothers to off-spring, called mitochondrial DNA. Such genes carry a molecular clock—if a single population splits into isolated groups, the buildup of random, but distinct, mutations allows geneticists to estimate how long the original groupings have been separated. "For the last five years, the genetic evidence has been saying early, early entry" into the Americas, says Theodore Schurr, a geneticist at Emory University in Atlanta. When Schurr counts the mutations accumulated among American Indians, the molecular data are consistent with departures from Asia between 15,000 and 30,000 years ago. The analysis revealed three distinct families of mutations common among American Indians and found elsewhere only in Siberia or Mongolia. Strangely, about 3 percent of Native Americans also have a genetic trait that occurs elsewhere only in a few places in Europe. This could mean either that some Asian populations migrated both west, into Europe, and east to the Americas, or that Ice Age Europeans may have trickled into the New World many thousands of years ago, perhaps by skirting the Arctic ice pack over the North Atlantic.

Linguists offer a remarkably parallel analysis. Johanna Nichols, a professor in the Slavic languages department of the University of California–Berkeley, counts 143 Native American language stocks from Alaska to the tip of South America that are completely unintelligible to one another, as different as Gaelic, Chinese, or Persian are from one another. The richest diversity of languages is along North America's Pacific coast, not along the Clovis group's supposed inland immigration route. California alone has dozens of dissimilar languages.

It takes about 6,000 years for two languages to split from a common ancestral tongue and lose all resemblance to each other, Nichols says. Allowing for how fast peoples tend to subdivide and migrate, she calculates that 60,000 years are needed for 140 languages to emerge from a single founding group. Even assuming multiple migrations of people using different languages, she figures that people first showed up in the Americas at least 35,000 years ago. If archaeologists haven't found proof of such ancient events, well, "as a linguist, that's not my problem," Nichols shrugs. Clovis-first, she says, is "not remotely possible."

The glacier highway. Even some geologists are taking a punch at Clovis primacy. "Recent work shows that the corridor [through the glaciers] was not open until 11,500 years ago," says Carole Mandryk, a geologist at Harvard University. "That is a pretty major problem for ideas that it was a highway for colonization within a few centuries." Mandryk's studies indicate the corridor would have been nearly impassable for a century or more, with little game or edible vegetation, and vast, boggy wetlands. "The corridor is 2,000 miles long," Mandryk says. "Let's say you are two young guys, and you carry as much food as you can, and you walk as fast as you can. It still takes you six months to get through. And then you run around and kill a lot of animals. Then you have to go back and tell everybody else to get their families and come on down." She blames the persistence of the Clovis-first theory on these "macho gringo guys" who "just want to believe the first Americans were these big, tough, fur-covered, mammoth-hunting people, not some fishermen over on the coast."

Just this summer, one longtime Clovis-firster abandoned the idea. For years, Albert Goodyear, associate director for research at the South Carolina Institute of Archaeology, has calmly supported Clovis. Monte Verde shook him just a bit. So in July, along the Savannah River at a site called Topper, he decided, just to be responsible, to keep digging below sediments dated to the Clovis era. All of a sudden, "we found a tool, and then another." For a solid yard down, scores of blades, flakes, and other human-crafted artifacts turned up. Goodyear told students and volunteers, yes, those sure look older than Clovis. "I had a paradigm crash right there in the woods. I felt like Woody Allen, like I had to turn and say to the audience, 'Why am I saying these things I'm not supposed to believe?' Just five years ago, nothing new was possible in American prehistory, because of dogma. Now everything is possible; the veil has been lifted."

Finds such as Goodyear's are cause for celebration among long-suffering Clovis doubters. "The Clovis-first model is dead," proclaims, with some overstatement, Robson Bonnichsen, director of the Center for the Study of the First Americans at Oregon State University. He has made the center a clearinghouse for information about alternatives to Clovis-first. "I've felt there were people here more than 12,000 years ago from the start," he says. "We're finally getting the evidence to back that up."

But not all Clovis-firsters are throwing in the towel. "I find Monte Verde quite unconvincing," says Frederick Hadleigh West, director of archaeology at the Peabody Essex Museum in Salem, Mass., and editor of a recent 576-page compendium on the archaeology of Alaska and eastern Siberia. "There is really no credible, undisputable evidence of anything prior to Clovis. But with Clovis you have an undeniable outburst of people, appearing on an empty continent, spreading like mad. There is absolutely no [incontrovertible] evidence of people coming into the New World before 12,000 [years ago], or 15,000 if you keep them in Alaska." For Monte Verde to unseat Clovis-first, he said, "Would be like Sudan conquering the United States."

Not enough stuff. Another longtime Clovis-first adherent, geoarchaeologist Vance Haynes of the University of Arizona, was among the experts who last year endorsed the 12,500-year-old Monte Verde finds as legitimate. But he argues there isn't enough evidence to support the Meadowcroft and Cactus Hill material. And even if he can't rule out Monte Verde, Haynes says it should take more than one site—scientific fallibility being what it is—to refute the primacy of Clovis. "It has just six artifacts [stone tools]. If it is as old as it looks, and the dates do look solid, then there should be others like it. Until we find those, there are still questions."

Those questions are profound. The Clovis people were real, but where did they come from? No tools in Alaska or Asia seem to foreshadow their distinctive fluted spear points. And how and when did people get to South America? Many authorities believe it would have taken people 7,000 years to have reached southern Chile from Alaska.

Others say it could have been faster by boat. But the fact remains that while Clovis traces are abundant, evidence of older cultures is terribly hard to find. "Where are they?" asks David Meltzer, an archaeologist at Southern Methodist University in Dallas, who thinks the Monte Verde dates are accurate but remains puzzled. "I don't know. That is the exciting part about all this."

No single, simple theory has yet emerged to replace Clovis-first. But some of the stories that are emerging in attempts to answer those questions are as arresting as the original Bering land bridge and inland invasion saga. For one, there's the mystery of the people who chipped that basalt point Daryl Fedje's team found this spring off Canada's Pacific shore.

The recovery of the tool was no random plunk with a bucket into the sea floor. Fedje and marine geologist Heiner Josenhans of the Geological Survey of Canada spent four years mapping the sea floor around the Queen Charlotte Islands. An array of sonar receivers revealed it as though it were viewed from a low-flying plane without any distortion from water; computer software let the researchers soar and loop low at will, as in a video game, among now-submerged valleys and hills. Fedje knew that if people were here more than about 10,000 years ago, they lived on that farther shore, near salmon, seals, shellfish, and other key food sources. Tribal lore of the present-day Haida nation includes tales of times when the islands were far larger and surrounded by grassy plains, and of subsequent, fast-rising oceans when a supernatural "flood tide woman" forced the Haida to move their villages to higher ground. Geologists agree with the traditional Haida view of their past: The islands were twice as large 11,000 years ago, and the Pacific rose more than an inch per year for a millennium after that, as the glaciers melted. The Haida have been on the islands, which they call Haida Gwaii, a very long time. Whether it was their ancestors who left the stone point is unknown. Fedje and Josenhans are now poring over the maps of the vanished landscape, hoping to return in the next year or so, if they get the funding, with remotely controlled submarines to prowl the places some of the earliest Americans may have called home.

But the origins of these coastal people remain a mystery. It seems unlikely that Clovis hunters could have scampered west along the ice sheet's southern edge, transformed themselves into a seagoing, salmon- catching, seal-spearing culture, and occupied Haida Gwaii within a few centuries of arrival. Hence the favorite hypothesis, first proposed more than 20 years ago but now supported by the Smithsonian's Stanford, Harvard's Mandryk, Fedje, and many others, is that many people migrated to the New World along the coast instead of overland. Travel may have been in small boats, perhaps covered in skin like traditional Eskimo and Aleut kayaks. If, as seems likely, people migrated during the height of the last Ice Age, between about 25,000 and 12,000 years ago, they would have avoided glaciers calving into the sea. "There was boat use in Japan 20,000 years ago," says Jon Erlandson, a University of Oregon anthropologist. "The Kurile Islands [north of Japan] are like steppingstones to Beringia," the then continuous land bridging the Bering Strait. Migrants, he said, could have then skirted the tidewater glaciers in Canada right on down the coast.

Evidence of other maritime cultures along the West Coast is coming in fast. Erlandson has uncovered remains of seagoing peoples who lived more than 10,000 years ago in the Channel Islands off Southern California. And last month, other scientists reported that two sites in Peru reveal people were living along its coast, subsisting almost entirely on seafood, nearly 11,000 years ago, too long ago for the Clovis migration to have gotten there and spawned a maritime way of life.

The Americas are big continents. Perhaps the earliest people just weren't very numerous and left little mark of their passing. Or, maybe most of them lived out on the then exposed continental shelf, retreating inland only when the end of the Ice Age raised the sea. Perhaps these people, driven inland, gave rise to the Clovis hunters. Well below the waves and under millenniums' worth of cold sediment, may lie the footprints, remains of meals, and discarded tools and campfire pits of a lost world. It is, indeed, a whole new ballgame in the search for the first Americans.

Unit Selections

5. **New Clues Show Where People Made the Great Leap to Agriculture,**
   John Noble Wilford
6. **New Dig at a 9,000-Year-Old City Is Changing Views on Ancient Life,**
   Edward DeMarco
7. **When No One Read, Who Started to Write?** John Noble Wilford
8. **A Tale of Two Cultures,** Charles Fenyvesi
9. **City of the Gods,** Michael D. Lemonick
10. **The Cradle of Cash,** Heather Pringle

Key Points to Consider

❖ What is "civilization"?

❖ What is the role of agriculture in the growth of civilization?

❖ Which came first—settlement or agriculture?

❖ What were the advantages and disadvantages of living in cities?

❖ What is the importance of writing in the development of civilization? Can there be civilization without literacy?

❖ Can there be civilization without money? Explain.

❖ What is the argument concerning diffusion and independent origins of ideas and technology? Give examples.

❖ Why would local people in Mexico be upset that the Chinese might have given culture to the Olmec?

 **Links** | **www.dushkin.com/online/**

These sites are annotated on pages 4 and 5.

Although the points are debatable, the characteristics of civilization include urbanization; literacy; complex economic, political, and social systems; and an advanced technology. The presence of cities, writing, and metallurgy are indications of this accomplishment. Civilization, it would seem, represents the highest level of human organization, but this strict definition can ignite arguments. If, for example, a tribe or society does not write, are they "uncivilized"? Since historians embrace written records as their main source of information, moreover, are illiterate people "prehistoric"? This can be a problem since the definition of civilization can imply a judgement about what is best or valuable. World historians usually avoid such value judgements, but they nonetheless use the history of civilizations as an organizing principle. Moreover, world historians often apply a looser definition of civilization so that a complex society, such as the Inca, is included as a "civilization."

The two great leaps of humankind in technology are the discovery of agriculture and the industrial revolution. The industrial revolution is a topic of the second half of world history, a phenomenon of the late eighteenth and nineteenth centuries. The discovery of agriculture, however, came hand-in-hand with the establishment of the earliest cities some 10,000 years ago. Although there is evidence that nomadic peoples planted seeds that they would later harvest, as crops became a common source of food the farmers stayed nearby to tend the fields; thus did towns and cities evolve. The great grain crops—corn in the Western Hemisphere, wheat in the Middle East, and rice in Asia—apparently evolved independently. Farming developed first, however, in the fertile crescent of the Middle East, as John Noble Wilford, a Pulitzer Prize–winning author, explains in his article on agriculture in the Middle East.

Farming changed the path of human development. Cities, trade, literacy, social and cultural complexity followed. Some scholars, such as Jacob Bronowski and Lewis Mumford, even argue that mass warfare also came with the development of farming and cities. After all, people had to build walls around their towns to protect their harvested food from marauders. A wall was built around Jericho, one of the first cities of the Middle East. Archaeological excavations at another early settlement, a Neolithic town in Turkey called Catalhoyuk, does not reveal evidence of warfare. There was a concern about death and destruction, however, and people entered their houses from the roof. An older interpretation of Catalhoyuk holds that it was a highly organized place with a mother-goddess fertility religion. These theories are explained in the brief article by Edward DeMarco.

The urban Sumerians began to experiment with writing about 5,000 years ago and established the line between history and prehistory. Apparently, literacy was an important aid for governing and dealing with the economy of kingdoms. So important was this tool that writing was independently invented in China and Mesoamerica, as examined by John Noble Wilford, who asked the question, "When no one read, who started to write?"

Along with writing came an advance in the sophistication of trade. Simple barter, the direct exchange of one item for another, did not work well in a marketplace of many items of different value. Thus, there was a need for some sort of money, which economists call a medium of exchange. Heather Pringle in "The Cradle of Cash" reveals that silver rings, gold, and ingots of precious metal served the purpose of cash as early as 2500 B.C.E.

Still, there is much to be discovered about early cities and societies. Charles Fenyvesi, in "A Tale of Two Cultures," raises the question of the diffusion of ideas. Were the ancient Olmec of southern Mexico influenced by the Shang Chinese? Or, did the Olmec develop their culture independently? Michael D. Lemonick, in addition, provides information about Teotihuacan, probably the largest city of the Americas in 500 C.E. The residents left behind huge pyramids, now a tourist site near Mexico City, and it is evident that they possessed a flourishing trade in obsidian, a hard, black flint-like rock. They were interested in human sacrifice, but much is still unknown about these urban people of the Western Hemisphere.

New Clues Show Where People Made The Great Leap to Agriculture

Scientists are figuring out where and how cereal grains were domesticated during agriculture's birth in the Fertile Crescent about 10,000 years ago. Taming meant some changes for the grains like einkorn wheat, perhaps the first to be domesticated, because harvesting methods favored plants that were less able to reproduce on their own. Plants with seeds that stayed attached to sturdy stalks, even after they ripened, were more likely to be gathered and stored for another year's planting.

By John Noble Wilford

The greatest thing *before* sliced bread, to reverse the cliché, was bread itself. The first cultivation of wild grains, that is, turned hunter-gatherers into farmers, beginning some 12,000 to 10,000 years ago. In the transition, people gained a more abundant and dependable source of food, including their daily bread, and changed the world forever.

Archeologists and historians agree that the rise of agriculture, along with the domestication of animals for food and labor, produced the most important transformation in human culture since the last ice age—perhaps since the control of fire. Farming and herding led to the growth of large, settled human populations and increasing competition for productive lands, touching off organized warfare. Food surpluses freed people to specialize in crafts like textiles and sup-

ported a privileged elite in the first cities, growing numbers of bureaucrats and scribes, soldiers and kings.

Excavations at more than 50 sites over the last half-century have established the Fertile Crescent of the Middle East as the homeland of the first farmers. This arc of land, broadly defined, extends from Israel through Lebanon and Syria, then through the plains and hills of Iraq and southern Turkey and all the way to the head of the Persian Gulf. Among its "founder crops" were wheat, barley, various legumes, grapes, melons, dates, pistachios and almonds. The region also produced the first domesticated sheep, goats, pigs and cattle.

But questions persist: Where in the Fertile Crescent were the first wheat and barley crops produced? What conditions favored this region? Why was the tran-

sition from hunting and foraging to farming so swift, occurring in only a few centuries?

New genetic studies suggest possible answers. They pinpoint the Karacadag Mountains, in southeast Turkey at the upper fringes of the Fertile Crescent, as the site where einkorn wheat was first domesticated from a wild species around 11,000 years ago. Moreover, they reveal that cultivated einkorn plants, as botanists had suspected, are remarkably similar genetically and in appearance to their ancestral wild varieties, which seems to explain the relatively rapid transition to farming indicated by archeological evidence.

A team of European scientists, led by Dr. Manfred Heun of the Agricultural University of Norway in As, reported these findings in the current issue of the journal Science. The researchers ana-

Grains resemble their wild cousins, with a few crucial differences.

lyzed the DNA from 68 lines of cultivated einkorn wheat, Triticum monococcum monococcum, and from 261 wild einkorn lines, T.m. boeoticum, still growing in the Middle East and elsewhere.

In the study, the scientists identified a genetically distinct group of 11 varieties that was also most similar to cultivated einkorn. Because that wild group grows today near the Karacadag Mountains, in the vicinity of the modern city of Diyarbakir, and presumably was there in antiquity, the scientists concluded, this is "very probably the site of einkorn domestication."

Knowing the site for the domestication of such a primary crop, the scientists said, did not necessarily imply that the people living there at the time were the first farmers. "Nevertheless," they wrote, "it has been hypothesized that one single human group may have domesticated all primary crops of the region."

Archeologists said that radiocarbon dating was not yet precise enough to establish whether einkorn or emmer wheat or barley was the first cereal to be domesticated. All three domestications occurred in the Fertile Crescent, probably within decades or a few centuries of each other. It was a hybrid of emmer and another species from the Caspian Sea area that produced the first bread wheat.

Dr. Bruce D. Smith, an archeobiologist at the Smithsonian Institution and author of "The Emergence of Agriculture," published two years ago by the Scientific American Library, praised the research as another notable example of new technologies' being applied in trying to solve some of archeology's most challenging problems. The einkorn findings, he said, made sense because they "fit pretty well with archeological evidence."

Not far from the volcanic Karacadag Mountains and also to the south, across the border in northern Syria, archeologists have exposed the ruins of prefarming settlements and early agricultural villages that appear to have existed only a few centuries apart in time. Sifting the soil turned up seeds of both wild and cultivated einkorn wheat. The ruins of Abu Hureyra, an especially revealing Syrian site on the upper Euphrates River, contained firm evidence of einkorn farming more than 10,000 years ago.

The European research team also pointed to this archeological evidence as supporting its conclusion that the domestication of einkorn wheat began in the Karacadag area.

But some archeologists may not readily accept the new findings. They have their own favorite areas where they think the first steps in plant domestication took place, and these happen to be to the west and south of the Turkish mountains. Mud-brick ruins at the edge of an oasis in the Jordan River valley near Jericho have often been cited as from the world's first known farming village, occupied by an ancient people that archeologists call the Natufians.

Dr. Frank Hole, a Yale University archeologist who specializes in early agriculture, thinks the major center for early plant domestication was more likely in the corridor running north from the Dead Sea to Damascus. Its Mediterranean-type climate, dry summers and mild but wet winters, which prevailed at the time of agricultural origins, would have favored the growth of annual plants like barley and both einkorn and emmer wheat. The Jericho site produced early evidence of barley cultivation.

Commenting on the new research, Dr. Hole said in an interview that "the location of domestication can't be determined by the present distribution of the wild plants." For example, einkorn does not grow wild today around Abu Hureyra, though excavations show that it must have more than 10,000 years ago. So it cannot be assumed, he said, that wild einkorn was growing in southeast Turkey at the time of domestication.

But Dr. Jared Diamond, a specialist in biogeography at the University of California at Los Angeles, disagreed, noting that the Karacadag Mountains supported "stands of wild einkorn so dense and extensive that they were being harvested by hunter-gatherers even before einkorn's domestication."

An experiment more than 25 years ago by Dr. Jack Harlan, an agronomist at the University of Illinois, demonstrated the likely importance of wild einkorn in the diets of post-ice age hunter-gatherers in the region and what might have encouraged them to domesticate it. Harvesting wild einkorn by hand in southeastern Turkey, Dr. Harlan showed that in only three weeks, a small family group could have gathered enough grain to sustain them for a full year.

In reaping the wild grain over a few decades, or at most three centuries, the hunter-gatherers unwittingly caused small but consequential changes in the plants. The new DNA analysis showed that an alteration of only a couple of genes could have transformed the wild einkorn into a cultivated crop.

In the wild, brittle stems hold the einkorn grains to the plant, making it easier for them to scatter naturally and reseed the fields. But natural mutations would have produced some semi-tough stalks that held the seeds more firmly in place. People cutting the plants with sharp stone sickles would have selected the stalks more laden with grain, and these would be stored as next year's seed stock. Birds would be more apt to consume the dispersed grain from brittle stalks, leaving less of it to germinate.

As Dr. Diamond pointed out, repeated cycles of harvesting and reseeding wild einkorn stands "would have selected automatically for those mutations." Those changes included plumper, more nutritious grains in denser clusters that cling to the stem until ripe, instead of scattering before they can be harvested.

"These few, simple changes during einkorn's domestication," Dr. Diamond wrote in a separate article in Science, "contrast sharply with the drastic biological reorganization required for the domestication of Native Americans' leading cereal, maize, from its wild ancestor."

This difference alone, he said, "helps explain why densely populated agricultural societies arose so much earlier and developed so much more rapidly in the Crescent than in the New World."

It was several thousand more years before maize, or corn, would become a cultivated crop in central Mexico. There were no native wild wheats and barley in the Americas that might have led to an earlier introduction of agriculture there. Such circumstances based on geographic location have often been critical in the timing and pace of cultural and economic development for diverse societies, as Dr. Diamond argued in "Guns, Germs, and Steel: The Fates of Human Societies," published earlier this year by W. W. Norton.

Nothing in the new einkorn research seems to alter current thinking about the timing and climatic circumstances for agriculture's genesis in the Fertile Crescent.

With the end of the ice age 14,000 to 12,000 years ago, retreating glaciers left the world warmer and wetter than before. Greater rainfall in many temperate zones nourished a spread of vegetation, including many grasses like wild wheat and barley. This attracted concentrations of grazing animals. Hunter-gatherers converged on the grasses and animals, in many cases abandoning their nomadic ways and settling down to village life. Such conditions were particularly favorable in the Middle East.

Then followed a brief return of colder, drier weather more than 11,000 years ago and lasting a few centuries. Dr. Ofer Bar-Yosef, an archeologist at Harvard University, thinks the stresses of coping with the Younger Dryas, as the dry spell is called, contributed to the beginning of plant domestication. With the sudden dearth of wild food sources, hunter-gatherers began storing grain for the lean times and learning to cultivate the fields for better yields. In any case, the earliest evidence for agriculture so far comes from the period immediately after the Younger Dryas.

In his book on early agriculture, Dr. Smith of the Smithsonian wrote, "Even in the absence of such an external pressure, gradual growth in their populations and expansion of their villages may have encouraged or necessitated a variety of economic changes, including experimenting with the cultivation of wild grasses."

Whatever the factors behind its origins, Dr. Diamond said, agriculture took a firm hold in the ancient Middle East because of the diversity of plants and animals suitable for domestication. The first farmers, he said in the journal article, quickly assembled "a balanced package of domesticates meeting all of humanity's basic needs: carbohydrate, protein, oil, milk, animal transport and traction, and vegetable and animal fiber for rope and clothing."

Eurasian geography probably favored the rapid spread of agriculture out of the Middle East and throughout much of the two continents. Referring to a thesis developed in his book, Dr. Diamond pointed out that the west-east axis of the Eurasian land mass, as well as of the Fertile Crescent, permitted crops, livestock and people "to expand at the same latitude without having to adapt to new day lengths, climates and diseases."

In contrast, the north-south orientations of the Americas, Africa and the Indian subcontinent probably slowed the diffusion of agricultural innovations. And that, Dr. Diamond contends, could account for the headstart some societies had on others in the march of human history.

New Dig at a 9,000-Year-Old City Is Changing Views on Ancient Life

By Edward DeMarco

KUCUKKOY, Turkey

The mound swells 65 feet above the vast, dusty, Konya Plain, an unremarkable bump to a motorist passing through this remote stretch of wheat and sugar beet fields 150 miles south of Ankara. But astonishing remnants of ancient life have been dug from this grassy mound, the signs of a 9,000-year-old settlement called Catalhoyuk, perhaps the largest settlement of the Neolithic age.

This was the crucial period when humans moved beyond hunting and gathering and began creating the first large settlements, inventing farming and domesticating animals. Catalhoyuk, first uncovered by archeologists in 1961, lay along a river that deposited rich soil for crops and created a lush environment for animals. Over the mound's 32 acres, as many as 10,000 people lived in cramped mudbrick dwellings packed so tightly that residents entered from their roofs.

The initial excavations at Catalhoyuk (pronounced cha-TAHL-huyook) in the early 1960's by the British archeologist James Mellaart suggested that city life revolved around ritual shrines festooned with bull horns and bizarre wall paintings depicting terrifying wild animals. Clay figurines and some wall art seemed to show powerful, voluptuous females,

implying that a mother goddess cult of fertility dominated.

Archeologists who have recently revived and expanded excavation of the site after a 30-year lull are offering a sharply different, and more puzzling, picture of life there in Neolithic times.

Some researchers now believe that Catalhoyuk's residents, though gathered in a city-like settlement, acted independently in family groups without any apparent control by a priestly or political elite. Moreover, they say, the spiritual life of the city probably was not built around the kind of mother goddess cult more common to the classical age, but may have sprung from a more primitive well of fear and preoccupation with death that resonated with the more recent hunter-gatherer past. This spiritual life was reflected in baffling wall art involving bulls and other images.

"Mellaart saw Catalhoyuk as divided into shrines and nonshrines," said the project director, Ian Hodder, a Cambridge University archeologist, as he paused near houses under excavation. "He saw shrines and an elite priestly group living in one area. Mellaart looked at the site through the eyes of Mesopotamia and later urban societies and viewed it as politically complex. We're seeing it as large but politically

simple without a class or elite with specialized functions."

The new excavation has found evidence that households devoted space to ritual as well as domestic uses. Ritual elements like bull horns and art painted on plaster walls were positioned along walls facing north, east or west, but never south. That area was reserved for cooking and other domestic tasks.

In a dwelling unearthed in August archeologists discovered a bull horn and, a few inches away, an eight-inch flint dagger with a bone handle carved into a bull's head. The dagger's finely serrated edges and superb condition suggest that it was a ceremonial offering.

Sifting of floor soil from excavated dwellings has shown that fragments of plants, bone and obsidian, a black volcanic glass used to make tools, are in far higher concentrations in cooking areas than in parts of the houses identified as ritual spaces.

Mr. Mellaart, who discovered Catalhoyuk in 1958, remains skeptical about the new view that ritual was confined to each household rather than organized along citywide lines. Describing evidence uncovered in the new dig, Mr. Mellaart said he did not believe the case for religious practice in houses had been made. "They haven't dug up a shrine yet," he said in an interview. But Dr. Hodder said that was precisely the point, that there were no separate shrines but simply places for religious ritual in individual dwellings.

Evidence for autonomy rather than centralized authority in Catalhoyuk also shows up in agriculture. Julie Near, a Berkeley researcher who is collecting ancient plant material like wheat, barley and edible tubers in soil removed from houses, has found no sign that food was stored and processed collectively. "Agriculture was not controlled in an idealistic or holistic way," she said. "It's much more small scale."

Only a fraction of the mound has yet been explored. The Turkish Government refused to grant Mr. Mellaart an excavation permit after 1965. A 1968 book by two British journalists, "The Dorak Affair," suggested that the ban sprang from murky allegations that Mr. Mellaart had smuggled precious artifacts out of Turkey from another ancient site. Mr. Mellaart, now 71 and sidelined, bitterly denies the accusations.

Perhaps the most controversial break with Mr. Mellaart's conception of Catalhoyuk is the disavowal of a mother goddess cult. Among the most famous artifacts Mr. Mellaart retrieved was a foot-high figurine depicting a lavishly plump woman seated on a throne flanked by leopards. The figurine has been claimed by mother goddess devotees as an icon. But Dr. Hodder contends mother goddess figures were not venerated at Catalhoyuk. "You never find them in a burial or in religiously significant situations," he said.

Naomi Hamilton, an Edinburgh University researcher who has reviewed all of Mr. Mellaart's humanoid figurines and recent finds, says the majority are not clearly female. And not until halfway through the thousand-year settlement history of Catalhoyuk do figurines thought of as mother goddess representations appear, perhaps because economic change reshaped sex roles.

Rather than fertility, Dr. Hodder says, the people of Catalhoyuk appear to have held a fascination with death and destruction. Two or three generations of a family typically are buried beneath the floors of a house. In one dwelling, scientists recovered 17 remains, mostly of children. Dozens of other burials are nearby.

At the end of the two- or three-generation burial cycle, ritual art like bull horns was removed, sometimes violently, and the dwelling was burned. Afterward the remains of the house were filled with fine dirt and the floor was laid for a new kinship dwelling above.

In a frenzy of digging from 1961 to 1965, Mr. Mellaart unearthed 156 structures, most no larger than a suburban American bedroom. He found wall paintings depicting huge bulls surrounded by Keith Haring-like stick figures running, dancing and sometimes hurling stones; nightmarish vultures attacking headless humans, and a startling frieze of human handprints under mounted bull horns.

David Lewis-Williams, a specialist in tribal rock art of southern Africa from the University of Witwatersrand in Johannesburg, recently concluded that Catalhoyuk's wall art resembled "membranes between this world and the spirit world."

In his view, painted animals were moving through the walls in shamanistic rituals of altered consciousness. "The town was a constructed cosmos with different levels, and going down into the rooms was like going down into an underworld," he said in an interview. People moved through crawl holes from one room to another "rather like crawling from one chamber of a cave to another," he added, "and the deeper you went, the richer the art became."

When No One Read, Who Started to Write?

Ancient art might have inspired early scribblers, or maybe it was the need to keep track of livestock.

By John Noble Wilford

PHILADELPHIA—The Sumerians had a story to explain their invention of writing more than 5,000 years ago. It seems a messenger of the king of Uruk arrived at the court of a distant ruler so exhausted from the journey that he was unable to deliver the oral message. So the king, being clever, came up with a solution. He patted some clay and set down the words of his next messages on a tablet.

A Sumerian epic celebrates the achievement:

> Before that time writing on clay had not yet existed,
> But now, as the sun rose, so it was!
> The king of Kullaba [Uruk] had set words on a tablet, so it was!

A charming just-so, or so-it-was, story, its retelling at a recent symposium on the origins or writing, held here at the University of Pennsylvania, both amused and frustrated scholars. It reminded them that they could expect little help—only a myth—from the Sumerians themselves, presumably the first writing people, in understanding how and why the invention responsible for the great divide in human culture between prehistory and history had come about.

The archeologists, historians and other scholars at the meeting smiled at the absurdity of a king's writing a letter that its recipient could not read. They also doubted that the earliest writing was a direct rendering of speech. Writing more than likely began as a separate and distinct symbolic system of communication, like painting, sculpture and oral storytelling, and only later merged with spoken language.

Yet in the story, the Sumerians, who lived in Mesopotamia, the lower valley of the Tigris and Euphrates Rivers in what is now southern Iraq, seemed to understand writing's transforming function. As Dr. Holly Pittman, director of the university's Center for Ancient Studies and organizer of the symposium, observed, writing "arose out of the need to store information and transmit information outside of human memory and over time and over space."

In exchanging interpretations and new information, the scholars acknowledged that they still had no fully satisfying answers to the most important questions of exactly how and why writing was developed. Many of them favored a broad explanation of writing's origins in the visual arts, pictograms of things being transformed into increasingly abstract symbols for things, names and eventually words in speech. Their views clashed with a widely held theory among archeologists that writing grew out of the pieces of clay in assorted sizes and shapes that Sumerian accountants had used as tokens to keep track of livestock and stores of grain.

The scholars at the meeting also conceded that they had no definitive answer to the question of whether writing was invented only once and spread elsewhere or arose independently several times in several places, like Egypt, the Indus Valley, China and among the Olmecs and Maya of Mexico and Central America.

But they criticized recent findings suggesting that writing might have developed earlier in Egypt than in Mesopotamia.

In December, Dr. Günter Dreyer, director of the German Archeological Institute in Egypt, announced new radiocarbon dates for tombs at Abydos, on the Nile about 250 miles south of Cairo. The dates indicated that some hieroglyphic inscriptions on pots, bone and ivory in the tombs were made at least as early as 3200 B.C., possibly 3400. It was now an "open question," Dr. Dreyer said, whether writing appeared first in Egypt or Mesopotamia.

At the symposium, Dr. John Baines, an Oxford University Egyptologist who had just visited Dr. Dreyer, expressed skepticism in polite terms. "I'm suspicious of the dates," he said in an interview. "I think he's being very bold in his readings of these things."

The preponderance of archeological evidence has shown that the urbanizing Sumerians were the first to develop writing, in 3200 or 3300 B.C. These are the dates for many clay tablets with a proto-cuneiform script found at the site of the ancient city of Uruk. The tablets bore pictorial symbols for the names of people, places and things for governing and commerce. The Sumerian script gradually evolved from the pictorial to the abstract, but it was probably at least five centuries before the writing came to represent recorded spoken language.

Egyptian hieroglyphics are so different from Sumerian cuneiform, Dr. Baines said, that they were probably in-

Early Writing: Cultures Make Their First Marks

Representing spoken languages in writing grew out of the transformation of pictures and random marks into images with consistent meaning. Among the earliest cultures to do this were:

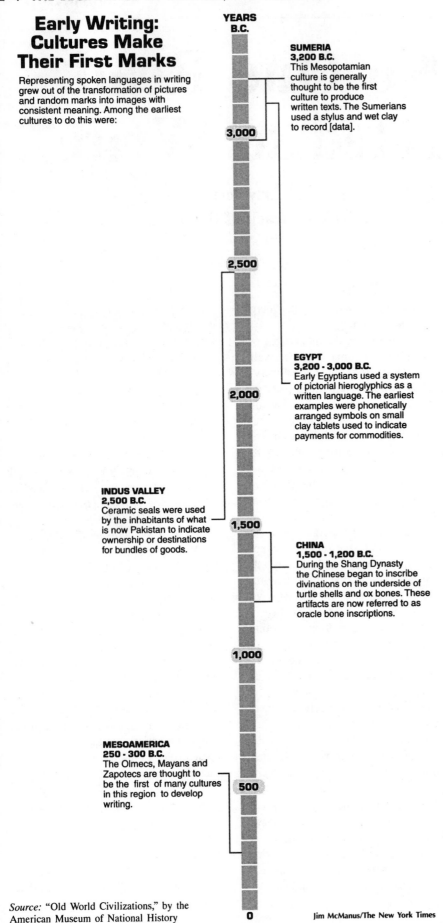

YEARS B.C.

SUMERIA 3,200 B.C.
This Mesopotamian culture is generally thought to be the first culture to produce written texts. The Sumerians used a stylus and wet clay to record [data].

3,000

2,500

EGYPT 3,200 - 3,000 B.C.
Early Egyptians used a system of pictorial hieroglyphics as a written language. The earliest examples were phonetically arranged symbols on small clay tablets used to indicate payments for commodities.

2,000

INDUS VALLEY 2,500 B.C.
Ceramic seals were used by the inhabitants of what is now Pakistan to indicate ownership or destinations for bundles of goods.

1,500

CHINA 1,500 - 1,200 B.C.
During the Shang Dynasty the Chinese began to inscribe divinations on the underside of turtle shells and ox bones. These artifacts are now referred to as oracle bone inscriptions.

1,000

MESOAMERICA 250 - 300 B.C.
The Olmecs, Mayans and Zapotecs are thought to be the first of many cultures in this region to develop writing.

500

0

Jim McManus/The New York Times

Source: "Old World Civilizations," by the American Museum of National History

vented independently not long after Sumerian writing. If anything, the Egyptians may have gotten the idea of writing from the Sumerians, with whom they had contacts in Syria, but nothing more.

In any event, the writing idea became more widespread at the beginning of the third millennium B.C. The Elamites of southern Iran developed a proto-writing system then, perhaps influenced by the proto-cuneiform of their Sumerian neighbors, and before the millennium was out, writing appeared in the Indus River Valley of what is now Pakistan and western India, then in Syria and Crete and parts of Turkey. Writing in China dates back to the Shang period toward the end of the second millennium B.C., and it dates to the first millennium B.C. in Mesoamerica.

Archeologists have thought that the undeciphered Indus script, which seemed to appear first around 2500 B.C., may have been inspired in part from trade contacts with Mesopotamia. But new excavations in the ruins of the ancient city of Harappa suggest an earlier and presumably independent origin of Indus writing.

In a report from the field, distributed on the Internet, Dr. Jonathan Mark Kenoyer of the University of Wisconsin and Dr. Richard H. Meadow of Harvard University showed pictures of marks incised on potshards that they interpreted as evidence for the use of writing signs by Indus people as early as 3300 B.C. If these are indeed proto-writing examples, the discovery indicates an independent origin of Indus writing contemporary with the Sumerian and Egyptian inventions.

Dr. Meadow, using E-mail, the electronic age's version of the king of Uruk's clay tablet, confirmed that the inscribed marks were "similar in some respects to those later used in the Indus script." The current excavations, he added, were uncovering "very significant findings at Harappa with respect to the Indus script."

At the symposium, though, Dr. Gregory L. Possehl, a Pennsylvania archeologist who specializes in the Indus civilization and had examined the pictures, cautioned against jumping to such conclusions. One had to be careful, he said, not to confuse potter's marks, graffiti and fingernail marks with symbols of nascent writing.

Of the earliest writing systems, scholars said, only the Sumerian, Chinese and Mesoamerican ones seemed clearly to be independent inventions. Reviewing the relationship between early Chinese bronze art, "oracle bones" and writing, Dr. Louisa Huber, a researcher at Harvard's Fairbanks Center for East Asian Research, concluded "Chinese writing looks to be pristine."

But few pronouncements about early writing go undisputed. Dr. Victor Mair, a professor of Chinese language at Penn, offered evidence indicating, he said, that "the Chinese writing system may well have received vital inputs from West Asian and European systems of writing and proto-writing."

Dr. Mair cited an intriguing correspondence between the Chinese script and 22 Phoenician letters and also Western-like symbols on pottery and the bodies of mummies found in the western desert of China. The recent discoveries of the mummies, wearing garments of Western weaves and having Caucasoid facial features, have prompted theories of foreign influences on Chinese culture in the first and second millennia B.C. It had already been established that the chariot and bronze metallurgy reached China from the West.

Though no one seemed ready to endorse his thesis, Dr. Mair said, "We simply do not know for certain whether the Chinese script was or was not independently created."

Dr. Peter Damerow, a specialist in Sumerian cuneiform at the Max Planck Institute for the History of Science in Berlin, said, "Whatever the mutual influences of writing systems of different cultures may be, their great variety shows, at least, that the development of writing, once it is initiated, attains a considerable degree of independence and flexibility to adapt a coding system to specific characteristics of the language to be represented."

Not that he accepted the conventional view that writing necessarily started as some kind of representation of words by pictures. New studies of Sumerian proto-cuneiform, he said, challenge this interpretation. The structures of this earliest writing, for example, did not match the syntax of a language. Proto-cuneiform seemed severely restricted, com-

Ancient writing is a field hot with controversy, and few scholarly conclusions go unchallenged.

pared with spoken language, dealing mainly in lists and categories, not in sentences and narrative.

This presumably reflects writing's origins and first applications in economic administration in a growing, increasingly complex society, scholars said. Most of the Uruk tablets were documents about property, inventory and, even then, taxes. The only texts that do not concern administrative activities, Dr. Damerow said, were cuneiform lexicons that were apparently written as school exercises by scribes in training.

For at least two decades, in fact, Dr. Denise Schmandt-Besserat, a University of Texas archeologist, has argued that the first writing grew directly out of a counting system practiced by Sumerian accountants. They used molded clay "tokens," each one specifically shaped to represent a jar of oil, a large or small container of grain, or a particular kind of livestock. When the tokens were placed inside hollow clay spheres, the number and type of tokens inside were recorded on the ball with impressions resembling the tokens. Finally, simplifying matters, the token impressions were replaced with inscribed signs, and writing was invented.

Though Dr. Schmandt-Besserat has won wide support, some linguists question her thesis and other scholars, like Dr. Pittman of Penn, think it too narrow an interpretation. They emphasized that pictorial representation and writing evolved together, part of the same cultural context that fostered experimentation in communication through symbols.

"There's no question that the token system is a forerunner of writing, and really important," Dr. Pittman said in an interview. "But I have an argument with her evidence for a link between tokens and signs, and she doesn't open up the process to include picture-making and all other kinds of information-storage practices that are as important as the tokens."

Dr. Schmandt-Besserat, who did not attend the symposium, vigorously defended herself in a telephone interview. "My colleagues say the signs on seals were a beginning of writing, but show me a single sign on a seal that becomes a sign in writing," she said. "They say that designs on pottery were a beginning of writing, but show me a single sign of writing you can trace back to a pot—it doesn't exist."

In its first 500 years, she asserted, cuneiform writing was used almost solely for recording economic information. "The first information that writing gives you is only the same information the tokens were dealing with," she said. "When you start putting more on the tablets, products plus the name of who has delivered and received them, that is where art would enter the picture. Then writing is out of the box, in all directions."

Dr. Damerow agreed that cuneiform writing appeared to have developed in two stages, first as a new but limited means of recording economic information, later as a broader encoding of spoken language for stories, arguments, descriptions or messages from one ruler to another.

Even so, it was a long way from the origin of writing to truly literate societies. At the symposium, scholars noted that the early rulers could not write or read; they relied on scribes for their messages, record keeping and storytelling. In Egypt, most early hieroglyphics were inscribed in places beyond the public eye, high on monuments or deep in tombs.

In this case, said Dr. Pascal Vernus of the University of Paris, early writing was less administrative than sacred and ideological, "a way of creating and describing the world as a dominating elite wants it to be."

Dr. Piotr Michalowski, professor of Near East civilizations at the University of Michigan, said the Uruk proto-cuneiform writing, whatever its antecedents, was "so radically different as to be a complete break with the past, a system different from anything else." It no doubt served to store, preserve and communicate information, but also was a new instrument of power.

"Perhaps it's because I grew up in Stalinist Poland," Dr. Michalowski said, "but I say coercion and control were early writing's first important purpose, a new way to control how people live."

A Tale of Two Cultures

*A Beijing scholar links an ancient Chinese dynasty
to the New World's earliest civilization*

Charles Fenyvesi

Abroad for the first time in his life, Han Ping Chen, a scholar of ancient Chinese, landed at Dulles International Airport near Washington, D.C., the night of September 18. Next morning, he paced in front of the National Gallery of Art, waiting for the museum to open so he could visit an Olmec exhibit—works from Mesoamerica's spectacular "mother culture" that emerged suddenly 3,200 years ago, with no apparent local antecedents. After a glance at a 10-ton basalt sculpture of a head, Chen faced the object that prompted his trip: an Olmec sculpture found in La Venta, 10 miles south of the southernmost cove of the Gulf of Mexico.

What the Chinese scholar saw was 15 male figures made of serpentine or jade, each about 6 inches tall. Facing them were a taller sandstone figure and six upright, polished jade blades called celts. The celts bore incised markings, some of them faded. Proceeding from right to left, Chen scrutinized the markings silently, grimacing when he was unable to make out more than a few squiggles on the second and third celts. But the lower half of the fourth blade made him jump. "I can read this easily," he shouted. "Clearly, these are Chinese characters."

For years, scholars have waged a passionate—and often nasty—debate over whether Asian refugees and adventurers might somehow have made their way to the New World long before Columbus, stimulating brilliant achievements in cosmogony, art, astronomy and architecture in a succession of cultures from the Olmec to the Maya and Aztec. On one side are the "diffusionists," who have compiled a long list of links between Asian and Mesoamerican cultures, including similar rules for the Aztec board game of *patolli* and the Asian pachisi (also known as Parcheesi), a theological focus in ancient China and Mesoamerica on tiger-jaguar and dragonlike creatures, and a custom, common both to China's Shang dynasty and the Olmecs, of putting a jade bead in the mouth of a deceased person. "Nativists," on the other hand, dismiss such theories as ridiculous and argue for the autonomous development of pre-Columbian civilizations. They bristle at the suggestion that the indigenous people did not evolve on their own.

Striking resemblances. For diffusionists, Olmec art offers a tempting arena for speculation. Carbon-dating places the Olmec era between 1,000 and 1,200 B.C., coinciding with the Shang dynasty's fall in China. American archaeologists unearthed the group sculpture in 1955. Looking at the sculpture displayed in the National Gallery, as well as other Olmec pieces, some Mexican and American scholars have been struck by the resemblances to Chinese artifacts. (In fact, archaeologists initially labeled the first Olmec figures found at the turn of the century as Chinese). Migrations from Asia over the land bridge 10,000–15,000 years ago could account for the Chinese features, such as slanted eyes, but not for the stylized mouths and postures particular to sophisticated Chinese art that emerged in recent millenniums.

Yet until Chen made his pilgrimage to the museum this fall, no Shang specialist had ever studied the Olmec. The scholar emerged from the exhibit with a theory: After the Shang army was routed and the emperor killed, he suggested, some loyalists might have sailed down the Yellow River and taken to the ocean. There, perhaps, they drifted with a current which skirts Japan's coast, heads for California, then peters out near Ecuador. Betty Meggers, a senior Smithsonian archaeologist who has linked pottery dug up in Ecuador to shipwrecked Japanese 5,000 years ago, says such an idea is "plausible" because ancient Asian mariners were far more proficient than they were given credit for.

But Chen's identification of the celt markings is likely to sharpen the controversy over origins even further. For example, Mesoamericanist Michael Coe of Yale University labels Chen's search for Chinese characters as "insulting to the indigenous people of Mexico." And some scholars who share Chen's narrow expertise are equally skeptical. There are only about a dozen experts worldwide in the Shang script, which is largely unrecognizable to readers of modern Chinese. Of the Americans, Profs. William Boltz of the University of Washington and Robert Bagley of Princeton recently looked at a drawing of the celts but dismissed as "rubbish" the notion that the characters could be Chinese. Those looking for a link between the two cultures, Bagley said, are Chinese, and "it no doubt gratifies their ethnic pride to discover that Mesoamerican civilization springs from China."

Others would like to see the celts before taking sides. David Keightley, University of California–Berkeley professor of history, said some characters on the celts "could, of course, be Shang, though I don't at present see it that way." His Chinese colleagues, he said "may just be onto something," and he noted that "it's important that scholars from China examine this material."

Chen, 47, is uninterested in the Mesoamericanists' war. When Prof. Mike Xu, a professor of Chinese history at the University of Central Oklahoma, traveled to Beijing to ask Chen to examine his index of 146 markings from pre-Columbian objects, Chen refused, saying he had no interest in anything outside China. He relented only after a colleague familiar with Xu's work insisted that Chen, as China's leading authority, take a look. He did and found that all but three of Xu's markings "could have come from China."

Xu was at Chen's side in the National Gallery when the Shang scholar read the text on the Olmec celt in Chinese and translated: "The ruler and his chieftains establish the foundation for a kingdom." Chen located each of the characters on the celt in three well-worn Chinese dictionaries he had with him. Two adjacent characters, usually read as "master and subjects," but Chen decided that in this context they might mean "ruler and his chieftains." The character on the line below he recognized as the symbol for "kingdom" or "country": two peaks for hills, a curving line underneath for river. The next character, Chen said, suggests a bird but means "waterfall," completing the description. The bottom character he read as "foundation" or "establish," implying the act of founding something important. If Chen is right, the celts not only offer the earliest writing in the New World but mark the birth of a Chinese settlement more than 3,000 years ago.

At lunch the next day, Chen said he was awake all night thinking about the sculpture. He talked about how he had studied Chinese script at age 5, tutored by his father, then director of the national archives. But Chen's father did not live to enjoy the honors the son reaped, such as a recent assignment to compile a new dictionary of characters used by the earliest dynasties—the first update since one commissioned by a Han emperor 2,000 years ago.

Color nuances. Chen was so taken with the Olmec sculpture that he ventured beyond scholarly caution. The group sculpture, he said, might memorialize "a historic event," either a blessing sought from ancestors or the act of founding a new kingdom or both. He was mesmerized by the tallest figure in the sculpture—made from red sandstone as porous as a sponge, in contrast to the others, which are highly polished and green-blue in hue. Red suggests higher status, Chen said. Perhaps the figure was the master of the group, a venerated ancestral spirit. The two dark blue figures to the right might represent the top noblemen, more important than the two others, carved out of pale green serpentine.

The Smithsonian's Meggers says that Chen's analysis of the colors "makes sense. But his reading of the text is the clincher. Writing systems are too arbitrary and complex. They cannot be independently reinvented."

Whether Chen's colleagues ultimately hail him or hang him, his theory yields a tale worthy of Joseph Conrad. And like Conrad, he cannot resist offering yet another footnote from the past: More than 5,000 Shang characters have survived, Chen says, even though the soldiers who defeated the Shang forces murdered the scholars and burned or buried any object with writing on it. In a recent excavation in the Shang capital of Anyang, archaeologists have found a buried library of turtle shells covered with characters. And at the entrance lay the skeleton of the librarian, stabbed in the back and clutching some writings to his breast.

The Olmec sculpture was buried under white sand topped with alternate layers of brown and reddish-brown sand. Perhaps it was hidden to save it from the kind of rage that sought to wipe out the Shang and their memory.

City of the Gods

**Who built Teotihuacán? Why did it fall? Thanks to a newly discovered
tomb, the secrets of Mexico's ancient metropolis may finally be revealed.**

By Michael D. Lemonick

For archaeologists and tourists alike, the monumental ruins of Mesoamerica are humbling testimony to the complex civilizations that once flourished there. Even the names of these peoples evoke power and mystery: Aztecs, Maya, Zapotecs, Toltecs, Olmecs. But of all the great pre-Columbian metropolises that dot the region, arguably the most magnificent of all belonged to a people who remain nameless. The Aztecs, who took over the area some 25 miles north of modern Mexico City in the 15th century, were convinced it was built by supernatural beings. Their name for the city, which we still use: Teotihuacán, or Place of the Gods.

With few clues to guide modern scientists, the origin and fate of the ancient rulers of Teotihuacán are a mystery to this day. But thanks to a discovery made this fall by an international research team, that mystery may finally be starting to unravel. In mid-October, archaeologists stumbled across a burial chamber deep inside Teotihuacán's massive Pyramid of the Moon. Inside they found a skeleton and more than 150 artifacts probably dating to about A.D. 150. It is, exults anthropologist Michael Spence of the University of Western Ontario, "a fantastic find."

Until the 1960s, no one realized that Teotihuacán's great Avenue of the Dead, anchored at its northern end by the Pyramid of the Moon and flanked by the even larger Pyramid of the Sun and other ceremonial buildings, was the core of a much larger metropolis. Indeed, at 8 sq. mi. and with an estimated population of 150,000, Teotihuacán was the largest city in Mesoamerica in its heyday (about A.D. 500) and one of the six largest in the world—larger even than Rome. Its political power reached all the way to Mayan city-states hundreds of miles away, with outposts as far away as Guatemala.

Unlike its Mayan counterparts, though, Teotihuacán has yielded very few inscriptions, and those are in a hieroglyphic language that archaeologists have not yet been able to decipher. The city's celebrated painted murals don't provide many clues either. "There are very few glimpses of daily life," complains Arizona State University anthropologist George Cowgill. The best information scientists have to date comes from a series of mass graves discovered about a decade ago in the so-called Feathered Serpent Pyramid by Cowgill, his Arizona State colleague Saburo Sugiyama and Rubén Cabrera of Mexico's National Institute of Anthropology and History. Most of the 150 skeletons found there were buried with their hands and feet bound, suggesting that they had been sacrificed; most of them were also dressed as soldiers and armed with obsidian-tipped spears and other weapons. More sacrificial victims were discovered within the Pyramid of the Sun by another team. But these finds raised as many questions as they answered about the culture of Teotihuacán.

Then, last year, Sugiyama and Cabrera decided to tackle the Pyramid of the Moon. Like most Mesoamerican pyramids, this one was built like an onion. Explains Cowgill: "They would build a small pyramid, then build a larger one over it and then build a third one after that." As a result, the interior is almost solid dirt and rubble, with no distinct passageways. This makes the going slow and expensive. It took the archaeologists 3 1/2 months to reach the burial chamber, which is about 90 ft. inside the pyramid.

It was worth the trouble. "No one has ever found a burial of this richness intact at Teotihuacán before," says Cowgill. Among the booty: two 1 1/2-ft.-high greenstone statuettes; a couple of larger human figurines fashioned from obsidian; at least 15 double-edged obsidian knives similar to those used in sacrifices; shell pendants in the form of human teeth; pyrite disks (which served as mirrors); the skeletons of two young felines (possibly jaguars) in the remnants of a wooden cage; and the scattered bones of at least seven large birds.

But it's the human bones that have Spence's attention. Once they have been fully extricated, he will try to determine the individual's age and gender (probably male). He'll also look for evidence of disease, malnutrition or developmental abnormalities as well as wounds, broken limbs or signs of hard labor and such status symbols as a deliberately shaped head or filed teeth. The absence of lavish body ornaments, the position of the skeleton's hand (which was belatedly found behind its back, as if the arms had been tied) and the location of

IN BRIEF

A New Key to the Family Tree

The bones unearthed at Teotihuacán are plenty ancient, but there's old and then there's *old*—and a find announced by South African scientists last week makes A.D. 150 seem like yesterday. Researchers at the University of the Witwatersrand reported that they've discovered the skeleton of a human ancestor that could be as much as 3.5 million years old.

That's even older than the celebrated Lucy, and comes from a time when humans still had many apelike characteristics. Best of all, this skeleton is almost complete; it even comes with a skull. There is no need to mix and match different specimens to guess what the entire creature looked like (Lucy, for example, was only 40% complete). Once the skeleton is fully excavated in a year or so, experts should be able to pin down the relative sizes of different body parts and see just which of the creature's features were apelike and which were human. It is, says paleontologist Alan Walker of Pennsylvania State University, "perhaps one of the best finds ever."

That's true even if, as some experts suspect, the specimen is really as little as 2.5 million years old. Complete skeletons are so rare that even such a relative youngster will inevitably flesh out the book of human evolution as few discoveries ever have. Says William Kimbel, science director of the Institute of Human Origins at Arizona State University: "It will give us what we got from Lucy, and more."—*By Michael D. Lemonick. Reported by Andrea Dorfman/New York*

the burial chamber all suggest to Sugiyama that the individual was bound and sacrificed. "We thought [the skeleton] might be a ruler or a person of high status, but it may not turn out to be that," he cautions.

In the long run, the scientists say, the individual's social status and the richness of the offerings may not be as important as the burial's age, which places it in a crucial time period only a couple of centuries after the city was founded. "We know almost nothing about Teotihuacán's early political history, so [this discovery] should shed a lot more light on that," says Cowgill.

But the real key to unraveling the secrets of Teotihuacán is more digging—a lot more—and Sugiyama's team is still hard at work. Despite this impressive discovery, says Cowgill, "95% of the city is still unexcavated. We're just scratching the surface."—*Reported by Andrea Dorfman/New York*

The Cradle of Cash

When money arose in the ancient cities of Mesopotamia, it profoundly and permanently changed civilization.

By Heather Pringle

THE SCENE IN THE SMALL, STIFLING room is not hard to imagine: the scribe frowning, shifting in his seat as he tries to concentrate on the words of the woman in front of him. A member of one of the wealthiest families in Sippar, the young priestess has summoned him to her room to record a business matter. When she entered the temple, she explains, her parents gave her a valuable inheritance, a huge piece of silver in the shape of a ring, worth the equivalent of 60 months' wages for an estate worker. She has decided to buy land with this silver. Now she needs someone to take down a few details. Obediently, the scribe smooths a wet clay tablet and gets out his stylus. Finally, his work done, he takes the tablet down to the archive.

For more than 3,700 years, the tablet languished in obscurity, until late-nineteenth-century collectors unearthed it from Sippar's ruins along the Euphrates River in what is now Iraq. Like similar tablets, it hinted at an ancient and mysterious Near Eastern currency, in the form of silver rings, that started circulating two millennia before the world's first coins were struck. By the time that tablet was inscribed, such rings may have been in use for a thousand years.

When did humans first arrive at the concept of money? What conditions spawned it? And how did it affect the ancient societies that created it? Until recently, researchers thought they had the answers. They believed money was born, as coins, along the coasts of the Mediterranean in the seventh or sixth century B.C., a product of the civilization that later gave the world the Parthenon, Plato, and Aristotle. But few see the matter so simply now. With evidence gleaned from such disparate sources as ancient temple paintings, clay tablets, and buried hoards of uncoined metals, researchers have revealed far more ancient money: silver scraps and bits of gold, massive rings and gleaming ingots.

In the process, they have pushed the origins of cash far beyond the sunny coasts of the Mediterranean, back to the world's oldest cities in Mesopotamia, the fertile plain created by the Tigris and Euphrates rivers. There, they suggest, wealthy citizens were flaunting money at least as early as 2500 B.C. and perhaps a few hundred years before that. "There's just no way to get around it," says Marvin Powell, a historian at Northern Illinois University in De Kalb. "Silver in Mesopotamia functions like our money today. It's a means of exchange. People use it for a storage of wealth, and they use it for defining value."

Many scholars believe money began even earlier. "My sense is that as far back as the written records go in Mesopotamia and Egypt, some form of money is there," observes Jonathan Williams, curator of Roman and Iron Age coins at the British Museum in London. "That suggests it was probably there beforehand, but we can't tell because we don't have any written records."

Just why researchers have had such difficulties in uncovering these ancient moneys has much to do with the practice of archeology and the nature of money itself. Archeologists, after all, are the ultimate Dumpster divers: they spend their careers sifting through the trash of the past, ingeniously reconstructing vanished lives from broken pots and dented knives. But like us, ancient Mesopotamians and Phoenicians seldom made the error of tossing out cash, and only rarely did they bury their most precious liquid assets in the ground. Even when archeologists have found buried cash, though, they've had trouble recognizing it for what it was. Money doesn't always come in the form of dimes and sawbucks, even today. As a means of payment and a way of storing wealth, it assumes many forms, from debit cards and checks to credit cards and mutual funds. The forms it took in the past have been, to say the least, elusive.

From the beginning, money has shaped human society. It greased the wheels of Mesopotamian commerce, spurred the development of mathematics, and helped officials and kings rake in taxes and impose fines. As it evolved in Bronze Age civilizations along the Mediterranean coast, it fostered sea trade, built lucrative cottage industries, and underlay an accumulation of wealth that might have impressed Donald Trump. "If there were never any money, there would never have been prosperity," says Thomas Wyrick, an economist at Southwest Missouri State University in Springfield, who is studying the origins of money and banking. "Money is making all this stuff happen."

Ancient texts show that almost from its first recorded appearance in the ancient Near East, money preoccupied es-

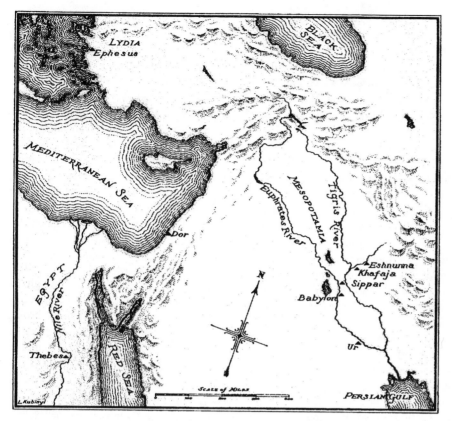

Cash first appeared in Mesopotamia then spread westward to the Mediterranean

Illustrations by Laszlo Kubinyi

stones across the plains and raising huge flat-topped platforms, known as ziggurats, on which to found their temples. Around their bases, they built street upon twisted street of small mud-brick houses.

To furnish these new temples and to serve temple officials, many farmers became artisans—stonemasons, silversmiths, tanners, weavers, boatbuilders, furniture makers. And within a few centuries, says Wyrick, the cities became much greater than the sum of their parts. Economic life flourished and grew increasingly complex. "Before, you always had people scattered out on the hillsides," says Wyrick, "and whatever they could produce for their families, that was it. Very little trade occurred because you never had a large concentration of people. But now, in these cities, for the first time ever in one spot, you had lots of different goods, hundreds of goods, and lots of different people trading them."

Just how complex life grew in these early metropolises can be glimpsed in the world's oldest accounting records: 8,162 tiny clay tokens excavated from the floors of village houses and city temples across the Near East and studied in detail by Denise Schmandt-Besserat, an archeologist at the University of Texas at Austin. The tokens served first as counters and perhaps later as prom-

tate owners and scribes, water carriers and slaves. In Mesopotamia, as early as 3000 B.C., scribes devised pictographs suitable for recording simple lists of concrete objects, such as grain consignments. Five hundred years later, the pictographs had evolved into a more supple system of writing, a partially syllabic script known as cuneiform that was capable of recording the vernacular: first Sumerian, a language unrelated to any living tongue, and later Akkadian, an ancient Semitic language. Scribes could write down everything from kingly edicts to proverbs, epics to hymns, private family letters to merchants' contracts. In these ancient texts, says Miguel Civil, a lexicographer at the Oriental Institute of the University of Chicago, "they talk about wealth and gold and silver all the time."

In all likelihood, says Wyrick, human beings first began contemplating cash just about the time that Mesopotamians were slathering mortar on mud bricks to build the world's first cities. Until then, people across the Near East had worked primarily on small farms, cultivating

barley, dates, and wheat, hunting gazelles and other wild game, and bartering among themselves for the things they could not produce. But around 3500 B.C., work parties started hauling

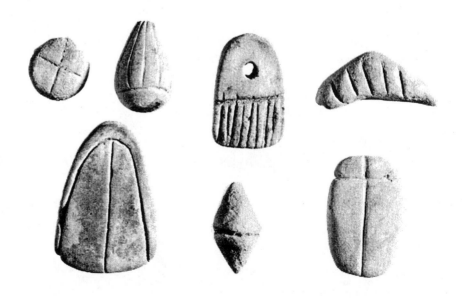

Courtesy Denise Schmandt-Besserat

These clay tokens from Susa, Iran, around 3300 B.C., represent (clockwise from top left): one sheep, one jar of oil, one garment, one measure of metal, a mystery item, one measure of honey, and one garment.

Ancient texts show that almost from its first recorded appearance in the ancient Near East, money preoccupied estate owners and scribes, water carriers and slaves.

issory notes given to temple tax collectors before the first writing appeared.

By classifying the disparate shapes and markings on the tokens into types and comparing these with the earliest known written symbols, Schmandt-Besserat discovered that each token represented a specified quantity of a particular commodity. And she noticed an intriguing difference between village tokens and city tokens. In the small communities dating from before the rise of cities, Mesopotamians regularly employed just five token types, repre-

senting different amounts of three main goods: human labor, grain, and livestock like goats and sheep. But in the cities, they began churning out a multitude of new types, regularly employing 16 in all, with dozens of subcategories representing everything from honey, sheep's milk, and trussed ducks to wool, cloth, rope, garments, mats, beds, perfume, and metals. "It's no longer just farm goods," says Schmandt-Besserat. "There are also finished products, manufactured goods, furniture, bread, and textiles."

Faced with this new profusion, says Wyrick, no one would have had an easy time bartering, even for something as simple as a pair of sandals. "If there were a thousand different goods being traded up and down the street, people could set the price in a thousand different ways, because in a barter economy each good is priced in terms of all other goods. So one pair of sandals equals ten dates, equals one quart of wheat, equals two quarts of bitumen, and so on. Which is the best price? It's so complex that people don't know if they are getting a good deal. For the first time in history, we've got a large number of goods. And

for the first time, we have so many prices that it overwhelms the human mind. People needed some standard way of stating value."

In Mesopotamia, silver—a prized ornamental material—became that standard. Supplies didn't vary much from year to year, so its value remained constant, which made it an ideal measuring rod for calculating the value of other things. Mesopotamians were quick to see the advantage, recording the prices of everything from timber to barley in silver by weight in shekels. (One shekel equaled one-third of an ounce, or just a little more than the weight of three pennies.) A slave, for example, cost between 10 and 20 shekels of silver. A month of a freeman's labor was worth 1 shekel. A quart of barley went for three-hundredths of a shekel. Best of all, silver was portable. "You can't carry a shekel of barley on your ass," comments Marvin Powell (referring to the animal). And with a silver standard, kings could attach a price to infractions of the law. In the codes of the city of Eshnunna, which date to around 2000 B.C., a man who bit another man's nose would be

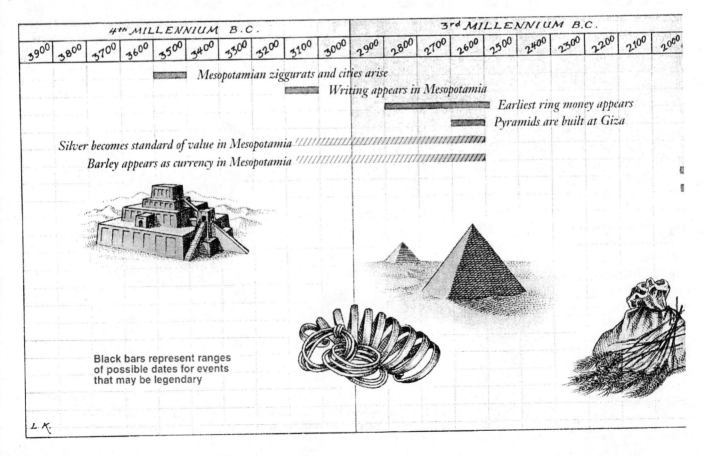

Black bars represent ranges of possible dates for events that may be legendary

L.K.

MONEYFACT

The Bartering Ape

William Hopkins and Charles Hyatt at Yerkes Regional Primate Center report that chimpanzees were observed swapping items for food from humans.

First, a human experimenter knelt down and begged in front of a chimp cage (chimpanzees customarily beg from one another in the wild). At the same time, the experimenter also pointed at an item—an empty food case—in the chimp's cage and held out desirable food, like an apple or half a banana. Of 114 chimpanzees, nearly half caught the trading spirit and pushed the item out. Some even traded much faster for more desirable food—taking just 15 seconds to trade for a banana versus nearly 3 minutes to trade for typical fare. And some chimpanzees negotiated on their own terms, notes Hopkins. He has worked with four who refused to cooperate in experiments for their usual food reward when other, more preferable food was in sight.

until they balanced a small carved stone weight in the other pan. Other members of the upper crust favored a more convenient form of cash: pieces of silver cast in standard weights. These were called *har* in the tablets, translated as "ring" money.

At the Oriental Institute in the early 1970s, Powell studied nearly 100 silver coils—some resembling bedsprings, others slender wire coils—found primarily in the Mesopotamian city of Khafaje. They were not exactly rings, it was true, but they matched other fleeting descriptions of *har*. According to the scribes, ring money ranged from 1 to 60 shekels in weight. Some pieces were cast in special molds. At the Oriental Institute, the nine largest coils all bore a triangular ridge, as if they had been cast and then rolled into spirals while still pliable. The largest coils weighed almost exactly 60 shekels, the smallest from one-twelfth to two and a half shekels. "It's clear that the coils were intended to represent some easily recognizable form of Babylonian stored value," says Powell. "In other words, it's the forerunner of coinage."

fined 60 shekels of silver; one who slapped another in the face paid 10.

How the citizens of Babylon or Ur actually paid their bills, however, depended on who they were. The richest tenth of the population, says Powell, frequently paid in various forms of silver. Some lugged around bags or jars containing bits of the precious metal to be placed one at a time on the pan of a scale

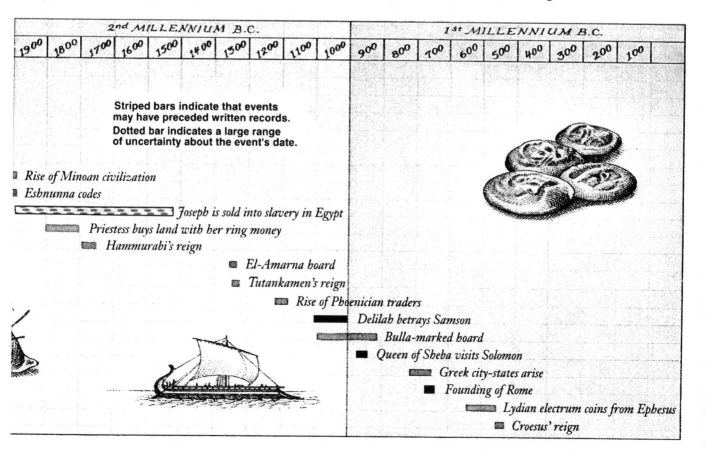

2nd MILLENNIUM B.C.										1st MILLENNIUM B.C.									
1900	1800	1700	1600	1500	1400	1300	1200	1100	1000	900	800	700	600	500	400	300	200	100	

Striped bars indicate that events may have preceded written records.
Dotted bar indicates a large range of uncertainty about the event's date.

Rise of Minoan civilization
Eshnunna codes
Joseph is sold into slavery in Egypt
Priestess buys land with her ring money
Hammurabi's reign
El-Amarna hoard
Tutankamen's reign
Rise of Phoenician traders
Delilah betrays Samson
Bulla-marked hoard
Queen of Sheba visits Solomon
Greek city-states arise
Founding of Rome
Lydian electrum coins from Ephesus
Croesus' reign

The masses in Mesopotamia, however, seldom dealt in such money. It was simply too precious, much as a gold coin would have been for a Kansas dirt farmer in the middle of the Great Depression. To pay their bills, water carriers, estate workers, fishers, and farmers relied on more modest forms of money: copper, tin, lead, and above all, barley. "It's the cheap commodity money," says Powell. "I think barley functions in ancient Mesopotamia like small change in later systems, like the bronze currencies in the Hellenistic period. And essentially that avoids the problem of your being cheated. You measure barley out and it's not as dangerous a thing to try to exchange as silver, given weighing errors. If you lose a little bit, its not going to make that much difference."

Measurable commodity money such as silver and barley both simplified and complicated daily life. No longer did temple officials have to sweat over how to collect a one-sixth tax increase on a farmer who had paid one ox the previous year. Compound interest on loans was now a breeze to calculate. Shekels of silver, after all, lent themselves perfectly to intricate mathematical manipulation; one historian has suggested that Mesopotamian scribes first arrived at logarithms and exponential values from their calculations of compound interest.

"People were constantly falling into debt," says Powell. "We find reference to this in letters where people are writing to one another about someone in the household who has been seized for securing a debt." To remedy these disastrous financial affairs, King Hammurabi decreed in the eighteenth century B.C. that none of his subjects could be enslaved for more than three years for failing to repay a debt. Other Mesopotamian rulers, alarmed at the financial chaos in the cities, tried legislating moratoriums on all outstanding bills.

While the cities of Mesopotamia were the first to conceive of money, others in the ancient Near East soon took up the torch. As civilization after civilization rose to glory along the coasts of the eastern Mediterranean, from Egypt to Syria, their citizens began abandoning the old ways of pure barter. Adopting local standards of value, often silver by

weight, they began buying and selling with their own local versions of commodity moneys: linen, perfume, wine, olive oil, wheat, barley, precious metals—things that could be easily divided into smaller portions and that resisted decay.

And as commerce became smoother in the ancient world, people became increasingly selective about what they accepted as money, says Wyrick. "Of all the different media of exchange, one commodity finally broke out of the pack. It began to get more popular than the others, and I think the merchants probably said to themselves, 'Hey, this is great. Half my customers have this form of money. I'm going to start demanding it.' And the customers were happy, too, because there's more than just one merchant coming around, and they didn't know what to hold on to, because each merchant was different. If everyone asked for barley or everyone asked for silver, that would be very convenient. So as one of these media of exchange becomes more popular, everyone just rushes toward that."

What most ancient Near Easterners rushed toward around 1500 B.C. was silver. In the Old Testament, for example, rulers of the Philistines, a seafaring people who settled on the Palestine coast in the twelfth century B.C., each offer Delilah 1,100 pieces of silver for her treachery in betraying the secret of Samson's immense strength. And in a well-known Egyptian tale from the eleventh century B.C., the wandering hero Wen-Amon journeys to Lebanon to buy lumber to build a barge. As payment, he carries jars and sacks of gold and silver, each weighed in the traditional Egyptian measure, the deben. (One deben equals 3 ounces.) Whether these stories are based on history or myth, they reflect the commercial transactions of their time.

To expedite commerce, Mediterranean metalsmiths also devised ways of conveniently packaging money. Coils and rings seem to have caught on in some parts of Egypt: a mural painted during the fourteenth century B.C. in the royal city of Thebes depicts a man weighing a stack of doughnut-size golden rings. Elsewhere, metalsmiths cast cash in other forms. In the Egyptian city

of el-Amarna, built and briefly occupied during the fourteenth century B.C., archeologists stumbled upon what they fondly referred to as a crock of gold. Inside, among bits of gold and silver, were several slender rod-shaped ingots of gold and silver. When researchers weighed them, they discovered that some were in multiples or fractions of the Egyptian deben, suggesting different denominations of an ancient currency.

All these developments, says Wyrick, transformed Mediterranean life. Before, in the days of pure barter, people produced a little bit of everything themselves, eking out a subsistence. But with the emergence of money along the eastern Mediterranean, people in remote coastal communities found themselves in a new and enviable position. For the first time, they could trade easily with Phoenician or Syrian merchants stopping at their harbors. They no longer had to be self-sufficient. "They could specialize in producing one thing," says Wyrick. "Someone could just graze cattle. Or they could mine gold or silver. And when you specialize, you become more productive. And then more and more goods start coming your way."

The wealth spun by such specialization and trade became the stuff of legend. It armed the fierce Mycenaean warriors of Greece in bronze cuirasses and chariots and won them victories. It outfitted the tomb of Tutankhamen, sending his soul in grandeur to the next world. And it filled the palace of Solomon with such magnificence that even the Queen of Sheba was left breathless.

But the rings, ingots, and scraps of gold and silver that circulated as money in the eastern Mediterranean were still a far cry from today's money. They lacked a key ingredient of modern cash—a visible guarantee of authenticity. Without such a warranty, many people would never willingly accept them at their face value from a stranger. The lumps of precious metal might be a shade short of a shekel, for example. Or they might not be pure gold or silver at all, but some cheaper alloy. Confidence, suggests Miriam Balmuth, an archeologist at Tufts University in Medford, Massachusetts, could be won only if someone reputable certified that a coin was both the promised weight and composition.

Balmuth has been trying to trace the origins of this certification. In the ancient Near East, she notes, authority figures—perhaps kings or merchants—attempted to certify money by permitting their names or seals to be inscribed on the official carved stone weights used with scales. That way Mesopotamians would know that at least the weights themselves were the genuine article. But such measures were not enough to deter cheats. Indeed, so prevalent was fraud in the ancient world that no fewer than eight passages in the Old Testament forbid the faithful from tampering with scales or substituting heavier stone weights when measuring out money.

Such wealth did the newly invented coins bring one Lydian king, Croesus, that his name became a byword for prosperity.

Clearly, better antifraud devices were needed. Under the ruins of the old city of Dor along northern Israel's coast, a team of archeologists found one such early attempt. Ephraim Stern of Hebrew University and his colleagues found a clay jug filled with nearly 22 pounds of silver, mainly pieces of scrap, buried in a section of the city dating from roughly 3,000 years ago. But more fascinating than the contents, says Balmuth, who recently studied this hoard, was the way they had been packaged. The scraps were divided into separate piles. Someone had wrapped each pile in fabric and then attached a bulla, a clay tab imprinted with an official seal. "I have since read that these bullae lasted for centuries," says Balmuth, "and were used to mark jars—or in this case things wrapped in fabric—that were sealed. That was a way of signing something."

All that remained was to impress the design of a seal directly on small rounded pieces of metal—which is precisely what happened by around 600 B.C. in an obscure Turkish kingdom by the sea. There traders and perfume makers known as the Lydians struck the world's first coins. They used electrum, a natural alloy of gold and silver panned from local riverbeds. (Coincidentally, Chinese kings minted their first money at roughly the same time: tiny bronze pieces shaped like knives and spades, bearing inscriptions revealing places of origin or weight. Circular coins in China came later.)

First unearthed by archeologists early this century in the ruins of the Temple of Artemis in Ephesus, one of the Seven Wonders of the ancient world, the Lydian coins bore the essential hallmarks of modern coinage. Made of small, precisely measured pieces of precious metal, they were stamped with the figures of lions and other mighty beasts—the seal designs, it seems, of prominent Lydians. And such wealth did they bring one Lydian king, Croesus, that his name became a byword for prosperity.

Struck in denominations as small as .006 ounce of electrum—one-fifteenth the weight of a penny—Lydia's coinage could be used by people in various walks of life. The idea soon caught on in the neighboring Greek city-states. Within a few decades, rulers across Greece began churning out beautiful coins of varied denominations in unalloyed gold and silver, stamped with the faces of their gods and goddesses.

These new Greek coins became fundamental building blocks for European civilization. With such small change jingling in their purses, Greek merchants plied the western Mediterranean, buying all that was rare and beautiful from coastal dwellers, leaving behind Greek colonies from Sicily to Spain and spreading their ideas of art, government, politics, and philosophy. By the fourth century B.C., Alexander the Great was acquiring huge amounts of gold and silver through his conquests and issuing coins bearing his image far and wide, which Wyrick calls "ads for empire building."

Indeed, says Wyrick, the small change in our pockets literally made the Western world what it is today. "I tell my students that if money had never developed, we would all still be bartering. We would have been stuck with that. Money opened the door to trade, which opened the door for specialization. And that made possible a modern society."

Unit Selections

11. **Indus Valley, Inc.,** Shanti Menon
12. **Saving Knossos,** Spencer P. M. Harrington
13. **Five Ways to Conquer a City,** Erika Bleibtreu
14. **Empires in the Dust,** Karen Wright
15. **Out of Africa: The Superb Artwork of Ancient Nubia,** David Roberts

Key Points to Consider

❖ What is the significance of archaeology in the study of history? Should historians rely solely on written records? Why or why not?

❖ What elements of urban planning can be found in the Indus Valley civilization? Why are these important? Compare Harappa and Mohenjo-Daro to Catalhoyuk (Unit 2).

❖ What were the ways to conquer a walled city?

❖ Why has Nubia been ignored by historians?

 **Links**   **www.dushkin.com/online/**

20. **Ancient City of Athens** http://www.indiana.edu/~kglowack/Athens/
21. **Exploring Ancient World Cultures** http://eawc.evansville.edu
22. **Reeder's Egypt Page** http://www.sirius.com/~reeder/

These sites are annotated on pages 4 and 5.

Cities and farming became human destiny. The cycle of more people and more food and more cities has continued to the present. Add to this the industrial revolution, when agriculture and urbanization both received a boost, and the result is like that of the United States where less than 2 percent of the population supplies the food for the rest of the people who live in or near cities. At the year 2000 about half the world will live in urban places. Urbanization is a finite process that started in the ancient world and continues into the present.

An amazing sophistication in urban design was expressed by the Indus Valley civilization, which provided some of the earliest examples of urban planning. Water supply, sewerage, toilets, straight streets, and standard-sized building bricks were all a part of their cities of Harappa and Mohenjo-Daro. These places flourished for 700 years and are described by Shanti Menon in "Indus Valley, Inc." The people of this civilization were practical and businesslike, in contrast to the more elaborate Minoan civilization symbolized by the palace at Knossos on the island of Crete. The Minoans represent Europe's first literate society, and their influence as seafaring traders in the Mediterranean Sea was enormous. The palace, which was made of soft stone and is now a major tourist site, is threatening to dissolve through erosion. Spencer Harrington outlines the importance of this palace in "Saving Knossos."

Most ancient cities or their civilizations did not survive into the present period. They were destroyed by war and conquest, and sometimes by nature. "Five Ways to Conquer a City" reveals the manner of Assyrian (900–600 B.C.E.) conquest. There were various means to breach the walls of a protected city, as depicted in Assyrian wall decorations. Drought, however, may explain the downfall of Mesopotamian civilization. Karen Wright writes about this ecological disaster in "Empires in the Dust." No city or civilization can survive without adequate water.

The most famous of the ancient civilizations known to Westerners is probably that of Egypt because of the enduring, awe-inspiring pyramids of Giza. Herodotus, the ancient Greek historian who traveled widely and set a standard for western historiography, visited Egypt and commented about the pyramids, the tombs of pharaohs. Much of the information about Egypt concerns the upper class

and comes from the tombs that survived. Kent Weeks, an archaeologist, for example, uncovered a vast burial chamber under a parking lot in the Valley of the Kings in 1995. Much less is known about the Egyptian people of the time, but excavations at the village of Deir el-Medina near the Valley of the Kings is revealing. This village housed the educated artisans who decorated the rich burial chambers in the nearby valley. They were unusually literate and left behind their own letters and messages.

The civilization of ancient Egypt is considered the most developed in Africa, but there is more to be learned about Nubia, an empire south of Egypt on the upper Nile River. The land is now barren, but it flourished at one time in competition with Egypt. The two nations often were at war with each other, and most of our information about Nubians comes from their enemies. Nubian writing has not been deciphered and, thus, historians are at a loss for information. History, therefore, may have been distorted. There is a current argument that the inspiration for Greek culture came from Nubia through Egypt. Most historians are waiting for proof of that assertion, but David Roberts in "Out of Africa: The Superb Artwork of Ancient Nubia," praises the quality of Nubian art, the extant artifacts through which this mysterious civilization is known.

Indus Valley, Inc.

No golden tombs, no fancy ziggurats. Four thousand years ago city builders in the Indus Valley made deals, not war, and created a stable, peaceful, and prosperous culture.

By Shanti Menon

THE RAILWAY LINKING LAHORE TO MULTAN IN PAKISTAN IS 4,600 YEARS OLD. In truth, the rails were laid down in the middle of the nineteenth century, but to build the railway bed, British engineers smashed bricks from crumbling buildings and rubble heaps in a town called Harappa, halfway between the two cities. Back in 1856, Alexander Cunningham, director of the newly formed Archaeological Survey of India, thought the brick ruins were all related to nearby seventh-century Buddhist temples. Local legend told a different story: the brick mounds were the remnants of an ancient city, destroyed when its king committed incest with his niece. Neither Cunningham nor the locals were entirely correct. In small, desultory excavations a few years later, Cunningham found no temples or traces of kings, incestuous or otherwise. Instead he reported the recovery of some pottery, carved shell, and a badly damaged seal depicting a one-horned animal, bearing an inscription in an unfamiliar writing.

That seal was a mark of one of the world's great ancient civilizations, but mid-nineteenth-century archeologists like Cunningham knew nothing of it. The Vedas, the oldest texts of the subcontinent, dating from some 3,500 years ago, made no mention of it, nor did the Bible. No pyramids or burial mounds marked the area as the site of an ancient power. Yet 4,600 years ago, at the same time as the early civilizations of Mesopotamia and Egypt, great cities arose along the floodplains of the ancient Indus and Saraswati rivers in what is now Pakistan and northwest India. The people of the Indus Valley didn't build towering monuments, bury their riches along with their dead, or fight legendary and bloody battles. They didn't have a mighty army or a divine emperor. Yet they were a highly organized and stupendously successful civilization. They built some of the world's first planned cities, created one of the world's first written languages, and thrived in an area twice the size of Egypt and Mesopotamia for 700 years.

To archeologists of this century and the last, Harappa and Mohenjo-Daro, a neighboring city some 350 miles to the southwest, posed an interesting, if unglamorous puzzle. Excavations revealed large, orderly walled cities of massive brick buildings, with highly sophisticated sanitation and drainage systems and a drab, institutional feel. The streets of Harappa, remarked British archeologist Mortimer Wheeler, "however impressive quantitatively, and significant sociologically, are aesthetically miles of monotony." The archeologist and popular author Leonard Cottrell, a contemporary of Wheeler's, wrote in 1956, "While admiring the efficiency of Harappan planning and sanitary engineering, one's general impression of Harappan culture is unattractive.... One imagines those warrens of streets, baking under the fierce sun of the Punjab, as human ant heaps, full of disciplined, energetic activity, supervised and controlled by a powerful, centralized state machine; a civilization in which there was little joy, much labor, and a strong emphasis on material things."

Superior plumbing and uniform housing, no matter how well designed, don't fire the imagination like ziggurats and gold-laden tombs. "But there's more to society than big temples and golden burials," argues Jonathan Mark Kenoyer, an archeologist at the University of Wisconsin in Madison. "Those are the worst things that ancient societies did, because they led to their collapse. When you take gold and put it in the ground, it's bad for the economy. When you waste money on huge monuments instead of shipping, it's bad for the economy. The Indus Valley started out with a very different basis and made South Asia the center of economic interactions in the ancient world."

Kenoyer, who was born in India to missionary parents, has been excavating at Harappa for the past 12 years. His work, and that of his colleagues, is changing the image of Harappa from a stark, state-run city into a vibrant, diverse metropolis, teeming with artisans and well-traveled merchants.

"What we're finding at Harappa, for the first time," says Kenoyer, "is how the first cities started." Mesopotamian texts suggest that cities sprang up around deities and their temples, and once archeologists found these temples, they didn't look much further. "People assumed this is how cities evolved, but we don't know that for a fact," says Kenoyer. At Harappa, a temple of the glitzy Mesopotamian variety has yet to be found. Kenoyer's archeological evidence suggests that the city got its start as a farming village around 3300 B.C. Situated near the Ravi River, one of several tributaries of the ancient Indus River system of Pakistan and northwestern India, Harappa lay on a fertile floodplain. Good land and a reliable food supply allowed the village to thrive, but the key to urbanization was its location at the crossroads of several major trading routes.

Traders from the highlands of Baluchistan and northern Afghanistan to the west brought in copper, tin, and lapis lazuli; clam and conch shells were brought in from the southern seacoast, timber from the Himalayas, semiprecious stones from Gujarat, silver and gold from Central Asia. The influx of goods allowed Harappans to become traders and artisans as well as farmers. And specialists from across the land arrived to set up shop in the new metropolis.

The city had room to expand and an entrepreneurial spirit driven by access to several sources of raw materials. "You had two sources of lapis, three of copper, and several for shell," says Kenoyer. "The way I envision it, if you had entrepreneurial go-get-'em, and you had a new resource, you could make a million in Harappa. It was a mercantile base for rapid growth and expansion." Enterprising Harappan traders exported finely crafted Indus Valley products to Mesopotamia, Iran, and Central Asia and brought back payment in precious metals and more raw materials. By 2200 B.C., Harappa covered about 370 acres and may have held 80,000 people, making it roughly as populous as the ancient city of Ur in Mesopotamia. And it soon had plenty of neighbors. Over the course of 700 years, some 1,500 Indus Valley settlements were scattered over 280,000 square miles of the subcontinent.

Unlike the haphazard arrangement of Mesopotamian cities, Indus Valley settlements all followed the same basic plan. Streets and houses were laid out on a north-south, east-west grid, and houses and walls were built of standard-size bricks. Even early agricultural settlements were constructed on a grid, "People had a ritual conception of the universe, of universal order," says Kenoyer. "The Indus cities and earlier villages reflect that." This organization, he believes, could have helped the growing city avoid conflicts, giving newcomers their own space rather than leaving

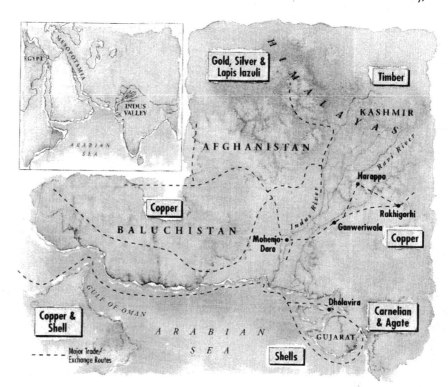

MAP BY BETTE DUKE

Indus Valley cities lay along major trade routes.

them to elbow their way into established territories.

Part of that ritual conception included a devotion to sanitation. Nearly every Harappan home had a bathing platform and a latrine, says Kenoyer, and some Indus Valley cities reached heights of 40 feet in part because of concern about hygiene. Cities often grow upon their foundations over time, but in the Indus Valley, homes were also periodically elevated to avoid the risk of runoff from a neighbor's sewage, "It's keeping up with the Joneses' bathroom," he quips, "that made these cities rise so high so quickly." Each neighborhood had its own well, and elaborate covered drainage systems carried dirty water outside the city. By contrast, city dwellers in Mesopotamian cities tended to draw water from the river or irrigation canals, and they had no drains.

The towering brick cities, surrounded by sturdy walls with imposing gateways, reminded early researchers of the medieval forts in Delhi and Lahore. But Kenoyer points out that a single wall, with no moat and with no sudden turns to lead enemies into an ambush, would have been ill-suited for defense. He

thinks the walls were created to control the flow of goods in and out of the city. At Harappa, standardized cubical stone weights have been found at the gates, and Kenoyer suggests they were used to levy taxes on trade goods coming into the city. The main gateway at Harappa is nine feet across, just wide enough to allow one oxcart in or out. "If you were a trader," he explains, "you wanted to bring goods into a city to trade in a safe place, so bandits wouldn't rip you off. To get into the city, you had to pay a tax. If you produced things, you had to pay a tax to take goods out of the city. This is how a city gets revenues."

THE IDENTITY OF THE TAX collectors and those they served remains a mystery. Unlike the rulers of Mesopotamia and Egypt, Indus Valley rulers did not immortalize themselves with mummies or monuments. They did, however, leave behind elaborately carved stone seals, used to impress tokens or clay tabs on goods bound for market. The seals bore images of animals, like the humped bull, the elephant, the rhinoceros, and the crocodile, which were probably emblems of

Unlike Mesopotamian cities, Indus Valley cities all followed the same basic plan, reflecting the people's ritual conception of universal order.

powerful clans. The most common image is the unicorn, a symbol that originated in the Indus Valley.

Frustratingly, though, those seals carry inscriptions that no one has been able to decipher. Not only are the inscriptions short, but they don't resemble any known language. From analyzing overlapping strokes, it is clear that the script reads right to left. It is also clear that the script is a mix of phonetic symbols and pictographs. Early Mesopotamian cuneiform, which used only pictographs, was thought to be the world's first written language, says Kenoyer, but the Indus Valley script emerged independently around the same time—at least by around 3300 B.C.

As long as the language remains a mystery, so too will the identities of the Indus Valley elites. Kenoyer thinks each of the large cities may have functioned as an independent city-state, controlled by a small group of merchants, landowners, and religious leaders. "They controlled taxation, access to the city, and communication with the gods," he says. While the balance of power may have shifted between these groups, they seem to have ruled without a standing army. Sculptures, paintings, and texts from Egypt and Mesopotamia clearly illustrate battles between cities and pharaonic wars of conquest. But in the Indus Valley, not a single depiction of a military act, of taking prisoners, of a human killing another human has been found. It's possible these acts were illustrated on cloth or paper or some other perishable and simply did not survive. Yet none of the cities show signs of battle damage to buildings or city walls, and very few weapons have been recovered.

Human remains show no signs of violence either. Only a few cemeteries have been found, suggesting that burial of the dead may have been limited to high-ranking individuals (others may have been disposed of through cremation or river burials). The bones from excavated burials show few signs of disease or malnourishment. Preliminary genetic studies from a cemetery in

Harappa have suggested that women were buried near their mothers and grandmothers. Men do not seem to be related to those near them, so they were probably buried with their wives' families. There is evidence that people believed in an afterlife: personal items like amulets and simple pottery have been recovered from a few burials. But true to their practical, businesslike nature, the Harappans didn't bury their dead with riches. Unlike the elites of the Near East, Harappans kept their valuable items in circulation, trading for new, often extraordinary ornaments for themselves and their descendants.

In spite of this practice, excavators have turned up some hints of the wealth an individual could accumulate. Two decades ago, in the rural settlement of Allahdino, near modern Karachi in Pakistan, archeologists stumbled upon a buried pot filled with jewelry, the secret hoard of a rich landowner. Among the silver and gold necklaces and gold bands, beads, and rings was a belt or necklace made of 36 elongated carnelian beads interspersed with bronze beads. Shaping and drilling these long, slender beads out of hard stone is immensely difficult and time-consuming. Indus craftsmen made a special drill for this purpose by heating a rare metamorphic rock to create a superhard material. Even these high-tech drills could perforate carnelian at a rate of only a hundredth of an inch per hour. Kenoyer estimates that a large carnelian belt like the one at Allahdino would have taken a single person 480 working days to complete. It was most likely made by a group of artisans over a period of two or three years.

Such intensive devotion to craftsmanship and trade, Kenoyer argues, is what allowed Indus Valley culture to spread over a region twice the size of Mesopotamia without a trace of military domination. Just as American culture is currently exported along with goods and media, so too were the seals, pottery styles, and script of the Indus Valley spread among the local settlements. Figurines from the Indus Valley also tes-

tify to a complex social fabric. People within the same city often wore different styles of dress and hair, a practice that could reflect differences in ethnicity or status. Men are shown with long hair or short, bearded or clean-shaven. Women's hairstyles could be as simple as one long braid, or complex convolutions of tresses piled high on a supporting structure.

Eventually, between 1900 and 1700 B.C., the extensive trading networks and productive farms supporting this cultural integration collapsed, says Kenoyer, and distinct local cultures emerged. "They stopped writing," he says. "They stopped using the weight system for taxation. And the unicorn motif disappeared." Speculation as to the reasons for the disintegration has ranged from warfare to weather. Early archeologists believed that Indo-Aryan invaders from the north swept through and conquered the peaceful Harappans, but that theory has since been disproved. None of the major cities show evidence of warfare, though some smaller settlements appear to have been abandoned. There is evidence that the Indus River shifted, flooding many settlements and disrupting agriculture. It is likely that when these smaller settlements were abandoned, trade routes were affected. In the Ganges River valley to the east, on the outskirts of the Indus Valley sphere of influence, the newly settled Indo-Aryans, with their own customs, grew to prominence while cities like Harappa faded.

But the legacy of the ancient Indus cities and their craftspeople remains. The bead makers of Khambhat in India continue to make beads based on Harappan techniques—though the carnelian is now bored with diamond-tipped drills. Shell workers in Bengal still make bangles out of conch shells. And in the crowded marketplaces of Delhi and Lahore, as merchants hawk the superiority, of their silver over the low-quality ore of their neighbors, as gold and jewels are weighed in bronze balances, it's hard to imagine that a 4,000-year-old Harappan bazaar could have been terribly different.

Saving Knossos

The struggle to preserve a landmark of Europe's first great civilization

by Spencer P. M. Harrington

ALEXANDRA KARETSOU SQUINTS into the late afternoon sun and points to a distant farmhouse perched on a wooded hill overlooking the minoan ruins of Knossos. "That house," she says, "violates our building codes. It's too large. So is that one, and that one." They look innocent enough, but to her they are an insult. A petite, fashionably dressed woman of about 50, Karetsou is ephor (director) of prehistoric and classical antiquities in central Crete, and as such is responsible for maintaining the most famous Minoan sites—Knossos, Mallia, and Phaistos—managing the Herakleion Museum, and issuing permits to those building near archaeological sites. In addition, her salvage teams must excavate in advance of construction projects, no small task in central Crete, where seaside hotels sprout like toadstools after a rain. Being ephor is a busy job, often fraught with pressures from developers and homeowners who view building as their right. "In Greece," she says, "protecting our culture and monuments should be a matter of love. In reality it's a matter of war."

As builders skulk along Knossos' boundaries like uninvited guests, a more immediate threat comes from the invited—the thousands of tourists who throng daily to the site to see the remains of Europe's first great civilization. Though 200 miles across the Aegean from Athens, Knossos has consistently drawn the most tourists of any archaeological site save the Acropolis, averaging a million visitors a year. This has meant prosperity for Cretans, among the richest of all Greeks, but great hardship for those entrusted with preventing the site from being trampled to dust. On the eve of the centenary of its initial excavation, there is little question that Knossos is imperiled by tourism, development and weathering.

The Minoans built their palaces with a coarse, soft limestone called *poros*, sandstone, and gypsum, presenting staggering problems for future conservators. According to Elias Mariolakos, a University of Athens geologist, the site will simply dissolve in two or three hundred years at current rates of erosion. Arthur Evans, Knossos' excavator earlier this century, attempted to save the remains by reconstructing large parts of the palace with reinforced concrete, permanently altering the site. In so doing, he not only assured his own fame but secured lasting preeminence for Knossos. Evans' concrete has cracked in the intervening years, exposing rusting steel, and Karetsou's ephorate is now faced with the task of restoring a reconstruction of the Minoans' architectural legacy.

Excavation of Minoan palaces on Crete and contemporary sites on the Cycladic Islands has shown that Knossos was the hub of Europe's first literate society, exerting a profound political, spiritual, and artistic influence throughout the Greek world in the later Bronze Age (2000–1100 B.C.). Clay tablets found at Knossos inscribed with Minoan hieroglyphs and Linear A, an undeciphered script, revealed that the Minoans were using writing sometime between 1900 and 1700 B.C., making them the first Europeans to do so. This undoubtedly helped organize their economic life. Knossos had capacious storerooms containing massive *phithoi* (jars) that once held foodstuffs for distribution throughout the island and the eastern Mediterranean. The Minoans are known to have exported pottery, wood, textiles, wine, and oil in exchange for precious metals and stones.

At its height in the Second Palace period (between 1700 and 1450 B.C.), Knossos' well-to-do inhabitants had an astonishing array of creature comforts, including latrines, water conduits for drainage, and skylights for illumination and ventilation. Commoners outside the palace grounds lived in multistory townhouses with windows. Many Minoan residences had sitting rooms with adjustable partitions, indoor pools to cool the summer air, and verandas with splendid views. Amenities like indoor plumbing that the Minoans took for granted were uncommon in later Crete, only reappearing in the early twentieth century.

"It's unbelievable how modern their buildings were in many ways," says Clairy Palyvou, an architect and Minoan specialist based in Athens. "Especially when you consider [the rectangular

Reprinted with the permission of *Archaeology* magazine, Vol. 52, No. 1, January/February 1999, pp. 30-40. © 1999 by the Archaeological Institute of America.

mud-brick houses] that existed before Minoan architecture. It is the first time you have a style that has all the basic traits for what we are so familiar with now in Western architecture."

ON FIRST INSPECTION, THE PALACE at Knossos appears to be a labyrinthine confusion of walls and low foundations interspersed with Evans' reconstructions of various residential and civic buildings. The ruins do not soar into the air like Mesoamerican pyramids, nor are they anywhere near as well preserved as some classical Greek monuments such as the temples at Agrigento in Sicily. But what Knossos does yield to scrutiny is something profoundly intriguing: a sense of activity—political, religious, commercial, domestic—all taking place within one structure. Minoan architectural specialist John McEnroe has described it as encompassing "the breadth and depth of its culture more eloquently than any other single building in the history of European architecture."

Bronze Age visitors to Knossos would have been impressed by the large size of the palace; it covered nearly five acres, several times bigger than Mallia, 20 miles to the east, the next largest Minoan palace. They would likely "have perceived the building as having no borders, as being virtually limitless," says Jeremy Rutter, a Dartmouth College archaeologist. The palace was composed of low buildings with boxy, rectangular chambers stacked upon it. Guests entering from the west, as tourists do today, would have walked through a hallway (the so-called Corridor of the Procession Fresco) paved with gypsum flagstones and decorated with a fresco showing visitors bearing gifts. The passage wended its way to the central court, measuring 164 by 82 feet, where public gatherings and ceremonies took place. Clustered around the court were residences housing the palace elite, reception rooms, treasuries and storerooms, chambers for ritual activity, potters' and smith's workshops, and administrative archives—in short, everything required of a sophisticated, literate society.

Around 1450 B.C., nearly all the Minoan palace-cities, villas, and towns on Crete were mysteriously destroyed by fire. Knossos escaped relatively unscathed. Pottery styles and the writing used on inscribed tablets at the site change at this point, reflecting the arrival of Mycenaean settlers from mainland Greece. Knossos appears to have been administered by the Mycenaeans into the fourteenth or thirteenth century B.C. By 1000 B.C. the island's primary settlement area was just northwest of the now-abandoned palace. A later Greek and Roman city was built less than a mile north of the palace, which by this time was probably in ruins. After the Arab conquest in the ninth century A.D., Herakleion, a fortified coastal city five miles north of Knossos, became the island's principal settlement.

Until 100 years ago the Minoans were known to us only in myth. An ancient Greek legend spoke of a King Minos, a wise leader and just lawgiver who ruled Crete from Knossos. According to legend, Minos defeated the Athenians in battle, demanding that they sacrifice seven young men and seven young women to the Minotaur, which was imprisoned in a labyrinth constructed by the architect Daedalus. The hero Theseus, volunteering as one of the seven male youths, slew the Minotaur and found his way out of the labyrinth with the aid of thread provided by Ariadne, Minos' daughter.

Heinrich Schliemann's excavations at Troy and Mycenae in the 1870s provided impetus for others to seek historical basis for such myths. One such scholar was Arthur Evans, the curator of Oxford's Ashmolean Museum. Fascinated by the legend, Evans was eager to dig at Knossos. No less important for him was the search for writing on Crete. Late nineteenth-century scholars considered writing one of the true marks of civilization. While Schliemann's work at Troy and Mycenae revealed monumental structures, beautiful artworks, and other evidence of a complex society, scholars were puzzled that the Mycenaeans had never developed a script. At the Ashmolean, Evans acquired artifacts from British archaeologist Flinders Petrie's excavations in Egypt and grew interested in Petrie's notion that there was an Aegean precursor to Mycenaean civilization. Evans had already acquired sealstones with pictographic and linear symbols for the Ashmolean and was impressed by German scholar Arthur Milchhoefer's suggestion that these stones originated in Crete. His interest was further piqued when he acquired Cretan sealstones in an Athenian bazaar inscribed with symbols he thought were part of a writing system.

EVANS MADE SEVERAL TRIPS TO Crete between 1894 and 1899 both to collect artifacts and to negotiate the purchase of olive groves that stood on the site of a palace that had been preliminarily investigated in 1878–1879 by Minos Kalokairinos, a Cretan businessman, and considered for purchase and excavation by Schliemann in the late 1880s. During this period Evans began publishing articles suggesting that writing was developed on Crete by a yet-to-be-discovered pre-Mycenaean civilization. In 1900, he began a largely self-financed excavation at Knossos to prove his theory. Clay tablets inscribed with what he would call Linear B were among his first discoveries. "There were no surprises," says Sandy MacGillivray, Evans' biographer, "not a single one. It's really extraordinary. Everything he dug confirmed his theories."

Though Evans was not an experienced excavator when he started to dig Knossos, he was guided by David G. Hogarth, then director of the British School of Archaeology at Athens, and Duncan Mackenzie, an experienced archaeologist who had dug at the Bronze Age site of Phylakopi on Melos. Mackenzie's diaries were impeccable, and he is credited with being one of the first scientific excavators in the Aegean. Every stage of the project was photographed, and Evans' architect, Theodore Fyfe, drew precise sketches of the site, a novelty at the time. Evans was also among the first to recognize the importance of archaeological stratigraphy. He documented each layer of earth as he removed it, recording the depth at which objects were found. This allowed Evans to create a chronology of successive stages in the palace's development.

The first trowelfuls of earth in Evans' first excavation season brought to the surface wall fragments decorated with frescoes. These belonged to what he called the Throne Room complex, which included an antechamber, a throne room, and a small black chamber thought to be a shrine. In the throne room was a large, stone-lined tank that Evans named "Ariadne's Bath"; the tank is now believed to have been a lustral basin used in ritual. Nearby was a stone chair set on a platform that Evans called the Throne of Ariadne, believing the wide seat to be suited to female anatomy. Just to the west, his team found a series of 18 narrow storerooms, in which were several clay *pithoi* that had probably held olive oil, wine, or grain.

But it was the discovery of written records in a chamber that would become known as the Room of the Chariot Tablets that was the most important find of the season. Evans uncovered what he described as "a kind of elongated clay bar, rather like a stone or bronze chisel in shape though broken at one end, with script and what appears to be numerals." He determined that Knossos had been an important administrative center where records were kept establishing ownership of property. Though he had come to Crete to find a script, and though he was to succeed in separating and classifying the three writing systems he found at the site (the Linear A, Linear B, and hieroglyphic scripts), he was never able to translate any of them. It was not until 1952 that Michael Ventris, an English architect inspired by one of Evans' lectures, was able to decipher Linear B, an early form of Greek. The other two scripts remain undeciphered.

In 1901 there were more dramatic discoveries: a multistory residential area for Knossos' rulers that Evans called the Domestic Quarter. These rooms were reached by a four-story gypsum stairway that became known as the Grand Staircase. Much of the Domestic Quarter and the Grand Staircase were well preserved because they had been built into the side of a hill, which provided support. Even though the wooden framework for these buildings had long since disintegrated and the upper floors had sagged, Evans was astonished to

While tourism is an obvious cause of wear at the site, weathering presents a less visible but more insidious danger.

find "gypsum paving slabs, door jambs, limestone bases, the steps of stairs, and other remains . . . on the upper level, almost at the height at which they had originally rested, though the intervening supports . . . were reduced to brittle masses of charcoal." Evans later described the preservation of the upper-story Domestic Quarter remains as "miraculous," because it allowed him to reconstruct almost perfectly the plan of the complex.

Even in the first years of excavation it became clear to Evans that he would have to take measures to preserve the structures he was excavating. He erected a roof over the Throne Room complex in early 1901 to save its gypsum floor. In 1905, heavy winter rains caused the second landing of the Grand Staircase to collapse. Evans launched an effort to rebuild parts of the site, both to protect excavated areas and to give visitors a better idea of how the palace might have looked. Though there was evidence of an older palace that had been destroyed by an earthquake ca. 1700 B.C., he chose to restore what has become known as the New, or Second, Palace, which was in use between 1700 and 1450 B.C.

The splendid preservation of parts of the site helped Evans in his reconstructions, and fresco fragments found in some of the rooms gave him a sense of how they were decorated and proportioned. Evans first used wood and brick to rebuild, then double-T steel bars, and finally, after World War I, reinforced concrete. He was among the very first

in Greece to use such material, and in so doing he was reflecting the architectural zeitgeist. Reinforced concrete was "the basis for Le Corbusier's New Architecture," says MacGillivray. "It was a time of reconstruction. The First World War was so horrible. Architects wanted to build a new world, and Knossos became part of that. Just as reinforced concrete gave modern architects the ability to create a new world for their living population, so it gave Evans exactly the same ability to create a new world for the ancients."

In a paper delivered to the Society of Antiquaries in London on December 9, 1926, Evans explained his extensive reconstructions: "To the casual visitor who first approaches the site and sees before him an acre or so of upper stories the attempt may well at times seem overbold, and the lover of picturesque ruins may receive a shock." The reconstruction work continued until 1930, and inevitably provoked criticism. A French journalist called Evans "the builder of ruins," while René Dussaud, author of a study on prehellenic civilization in the Aegean, was troubled by "the brazenness of Evans actions . . . it is generally believed that this clever archaeologist is completely rebuilding the palace of Minos from scratch. It would certainly have been preferable if the restoration of certain portions had not gone too far and if the visitor could have been spared the unpleasant impression of entering a completely redecorated apartment."

Though most scholars acknowledge that Evans was conscientious and scientific in his reconstructions, some of this work was inevitably speculative and drew on his intuition of what the palace might have looked like. Evans' use of concrete, rather than wood, for support beams and columns rankles some modern experts. "You have to press your imagination hard to imagine that these [beams and columns] were all wood," Palyvou says. "This has completely changed the feeling of Minoan architecture. Concrete is such a different material. No matter how you paint concrete, you just can't give the impression of wood."

For the visitor, there is one obvious benefit to the rebuilt Knossos: it is the only Minoan site where one can see a full-scale representation of what the architecture might have looked like. "This legitimate process of reconstitution... must appeal to the historic sense of the most unimaginative," wrote Evans in the *Times* in 1905. Guidebooks advise seeing Knossos before journeying to Phaistos and Mallia, where only walls and foundations remain. "Though modern restorers would never rebuild to the extent Evans did," says Palyvou, "deep inside, most of us are not that upset with what he did."

TODAY, NOT ONLY ARE THE ANCIENT building materials at risk, but so are Evans' reconstructions. Excited by the possibilities of reinforced concrete, Evans was sometimes indiscriminate in its use. "The upper stories were probably made with dried mud brick," says MacGillivray. "By putting steel-reinforced concrete on top of the ancient material, Evans put a massive load that is not being distributed properly and that is forcing the ancient foundations to crumble."

Even worse, both Evans' concrete and his steel were fairly primitive by modern standards. Water has seeped into exposed concrete, rusting the steel bars inside; inch-thick chunks of concrete have been known to fall from the bottom of roof beams, posing obvious hazards for tourists. Karetsou estimates that more than half the complex is now off limits. Recently, the Grand Staircase, the jewel of Evans' reconstructed Domestic Quarter, was closed. As the main access to the quarter, it was attracting so many visitors that it was beginning to resemble a ramp. Palyvou wrestled with the idea of putting a wooden staircase over the original, but noted that other parts of the stairwell were being harmed by tourists traipsing up and down.

"It was not just the steps that were suffering," she says. "It was the side walls as well. It was the colonnade that flanks the staircase. It was everything in this narrow space because people touch everywhere." Without any organized pathway, says Palyvou, "people went up and down not because they had to, but because they didn't know otherwise." Though the Domestic Quarter is now entirely closed, visitors can view the staircase and different rooms in the residential area from several vantage points outside it.

Karetsou estimates that more than half the damage to Knossos has resulted from "an illogical use of the site." By this she means that visitors without guides often get lost and end up climbing over ancient walls. "Visitors would jump from one wall to another, go through very narrow doors, and step on exposed areas of soft stone that Evans left without any protection," says Palyvou. "It was a very bad situation."

A visitors' pathway designed by Palyvou, the first major site management plan of its kind in Greece, has been installed and should make it easier to get around. More problematical are the thousands of people disembarking from cruise ships during the summer months. Karetsou says that as many as 5,000 people from several boats sometimes enter Knossos during a three-hour period, creating impossible site management problems: "Even if we had 50 guards during those hours, it would be useless," she says. "The tour operators earn millions, and they give nothing back for the upkeep of the monuments."

This is a formidable problem because the solution—forcing tour groups to make reservations—will draw howls of protest from cruise companies and tour operators, who operate on tight schedules. Groups from cruise ships often have only three hours to visit Knossos, the Herakleion Museum, and go shopping, says Yannis Tzedakis, director of archaeology at the Greek Ministry of Culture. While he disapproves of the way tour operators plan their daily programs, he does concede that "the power is in their hands. They can always say, 'If you don't do things our way we'll skip Herakleion and go to Turkey.'" Putting pressure on the tourist industry is not the business of the Ministry of Culture, he insists, but the responsibility of the Ministry of Tourism.

For its part, the Ministry of Tourism is reluctant to implement changes that might interfere with people visiting Knossos. "Greece is a democratic country," says Angela Varela, a ministry spokeswoman. "It's against the principles of the country to prevent tourists from visiting the site." Still, the ministry is under pressure from the Federation of Greek Guides, a group representing guides at archaeological sites throughout the country, to control tourist flow at Knossos. "We would like it if all the boats didn't arrive on the same day and at the same time," says Dora Spachi, the federation's general secretary.

Archaeologists who worked at Knossos in the late 1950s and early 1960s say the site received few visitors then. The arrival of a cruise ship made local news. Excavators at the Minoan palace at Zakros in eastern Crete in the 1960s recount 11- to 14-hour journeys over rough roads, during which they saw no hotels and only a few modest houses with no indoor plumbing. Tourists started arriving in large numbers in the late 1960s. Cretans were quick to realize that hotels and restaurants were a more profitable use of their land than farming, and many were soon serving coffee and turning down sheets instead of cultivating grapes and olives. The islanders grew wealthy and started building hotels, especially along the north coast. By the 1970s development was encroaching upon some of the coastal archaeological sites. Costis Davaras was ephor of prehistoric and classical antiquities in eastern Crete at the time and was the first to restrict land use around sites; acres of land in eastern Crete were suddenly off limits to hotel developers.

Those owning land within restricted zones "were furious," recalls Davaras, "and they had a right to be." The government wasn't offering them any compensation. "But I felt my duty as an ephor was not to be concerned with the social aspects of the issue. My duty was to protect the sites." Soon land-use laws were adopted throughout Crete, and archaeologists, many from the mainland, have since found themselves in the uncomfortable position of telling islanders how they can and cannot develop their land. "They're really complaining and sometimes you're afraid," recalls Davaras. "Some have a tendency to get violent." Now a professor at the University of Athens, Davaras says the job became too stressful. "I should have left the service years ago," he says. "When you're an ephor, you have the feeling that you're the only one who cares about these issues."

Greeks who knew Crete in the 1960s say they don't recognize it now. Davaras describes the prosperity as sudden and jarring, with families making the transition from donkey to Mercedes in the space of a generation. Herakleion today is a city of 102,000 with a swank downtown commercial area. The cafes at the corner of Ioannis Perdikari and Androgeo streets are elegantly decorated, and by 1:00 P.M. are full of fashionable young people sipping Nescafé frappés and playing backgammon. With its relaxed pace and array of upscale shops, the city has the feel of a *ville bourgeoise*. On a recent trip, I wandered into a Herakleion rug shop and mentioned that, even in the off-season, the town was full of tourists. "This is nothing," the proprietor said. "In August we have ten times this number!"

WITH NO RESTRICTIONS ON tourist access to Knossos planned for the foreseeable future, Palyvou says the roped off pathways that distance visitors from the building are the best defense against site destruction. "The more visitors are free to walk around," she says, "the more they damage the ruins."

In planning the pathways, Palyvou talked to guides and realized that the routes they had already selected were the most logical. She then tailored the most basic route, a 90-minute walk through the major buildings, to the site's largest clientele: elderly people who tire easily and arrive in large groups pressed for time. She also provided secondary pathways for visitors with more time to spare. A nature walk running along the site's periphery is planned for those who want to make a day of it.

Informational panels will be placed throughout the site to identify buildings and show what they were like before and after Evans' restoration. Guidebooks to the palace do not always indicate what Evans tinkered with, and most tourists walking around the ruins must find it difficult, as I did, to distinguish between old and new building material. Certain buildings are obviously recon-

structed, but are their foundations original? As careful as he was in his restoration, Evans did not indicate different time periods in the building's history, nor did he make the distinction between ancient materials and modern reconstructions absolutely clear. According to MacGillivray, Evans "assumed that the educated visitor would instantly know the difference between reinforced concrete and calcite alabaster in the walls. But at the same time he reused a lot of the original collapsed material in his rebuilds, so that even trained scholars can be deceived into thinking that some of the walls they're looking at are ancient, whereas they were built in the 1920s."

WHILE TOURISM IS AN OBVIOUS cause of wear at the site, weathering presents a less visible, but more insidious danger. University of Athens geologist Elias Mariolakos estimates that parts of the site are eroding by as much as 0.1 millimeter annually, especially in areas exposed to the windborne salt water of the Sea of Crete. "Our lives are too short to notice these sorts of changes," he says, "but over hundreds of years this means a lot of erosion. It's not an earthquake or a volcanic eruption, but these small changes are more dangerous." Scientists at the Stone Conservation Institute in Athens have developed a compound that will be applied to the stone this year. The solution, which does not discolor the stone, provides only a 30 percent increase in resistance to the elements. "That's very low," says Iordanis Dimakopoulos, director of restoration at the Ministry of Culture. "It means that after a period of time you will have the same problem again. But it's better than doing nothing."

Preservation specialists familiar with Knossos have explored, and rejected, the idea of building a roof over the site. "[University of Cincinnati archaeologist Carl] Blegen built a roof over Nestor's Palace at Pylos," says Dimakopoulos. "But imagine at Knossos—you'd have to build a roof 20 times that size. It couldn't be done. At Knossos you have an area of approximately 20,000 square meters [5 acres] instead of 1,500 [¼acre] at Pylos." While a roof does

cover the crypt near the agora at Mallia, Dimakopoulos estimates that this roof is one-tenth the size that would be required to protect Knossos. He also fears that a roof would not only be unsightly, but might damage the site: "You would have to create space for columns to support such a huge roof. And these columns would be raised on archaeologically sensitive ground."

In 1992–1993, Dimakopoulos began a pilot project to reinforce Evans' restorations on the South House, a Minoan villa south of the main palace complex. Contractors sprayed a quick-drying plaster-cement mixture designed to stabilize the cracking concrete. Karetsou and Dimakopoulos were satisfied with the results, and all of Evans' restorations are now undergoing the same treatment, at a cost of $1 million. This project is viewed as a temporary fix in advance of a much more massive project: dismantling Evans' cracking concrete beams. This work must await both funding and the completion of an exhaustive site index cataloging structural features Evans excavated and rebuilt at the site.

The South House restoration highlighted the importance of a readily accessible archive of all previous excavation and conservation work. Karetsou says that restorers were unable to identify some of the trenches uncovered during drainage work on the South House. In 1992 a researcher was assigned to Oxford's Ashmolean Museum to index Evans' Knossos archive, which includes 26 volumes of daybooks kept by Mackenzie, 25 volumes of notes and sketches kept by Evans, four volumes of sketches of structural remains by Fyfe, and some 700 site photographs. Karetsou says the project has been slowed somewhat by the fact that "Evans' handwriting was terrible. Even for the British it's difficult [to decipher]." All information about the South House and the site's East Wing has now been bound into nearly a dozen volumes that include photocopies of the original manuscripts on one side and Greek translations on the other. The index on the west wing is still in progress.

Greek archaeologists who have worked on Crete say privately that the Ministry of Culture has in the past lavished more resources on mainland classical sites than on the Minoan palaces. There is little doubt that the Cretan ephorates are strapped for cash, which has precluded much thought about large-scale restoration projects. With the coastline to the east of Herakleion lined with hotels and restaurants, many under construction, rescue excavations are by far the largest drain on the ephorate's resources and manpower. Karetsou says she currently has 65 properties to excavate. She estimates that some 700 million drachmas ($2.4 million) are needed yearly for rescue excavations, but says she can only allot 20 million of her 500 million drachma ($1.7 million) budget. The rest must go to salaries and upkeep on archaeological sites and the Herakleion Museum. As a result, the ephorate can only excavate between eight and ten sites a year.

Karetsou blames bad city planning for her workload: "If 20 or 25 years ago politicians had respected the archaeological sites, or taken into account what they meant for the future, we wouldn't have had any problems." She estimates that nearly one-third of the builders in outlying areas of protected archaeological zones do not comply with building laws; noncompliance jumps to two-thirds during election years, when politicians are currying favor. "Why," she asks, "in the [Roman] harbor of Chersonissos [15 miles east of Herakleion] do you have 30 properties that are our obligation to excavate? They should have listened to us screaming 'No! Leave this place in peace because it is an archaeological site, and organize new cities and settlements in such a way as not to disturb them. Go away. Go far away."

Also frustrating restoration initiatives have been laws mandating that architects and engineers sign off on all studies and proposals for work at the sites. Karetsou says that ephors, who are usually archaeologists, often know what work is required and how to carry it out, but must wait for Ministry of Culture specialists to fly in from Athens. Only after they sign a work order can it be submitted for consideration to the Central Archaeological Council (CAC), a decision-making body in Athens that holds the purse strings. Ephorates can hire their own architects and engineers, but the salaries they are able to offer are too low to attract experienced professionals. Ephors are burdened with additional budgetary constraints; they can initiate no new work that costs more than 4 million drachmas without CAC approval.

IN A HOPEFUL SIGN FOR THE Ephorates, Evangelos Venizelos, the minister of culture, has promised that they will be able to keep ten percent of gate receipts from local sites. The Greek move follows a decision by the Italian parliament to grant Pompeii administrative, scholarly, and fiscal autonomy from the Ministry of Culture. While no such freedom of action is anticipated from the Greek Ministry of Culture, Karetsou welcomes the modicum of autonomy, though she says, "We haven't seen any of the money yet."

Even with the bureaucratic restrictions placed on the ephorate, Karetsou has been able to persuade the Ministry of Culture to create two highly paid positions for architects and engineers at Knossos, and to hire an accountant to keep her books. In the early 1990s, she oversaw the complete redesign of the site's entrance, installing a new box office, gift shop, restaurant, and grape arbor leading from the entrance area to the site. At her urging, the ministry is negotiating the purchase of a parcel of land north of the site that will be used to consolidate parking. Automobiles now park in a lot to the south of the site, tour buses just to the left of the entrance in a space once occupied by vineyards. Karetsou wants to replant the vineyards once the tour buses are relocated. In the more distant future, she would like to build a small theater at the entrance to show films introducing the site.

A graduate thesis I read on the conservation of Knossos suggested reburying parts of the site to preserve it. This is, of course, a responsible approach if preservation is the only goal, but the site's national significance makes this impossible. The gradual decay that Elias Mariolakos, describes seem to make conservation a Sisyphean task, but one that must proceed. The hundreds of thousands of pilgrims to Knossos deserve a chance, albeit momentary, to commune with the world of the Minoans.

SPENCER P.M. HARRINGTON *is a senior editor of* ARCHAEOLOGY.

Five Ways to Conquer a City

Erika Bleibtreu

In the spring of 1843, Paul-Emile Botta, the French consul at Mosul in present-day Iraq, invited Austen Henry Layard, then 26 years old and the British ambassador's secretary in Constantinople, to join him at a site Botta thought was ancient Nineveh: "Come, I pray you," Botta wrote, "and let us have a little archaeological fun at Khorsabad!"

Although Layard's notes indicate he was "anxious to visit" the site, he did not actually do so until August 1846. He found it an unhealthy place: "During M. Botta's excavations, the workmen suffered greatly from fever, and many fell victims to it."[1] He was also somewhat critical of Botta's excavation methods and was not very impressed with the remains.

For himself, Layard chose the site of Nimrud, about 35 miles south of Khorsabad. He began excavating Nimrud in 1845 and was soon as handsomely rewarded as Botta with monumental sculptures and other Assyrian treasures—now on display at the British Museum in London.

In 1849 Layard turned his attention to the ruins of Kuyunjik, on the other side of the Tigris River, opposite modern Mosul. Ironically, Botta had been here earlier, in 1842, but he had abandoned the site after a few months without discovering any remarkable remains.[2]

It turned out that Layard's site of Kuyunjik, not Botta's site at Khorsabad, was actually Nineveh. But when Botta

published the results of his excavations at Khorsabad, it was under the title *Monument de Ninive* (five volumes, 1849–1850). Actually Khorsabad was Dur-Sharrukin, literally "town of Sargon" or "Sargonsburg"; Botta had excavated the capital of Sargon II of Assyria, who reigned from 722 to 705 B.C. In 1849, 1850 and 1853, Layard published his own volumes on Nineveh containing most of the reliefs he had excavated at Kuyunjik and at Nimrud (*The Monuments of Nineveh* [two volumes, 1849 and 1853], *Nineveh and Its Remains* [two volumes, 1850] and *Discoveries in the Ruins of Nineveh and Babylon* [1853]).

Despite their stupendous finds, Botta and Layard both left much to be desired in excavation technique. Botta was an Italian-born physician turned diplomat, not a trained excavator at all. By modern standards, Layard was only marginally better. He excavated by tunneling along the walls of halls revealed by the discovery of sculptured slabs.

Nevertheless, at all three sites, the two men made discoveries still in many ways unsurpassed—monumental palaces, huge sculptures, major libraries of cuneiform texts and, most important for purposes of this article, miles of sculptured slabs that formed the decorations on the walls of the palaces.

At the real Nineveh, for example, Layard recovered almost two miles of sculptured slabs made of Mosul alabaster, in addition to 27 pairs of colossal, human-headed, winged bulls and lions that flanked the entrances to the Southwest Palace. The sculptured slabs formed the wall decorations of a palace with

more than 70 rooms and courts. It was built for Sennacherib (704–681 B.C.), who led a major military campaign against Judah in the late eighth century B.C. By his own account, he destroyed 46 Judean cities including Lachish* and even besieged Jerusalem, although for some reason failed to conquer it. (The Bible describes all this in 2 Kings 18.) Sennacherib decorated several rooms of his palace at Nineveh to celebrate his victory in this campaign. He called it "Palace Without Equal" and intended it to surpass the palaces of all his predecessors.

At Nimrud, Layard discovered two other palaces: one built by Ashurnasirpal II (883–859 B.C.), covering about 6.5 acres, and the other built by Tiglath-pileser III (744–727 B.C.).

Soon thereafter, another palace was excavated at Nineveh by Hormuzd Rassam and William Kennett Loftus. Called the North Palace, it was constructed during the reign of Sennacherib's grandson, Ashurbanipal (668–627 B.C.), who probably moved there from his grandfather's palace.

All together, these 19th-century excavations uncovered six Assyrian kings' palaces decorated with wall reliefs, dating from the early ninth to the late seventh centuries B.C.:

Ashurnasirpal II	883–859 B.C.
Tiglath-pileser III	744–727 B.C.
Sargon II	722–705 B.C.
Sennacherib	704–681 B.C.
Esarhaddon	680–669 B.C.
Ashurbanipal	668–627 B.C.

---

[1] Austen H. Layard, *Nineveh and Its Remains* (London, 1850), p. 148.

[2] The reason was that a deep accumulation of rubbish from later occupations covered the most impressive Assyrian remains.

---

* See Hershel Shanks, "Destruction of Judean Fortress Portrayed in Dramatic Eighth-Century B.C. Pictures," **BAR**, March/April 1984.

Reprinted from *Biblical Archaeology Review*, May/June 1990, pp. 36–44. © 1990 by the Biblical Archaeology Society.

Assyrian Palaces Where Wall Reliefs Were Found

Ancient Name of Site	Modern Name of Site	Assyrian Ruler	Excavators*	Date of Excavation
Dur-Sharrukin (Botta thought it was Nineveh. The city was founded by Sargon II and named after him.)	Khorsabad	Sargon II (721–705 B.C.) Palace	**Paul-Emile Botta and Eugène Flandin** Victor Place Henri Frankfort Gordon Loud Directorate General of Antiquities, Baghdad, Iraq	**1843–44** 1852–54 1929–32 1938–39
Kalhu (Calah of the Bible— see Genesis 10:11–12)	Nimrud	Ashurnasirpal II (883–859 B.C.) Northwest Palace	**Austen Henry Layard** **Hormuzd Rassam** Sir Max Mallowan Directorate General of Antiquities, Baghdad, Iraq Janusz Meuszynski	**1845–47, 1849–51** **1853–54** 1949–53 1959–60, 1969–74 1974–75
Kalhu	Nimrud	Tiglath-pileser III (744–727 B.C.) Central Palace	**Austen Henry Layard** **Hormuzd Rassam** **William Kennett Loftus** **Hormuzd Rassam** Sir Max Mallowan Janusz Meuszynski	1845–47, 1849–51 **1853–54** **1854** **1878–79** 1952 1975–1976
Kalhu	Nimrud	Esarhaddon (680–669 B.C.) Southwest Palace (Slabs sculptured for the Northwest Palace of Ashurnasirpal II and for the Central Palace of Tiglath-pileser III were found here ready to be reused and recarved.)	**Austen Henry Layard** **William Kennett Loftus** George Smith Sir Max Mallowan	**1845–47, 1849–51** **1854** 1873 1951
Nineveh Citadel	Kuyunjik	Sennacherib (704–681 B.C.) Southwest Palace (partly redecorated under the reign of his grandson Ashurbanipal)	**Austen Henry Layard** Henry Ross Christian Rassam **Austen Henry Layard** Christian Rassam **and his brother Hormuzd** **William Kennett Loftus** George Smith **Hormuzd Rassam** and his nephew Nimroud E. A. Wallis Budge Leonard William King R. Campbell Thompson Tariq Madhloom	**1846–47** 1847–48 1848 **1849–51** **1851–54** **1854** 1873–74 **1878** 1889–91 1903–05 1904–05, 1927, 1931–32 1965–67
Nineveh Citadel	Kuyunjik	Ashurbanipal (668–627 B.C.) North Palace	**Hormuzd Rassam William Kennett Loftus** and William Boutcher Christian Rassam E. A. Wallis Budge R. Campbell Thompson	**1853–54** **1854** 1854–55 1889–91 1904–05

* Excavators in boldface are mentioned in the accompanying article.

Before this period, palace walls had simply been painted. However, during this period, palace walls in most of the capital cities of Assyria were decorated with sculptured slabs of alabaster and limestone. These slabs were carved in flat relief and then, for the most part, painted and finally aligned along the walls constructed of unbaked brick.

Botta and Layard managed to send some hundreds of tons of Assyrian sculptures back to Paris and London. Even so, only the most magnificent and better-preserved pieces were selected for transport. Many of the smaller fragments—which were less important from the 19th-century treasure-hunting perspective—found their way to the antiquities market, eventually coming to reside in more than 50 museums and galleries on three continents.

Some of the major pieces were lost in transport. Botta's first shipment from Sargon's palace at Khorsabad, intended for the Louvre, sank in the Tigris River when the rafts upon which it had been loaded overturned in treacherous rapids on the way to the Persian Gulf.

Fortunately, we have in public museums not only the pieces that survived, but also the original drawings made on the spot by superb artists who were both talented and careful.

A young artist named Eugène Napoléon Flandin copied the sculptures found at Khorsabad. Between May and October 1844, he made about 150 drawings of the wall reliefs of Sargon's palace. These drawings are undoubtedly the best ever made of Assyrian wall reliefs, and were published as engravings in Botta's *Monument de Ninive.* Recently, in 1986, Flandin's original drawings—now kept in the Bibliothèque de l'Institut de France in Paris—were published for the first time in Pauline Albenda's *The Palace of Sargon, King of Assyria* (Paris, 1986).

In addition, the Department of Western Asiatic Antiquities in the British Museum has about 500 original drawings of Assyrian wall reliefs from the ninth to the seventh centuries B.C. Layard himself probably made about half of these. Although Layard was not a professional artist, he was a very gifted amateur. His drawings are of a high standard and very faithful.

Many of the drawings illustrate remains that have since disappeared. Most of the slabs not chosen for transport to a European museum by the 19th-century excavators were reburied in the rubbish of the site.

The slabs that decorated the walls are masterpieces of Assyrian art. It took enormous effort and talent to create them. The slabs first had to be transported from the quarries to the capital cities of the Assyrian empire, then carried through courts and corridors to the rooms in which they were to be used. The slabs were attached to the walls of the palaces by sinking them partly below floor-level. Clamps were probably used to tie them to the walls at the top.

To decorate the slabs, outlines of the scenes were first sketched on the flattened stone, probably following a model in clay that had been approved by the king. Thereafter a team of artisans executed the main scenes by carving away the background around the figures. Another group of stonemasons probably added the minor details, such as the mountain-scale pattern and the pattern of foliage on the trees. Still another team of artisans painted certain details in the reliefs; traces of red and black paint can still be seen on some of the slabs, for example on the shoes of the king and his courtiers in the Nimrud Gallery of the British Museum.

The result was a massive pictorial record of major events in the kings' reigns and the illustration of important ritual activities in which the kings took part.

Pictorial means of communication were more immediately effective than oral or even written storytelling. Pictures could reach illiterate people and people who spoke languages other than the Akkadian used by their Assyrian overlords. We do not know who was allowed to enter the palace, apart from the king's family and his courtiers. Therefore, we cannot say whether these wall decorations served as a kind of political propaganda to impress foreign visitors, or whether they were meant as a kind of religious demonstration to show that the will of the gods was being continually fulfilled in glorious Assyrian victories.

Scenes of warfare and Assyrian victory provide the themes of the reliefs— the conquest of foreign peoples, the deportation of prisoners, the inspection of spoil and booty and its transportation to Assyria. But above all was the superiority of the Assyrian army, whose victory was ordained by her gods, according to whose command the Assyrian kings led their campaigns.

The realistic representations on the wall reliefs depict various units of the Assyrian army—infantry, chariotry and cavalry. We see well-trained Assyrian soldiers fighting alongside auxiliaries from all parts of the Near East. We see too the enemies of the Assyrians. The wall reliefs also depict the tactics and strategies employed in order to conquer so many fortified cities.

Obviously, there is an enormous amount to be learned from these extraordinary reliefs. Here we shall concentrate on one aspect of them—what they teach us about the means by which walled, strongly fortified cities were conquered.

Five different methods can be distinguished. However, a combination of two or more of these methods can usually be observed at each site of attack.

We will describe these methods generally and illustrate them more particularly from the Assyrian palace reliefs:

1. One way to penetrate a fortified walled city was to use ladders to get over the top of the wall and inside the city. Scaling ladders were used to break the resistance of the defenders who fought from the city's towers and parapets. By this method, at least some of the attackers could enter the city from the top of the fortifications. Prior to the attack, however, trees had to be cut and ladders constructed to a suitable height for the walls surrounding the besieged city.

In some of the reliefs, archers and spearmen are shown climbing up the ladders. Helmets, shields and different kinds of body armour protect the attackers from the missiles that the defenders throw from above. Soldiers on the ground, shooting arrows, provided additional protection to those on the ladders.

2. A second method of attack involved penetration through a city wall or a city gate, the latter being the weakest point in the fortification. The wooden doors of a city gate could be easily demolished by setting them on fire, even when they were sheathed with bronze.

A wall or gate could also be forcibly penetrated by means of battering rams. In the Judahite cities Sennacherib says he conquered, he claims to have used battering rams, a claim consistent with the portrayal of the conquest of Lachish depicted on his palace walls, where several battering rams can be seen.

Battering rams from the ninth century B.C. are depicted as being heavy, six-wheeled engines. Later they became lighter and more mobile. The later battering rams were covered with raw hides to protect them against fire.

Before a battering ram could be used, a path had to be created to get it to the appropriate place at the appropriate height in the wall. To accomplish this, a siege ramp had to be built so that the battering rams could be rolled up it to the upper part of the wall.

Several carvings on the reliefs show different methods of building these ramps. In some cases they were built of rows of bricks. In others, regularly shaped stones appear to have been used with branches of trees as fillers between the layers. The quantity of stones needed to build a siege ramp was enormous. That is why bricks had to be used in Mesopotamia, which is a largely stone-less area. In some cases wooden tracks were used on the surface of siege ramps, as the ramps had to be smooth for the wheels of the battering rams.

3. It was possible for an attacker to go not only over the wall and through the wall, but also under the wall. To penetrate the city wall from underground was less dangerous for the attacker, but it was technically more difficult. Iron implements were used to dig what was in effect a tunnel from which the wall could be undermined. At the beginning of this effort, it was especially important to protect the diggers from attacks from above. Shield-bearers provided this protection. The great body-shields with curving tops, as shown in the reliefs, proved particularly useful in this regard.

4. A city could also be conquered without having its walls attacked by force. To conquer a strongly fortified city without attacking its walls by force, it was necessary to lay siege to it for as long as required. A siege could last several months or even years. Much depended on the supply of water and food inside the besieged city. Outside the city, the besieging army established its own fortified camp (or camps). The site of the besiegers' camp was on raised ground whenever this was available. This offered some security from counterattack by foraging city defenders.

The siege camps are always shown in the reliefs in a maplike representation. In the ninth century B.C., the groundplans are generally circular, square or rectangular; in the seventh-century reliefs, they all have oval shapes and are surrounded by their own fortified walls.

The reliefs depict two different types of tents inside the siege camps. The more elaborate are closed tents that are open to the sky in the middle. This type was used by the king, or by the chief commander of the army, or by high-ranking officers. The soldiers used ordinary tents with open sides. In the reliefs, we see inside these tents and thus observe the daily life of the soldiers—slaughtering animals or cooking and baking. In one fragment of a slab, a returning Assyrian archer is seen drinking beside his open bed.

5. The final method of conquering a fortified city involved cutting off its water supply. A scene from the palace of Ashurnasirpal II probably depicts the cutting off of the water supply of a city under siege. (It is certainly not so easy to illustrate ruses that were sometimes used to conquer a city.)

Once a city was conquered, much of it was destroyed, especially its fortifications. Soldiers of various units are seen in the reliefs systematically demolishing city walls. Then the city itself was put to the torch.

Once the battle was over, the Assyrians boasted of their prowess and bravery by delivering severed heads to a scribe, who registered the heads for a special reward. Usually a pair of scribes is illustrated, one using a two-part writing board covered with wax, and the other using a scroll of leather or papyrus. Thus, Assyrian valor was recorded for posterity and for the gods.

Bleibtreu wrote her doctoral thesis on Neo-Babylonian inscriptions and later studied under Sir Max Mallowan at Oxford. Since 1963, she has worked as research assistant at the Oriental Institute of Vienna University, where she has also served, since 1978, as senior lecturer in ancient Near Eastern art history and archaeology. Her excavations include sites in eastern Anatolia (Turkey) and in Austria. In collaboration with Geoffrey Turner and the late Richard D. Barnett, she is preparing a catalogue titled *The Sculptures of Sennacherib (705–681 B.C.) and Ashurbanipal (668–627 B.C.) from the Southwest Palace at Nineveh.*

Empires in the Dust

Some 4,000 years ago, a number of mighty Bronze Age cultures crumbled.
Were they done in by political strife and societal unrest?
Or by a change in the climate?

By Karen Wright

Mesopotamia: cradle of civilization, the fertile breadbasket of western Asia, a little slice of paradise between the Tigris and Euphrates rivers. Today the swath of land north of the Persian Gulf is still prime real estate. But several millennia ago Mesopotamia was absolutely The Place to Be. There the visionary king Hammurabi ruled, and Babylon's hanging gardens hung. There the written word, metalworking, and bureaucracy were born. From the stately, rational organization of Mesopotamia's urban centers, humanity began its inexorable march toward strip malls and shrink-wrap and video poker bars and standing in line at the DMV. What's more, the emergence of the city-state meant that we no longer had to bow to the whims of nature. We rose above our abject dependence on weather, tide, and tilth; we were safe in the arms of empire. Isn't that what being civilized is all about?

Not if you ask Harvey Weiss. Weiss, professor of Near Eastern archeology at Yale, has challenged one of the cherished notions of his profession: that early civilizations—with their monuments and their grain reserves, their texts and their taxes—were somehow immune to natural disaster. He says he's found evidence of such disaster on a scale so grand it spelled calamity for half a dozen Bronze Age cultures from the Mediterranean to the Indus Valley—including the vaunted vale of Mesopotamia. Historians have long favored political and social explanations for these collapses: disruptions in trade routes, incompetent administrators, barbarian invasions. "Prehistoric societies, single agriculturists—they can be blown out by natural forces," says Weiss. But the early civilizations of the Old World? "It's not supposed to happen."

Yet happen it did, says Weiss, and unlike his predecessors, he's got some data to back him up. The evidence comes from a merger of his own archeological expertise with the field of paleoclimatology, the study of climates past. His first case study concerns a series of events that occurred more than 4,000 years ago in a region of northern Mesopotamia called the Habur Plains. There, in the northeast corner of what is present-day Syria, a network of urban centers arose in the middle of the third millennium B.C. Sustained by highly productive organized agriculture, the cities thrived. Then, around 2200 B.C., the region's new urbanites abruptly left their homes and fled south, abandoning the cities for centuries to come.

Weiss believes that the inhabitants fled an onslaught of wind and dust kicked up by a drought that lasted 300 years. He also believes the drought crippled the empire downriver, which had come to count on the agricultural proceeds of the northern plains. Moreover, he contends, the long dry spell wasn't just a local event; it was caused by a rapid, region-wide climate change whose effects were felt by budding civilizations as far west as the Aegean Sea and the Nile and as far east as the Indus Valley. While the Mesopotamians were struggling with their own drought-induced problems, he points out, neighboring societies were collapsing as well: the Old Kingdom in Egypt, early Bronze Age cities in Palestine, and the early Minoan civilization of Crete. And in the Indus Valley, refugees fleeing drought may have overwhelmed the cities of Mohenjo-Daro and Harappa. The troubles of half a dozen Bronze Age societies, says Weiss, can be blamed on a single event—and a natural disaster at that.

Weiss first presented this scenario in 1993, when soil analyses showed that a period of severe dust storms accompanied the mysterious Habur hiatus. "I was thinking you can't have a microregion drought," he recalls, "because that isn't how climate works. It's got to be much bigger. And I said, 'Wait a minute, didn't I read about this in graduate school? Weren't there those who, 30 years ago, had said that drought conditions were probably the agency that accounts for all these collapses that happened in contiguous regions?'" says Weiss. "Back in the late sixties, we had read this stuff and laughed our heads off about it."

In 1966, British archeologist James Mellaart had indeed blamed drought for the downfalls of a whole spectrum of third-millennium civilizations, from the early Bronze Age communities in Palestine to the pyramid builders of Egypt's Old Kingdom. But when Mellaart first put forth this idea, he didn't have much in the way of data to back him up. Weiss, however, can point to new paleoclimate studies for his proof. These studies suggest that an abrupt, widespread change in the climate of western Asia did in fact occur at 2200 B.C. Samples of old ocean sediments from the Gulf of Oman, for example, show signs of extreme drought just when Weiss's alleged exodus took place. A new model of air-mass movement explains how subtle shifts in atmospheric circulation could have scorched Mesopotamia as well as points east, west, and south. And recent analyses of ice cores from Greenland—which offer the most detailed record of global climate change—reveal unusual climatic conditions at 2200 B.C. that could well have brought drought to the region in question.

I've got some figures I can show you. Figures always help," says paleoclimatologist Peter deMenocal, swiveling his chair from reporter to computer in his office at Columbia University's Lamont-Doherty Earth Observatory, just north of New York City. On the monitor, deMenocal pulls up a graph derived from the research project known

as GISP2 (for Greenland Ice Sheet Project 2). GISP2 scientists, he explains, use chemical signals in ice cores to reconstruct past climates. There are two kinds of naturally occurring oxygen atoms, heavy and light, and they accumulate in ice sheets in predictable ratios that vary with prevailing temperatures. In a cool climate, for example, heavy oxygen isotopes are less easily evaporated out of the ocean and transported as snow or rain to northern land masses like Greenland. In a warm climate, however, more heavy oxygen isotopes will be evaporated, and more deposited in the Greenland ice sheets.

By tracking oxygen-isotope ratios within the ice cores, the GISP2 graph reflects temperatures over Greenland for the past 15,000 years. Near the bottom of the graph, a black line squiggle[s] wildly until 11,700 years ago, when the last ice age ended and the current warm era, the Holocene, began. The line then climbs steadily for a few thousand years, wavering only modestly, until 7,000 years before the present. From then until now, global temperatures appear rela-

tively stable—"then until now" comprising, of course, the entire span of human civilization.

"The archeological community—and actually segments of the paleoclimate community—have viewed the Holocene as being climatically stable," says deMenocal. "And so they imagine that the whole drama of civilization's emergence took place on a level playing field in terms of the environment."

Until he met Harvey Weiss, de-Menocal wasn't much interested in studying the Holocene; like most of his peers, he was more drawn to the dynamic climate fluctuations that preceded it. In fact, the Holocene had something of a bad rep among climatologists. "It was thought of as kind of a boring time to study," says deMenocal. "Like, why would you possibly want to? All the action is happening 20,000 years earlier."

Then a few years ago he read an account of Weiss's drought theory and had an epiphany of sorts. It occurred to him that even the smallest variations in climate could be interesting if they had in-

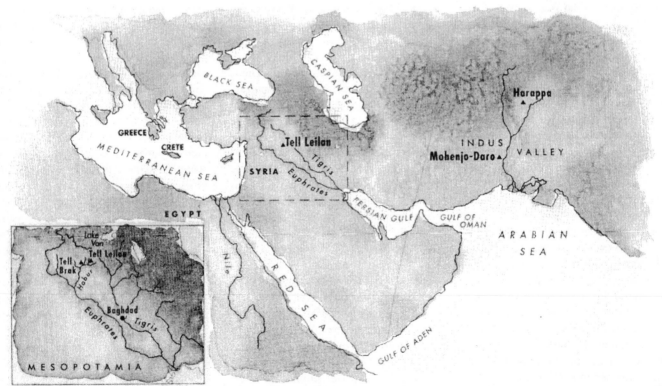

MAP BY BETTE DUKE

BRONZE AGE cultures possibly crippled by drought: The early Minoan in Crete, the old Kingdom in Egypt, the cities Mohenjo-Daro and Harappa, and the Akkadian Empire in Mesopotamia.

fluenced the course of history. What if something was going on in the Holocene after all? He looked up the 1993 paper in which Weiss had laid out the evidence for the Habur hiatus and reported the results of the soil analysis.

"I was pretty skeptical," says deMenocal. "I mean, what would you expect if everyone left a town? It would get dusty. Especially in the world's dustiest place. Big surprise."

Weiss, meanwhile, was getting a similar response from many of his peers. But when he and deMenocal met at a conference in 1994, they hit it off right away—largely because Weiss, too, was dismayed at the paucity of his own evidence. "Peter was immediately sensitive to my moaning about how we needed additional data, different kinds of data," says Weiss. "And he immediately understood where such data could be obtained."

DeMenocal told Weiss that if a large-scale drought had in fact occurred, it would have left a mark in the sediments of nearby ocean floors—the floor of the Gulf of Oman, for example. Lying approximately 700 miles southeast of ancient Mesopotamia, the gulf would have caught any windblown dust that swept down from the Tigris and Euphrates valleys. (The Persian Gulf is closer, but because it's so shallow, its sediments get churned up, thereby confusing their chronology.) And deMenocal just happened to know some German scientists who had a sediment core from the Gulf of Oman.

Analysis of the gulf core is ongoing, but deMenocal has already extracted enough information to confirm Weiss's suspicions. To track dry spells in the sediments, he and his colleague Heidi Cullen looked for dolomite, a mineral found in the mountains of Iraq and Turkey and on the Mesopotamian floodplains that could have been transported to the gulf only by wind. Most of the Holocene section of the core consists of calcium carbonate sediments typical of ocean bottoms.

"And then all of a sudden, at exactly 4,200 calendar years, there's this big spike of dolomite," says deMenocal—a fivefold increase that slowly decays over about three centuries. The chemistry of the dolomite dust matches that of the dolomite in the Mesopotamian mountains and plains, verifying the mineral's

source. And not only did deMenocal and his colleagues figure out what happened, they may have figured out how. Studies by Gerard Bond at Lamont-Doherty have shown that the timing of the drought coincided with a cooling period in the North Atlantic. According to a survey by Cullen of current meteorological records, such cooling would have dried out the Middle East and western Asia by creating a pressure gradient that drew moisture to the north and away from the Mediterranean.

The curse of Akkad describes "large fields" that "produced no grain" and "heavy clouds" that "did not rain." Scholars had decided that these expressions were mere metaphor.

"The whole disruption, collapse bit, well, I just have to take Harvey at his word," says deMenocal. "What I tried to do is bring some good hard climate data to the problem." Why hasn't anybody seen this signature of calamity before? Simple, says deMenocal. "No one looked for it."

Weiss's first hints of climate-associated calamity came from a survey of his principal excavation site, a buried city in northeastern Syria called Tell Leilan. Tell Leilan (rhymes with "Ceylon") was one of three major cities on the Habur Plains to be taken over by the Akkadian Empire around 2300 B.C. The city covered more than 200 acres topped by a haughty acropolis, and was sustained by a tightly regulated system of rain-fed agriculture that was co-opted and intensified by the imperialists from the south. Weiss had asked Marie-Agnès Courty of the National Center for Scientific Research in France to examine the ancient soils of Tell Leilan to help him under-

stand the agricultural development of the region. She reported that a section dating from 2200 to 1900 B.C. showed evidence of severe drought, including an eight-inch-thick layer of windblown sand and a marked absence of earthworm tunnels.

In his own excavations of the same period, Weiss had already found evidence of desertion: mud-brick walls that had fallen over clay floors and were covered with, essentially, 300 years' worth of compacted dust. And once he made the drought connection at Tell Leilan, he began turning up clues to the catastrophe everywhere he looked. In 1994, for example, Gerry Lemcke, a researcher at the Swiss Technical University in Zurich, presented new analyses of sediment cores taken from the bottom of Lake Van in Turkey, which lies at the headwaters of the Tigris and the Euphrates. The new results indicated that the volume of water in the lake—which corresponds to the amount of rainfall throughout western Asia—declined abruptly 4,200 years ago. At the same time, the amount of windblown dust in the lake increased fivefold.

Weiss came to believe that the effects of the drought reached downriver to the heart of Mesopotamia, causing the collapse of the Akkadian Empire. The collapse itself is undisputed: written records describe how, soon after it had consolidated power, Akkad crumbled, giving way to the Ur III dynasty in—when else?—2200 B.C. The cause of this collapse has been the subject of considerable speculation. But Weiss's studies of early civilizations have convinced him that their economies—complex and progressive though they may have been—were still fundamentally dependent on agricultural production. In fact, he notes, one hallmark of any civilization is that it requires a life-support system of farming communities toiling away in the fields and turning over the fruits of their labor to a central authority. The drought on the Habur Plains could have weakened the Akkadian Empire by drastically reducing agricultural revenues from that region. People fleeing the drought moved south, where irrigation-fed agriculture was still sustainable. For want of a raindrop, the kingdom was lost.

"Well, believe it or not, all my colleagues had not figured that out," says Weiss. "They actually believed that somehow this empire was based on bureaucracy, or holding on to trade routes, or getting access to exotic mineral resources in Turkey." But the drought itself is documented, Weiss says, in passages of cuneiform texts. Images from a lengthy composition called the Curse of Akkad, for example, include "large fields" that "produced no grain" and "heavy clouds" that "did not rain." Scholars had decided that these expressions were mere metaphor.

And many still stand by their interpretations. "I don't agree with his literal reading of the Mesopotamian texts, and I think he has exaggerated the extent of abandonment in this time period," says Richard Zettler, curator of the Near East section at the University of Pennsylvania's Museum of Archaeology and Anthropology in Philadelphia. Zettler doesn't question the evidence for drought, but he thinks Weiss has overplayed its implications. Although Tell Leilan may well have been deserted during the putative hiatus, for example, nearby cities on the Habur Plains show signs of continuing occupation, he says. As for the Curse and other Mesopotamian passages describing that period, says Zettler, "there are a lot of questions on how to read these texts—how much of it is just literary license, whatever. Even if there is a core of historical truth, it's hard to determine what the core of truth is."

Instead of backing down in the face of such commentary, Weiss has continued to document his thesis. Echoing Mellaart, he points out that 2200 B.C., saw the nearly simultaneous collapses of half a dozen other city-based civilizations in Egypt, in Palestine, on Crete and the Greek mainland, and in the Indus Valley. The collapses were caused by the same drought, says Weiss, for the same reasons. But because historians and archeologists look for internal rather than external forces to explain civilizations in crisis, they don't communicate among themselves, he says, and many aren't even aware of what's going on next door, as it were.

"Very few people understand that there was a synchronous collapse and probably drought conditions in both Egypt and Mesopotamia," let alone the rest of the Old World, says Weiss.

It didn't help Weiss's extravagant claims for third-millennium cataclysm that his alleged drought didn't appear in the GISP2 oxygen-isotope record. The graph in deMenocal's office, for example, has no spikes or dips or swerves at 2200 B.C. just a nice flat plateau. That graph was drawn from an interpretation of the ice-core data. But according to Paul Mayewski of the University of New Hampshire in Durham, who is chief scientist of GISP2 there are plenty of reasons a drought in western Asia might not make it into the oxygen-isotope record in the Greenland glacier. Greenland might be too far away to "feel" the regional event, or the drought may have left a different kind of chemical signature. Only a climatologist like Mayewski could explain these reasons however. And no one asked him to.

"As a consequence, a lot of people called Harvey Weiss and said, 'Well, the GISP2 record is the most highly resolved record of Holocene climate in the world. And if it's not in there, you're wrong, Harvey,'" says Mayewski. "I didn't realize that poor Harvey was being abused for not existing in our record."

Fortunately Mayewski, like deMenocal, is a curious sort with interests a bit broader than his own specialty. When he happened upon Weiss's 1993 paper, he'd already lent a hand on a few archeological projects, including one on the disappearance of Norse colonies from Greenland in the mid-1300s. But he figured other scientists had already looked for the Mesopotamian drought in the climate record. When he finally met Weiss in 1996, he learned otherwise. Mayewski began reanalyzing his core data with Weiss's theory in mind, and he uncovered a whole new Holocene.

"We can definitely show from our records that the 2200 B.C. event is unique," says Mayewski. "And what's much more exciting than that, we can show that most of the major turning points in civilization in western Asia also correlate with what we would say would be dry events. We think that we have found a proxy for "aridity in western Asia."

Earlier interpretations of the GISP2 data had measured a variety of ions in ice cores that would reveal general information about climate variability. To look for the 2200 B.C. drought in particular, Mayewski used tests based on 2.5-year intervals in the climate record instead of 50- to 100-year intervals. He also collected a broader set of data that allowed him to reconstruct specific patterns of atmospheric circulation—not only over land but over land *and* oceans. When Mayewski focused on the movement of air masses over oceans, he found that air transport from south to north in the Atlantic—so-called meridional circulation—hit a significant winter low some 4,200 years ago. Mayewski and deMenocal are studying how this event relates to drought in western Asia.

"But it seems on the basis of the paleoclimatic data that there is no doubt about the event at 2200 B.C.," says Weiss. "What the qualities of this event were, and what the magnitude of this event was, that is the current research frontier now."

Trouble is, even though the drought may seem like a sure thing, its effects on Mesopotamia are still unproved, as Zettler points out. They will remain controversial, Weiss admits, until archeologists better understand the contributions of politics, agriculture, and climate in the formation of ancient societies. That mission grows more urgent as more archeologists seem ready to grapple with models of "climatic determinism." In the past few years, drought and flooding have been cited in the demise of several New World civilizations, including the Maya of Central America, the Anasazi of the American Southwest, and the Moche and Tiwanaku of Peru and Bolivia.

"Until climatic conditions are quantified, it's going to be very difficult to understand what the effects of climate changes—particularly controversial, abrupt ones—were upon these societies," says Weiss. The precise constellation of forces that led to the collapse of Bronze Age cultures around 2200 B.C. will probably be debated for a very long time. But paleoclimatology has assured Mother Nature a place in that constellation. And the notion that civilizations are immune to natural disaster may soon be ancient history.

Out of Africa:
The superb artwork
of ancient Nubia

*The rich heritage and tradition of this venerable, long-neglected civilization
beside the Nile is now celebrated in four great Western museums*

David Roberts

David Roberts' latest book, Once They
Moved Like the Wind: Cochise, Geroni-
mo and the Apache Wars, *is published
by Simon & Schuster.*

To the ancient Greeks and Romans,
Nubia was one of the foremost civilizations of the world. Because its domain
lay on the edge of the unknown—south
of Egypt, along the tortured cataracts of
the upper Nile, where few Greek or Roman travelers had ventured—Nubia
shimmered with legend. But there was
no mistaking the area's might or wealth.

For centuries, exotic goods had
flowed north in an inexhaustible stream
from this African font: gold, frankin-
cense, ebony, ivory, panther skins, gi-
raffe tails and hippopotamus teeth.
Brave mercenary soldiers, virtuosos of
the bow and arrow, also traveled north
out of the storied land. Herodotus described Nubians as the "tallest and hand-
somest" people in the world, adding that
they reputedly lived to an age of 120,
thanks to a diet of boiled meat and milk.
Roman chroniclers reported that the
southern empire was ruled by queens.
From their own artwork, we know that
the Nubian ideal of female beauty put a
premium on fatness. Indeed, the sar-
donic Juvenal claimed that the breasts

of Nubian women were bigger than their
chubbiest babies. Writing in the third
century A.D., a romantic biographer of
Alexander the Great insisted that in Nubia there were whole temples carved
from a single stone, and houses with
translucent walls; the queen traveled in
a mobile palace on wheels drawn by 20
elephants.

Although these accounts veered into
the fabulous, Nubia was no mere phan-
tasm of the poets, no El Dorado. Within
Nubia, stretching along the Nile from
present-day Aswan in Egypt to Khar-
toum in the Sudan, at least six distinct,
supremely accomplished cultures
evolved between 3800 B.C. and A.D. 600.
Nubian civilizations lasted far longer
than either classical Greece or Rome.
Always a rival to the kingdom to its
north, Nubia conquered Egypt around
730 B.C. and ruled it for the following
60 years.

TA-SETI OR YAM OR WAWAT

Why is it, then, that most of us today
have barely heard of Nubia?

One reason is semantic. Over millennia, Nubia was known under many different names. To the early Egyptians, it
was Ta-Seti or Yam or Wawat. Later it

appears as Meroe. The Greeks and Romans called it Aethiopia (today's Ethiopia being Abyssinia to them). In the
Bible it appears as Kush.

Another reason has to do with prejudice. Nubia has always been exceedingly remote and difficult of access.
From its Christianization in the 6th century A.D. all the way down to the 19th,
the kingdom vanished from the European record: only the glowing reports of
the classical authors kept its memory
alive. This neglect had everything to do
with race—for Nubia had been an African empire, and a black African one at
that. Even the Greeks perpetrated the
prejudice. An early biographer of Alexander the Great records the queen of
Nubia responding to an inquisitive letter
from the youthful conqueror in the following words: "Do not despise us for
the color of our skin. In our souls we
are brighter than the whitest of your
people."

The first archaeologists to document
the glory that was Nubia succumbed to
a kindred bias. Even as he dug the remarkable royal cemeteries of El Kurru
below the Fourth Cataract, George A.
Reisner, working for Harvard University
and the Boston Museum of Fine Arts,
concluded that the rulers whose tombs

From *Smithsonian* magazine, June 1993, pp. 90–96, 98, 100. © 1993 by David Roberts. Reprinted by permission of the author.

he unearthed must have been an offshoot of a dynasty of Libyan (thus, white-skinned) pharaohs. For decades, everything Nubian was regarded as derived from the Egyptian, hence "decadent" and "peripheral."

Only now, perhaps, is the Western world beginning to acknowledge the achievements of ancient Nubia, as signaled by four dazzling new exhibitions at major North American museums. At the Boston Museum of Fine Arts (MFA)—which, thanks to Reisner and his colleagues, owns one of the finest collections of Nubian treasures in the world—a permanent display opened in 1992. Another permanent installation was unveiled the year before at the Royal Ontario Museum in Toronto. Through September 1993, the Oriental Institute Museum in Chicago will host "Vanished Kingdoms of the Nile: The Rediscovery of Ancient Nubia." And at the University of Pennsylvania's Museum of Archaeology and Anthropology, "Ancient Nubia: Egypt's Rival in Africa" recently opened. After closing in Philadelphia in October 1993, the exhibition will travel to seven other museums around the country, through 1996.

The exhibitions have had strong attendance, particularly among African-Americans, many of them in school groups. And there's evidence that awareness of Nubia is seeping into the popular culture. A new comic-book character called "Heru: Son of Ausar," which was created by cartoonist Roger Barnes, is a Nubian hero. A rap band out of New York City calls itself Brand Nubian.

The surge of interest in Nubia did not arise in a vacuum. For the past 30 years, scholars in Europe and the United States have been piecing together a vivid but tantalizing picture of the neglected civilization. Yet it took the building of a dam to stimulate this new appraisal of ancient Nubia.

Reisner, the pioneer of Nubian archaeology, was an Egyptologist working on the lower Nile in 1906 when the Egyptian government decided to raise the dam at Aswan by 16.5 feet. Before the resultant flooding could drown forever many unexcavated sites, Reisner was invited to survey and dig upriver. Thus was launched what one scholar calls the "earliest program of extensive salvage archaeology" in the world.

Close on Reisner's heels came two British archaeologists working for the University of Pennsylvania, David Randall-MacIver and Leonard Woolley. The rich collections existing today in Boston and Philadelphia derive from the seminal fieldwork of these scholars. Yet so strong was the lingering condescension toward Nubia as a kind of second-rate Egypt, that as late as 1960 only one American scholar—Dows Dunham, Reisner's protégé and successor at the MFA—was working in Nubian studies.

In 1959 Egypt announced plans to build a huge new dam at Aswan. The waters of the Nile would create Lake Nasser, stretching 300 miles south to the Second Cataract, just across the border in the Sudan. UNESCO launched an all-out appeal to the archaeologists of the world, who responded with scores of energetic expeditions, sowing the seeds of our current understanding of ancient Nubia.

The disruption wrought by the dam was tragic. Nubians whose ancestors had lived along the middle Nile for as long as the oldest tales could testify gathered their belongings and made their exodus north to the planned villages that would replace their own. They kissed the graves of their ancestors; many filled their pockets with sand, their only keepsake of the lost homeland.

LOSING ONE'S WAY COULD MEAN LOSING ONE'S LIFE

On the face of it, Nubia seems an unlikely place for a major civilization to sprout. It lies in the middle of the hottest and driest area on Earth's surface; in much of Nubia, rain never falls. Farther north, in classical Egypt, the Nile creates a generous floodplain up to 15 miles wide, but in Nubia the fertile land bordering the river comes only in intermittent patches rarely exceeding 1,600 yards in width. The cataracts—canyons seamed with big rapids—as well as long, tormented passages such as Batn el Hajar, the "Belly of Rocks"—make continuous navigation up and down the Nile impossible. In the Sudan, where the river makes two great loops in the shape of an S, the ancient trade routes struck off on bold shortcuts across the empty desert. To lose one's way often meant to lose one's life. Even today, travel here remains as difficult and as dangerous as anywhere in Africa.

As Reisner plunged into this archaeologically pristine wilderness, where he worked tirelessly from 1907 to 1932, he slapped provisional names on the various cultures he began to identify. Unfortunately, these temporary labels have stuck. Thus we still allude to some Nubian cultures—each as complex and impressive as, say, that of the Hittites or the Etruscans—as the A-Group, the C-Group and the X-Group.

With the emergence of the A-Group around 3800 B.C., Nubia takes its place on the prehistoric stage. We still know relatively little about this early civilization, which became a serious rival to Pre-Dynastic Egypt. The A-Group's most distinctive artifact is a handsome "eggshell" pottery, named for its thin walls. Crisscross hatches and geometric patterns in red and cream seem to conjure up weaving; it is as if the potters were celebrating the discovery of the vessel that worked better than basketry.

Toward the end of its thousand-year sway, the A-Group emerges also in the written record, as the Egyptians invented their hieroglyphic script. The domain of the blacks in the Lower Nubia was known as Egypt as Ta-Seti—the "Land of the Bow." Eventually the pharaohs waged war with Ta-Seti. A great victory around 2600 B.C. was won by the pharaoh Sneferu, who bragged that he took 7,000 Nubians and 200,000 domestic animals captive.

Bruce Williams of Chicago's Oriental Institute believes that the earliest definite evidence anywhere in the world of the institution of kingship may be among the A-Group of Nubia. Williams' argument hinges upon a handful of extraordinary objects found in royal A-Group graves. During my own visit to the Oriental Institute, Williams showed me a beautiful stone incense burner found at Qustul (just north of the Sudanese border), dated to around 3300 B.C.

The cylindrical burner is encircled by a frieze of incised figures.

Peering through the display glass, I followed Williams' pointing finger. "The falcon means a god," he said. "That's definitely a representation of a king, and he's wearing a crown. The bound prisoner is going to be bashed in the head in front of the god. The burner is definitely a typical Nubian, not an Egyptian, object."

Other scholars, however, reject Williams' theory. Says David O'Connor of the University of Pennsylvania, "I think there may well have been an elite group in Nubia at the time, in charge of a complex chiefdom. But the objects Williams' argument depends on are almost certainly Egyptian, not Nubian-traded to Nubia in early pharaonic times. The kings he sees were Egyptian kings."

One of the most formidable obstacles to an appreciation of ancient Nubia is that, in terms of the written record, we learn about the civilization almost entirely in the words of its enemies—Egyptians above all, but also Hebrews, Assyrians, Persians and Romans. Thus, for the Egyptians, Nubia is always "vile," "miserable," "wretched." The pharaohs had images of Nubians carved on their footstools and on the bottom of their sandals so that they could trample on their enemies daily.

The aggression of Egypt throughout the third millennium B.C. seems to have driven A-Group survivors south into the little-known lands above the Second Cataract. Around 2300 B.C., a pair of new cultures springs into view. One, appearing in Lower Nubia, was called by Reisner the C-Group. Elaborate tombs suggest these people were skilled pastoralists, raising huge herds of livestock and perhaps worshiping their gods through a cattle cult.

The C-Group kept peace with the kingdom to the north for centuries, during which time trade flourished and ideas flowed both ways. Then, in the 19th century B.C., the pharaohs turned belligerent again. Their motive may have been to control the gold mines that were being opened in the eastern desert. Thrusting above the Second Cataract, Egyptian armies built a series of colossal fortresses along the tortuous Belly of Rocks. These fortresses were placed so that line-of-sight signals could be flashed from one to the next.

Meanwhile, 170 miles beyond the southernmost Egyptian fortress, the most powerful empire Nubia had yet seen was flourishing. Named the Kerma culture by Reisner, who in 1913 excavated tombs close to the modern town of that name, it was known to the Egyptians as the Kingdom of Kush. An ancillary motive for erecting the Egyptian fortresses, with their intensely defensive character, was no doubt fear of Kush.

A FLAMBOYANT AND GRANDIOSE GLORY

After 1700 B.C., racked by internal struggles, Egypt retreated from Nubia, abandoning its fortresses along the Belly of Rocks. In the void, Kerma grew magnificently. Nothing declares the flamboyant, even grandiose glory of Kerma more forcefully than its royal tombs. The king was buried under a huge tumulus—a circular mound—with the diameter nearly the length of a football field. He was laid on a gold-covered bed, and the finest objects wrought of gold, bronze, ivory and faience were placed beside him. Into the tomb's central corridor crowded a host of followers and concubines (400 of them in one king's tomb), who, dressed in their best clothes, came willingly to be buried alive in honor of their master.

All through Nubia, from Reisner until the present day, burial sites have monopolized archaeologists' attention. This has been true in part because the remains of habitation sites are so hard to find; houses were made of perishable stuff, but tombs were built to last. Only two large villages from the C-Group, for instance, have ever been excavated. Consequently we know much more about the rulers of Nubia than about the commoners.

At Kerma, however, for the past 28 years an international team under Charles Bonnet, of the University of Geneva, has carried out one of the most ambitious digs in Africa. In the process, they have revealed not only the palaces and cemeteries but the main town of Kerma.

When I visited Bonnet in Geneva last fall, he showed me the plan of the settlement. Tapping an outlying area with his pencil, he said, "Just last year we found a whole new section of houses here. It goes on and on!" Bonnet's work documents the oldest city that has ever been found in Africa outside Egypt.

Many of the houses Bonnet's team excavated were rectangles of mud bricks, but the most characteristic domicile was a circular hut made of wood (always a rare substance along the Nile), topped with a thatched roof. Each hut was ingeniously designed to allow the prevailing north wind to blow through it during the desperate heat of summer; in winter, a temporary wall blocked the same breeze. Small neighborhoods of huts were bordered by fields and gardens where crops (chiefly wheat and barley) were raised, and cattle and goats pastured. No general plan governed the shape of the sprawling city, but a defensive palisade surrounded it.

Once more the tides of empire shifted. Around 1550 B.C., a newly invigorated Egypt invaded Nubia. The struggle against Kerma lasted 100 years, but at last the pharaohs conquered all but the southernmost reaches of Nubia. Their sway lasted another 350 years, during which the Nubian upper class became thoroughly Egyptianized, decorating their tombs with images of workers on date palm plantations and with performing dancers and musicians.

But the tides shifted again. At the end of the New Kingdom, about 1080 B.C., Egypt was torn by conflict between the pharaohs and the priesthood. The country began to fragment into city states, among them several in Nubia that became all but autonomous. What happened after 1080 remains a great mystery.

According to Timothy Kendall of the MFA, "the greatest gap in our knowledge of ancient Nubia is the period from 1000 to 850 B.C. We know almost nothing about it. Only one or two sites in Nubia can be dated to this period, and then, only to the latter part of it. Some experts believe Nubia was growing stronger and politically independent; others think that Egyptian enclaves and temple estates persisted. But these are theories spun out of thin air. Nobody really has a clue, except that a series of elaborate tombs began to be built in 850 B.C."

When Nubia emerged from this historical void in the eighth century B.C., it did so dramatically, achieving the greatest triumph in all its long history. By this time the center of power lay at Napata, which was just below the Fourth Cataract. Here a holy mountain called Jebel Barkal was believed to be the home of the ram-headed god Amun, who spoke oracles through statues and even selected the country's rulers.

Whatever their motive, after 750 B.C. the Napatan kings pushed boldly north. Around 730, a great army under a king named Piye conquered all of Egypt. He and his successors became the pharaohs of the 25th Dynasty, the later kings moving from Napata to Memphis to govern. The Nubian empire now stretched all the way from the junction of the Blue and White Niles to the delta (present-day Alexandria)—1,200 miles as the crow flies.

Although the inscribed victory stela Piye erected to proclaim his triumph alludes to him in Egyptian hieroglyphs as "raging like a panther" and bursting upon his enemies "like a cloudburst," the Nubian pharaohs of the 25th Dynasty ruled with an enlightened benevolence. They were Medicis, rather than Caesars, who awoke Egypt to the artistic and cultural splendor of its own past as they patronized artists, revived lost learning and rebuilt derelict temples.

Piye was also a great lover of horses, the first of four successive pharaohs to have whole chariot teams buried near his grave. The horses, interred in a standing position, were decked with bead nets and brilliant jewelry. When Piye conquered Hermopolis, the defeated King Nemlot opened his harem. But Piye averted his eyes from the women and demanded to see the king's horses instead. These he found nearly starved to death. "That my horses were made to hunger," he thundered at Nemlot (as recorded on Piye's stela), "pains me more than any other crime you committed in your recklessness. Do you not know God's shadow is above me?"

The brilliance of the Napatan empire speaks in many of the objects now on display in Boston, Philadelphia, Chicago and Toronto. In the MFA, I gazed at haunting rows of *shawabtis*, part of a cache of 1,070 found in the tomb of King Taharqo, Piye's son. Figurines carved out of alabaster and gray or black granite, ranging from seven inches to two feet in height, these sober-looking humans with arms crossed were "answerers" who would perform for the deceased king the work the gods commanded of him. (Here, I thought, was a humane alternative to the retainers buried alive at Kerma!)

One of the most exquisite objects ever recovered from Nubia is also on display in Boston. It is a small pendant from the tomb of one of Piye's wives, a gold head of Hathor, goddess of beauty, mounted on a ball of rock crystal, thought to have magical properties.

The Napatan supremacy was short-lived. By 667 B.C. the Nubian pharaohs had abandoned Egypt to another raging panther, King Esarhaddon of Assyria. Once again, we learn of a profoundly pivotal moment in Nubian history only in the contemptuous boasts of its enemies: "I tore up the root of Kush," crowed Esarhaddon, "and not one therein escaped to submit to me."

Gradually through the next four centuries, the Nubian political and cultural center shifted south beyond the Fourth Cataract. In isolation and relative obscurity, the last Nubian empire evolved. Its center was the town of Meroe, halfway between the Fifth Cataract and the junction with the Blue Nile.

Meroe, which flourished from about 270 B.C. to A.D. 350, is in many respects the most intriguing of all the incarnations of Nubian greatness. Cambyses of the Persians, as well as Petronius among the Romans, sent out armies to conquer the distant country, without success. Even Nero contemplated the possibility of an attack. Despite all this contact, the veil of mystery that clung to the legendary southern land never really lifted.

One reason was linguistic. In their isolation from Egypt, the Meroites lost the use of Egyptian hieroglyphs. By 170 B.C. they had developed their own written language, a quasi-cursive script now called Meroitic. Stelae and plaques covered with this writing abound. By 1909 scholars had proved that it was an alphabetic script (unlike the hieroglyphs, which are part ideographic, part phonetic and part alphabetic). Thanks to a few parallel inscriptions, they had learned the sound values for each of the 23 Meroitic letters. Yet more than eight decades later, the language remains undeciphered.

At first, scholars were confident that Meroitic would turn out to be a cognate of the Nubian tongues spoken today along the Nile. That hope faded, and all that the experts can now assert is that Meroitic seems to be related to no other known language. Decipherment must await the discovery of a Nubian Rosetta Stone—a stela with lengthy parallel texts in Meroitic and Egyptian or Meroitic and Greek.

A ROYAL OFFERING TO AMUN

In the MFA, I walked around and around a five-foot-tall stela found at Jebel Barkal; covered on all sides with writing, the stone bears the longest known inscription in Meroitic. We know the text has something to do with an offering by King Tanyidamani to the god Amun, and we can see places where lines have been deliberately erased. The rest is enigma.

Timothy Kendall tantalized me further by describing the second-longest Meroitic inscription known, found on a stela now in the British Museum. "If we could read it," he sighed, "we'd have the Meroitic version of the war against Petronius and the Romans in 24 B.C."

In its drift away from Egyptian culture over the centuries, Meroitic art developed its own idiosyncratic genius. At the Oriental Institute, Emily Teeter explained to me its quirks. "It becomes a very spontaneous art, full of free-flowing improvisation," she said, pausing before a Meroitic pot. "You see that?" She pointed to a curling snake painted on the vessel, holding in its mouth a drooping flower. "The flower is obviously an *ankh*."

I gasped in sudden recognition. I had seen many an *ankh* on Egyptian objects: a cross-shaped symbol topped with an oval, which is the hieroglyph for the verb "to live." In Egyptian art, the *ankh* appears alone or in rows of declarative rigidity. On the Meroitic pot, the snake stings the world to life with a flower. "The Egyptians are too staid for this," Teeter said. "They don't like loopy things."

At the University of Pennsylvania museum, David O'Connor guided me through several hundred Meroitic objects from the provincial capital of Karanog, excavated by MacIver and Wooley in 1907–08. The same freedom—a set of wild variations on Egyptian themes—graced these priceless objects. In Egypt, O'Connor explained, the *ba* statue, which represents a dead person's spirit, is a formal-looking bird with a human head; in Meroe, the *ba* becomes a human with wings. The pots dance with two-legged crocodiles, with giraffes ranging from the lordly to the comic, with deer darting through shadows. There are abstract designs made of endless waves of draped festoons and floral curlicues.

The sheer exuberance of Meroitic art proclaims a civilization that believed in pleasure and playfulness. The pots were largely used for wine drinking. At certain Meroitic sites, whole barrooms have been excavated.

At the end of the fourth century A.D., Meroe declined. The distinctive script fell out of use, and no new temples were built. It has long been the fashion to regard the 250-year interim before Christianity, whose culture Reisner called the X-Group, as a Nubian Dark Age; but recent scholars point to the continued excellence of pottery and jewelry, to a flowering of brilliant work in bronze and iron, as well as to the magnificent royal tombs at Ballana and Qustul, as signs of a healthy culture, original in its own right.

Although the Meroitic language seems to have been lost forever, scholars who travel in the Sudan have been struck by the remarkable survival in living cultures of traits and belongings they know also from archaeology. The wood-and-palm-fiber bed a Sudanese sleeps on today looks very much like ones found in royal tombs in Kerma. The throw-stick, a proto-boomerang still used for hunting today, is identical to ones retrieved by Reisner from a Kerma tomb. Even current Sudanese fashions in hairstyle and facial scarification find their counterparts in ancient paintings of Nubians.

Thus the discipline of ethnoarchaeology, still in its infancy, may yield new insights into Nubia, as scholars ask living informants to comment on ancient relics. Emily Teeter told me of a pair of small revelations. Shortly after the Oriental Institute's exhibition opened, she met Awad Abdel Gadir, a Sudanese teaching in Texas. He took her aside, pointed to a stone object and said politely, "That's not an incense burner. We have those in our village. It's a receptacle for a liquid offering." Teeter changed the label. He paused before a "thorn-removal kit" from the X-Group—a kind of Swiss Army Knife of iron tools on a chain, including tweezers, picks and scrapers. "I remember," said Abdel Gadir, "my grandmother used to wear a set like that on her belt."

Meanwhile, the archaeological surface of ancient Nubia has barely been scratched. The sites that lie in lower Nubia, north of the Egypt-Sudan border, are gone forever, swallowed by Lake Nasser. In the Sudan, the 1989 coup that brought Islamic fundamentalists to power, as well as the civil war that continues to rage in the country's south, have made it harder than ever for Western archaeologists to work there.

Yet, in the Sudan, a French survey has counted one million ancient mounds, only a fraction of which have been excavated. There are more royal pyramids in the Sudan than in all of Egypt. I asked Timothy Kendall, who has done breakthrough work at Jebel Barkal, where he would dig if he had carte blanche to choose among the Sudan's best Nubian sites.

He leaned back in his chair, put his hands behind his head and smiled. "I'd go to Naga," he said, "although it's just a pipe dream, because the Sudanese Antiquities Service is saving it for themselves."

I knew Naga as a Meroitic site that, uncharacteristically, lay inland in the Butana Desert, some 25 miles south of the Nile. "Why Naga?"

"It's a complete Meroitic city founded about the first century A.D., with important temples, a settlement and a cemetery," Kendall answered. "The residents built an artificial reservoir of water. Not a single spadeful of earth has ever been turned there.

"Of course," he added, gazing off into space at the eternal dilemma that bedevils archaeologists, "you'd need a lot of money, a big team, a lot of cooperation, extreme physical endurance." He paused. "And a very, very long life."

ADDITIONAL READING

Nubia: Corridor to Africa by William Y. Adams, Princeton University Press, 1977
Meroe by Peter L. Shinnie, Praeger (New York), 1967
Nubia Under the Pharaohs by Bruce G. Trigger, Westview Press (Boulder, Colorado), 1983
The African Origin of Civilization: Myth or Reality by Cheikh Anta Diop, Lawrence Hill, 1974

Unit 4

Unit Selections

Key Points to Consider

❖ Compare the work of archaeologists in Peru with those in Turkey and Mexico (Unit 2).

❖ Where are the places in modern life that serve the purpose of an agora?

❖ What do the sports of a society tell you about the interests of the society?

❖ Why have people throughout time been interested in Cleopatra? What are the historical problems in finding the truth about Cleopatra?

❖ How have humans constructed ideas about days, weeks, months, and years? Why are we so concerned about time?

 **Links**   **www.dushkin.com/online/**

These sites are annotated on pages 4 and 5.

Life in the ancient world was likely to be short and brutal. Poor nutrition, disease, hazards of childbirth, warfare, and violence all took their toll. In the Roman Empire, for example, only one child in eight could be expected to reach 40 years of age. Since people were often judged by their usefulness, long life was not necessarily a blessing. Women were often subservient and mistreated, criminals and slaves were publicly slaughtered, and unwanted children were abandoned to die. Yet, at the same time, humankind built splendid cities, formed empires, wrote history, invented sports, and created great art. Aspects of this growing diversity is examined in this section.

In the New World, civilization evolved later than in the Old World, perhaps due to the pattern of migration to that hemisphere and the later development of agriculture. The Aztecs, Maya, and Inca, nonetheless, constructed magnificent stone cities and developed complex social and economic institutions. Unfortunately, most of these accomplishments were destroyed during the Spanish invasion. In addition, many of the native people died due to widespread disease brought by the Europeans (see Unit 7, "How Many People Were Here before Columbus?"). The achievements of Inca civilization have been seen in the ruins of their cities and road system, but recently young sacrificial victims, frozen for 500 years on high Andean mountain peaks, have been recovered. The mummies of these children should reveal more about the culture and the genetic origins of the Inca people.

Athens, in the Old World, developed into one of the most interesting of the ancient Greek city-states and was important for the origin of modern ideas about government, art, and sport. At the center of the city was the agora, a plaza surrounded by civic and religious buildings. The modern word "agoraphobia," the fear of open places, comes from this place in Greek cities. In Athens the agora served as a meeting place for merchants and scholars, as John Fleischman points out in his article, "In Classical Athens, a Market Trading in the Currency of Ideas."

From the decorations on Athenian pots, modern sports historians have found illustrations of Greek sports. The Greeks represent the highest level of development in ancient sports, but other peoples—Minoans, Egyptians, Etruscans, Romans—also enjoyed sporting events. Allen Guttmann, one of the leading scholars in sports history, reviews this sporting interest in his article, "Old Sports." The most important development was the Olympic Games of Greece that lasted 1,100 years until the fourth century C.E. Even with the Greek emphasis on the harmony of body and mind, most of these early sports had a basis in military or survival skills. It was these old competitions of throwing, running, and wrestling, however, that inspired the Olympic Games of the present time.

In ancient Rome the average lifespan of a female was 25 years, and for a male it was only 23 years. There were numerous hazards, such as the smallpox pandemic that struck in 165 C.E. Some 2,000 people a day died in Rome. Life was short also for one of the most famous women of the ancient world, Cleopatra. She died at age 39 after enrapturing the most powerful men of her time. Cleopatra's story has been told by others, not by her, with the result that her history may never obtain objectivity. Barbara Holland, with a wry skepticism, relates what happened to Cleopatra's history at the hands of Hollywood producers as well as of playwrights and historians.

In our current frenzy about the impact of time counting and our computers, the infamous Y2K problem, we often forget the origins of our interest in the passage of time. In "Countdown to the Beginning of Time-Keeping," by Robert Garland, can be found the roots of our millennium fears. It will not solve our computer woes, but it is worthwhile to understand that the measurements of time are of longtime human construction. We have gotten ourselves into the Y2K mess and we will have to figure our way out of it. It is a problem that we have inherited from the distant past.

Tiny Sacrifices at 22,000 Feet

Archaeologists find mummified Incan children on an Andean peak

By Jonah Blank

At the peak of an Andean volcano, three children were found cold, with gold—and 500 years old. They certainly didn't look their age: The ice mummies unveiled in Argentina last week may be the best-preserved ancient human remains ever discovered. The bodies, two girls and one boy, ages between 8 and 15, were probably left at this towering height as sacrificial victims offered to Incan deities. One wore a white feather headdress and a yellow mantle with ornate geometric patterns.

Gasping for breath in the oxygen-poor atmosphere 22,057 feet above sea level, nine archaeologists, workers, and guides spent nearly two weeks battling adverse conditions, including ferocious blizzards and 70-mph winds. For three days the team members were trapped in their tents under about 3 feet of snow, with the temperature at times 20 degrees below zero. "Even taking off my gloves to write notes was a major ordeal," expedition co-director Maria Constanza Ceruti recalled from Argentina. The altitude of the summit—only 6,971 feet lower than that of Mount Everest—can cause the brain to swell and the lungs to fill with fluid.

Johan Reinhard, primary organizer of the American-Argentine-Peruvian expedition sponsored by the National Geographic Society, had been scouting out this mountain peak since 1983 and had already brought 16 ice mummies down

from other Andean summits. He knew the Incas were inclined to offer human sacrifices on the highest possible spots. "You feel like you're on the top of the world there," he said, after bringing the mummies down last week.

The weight of history. After using picks and shovels to dig through 5 feet of rock and frozen earth, the crew had to lower a graduate student into the pit by his ankles to lift the mummies out of their sanctuary. The team wrapped the bodies in protective foam and ice and carried the 80-pound burdens down the mountain in backpacks. Ceruti said she knew the find was remarkable when she saw the children's fingernails and the fine hairs on their arms, still preserved after five centuries. But the discovery's full import wasn't clear until CT scans revealed all the internal organs in two of the bodies to be intact.

David Hunt, a biological anthropologist at the Smithsonian Institution, said the find would probably prove to be even more impressive than "Juanita," the Incan "Ice Maiden" Reinhard discovered in Peru four years ago.

Unlike most mummies found elsewhere, the children's bodies have been in near-perfect states since the time of their deaths: The permafrost of ice-packed rock and dirt kept the internal organs and bodily fluids frozen rather than freeze-dried. Normally, the fluids in a corpse quickly bring about decay.

Embalmers of Pharaonic Egypt and other ancient cultures painstakingly removed fluids to ensure preservation in hot, dry climates.

"Accidental" mummies have survived when nature served as an embalmer instead. The Ice Maiden Juanita—whom President Bill Clinton once jokingly said he might be tempted to ask out on a date—and the famous 5,300-year-old "Ice Man" discovered in the Italian Alps in 1991 were desiccated by exposure or repeated cycles of thawing and refreezing. The 1,000-year-old Bog People found at various sites in Northern Europe were turned to leather by the tannic acid of the peat into which they'd been cast. The newly discovered ice mummies, however, were saved from dehydration by the perpetual cold of their high-altitude burial site.

The fact that these mummies have not been desiccated makes them a particularly valuable source of information: Scientists can examine the corpses the same way that a coroner would perform an autopsy on a murder victim. Arthur Aufderheide, a University of Minnesota-Duluth expert on New World mummies who also worked as a pathologist, says the plasma of these bodies might reveal what diseases were present in the pre-Columbian Andes.

"This is the sort of thing folks like me dream about," says Aufderheide, whose research on 1,000-year-old mummies proved that tuberculosis was present in the New World 500 years before its widespread distribution by Europeans. Studying historical patterns of disease, Aufderheide says, can help predict future outbreaks, and the DNA of ancient microbes could assist doctors fighting their modern descendants.

Keys to kinships. DNA fingerprinting of the mummies might also help trace genetic links between the Incas and other societies. "Blood serum can show relations between distant populations," says the Smithsonian's Hunt. Analysis of samples drawn from modern individuals is complicated by the social mobility and subsequent genetic intermingling of the past five centuries. The DNA of a pre-Columbian population would be more homogeneous. "If we found a rare genetic marker shared with a group as far off as the Arctic Circle or Asia," Hunt says, "that could tell us a lot about how and when South America was settled."

For cultural anthropologists, the discovery provides striking details about the ritual life of the Incas. For nearly a century prior to the Spanish conquest of 1532, the Incan empire encompassed much of what is now Peru, Ecuador, Bolivia, Chile, and Argentina. That period remains shrouded in mystery: Unlike earlier Central American peoples such as the Maya, the Incas had no written language. Highly skilled as mathematicians and builders, they kept the records of a vast kingdom with a complex system of knots tied in strings of varying lengths and colors. Apart from archaeological artifacts, the only evidence modern scholars have about the culture of the Incas comes from accounts written during the time of the Spanish invasion. Those accounts often focused solely on recording "idolatrous" practices as a prelude to obliterating them.

The Incas' most controversial custom was human sacrifice. They did not practice it nearly as often as did the Maya, Aztecs, and Toltecs (the Incas preferred to slaughter llamas or guinea pigs). But on occasions of special importance such as coronations or natural disasters, young children were offered up in a rite called *capac cocha*. The Incas also gave their gods the most valuable gifts they could—the burial site unearthed last week included statuettes made of gold, silver, and rare shells from the far-distant ocean—so the sacrifice of an unblemished, aristocratic child was seen as a particularly auspicious offering. "This find could answer many questions about the *capac cocha* ritual," says Richard Burger, a specialist in Peruvian archaeology at Yale University.

The Incas considered mountains sacred: The higher the mountain, the closer to divinities represented by the sun and the moon. "It was almost a spiritual moment when we saw the face of the first girl," said Ceruti. "At the summit, I looked at her and tried to imagine her last moments." For Ceruti, Reinhard, and the rest of the team, however, the search is far from over. They know the high Andes have many secrets left to tell. The day after announcing their find, the crew set out again for Mount Llullaillaco to continue their search.

In Classical Athens, a market trading in the currency of ideas

For 60 years, archaeologists have pursued secrets of the Agora, where Socrates' society trafficked in wares from figs to philosophy

John Fleischman

John Fleischman, who wrote about the excavation of the legendary site of Troy in a past Smithsonian, *braved Athens' summer heat on the trail of his story.*

Athens on an August afternoon: the clear radiant light of Greece suffuses every stone and walkway. From my vantage point, I squint upward to the outcropping of the Acropolis, crowned by Athena's temple, the Parthenon; hordes of tourists lay constant siege to the site. Standing at the base of that fabled rampart, I begin to traverse a quiet, heat-baked square, crisscrossed by gravel paths, dotted with the stubs of ancient walls and scrubby pomegranate and plane trees.

This dusty archaeological park, a sanctuary amid the roar of overmotorized Athens, is in fact one of the most remarkable sites in Classical archaeology. I am crossing the Agora—or central marketplace—of ancient Athens. That this place still exists seems nothing short of miraculous. I am walking in Socrates' footsteps.

The gadfly philosopher frequented this very square—as did his compatriots in the extraordinary experiment that was Classical Athens. Shades of Pericles, Thucydides, Aristophanes, Plato. They

all strolled in this place—the Agora, where philosophy and gossip were retailed along with olive oil. And where Classical Athens actually lived, traded, voted and, of course, argued. The Agora was the city's living heart. Here, politics, democracy and philosophy (their names, after all, are Greek) were born.

For every ten tourists who climb to the Parthenon, only one discovers the precincts of the serene archaeological site at its base. Those visitors are in fact missing an excursion into history made palpable, as well as a glimpse into what must be acclaimed as one of this century's most triumphant urban archaeology undertakings.

Since 1931, the American School of Classical Studies has been digging here, unearthing a dazzling array of artifacts from the layers of history compacted under this earth: Neolithic, Mycenaean, Geometric, Classical, Hellenistic, Roman, Byzantine and more—all collected from this 30-acre site. Still, it is the objects from Classical Athens that seem to speak with greatest resonance.

And fortunately for those of us unable to make it to Athens anytime soon, we have a chance to see for ourselves some of the Agora's most celebrated artifacts. The occasion of this opportunity

is a striking anniversary: 2,500 years ago, the Athenian reformer Cleisthenes renounced tyranny and proclaimed the birth of a radically new form of government, democracy. His genius was to offer a straightforward plan. To diffuse powerful political factions, Cleisthenes reshuffled the Athenian city-state into ten arbitrary tribes and called 50 representatives from each to a senate, or boule, of 500. This, then, was the beginning of democracy, however imperfect and subject to subversion and strife it might have been.

Hence the arrival of the exhibition "The Birth of Democracy," which opened recently in the rotunda of the National Archives in Washington, D.C. and continues there through January 2, 1994. A few steps from our own Declaration of Independence, Constitution and Bill of Rights lie the humble tools of Athenian self-government, nearly all of them unearthed in the Agora over the past 60 years by American excavators.

You can look upon actual fourth-century B.C. Athenian jurors' ballots, discovered still inside a terra-cotta ballot box. The ballots, stamped "official ballot," look like metal tops. Each juror was handed two; the spindle shafts designated the vote, solid for acquittal and hollow for guilty. Taking the spindle ends between thumb and forefinger, an Athenian juror was assured that no one could see which spindle he deposited in the ballot box.

FOR THE TOO POWERFUL, A DECREE OF EXILE

Also on view are ostraca, pottery fragments on which Athenians inscribed the names of persons they felt too powerful for the good of the city and deserving of ostracism, or ten years' exile, a procedure formalized by Cleisthenes. More than 1,300 ostraca, condemning many famous figures—Pericles, for instance, and Aristides and Themistocles—have been found in the Agora. Looking closely at the sherds, you can spell out the names straight from the history books and realize that these ostraca were written out by contemporaries who knew these men personally. And in some cases hated them.

Ostracism was not the worst punishment the democracy could decree. The National Archives also displays a set of distinctive pottery vials uncovered from the fifth-century B.C. Athenian state prison. These tiny vials were used to hold powerful drugs, such as lethal doses of hemlock. Socrates swallowed just such a dose, voted for him in 399 B.C. by his fearful fellow citizens. Archaeologists say the death scene of Socrates described in Plato's *Phaedo* fits the layout of a precise location in the Agora—a building near the southwest corner of the market square.

Plato recounts that after Socrates took the poison, he walked about, then lay down, telling his friends to stop weeping "for I have heard that one ought to die in peace." When the numbness spread from his legs upward to his abdomen, he covered his face. His last words were, as always, ironic. Socrates claimed he had a debt to the god of medicine. "I owe a cock to Asclepius," he informed a companion, "do not forget, but pay it."

The exhibition contains several other objects associated with Socrates, including part of a small marble statue, thought to be of the philosopher, that

was also recovered from the prison. Visitors can find, as well, actual hobnails and bone eyelets from the Agora shop of one Simon the cobbler. Socrates is known to have met at such a shop with young students and prominent Athenians alike.

The boundaries of the Agora were clearly marked, and entrance was forbidden to Athenian citizens who had avoided military service, disgraced themselves in the field—or mistreated their parents. Around the open square, but outside its actual boundaries, lay the key civic buildings—courts, assembly halls, military headquarters, the mint, the keepers of the weights and measures, commercial buildings and shrines to the city gods. One such shrine, the Altar of the Twelve Gods, stood within the Agora and marked the city's center.

On business days, the square was filled with temporary wicker market stalls, grouped into rings where similar wares were offered. There was a ring for perfume, for money changing, for pickled fish, for slaves. The Agora was a constantly changing mix of the mundane and the momentous—pickled fish and the world's first democracy. The comic poet Eubulus described the scene: "You will find everything sold together in the same place at Athens: figs, witnesses to summonses, bunches of grapes, turnips, pears, apples, givers of evidence, roses, medlars, porridge, honeycombs, chickpeas, lawsuits, beestings-puddings, myrtle, allotment machines, irises, lambs, water clocks, laws, indictments."

"The Agora was a place for hanging out," according to archaeologist John M. Camp, who is my patient guide this afternoon. "You'd have men of affairs doing a little business, conducting a little politics and stirring up a little trouble." Camp has spent most of his adult life digging here, and he's tireless even in the heat. (He's also the author of *The Athenian Agora*, an erudite and delightful guide to the site, written for a general audience.) The real pleasure of studying this site, he says, is the shock of recognition. "Our own ideas, our own concepts originated right *here*," he told me, gesturing toward the bright open square of the Agora. "It's not only democracy, it's virtually all of Western

drama, law—you name it. Over and over again, you find the only thing that's really changed is the technology. Everything else, they thought of it before. They did it before, and it all happened *here*."

IN THE BEGINNING, ARCHAEOLOGISTS BANKED ON HOPE

The open Agora at midday is suited only for mad tourists and foreign archaeologists, both on tight schedules. The tourists can see the Agora today because American archaeologists (funded in large part by American philanthropists—principally John D. Rockefeller jr. and the David and Lucile Packard Foundation) saved the site from total obliteration. At the outset, the archaeologists who began nosing around here in the late 1920s were banking on educated hope. Although the memory of the Agora was preserved by sources such as Plato and the historian Xenophon, tantalizing description was all that remained. That celebrated site had vanished at least 1,400 years before, lost to waves of pillaging barbarians, buried under layers of settlement from medieval times on.

In short, no one knew for sure where the ancient Agora really was. (Greek and German archaeologists had made some tentative beginnings in the 19th century, but their efforts had shed little light on the actual location.) The most likely site, authorities agreed, was at the foot of the northwestern slopes of the Acropolis. That area, however, was buried beneath a dense neighborhood of 19th-century houses and shops.

The debate remained largely academic until 1929, when the Greek government offered to the American School of Classical Studies a dig-now-or-forever-hold-your-peace deal. The Americans would have to demolish 300 houses and relocate 5,000 occupants. The Greek government required that a permanent museum be built for any finds and that the Agora be landscaped as a park.

The American School finally commenced excavations in 1931. As archaeologists have labored here for more than

60 years, we can read the life and times of Classical Athens in the spaces they have cleared and excavated.

Take the Panathenaic Way, for example, a diagonal street running uphill to the Acropolis. The roadway is packed gravel today, as it was in the days of the Panathenaia, the city's great religious festival. The celebrations began with the Athenian cavalry leading a procession of priests, sacrificial animals, chariots, athletes and maidens across the Agora to the temples of the gods above. All of Athens would have gathered along this route to witness the splendid parade wending across the marketplace. One Panathenaic event, the *apobates* race, in which a contestant in full armor leapt on and off a moving chariot, continued in the Agora well into the second century B.C.

With or without armor, walking uphill is not a recommended Athenian summer-afternoon activity. But taking your time and picking your shade, you can cut across the square to the base of a sharply inclined hill and look upward at a large Doric temple just beyond the western limit of the Agora. This is the Hephaisteion—a temple dedicated to Hephaestus, the god of the forge, and to Athena, patron deity of the city and of arts and crafts. Excavations have shown that it was once surrounded by shops where bronze sculpture, armor and fine pottery were made. Today the world's best-preserved Classical temple, it is a marvel unto itself. Somehow it has survived from Pericles' time onward, a marble monument to the miracle of Athens.

The temple's friezes are carved with scenes that spoke to the imagination of every Athenian. Theseus battling the Minotaur, the labors of Hercules, the Battle of the Centaurs—all images from a world where gods and men resided in a kind of rarefied complicity.

Below the Hephaisteion stood the most important buildings of the Athenian city-state. Here was the Bouleuterion where the 500 representatives of the tribes met. (An older assembly hall stood next door.) Nearby was the round, beehive-shaped Tholos where the 50 members of the executive committee of the Boule served 35- or 36-day terms of continuous duty, living and dining in the Tholos at state expense. (Those early practitioners of democracy apparently subsisted on simple fare—cheese, olives, leeks, barley, bread and wine. No lavish state dinners yet.)

In front of the Bouleuterion stood the statues of the Eponymous Heroes, the ten tribal namesakes chosen by the Delphic Oracle (and the source of our word for a group or thing named after a real or mythical person). Athenians tended to throng before this monument—not out of piety but because this was the site of the city's public notice board, a kind of proto-daily-paper for ancient news junkies. Nearby lay the Strategeion where the ten military leaders of the tribes made their headquarters (and gave us a Greek word for military planning).

North of the Bouleuterion complex rose the Stoa, or covered colonnade, of Zeus, a religious shrine but apparently an excellent place to practice philosophy. Both Plato and Xenophon said that the Stoa of Zeus was a favorite teaching post of Socrates. No one is more closely associated with the Agora than Socrates. He lived his life here. He met his death here. Xenophon remembered his former teacher moving among the market tables and stoas: "he was always on public view; for early in the morning he used to go to the walkways and gymnasia, to appear in the agora as it filled up, and to be present wherever he would meet with the most people."

As much as Socrates enjoyed the public scene in the Agora, he made it clear, according to Plato, that he was not a "public" person, that is, he was not interested in politics. This was a scandalous opinion to hold in Athens, where the real work of every Athenian citizen was just that—being a citizen. In Plato's *Apology,* Socrates rounded on his critics: "Now do you really imagine that I could have survived all those years, if I had led a public life, supposing that . . . I had always supported the right and had made justice, as I ought, the first thing?"

He had learned the hard way. Allotted to a turn in the Bouleuterion in 406–05 B.C., he was assigned to the Tholos as a member of the executive committee. And thus it fell to Socrates to preside over a wild meeting of the mass Athenian Assembly when word arrived of the sea battle at Arginusae. It was an Athenian win, but the victorious generals were accused of leaving their own dead and dying behind. The majority moved to condemn the generals to death as a group without individual trials. Socrates resisted. "Serving in the Boule and having sworn the bouleutic oath [to serve in accordance with the law], and being in charge of the Assembly, when the People wished to put all nine [actually eight of the ten] generals to death by a single vote, contrary to the laws, he refused to put the vote," according to Xenophon. "He considered it more important to keep his oath than to please the People by doing wrong."

That was the sort of behavior that could earn you a great many enemies. Eventually, three citizens brought charges against Socrates for mocking the gods and corrupting Athenian youth. The exact location of the courtroom where Socrates stood trial still eludes identification, but the place of his indictment, the Royal Stoa, has been excavated. As for the place of his death, if you hunt carefully on the rising slope beyond the Tholos, you can find the low precinct of exposed stones that archaeologists believe was the site of his demise.

The precise forces and circumstances that led to the jury's death sentence have never been elucidated completely. What is clear is that the questions raised by that trial so long ago are not dead letters. Dissent versus consent, public good versus private conscience, they still buzz about the ears of modern democracies. "I am the gadfly which the god has given the state," Socrates told his jury in the *Apology,* "and all day long and in all places am always fastening upon you, arousing and persuading and reproaching you."

The Athenian Agora still buzzes with surprises and mysteries. In 1981, on the northern edge of the Agora, Princeton archaeologist T. Leslie Shear jr. hit the corner of one of the most famous buildings of ancient Athens, the Poikile, or Painted, Stoa. This discovery was stunning good news for Agora archaeology. The structure had been renowned throughout the ancient world for its spectacular wall paintings. The glowing images, covering enormous wooden panels, lionized Athenian victories both mythological (over the Amazons, for instance) and historical (over the Persians at Marathon).

The fabled paintings were removed by the Romans in the fourth century A.D. but survived long enough to have been described by the second-century A.D. chronicler Pausanias. "The last part of the painting," he recorded, "consists of those who fought at Marathon.... In the inner part of the fight the barbarians are fleeing and pushing one another into the marsh; at the extreme end of the painting are the Phoenician ships and the Greeks killing the barbarians who are tumbling into them."

For Athenians, the Painted Stoa was the arena of their triumphs made visible. It was also a hotbed of philosophical speculation, eventually turning up as the gathering place of the third-century B.C. followers of Zeno of Citium. Zeno preached that the wise man should remain indifferent to the vanities of the transient world. The people of Athens associated the school of thought with the building, calling Zeno's disciples Stoics and their philosophy Stoicism. And 2,300 years later, so do we.

Stoicism is a necessity in Agora archaeology. As Leslie Shear explains, his father had, in some ways, an easier time of it here. The elder Shear supervised the original excavations during the 1930s. He had a squad of colleagues and 200 paid workmen to take down a whole neighborhood at a time. This summer, Shear has John Camp, his coinvestigator and colleague of 25 years, a nine-week season, and 33 student volunteers (American, Canadian and British) in addition to a small crew of Greek workmen who handle the heavy machinery and earthmoving. And he has his wife, Ione, a highly trained archaeologist in her own right, who has also worked at the site for 25 years.

Pursuing the Agora in the present Athens real estate market is tedious and expensive. It is house-to-house archae-ology—negotiation, demolition and then excavation. While he has been busy elsewhere on the site, Shear is still waiting patiently to acquire the five-story building that is standing on the rest of the Painted Stoa.

Meanwhile, every water jug, bone or loom weight excavated anywhere in the Agora must receive a numbered tag. Every number goes into the dig's records, meticulously kept in special 4-by-6-inch clothbound notebooks. When in use in the field, these notebooks reside in an old, cheap suitcase that sits on a rough wooden desk that looks even older and cheaper. With a folding umbrella for shade, this is the nerve center for the dig. The senior archaeologists sit here, drawing tiny diagrams of the strata and the find location for every tagged item.

MAY 28, 1931: "H. A. THOMPSON COMMENCED..."

It is, as Camp puts it, "dinosaur-age" archaeology in the era of field computers, but it works. Completed notebooks go into filing cabinets in offices inside the Stoa of Attalos. (This colonnade, originally a great commercial arcade in the second century B.C., was completely reconstructed in the 1950s to house the excavation's museum, laboratories, offices and storage vaults.) There the records march back in unbroken order through the decades to May 28, 1931, and the very first entry: "In the afternoon, H. A. Thompson commenced the supervision of Section A."

Looking back over more than 60 years, from the other side of the Atlantic, Homer Thompson smiled when he heard again that clipped description of the first day. He was a young, relatively inexperienced archaeologist then. Today he is a vigorous professor emeritus at the Institute for Advanced Study in Princeton, New Jersey. He oversaw the Agora excavations from 1947 to 1967.

Back in the '30s, he recalls, it took seven years to find the first boundary stone that used the word "Agora." It wasn't a thrill so much as a relief, says Thompson, who was in charge of the crew that uncovered the marker, wedged in by the wall of Simon the cobbler's shop. "We believed we were working in the Agora, but we had so little to show for it—in inscriptions—that some of our colleagues would come by and ask 'How do you know that you're in the Agora?' Well, this settled it."

Finding the second boundary stone took another 30 years. The marker lies on the southwest corner of the square. Ione Shear uncovered it one afternoon in 1967.

It is a very ordinary marble block. The faintly visible lettering runs across the top and then down one side. The important thing, says Leslie Shear, is that this block and the one found near Simon's shop have not been moved in 2,500 years. Other boundary stones have been found uprooted, buried in rubble fill. "But these two stand where they've stood since the sixth century B.C.," he observes. "They were set out at about the time the democracy was founded. In a very real sense, democracy as we understand it was invented in the Agora of Athens." He leaned down to trace the letters.

Stones can speak, although they rarely speak in the first person. This one spoke loud and clear: "I am the boundary of the Agora." There was no dispute after that. This was the word. This was the place.

ADDITIONAL READING

The Athenian Agora: Excavations in the Heart of Classical Athens by John M. Camp, Thames and Hudson (London), 1986

The Birth of Democracy: An Exhibition Celebrating the 2500th Anniversary of Democracy, edited by Josiah Ober and Charles W. Hedrick, American School of Classical Studies at Athens (Princeton, New Jersey), 1993

The Athenian Agora: A Guide to the Excavation and Museum, American School of Classical Studies at Athens, 1990

The Agora of Athens, The Athenian Agora, Volume XIV by H. A. Thompson and R. E. Wycherley, American School of Classical Studies at Athens, 1972

Old Sports

The Olympic Games were not the earliest athletic rituals in the eastern Mediterranean

Allen Guttmann

Guttman has completed an English translation of Sports and Games of Ancient Egypt, *by Wolfgang Decker. A professor of English and American studies at Amherst College, he has also examined the diffusion of modern sports from England and America as a case of cultural imperialism*

Every four years at Olympia, the athletes of ancient Greece paid homage to Zeus by demonstrating their *arete*, their excellence of mind and body. According to Hippias of Elis, the nearby city-state that organized the competitions, the Olympic Games began in 776 B.C. with a simple footrace, and other events were subsequently added. But the list of victors Hippias compiled, sometime about 400 B.C., exaggerated the age of the games, apparently to aggrandize the glory of his native city. Plutarch admonished that Hippias "had no fully authoritative basis for his work," and historians now believe that the games began, with as many as five different sports, about 600 B.C., more or less at the same time as the sacred games at Delphi, Corinth, and Nemea, which rounded out the four-year cycle of Greek athletics. (Isaac Newton anticipated modern scholars, estimating the games' later origin by recalculating the duration of royal reigns and accurately dating eclipses referred to by ancient astronomers.)

The true precursors of the sixth-century games remain elusive, but we do know that the Greeks were not the only people of the eastern Mediterranean to emphasize athletic ritual as a religious and political statement. In ancient Egypt, for example, from at least 3000 B.C., physical prowess was a necessary sign of a pharaoh's fitness to rule. As a representative of divinity on earth, his role required him to maintain order against the forces of chaos. A pharaoh commemorating the thirtieth anniversary of his enthronement would formally prove his fitness by executing a ceremonial run in the jubilee known as the Festival of Sed. The course, from one mark to another and back, symbolized the boundaries of the kingdom he protected. The earliest known turn markers, at the pyramid of Djoser (ca. 2600 B.C.), lie about sixty yards apart.

There were numerous other occasions for a pharaoh to display his strength and stamina. Inscriptions and reliefs testify to almost superhuman demonstrations of hunting skill, events that may or may not have actually occurred. Tuthmosis III, for example, one of the monarchs of the Eighteenth Dynasty (1552–1306 B.C.), boasted, "In an instant I killed seven lions with my arrows." Similarly, he and several other monarchs of that dynasty were said to have so mastered the composite bow (made of hardwood, softwood, and horn) that their arrows were able to transfix sheets of copper "three fingers thick." (Modern attempts to replicate this feat have failed.) The pharaoh had to be seen as the mightiest archer, most successful hunter, and swiftest runner. An American president can lose a tennis match without unleashing the forces of chaos, but Tuthmosis III was required to surpass all mortal achievements.

In the biography of Cheti, prince of Siut, who lived during the Eleventh Dynasty (2134–1991 B.C.), we read that "he learned to swim together with the children of the pharaoh." But despite the central role of the Nile in Egyptian life, there is no evidence that the pharaoh was expected to demonstrate his prowess at swimming. Or perhaps Egyptian artists considered the physical movements too undignified to show in a representation of divinity. There is, however, an inscription telling of the amazing boating exploits of the Eighteenth Dynasty monarch Amenophis II, who was said to have steered his "falcon ship" for three *itrw* (about 18.6 miles), when others gave up in exhaustion after a mere half *itrw*. And according to Egyptian legend, the gods Horus and Seth, both of whom claimed the right to rule the universe, agreed to settle their dispute with a diving contest.

If the quantity of visual evidence is any indication, wrestling was among the most popular Egyptian sports. Murals discovered in the eleventh-century tombs at Beni Hasan depict nearly every hold known to modern wrestlers. Although the sport has a religious character in many cultures, including those of Africa south of the Sahara, for the ancient Egyptians it seems to have been a purely secular contest. A pharaoh thrown roughly to the ground would have been a terrifying portent of disaster.

The pharaohs most celebrated for their athletic achievements were the martial monarchs of the Eighteenth Dynasty, especially Tuthmosis III, Amenophis II, Tuthmosis IV, and Amenophis III. These were the immediate successors of the Hyksos, a seminomadic people whose warriors swept from the northeast into the valley of the Nile

Reprinted with permission from *Natural History*, July 1992, pp. 51–56. © 1992 by the American Museum of Natural History.

about 1650 B.C. Their war chariots spread terror among the Egyptians of the time, for whom this was an unknown weapon. For more than a century, the Hyksos usurpers ruled Egypt; once they were expelled, more emphasis than ever was placed on the pharaoh's physical prowess. Even Queen Hatshepsut, an Eighteenth Dynasty monarch who ruled as if she were a man, had to prove her fitness with the time-honored ceremonial run. A relief discovered at Karnak depicts her in the middle of the ceremony, accompanied by the bull-god Apis. The great exception was the pacific Amenophis IV (who ruled as Akheneten), best remembered for his heretical monotheistic religious views.

The Hyksos were expelled; the chariot remained. It was used for hunting as well as for waging war, and pharaohs were often portrayed wielding spears or drawing bows from the basket of a chariot. Chariot races as such were not part of ancient Egyptian culture, despite the suitability of the terrain. But later, during the Hellenistic age (fourth to first centuries B.C.), when Alexander the Great and his successors spread Greek culture throughout the eastern Mediterranean, chariot races became immensely popular in Alexandria and elsewhere in Egypt.

The Egyptians seem never to have been as passionate about horses as were the Hyksos, the Hittites (of what is now central Turkey), the Assyrians of Mesopotamia (modern Iraq), and other peoples of the Near East, who devoted enormous amounts of time and energy to their care and breeding. An obscure fourteenth-century Hittite named Kikkuli has left us a detailed account of these matters in writings sometimes referred to as *The Book of Horses*. The later Persian empire, which came close to overwhelming Greek civilization in 490 B.C., had similar roots. As Xenophon and other Greek historians made clear, equestrianism was an essential aspect of the education of a Persian prince, whose skill as a rider and hunter was a warranty of fitness to rule.

We know little about the role of sports in the great Minoan civilization, which reached its height on the island of Crete between 2200 and 1400 B.C.

The written language remains mostly a mystery. But few frescoes have engendered more speculation than the one excavated at the Palace of Minos in Knossos, which shows adolescents, a boy and two girls, seizing the horns of a charging bull and somersaulting over its back. Ever since Arthur Evans discovered the image in 1900, scholars have wondered whether people really performed this dangerous stunt and, if so, what it signified. Was it a contest in which youths competed against each other, like modern gymnasts, or was the bull their adversary, as in a Spanish *corrida de toros*? Another fresco from Knossos, now at the National Museum in Athens, depicts a group of male and female spectators arranged on terraces, or tiers. Whether the audience consists of assembled worshipers or sports enthusiasts is not clear, but some scholars believe they are attending a bull-vaulting performance.

Vases, statuettes, coins, and other remains of Minoan culture attest to the popularity of hunting, boxing, and wrestling. Among the most tantalizing discoveries is a fresco from the island of Thera, a Minoan outpost, that shows two boys wearing some kind of boxing gloves, squaring off as if in a modern ring. The guides in Thera call them the "boxing princes," but whether they really were princes proving their fitness for rule or merely two boys at play remains the artist's secret.

The Etruscans, whose civilization flourished during the seventh century B.C. in the region north and west of Rome, were enthusiastic about sports, perhaps as a result of Greek influence. The murals inside the so-called Tomb of the Monkey and other burial sites feature Etruscan wrestling and boxing, while chariots race across the walls of the Tomb of the Olympics, Tomb of the Two-Horse Chariots, and others. The murals of the chariot races include the spectators and perhaps the officials, at least one of whom seems to have been female. Jean-Paul Thuillier, the leading authority on Etruscan sports, argues that these types of murals represented funeral games, traditionally held to honor the dead. This is plausible for many sports, but one wonders about the scenes

in the Tomb of Hunting and Fishing, which include a fine picture of a man diving.

A mysterious Etruscan sport appears in the Tomb of the Augurs and Tomb of the Olympics. Known as the Phersu combat, from a word inscribed in the latter tomb, it pitted a masked man against a dog held on a leash by a second man. It may have inspired the later Roman combats of men and animals (*venationes*).

Scholars once believed that the Etruscans also gave the Romans the idea for their *munera*, combats between pairs of armed gladiators. An origin in Campania, south of Rome, or Samnia, east of Rome, now seems more likely. The precedent may have been a deadly funeral contest that had evolved from a still earlier ritual of human sacrifice. Such sacrifices would have been made to provide dead heroes with an entourage and appease the gods of the underworld. Eventually, death in combat might have been deemed a better offering than the less thrilling sacrifice of a passive victim. The Romans took the ultimate step of making a fight to the death a gruesome form of entertainment. (The religious trappings of Rome's pagan games, incidentally, were what horrified Christian theologians like Tertullian, who deplored idolatry more than the martyrdom of his fellow believers.)

Funeral games may also have been the chief precursors of the Greek Olympics. Our best early source is not visual art or archeology but literature: Homer's *Iliad*, a ninth-century account of the Trojan War, which probably occurred in the thirteenth century B.C. In Book XXIII, the Greeks, who have not yet captured the city of Troy, celebrate funeral games for Patroklos, who has been slain by the Trojan hero Hektor. Lavish prizes are offered by the great Achilles, Patroklos's bosom friend.

The first event of the games is a chariot race, for which Achilles offers five prizes, chief of which is "a woman skilled in fair handiwork." Although Greece was not the ideal place to breed horses, chariot races were apparently common in Attica, Thessaly, and other places where the terrain was not too forbidding. The plain before "the topless towers of Ilium" provides a suitable course, but the race is a rough one, with the goddess Athene intervening to assure victory for her favorite, Diomedes. (Fair play, which requires that everyone compete under the same rules, is as much a nineteenth-century concept as the nearly defunct amateur rule of the modern Olympics.)

The chariot race is followed by the boxing and wrestling contests. The first is won by Epeius, who fells his opponent with a mighty blow to the cheek. The second is declared a draw when neither Odysseus nor Ajax can throw the other. Then comes the footrace, in which Athene again intervenes, this time to favor Odysseus, whose limbs she lightens. The oafish Ajax she causes to slip and fall on offal left from the ritual slaughter of oxen.

When Ajax recovers, he is matched against Diomedes in potentially deadly armed combat, but the spectators stop the fight when Diomedes thrusts fiercely at Ajax's throat. Ajax has apparently suffered enough for a single day. The games conclude with the hurtling of the discus and with an archery contest in which the target is a dove tethered to a ship's mast. (The javelin contest, which was supposed to end the games, is canceled when Achilles, deciding that Agamemnon is certain to win anyway, gives him the prize.)

In Homer's dramatization, we can see that the games were a form of religious ritual, an appropriate way to worship the gods and to honor a fallen warrior. The contests also emphasized the skills and accomplishments of warriors. Both themes were eventually incorporated in the Greek Olympics, although the nature of the contestants changed somewhat. At first they were aristocratic warriors, but later, ordinary Greek men also competed and the role of the full-time athlete grew.

Pelops, a local hero said to be buried at Olympia, may have been honored by funeral games, and subsequent commemorative contests may explain why the site was chosen when the official games were instituted about 600 B.C. Originally, the Olympics probably consisted of a number of events, foremost of which was the short-distance race, or stade, from one end of the field to the other (a stadium for the footrace built later at Olympia may still be visited). The other events may have included a chariot race and the pentathlon or its constituents—a footrace, the discus, long jump, javelin, and wrestling. Other contests added over the years included longer footraces, a race in armor, and boys' events.

Neither the *Iliad*'s archery contest nor its armed combat were a part of the Olympic Games. Nor, despite the location of most Greek cities on the shores of the Aegean or on the banks of a river, were there swimming events at Olympia or any of the other sacred games. This was true even of the Isthmian Games, held at Corinth in honor of Poseidon, god of the sea.

Although the Greek athletic festivals were not the only, or even the earliest, ritualized sports of antiquity, they, more than any others, characterized an entire culture and embodied many of its people's highest aspirations. When, nearly a century ago, Pierre de Coubertin championed ancient Greece as an inspiration for modern games, he chose his model wisely. Amenophis II proved his divinity by his superhuman (and probably imaginary) athletic performance. Olympic victors, true exemplars of human physical excellence, won their immortality the hard way.

Cleopatra: What Kind of a Woman Was She, Anyway?

Serpent of the Nile? Learned ruler? Sex kitten? Ambitious mom? African queen? History is still toying with the poor lady's reputation

Barbara Holland

Barbara Holland, who often writes wryly about history and politics for the magazine, is the author of several books, including Endangered Pleasures *(Little, Brown).*

Until now, everyone has had pretty much the same fix on Cleopatra: passion's plaything, sultry queen, a woman so beautiful she turned the very air around her sick with desire, a tragic figure whose bared bosom made an asp gasp when she died for love. Inevitably, the best-known incarnation of her is Hollywood's: Theda Bara, Claudette Colbert, Elizabeth Taylor, telling us what fun it was to be filthy rich in the first century B.C., spending days in enormous bathtubs and nights in scented sheets. Drinking pearls dissolved in vinegar. (Do not try this at home; it doesn't work.) Lounging around on a barge, being waited on hand and foot.

Sometimes the asp looks like a small price to pay.

Hollywood's queen rests less on George Bernard Shaw's Cleopatra, who is a clever sex kitten, than on William Shakespeare's; in the Bard's *Antony and Cleopatra* she's a fiercer soul, downright unhinged by love for Mark Antony. Of course, they both had to leave out her children. Everyone does. It's tough being the world's top tragic lover with four kids underfoot. Even if you can get a sitter, it doesn't look right.

The latest version, part of the current debate about the possible influences of Africa on Greek and Roman culture, suggests that she was black. The last time we looked she was a Macedonian Greek, but the black-Cleopatra advocates like to point out that since nobody knows anything about her paternal grandmother except that she wasn't legally married to Ptolemy IX, it is possible that she was black.

Most classical scholars disagree. Some note that though Ptolemy II, more than a century earlier, had an Egyptian mistress, the Ptolemies were wicked snobs, so proud of their bloodline, not to mention the line of succession to their throne, that they tended to marry their brothers and sisters to keep it untainted. When they picked mistresses, they customarily chose upper-class Greeks. They felt so superior to the Egyptians, in fact, that after 300 years in Alexandria, they couldn't say much more than "good morning" to the locals in their native tongue; Cleopatra was the first in her family to learn the language.

Nobody should be surprised at such claims, however. For the fact is that for purposes political and otherwise, people have been fooling around with Cleopatra's image to suit themselves for centuries. In *All for Love* John Dryden gives us a traditional Cleo less a queen and a ruler than an addictive substance. Shaw made her stand for everything unBritish and thus deplorable. In the course of his *Caesar and Cleopatra* she evolves from a superstitious, cowardly little girl into a vengeful, bloodthirsty little girl. To underline his point he lops five years off her actual age and leaves her under the thumb of a sturdy Roman governor, forerunner of the wise and kindly British administrators of later colonies full of childish foreigners.

Of course, nearly everyone's story goes back to Plutarch, the first-century Greek biographer, who included two versions of Cleo. He knew the writings and stories of people in her part of the world who remembered her as a scholar in their own refined tradition, so unlike the ignorant, loutish Romans; a mothering goddess; a messiah sent to liberate the East from under the jackboots of Rome. On the other hand, he had the Roman story, largely attributed to her enemy in war, and conqueror, Octavian (who later became the emperor Augustus—portrayed as the clueless husband of the evil Livia in the television series *I, Claudius*). Octavian worked hard to set her up as everything scheming, treacherous, female, foreign and, most of all, sexually rapacious. His Queen Cleopatra was a drunken harlot, the wickedest woman in the world.

Actually, where we can reasonably deduce them, the facts are more interesting than these exotic scenarios.

Cleopatra VII was born in 69 B.C, the third child of Ptolemy XII, called Auletes, known as the Flute Player. Egypt was still rich, then, but its ancient empire had been nibbled away, and the natives, unfond of their Macedonian masters, were restless. The Flute Player kept going to Rome to get help in holding onto his throne. He may have taken Cleopatra along when she was 12; she may have watched the Roman loan sharks charge him 10,000 talents, or nearly twice Egypt's annual revenue, for services to be rendered.

Not only couldn't he control his subjects, he couldn't do a thing with his children. While he was away his eldest daughter, Tryphaena, grabbed the throne. After she got assassinated, second daughter Berenice grabbed it next—until Ptolemy came back with Roman

help and executed her. Cleopatra, now the eldest, had cause to ponder. She knew Egypt needed Roman help, but paying cash for help was beggaring the state. She knew she had to watch her back around her family. I suppose you could call it dysfunctional.

She seems to have found herself an education. Cicero, like most Romans, couldn't stand her, but he grudgingly admits she was literary and involved like him in "things that had to do with learning." The Arab historian Al-Masudi tells us she was the author of learned works, "a princess well versed in the sciences, disposed to the study of philosophy." According to Plutarch she spoke at least seven languages.

In 51 B.C., when Cleopatra was 18, the Flute Player died and left the kingdom to her and her 10-year-old brother (and fiancé) Ptolemy XIII. The reign got off on the wrong foot because the Nile refused to flood its banks to irrigate the yearly harvest. A court eunuch named Pothinus reared his ugly head; he'd got himself appointed regent for little Ptolemy, squeezed Cleopatra clear out of town and began giving orders himself.

Cleopatra's looks are one of the burning issues of the ages.

Rome, meanwhile, was in the process of shedding its republican privileges to become an empire. An early phase involved the uneasy power-sharing device called the First Triumvirate, with Caesar, Pompey and Crassus (a money man) jointly in charge. It wasn't Rome's brightest idea. Caesar and Pompey quarreled, Caesar defeated Pompey in Greece, Pompey took refuge in Egypt.

Not wanting to harbor a loser, the Egyptians had him murdered and cut off his head and presented it to victorious Caesar when he sailed into Alexandria to collect the defunct Flute Player's debts. Pothinus had reason to hate and fear Rome. He was very likely plotting to do in Caesar, too, who took over the palace and stayed on with a guard of 3,000 Roman soldiers. He couldn't take his ships and go home; the winds were unfavorable.

Cleopatra needed a secret word with him, so as we've all heard, she got herself rolled up in some bedding and had herself delivered to Caesar as merchandise. According to Plutarch, Caesar was first captivated by this proof of Cleopatra's bold wit, and afterward so overcome by the charm of her society that he made a reconciliation between her and her brother. Then he killed Pothinus. So there was Cleopatra, at the price of being briefly half-smothered in bedding, with her throne back. And of course, sleeping with Caesar, who was in his 50s and losing his hair.

How did she do it? Cleopatra's looks are one of the burning issues of the ages. European painters tend to see her as a languishing blue-eyed blonde with nothing to wear but that asp. However, there's a coin in the British Museum with her profile on it, and she looks more like Abraham Lincoln than a voluptuous queen. Most people who have written about her agree that she commissioned the coins herself and, being a woman, was vain of her looks, so even this profile could have been downright flattering. In any case, it launched a lot of cracks about her proboscis. Had Cleopatra's nose been shorter, according to 17th-century French writer Blaise Pascal, the whole face of the world would have been changed. However, there's no evidence that Antony was unhappy with her nose the way it was.

Or maybe it wasn't so long. Maybe she thought more of her kingdom than her vanity and wanted to scare off possible enemies by looking fierce. Considering the speed with which she corrupted Rome's top commanders—both of them widely traveled, experienced married men—it's possible she looked more like a woman and less like Mount Rushmore than she does on the coins. Besides, the second-century Greek historian Dio Cassius says Cleopatra seduced Caesar because she was "brilliant to look upon . . . with the power to subjugate everyone." (She knew a few things about fixing herself up, too, and wrote a book on cosmetics full of ingredients unknown to Estee Lauder, like burnt mice.) And Plutarch reports that "It was a pleasure merely to hear the sound of her voice, with which, like an instrument of many strings, she could pass from one language to another. . . ."

She bowled Caesar over, anyway, and when reinforcements came he squelched the rebellious Egyptian army for her. In the process he had to burn his own ships, and the fire spread and took out part of Alexandria's famous library, which housed most of what had been learned up to the time—Shaw called it "the memory of mankind." When the smoke cleared they found Ptolemy XIII drowned in the Nile in a full suit of golden armor, but as far as we know, his sister hadn't pushed him. Caesar then married her to her youngest brother, Ptolemy XIV, age 12, whom she ignored. When Caesar left, she was pregnant. Anti-Cleopatrans scoff at the notion that Caesar was the father, claiming he never admitted it himself, but there was plenty he never admitted, including his whole Egyptian fling, and somehow it seems likely. Giving the childless Caesar a son was a much shrewder move than getting pregnant by your 12-year-old brother; as policy it might have done wonders for Egypt. She named her son Ptolemy Caesar, always referred to him as Caesarion, and took him with her to Rome in 46 B.C. Mindful of her father's mistake, she took Ptolemy XIV, too, so she could keep an eye on him.

In Rome she was Caesar's guest. They gave fabulous parties together. He put up a golden statue of her in the temple of Venus Genetrix, causing a scandal that made him more vulnerable to the people who were plotting to kill him, as they did in March of 44. After he got stabbed, it turned out that he hadn't named Caesarion as his heir, but his great-nephew Octavian, so Cleopatra had to pack up and go home. When brother Ptolemy XIV conveniently died,

she appointed the toddler Caesarion as coruler.

Here the record loses interest in her for several years, between lovers, but she must have been busy. She'd inherited a country plagued by civil wars, Egypt was broke, and twice more the Nile floods misfired. Somehow, though, by the time the West began to notice her again, peace reigned even in fractious Alexandria. She'd played her cards deftly with Rome and her subjects loved her. According to the first-century A.D. Jewish historian Josephus, she'd negotiated a sweetheart real estate deal with the Arabs and in general managed the economy so well that Egypt was the richest state in the eastern Mediterranean. So rich that Mark Antony came calling in 41 B.C. in search of funds to finance an attack on the Parthians.

. . . like any Washington lobbyist with a pocketful of Redskins tickets, she was putting her time and money where they mattered most.

By then the Romans were pigheadedly pursuing the triumvirate notion again, this time with Octavian, Lepidus and Antony. If you believe Plutarch, Antony was simple, generous and easygoing, though a bit of a slob. Cicero says his orgies made him "odious," and there's a story that, after an all-night party, he rose to give a speech and threw up into the skirt of his toga while a kindly friend held it for him. Still, he was doing all right until Cleopatra came along, when he was, as Dryden laments, "unbent, unsinewed, made a woman's toy."

Plutarch's description of their meeting on her barge makes poets and movie producers salivate. Who could resist those silver oars and purple sails, those

flutes and harps, the wafting perfumes, the costumed maidens, and the queen herself dressed as Venus under a canopy spangled with gold? Not Antony, certainly. She knew what he'd come for and planned to drive a hard bargain. Naturally, they became lovers; they also sat down to deal; she would pay for his Parthian campaign, he would help fight her enemies and, for good measure, kill her sister Arsinoe, her last ambitious sibling.

Antony came for money and stayed to play. A sound relationship with Rome was tops on the whole world's agenda at the time. So, like a perfect hostess, Cleopatra lowered her standards of decorum and encouraged her guest in rowdy revels that have shocked the ages. The ages feel that all that frivoling means she was a frivolous woman, and not that, like any Washington lobbyist with a pocketful of Redskins tickets, she was putting her time and money where they mattered most.

She drank and gambled and hunted and fished with him. Sometimes they dressed as servants and roamed the town teasing the natives. Plutarch's grandfather knew a man who knew one of her cooks and reported that each night a series of banquets was prepared. If Antony wanted another round of drinks before dinner, the first banquet was thrown out and a second was served up, and so on. Anyone standing outside the kitchen door must have been half-buried in delicacies.

Back in Rome, Antony's third wife, Fulvia, and his brother raised an army against Octavian. (Lepidus, like Crassus, fizzled out early.) She got whipped, and Antony had to bid the fleshpots farewell and go patch things up. Then Fulvia died, and Antony sealed a temporary peace by marrying Octavian's sister, Octavia. Within weeks of that ceremony in Rome, Cleopatra had twins, Alexander Helios and Cleopatra Selene.

At the news of Antony's marriage, Shakespeare's queen has hysterics and tries to stab the messenger, but the Bard is guessing. The real queen probably took it in stride. She could recognize a political move when she saw it; she had Antony's alliance and a son to prove it, and a country to run besides.

SHE HAD NO TIME TO LOLL IN ASS'S MILK

No one suggests that she had a prime minister, and after Ponthinus, who would? No one denies, either, that Egypt was in apple-pie order. So there sits our drunken harlot, with Caesarion and the twins in bed, working late by oil light, signing papyri, meeting with advisers, approving plans for aqueducts, adjusting taxes. Distributing free grain during hard times. Receiving ambassadors and haggling over trade agreements. She may hardly have had time to put eyeliner on, let alone loll in ass's milk, and apparently she slept alone.

Antony finally got it together enough to invade Parthia. He needed help again, so he sent for Cleopatra to meet him at Antioch and she brought the children. Some see this as strictly business, but Plutarch insists his passion had "gathered strength again, and broke out into a flame." Anyway, they were rapturously reunited, and she agreed to build him a Mediterranean fleet and feed his army in exchange for a good deal of what is now Lebanon, Syria, Jordan and southern Turkey.

Did she really love him, or was it pure ambition? Ambition certainly didn't hurt, but it seems she was fond of him, though he probably snored after parties. Sources say she tried to introduce him to the finer things in life and dragged him to learned discussions, which at least sounds affectionate.

After a happy winter in Antioch, he went off to attack Parthia and she was pregnant again. The Parthian campaign was a disaster, ending with the loss or surrender of nearly half his army.

But for Cleopatra it was another boy, Ptolemy Philadelphus. When she'd recovered, she went to Antony's rescue with pay and warm clothes for the survivors. Presently Octavia announced that she, too, was coming to bring supplies. Antony told her to forget it and stay home. Octavian felt his sister had been dissed and suggested to the Romans that Antony was a deserter who planned to move the capital of the empire to Alexandria and rule jointly with his queen from there.

You could see it that way. In a public ceremony in Alexandria, Antony assembled the children, dressed to the teeth and sitting on thrones, and proclaimed Cleopatra "Queen of Kings" and Caesarion "King of Kings." He made his own three kids royalty, too, and gave them considerable realms that weren't, strictly speaking, his to give. Worst of all, he announced that Caesarion, not Octavian, was Julius Caesar's real son and the real heir to Rome.

Then he divorced Octavia.

All hands prepared for war. If the lovers had been quick off the mark, they might have invaded Italy at once and won, but instead they retired to Greece to assemble their forces, including Cleopatra's fleet. She insisted on sailing with it, too; her national treasury was stowed in the flagship. The upshot was that in 31 B.C. they found themselves bottled up at Actium, facing Octavian across the Ambracian Gulf. The standard version of the Battle of Actium is that while the fight hung in the balance, Cleopatra took her ships and left, because, being a woman, she was a coward and deserted in battle. The besotted Antony, we're told, followed her like a dog, and the fight turned into a rout.

With battles, the winner gets to tell the tale. Octavian was the winner, and he saw Cleopatra as a threat to Rome, a lascivious creature, and himself as a noble Roman able to resist her Eastern blandishments. All we really know is that it was a bloody mess, from which she managed to retreat with the treasury intact, enough to build another fleet with change left over. Octavian wanted that money to pay his troops. She wanted Egypt for her children. Perhaps deals could be made. Antony even suggested killing himself in trade for Cleopatra's life, but Octavian was bound for Egypt and he wouldn't deal.

Thus threatened, the queen swiftly stuffed a big mausoleum with treasure, along with fuel enough to burn it down if all else failed, and locked herself in with her serving maids. It's unclear whether Antony was told she was dead or he just felt depressed, but anyway he disemboweled himself. He botched the job—it's harder than you'd think—and lingered long enough to be hauled to the mausoleum and hoisted through the upstairs window, where presumably he expired in Cleopatra's arms. Victorious Octavian marched into town. He sent his henchmen to the queen, and they tricked their way in, snatched away her dagger, taking her—and her treasure—prisoner.

... she and her ladies dressed up in their best finery and killed themselves. Octavian did the handsome thing and had her buried with Antony.

According to Plutarch, at 39 "her old charm, and the boldness of her youthful beauty had not wholly left her and, in spite of her present condition, still sparkled from within." It didn't help, so she and her ladies dressed up in their best finery and killed themselves. Octavian did the handsome thing and had her buried with Antony. Then he tracked down and killed Caesarion and annexed Egypt as his own personal colony.

The best-remembered Cleo story is the asp smuggled in with the basket of figs. Plutarch, who saw the medical record, mentions it as a rumor, wrestles with the evidence and concludes that "what really took place is known to no one, since it was also said that she carried poison in a hollow comb ... yet there was not so much as a spot found, or any symptom of poison upon her body, nor was the asp seen within the monument. ..."

Later it was suggested—probably by Octavian—that she'd tried various substances on her slaves and, so the story usually goes, opted for the asp, but in truth its bite is even less fun than disemboweling. Maybe she used a cobra, whose effects are less visible. But where did it go? Some people claimed there were two faint marks on her arm, but they sound like mosquito bites to me. Others insist they saw a snake's trail on the sand outside; fat chance, with all those guards and soldiers and distressed citizens milling around shouting and trampling the evidence.

It looks likelier that she'd brewed up a little something to keep handy. She was clever that way; remember the second brother. Octavian's men had patted her down—"shook out her dress," Plutarch says—but she was smarter than they were. And why gamble on the availability of snakes and smugglers when you could bring your own stuff in your suitcase? When Octavian led his triumph through Rome, lacking the actual queen, he paraded an effigy of her with her arm wreathed in snakes, and the asp theory slithered into history. Maybe he'd heard the rumor and believed it, or maybe he started it himself. It would have played well in Rome. In Egypt the snake was a symbol of royalty and a pet of the goddess Isis, but in Rome it was strictly a sinuous, sinister reptile, typical of those Easterners, compared with a forthright Roman whacking out his innards.

History has always mixed itself with politics and advertising, and in all three the best story always carries the day. But why did the man who was now undisputed ruler of the known world work so hard to ruin a dead lady's reputation? Maybe she'd been more formidable than any of our surviving stories tell. We do know she was the last great power of the Hellenistic world, "sovereign queen of many nations" and the last major threat to Rome for a long time. She might have ruled half the known world or even, through her children, the whole thing, and ushered in the golden age of peace that she believed the gods had sent her to bring to the Mediterranean.

At least she would have left us her own version of who she was, and maybe it would be closer to the truth than the others. And then again, given the human urge to tell good stories, maybe not.

Countdown to the Beginning of Time-Keeping

Robert Garland investigates the ancient origins of the calendar and time-keeping systems of the Western world.

OUR PRESENT system of time-keeping provides us with a year of fixed and unalterable length which requires only the intercalation of a single (leap) day every four years. We seem to hold the passage of time so securely within the palms of our hands that we can almost hear its quiet heartbeat. Our present calendar has become so accurate that it will take 44,000 years before it falls out of step with the sun by so much as a single day.

We are also agreed about our precise place within chronological time. There is no country on Earth that fails to concede the practicality of an absolute dating system based on a commonly agreed era date. It is true that some resent using the birth of Christ as their chronological benchmark and who continue to maintain their own idiosyncratic systems. Right-wing traditionalist Japanese, for instance, sometimes seek to reintroduce the system of dating in accordance with the year of the emperor's reign. Orthodox Jews date events from the day that the world was created, i.e. October 6th, 3761 BC. Muslims calculate from the year after the Hegira or flight of Mohammed to Mecca in AD 622, which makes the current year Ab Hegira, or AH, 1419. Hindus calculate from the birth of Bramha. No society, however, can any longer ignore the countdown of

the Western calendar towards the year AD 2000. As the whole human race moves inexorably towards its encounter with the third Christian millennium, it may be timely to consider for a few moments how we come to be heading there in the first place. Our dating system is the construct of a variety of religious needs, pagan as much as Christian, including the need to establish fixed points in the solar year for the celebration of annual festivals.

Pre-industrial societies base their estimate of the year's length on a variety of repetitive occurrences in the natural world. These occurrences include changes in vegetative growth, the phases of the moon, the solstices, and the movement of the stars. Thus the Greek poet Hesiod, who lived in the seventh century BC, advised farmers in *Works and Days* to begin the harvest when the constellation known as the Pleiades was rising and to begin ploughing when it was setting, but to sharpen their agricultural implements when snails began climbing up plants.

For religious purposes, the phases of the moon provide a particularly convenient unit of time. The Greek religious year consisted of twelve lunar months, each twenty-eight or twenty-nine days in length from earliest times. A lunar calendar is useful for arranging the dates of monthly festivals and, perhaps, the

payment of debts. But as a basis for determining the length of the solar year, the lunar calendar is virtually useless. Every two or three years it becomes necessary to insert (intercalate) an extra month. For civic purposes, therefore, the Athenians introduced a second calendar which divided the year into ten months, each thirty-six or thirty-seven days in length. The Egyptians used a calendar of twelve months, each of thirty days; at the end of the year they added five extra days. The decision not to base their calendar solely on the lunar cycle was prompted by the necessity to be alert to the annual inundation cycle of the Nile, which was sufficiently predictable to give them a more direct way of observing the solar year than was available to most early civilisations. Though even this calendar fell one day behind solar time every four years, it was the system, adopted and modified by the Romans, upon which our own calendar was ultimately to be based.

The earliest Roman calendar, dating perhaps as far back as the eighth century BC, consisted of ten lunar months, corresponding to the months later named Martius to December. Januarius and Februarius were added by Numa Pompilius (c.700), the second king of Rome, according to tradition, as the winter was

This article first appeared in *History Today*, April 1999, pp. 36-42. © 1999 by History Today, Ltd. Reprinted by permission.

originally excluded from the calendar altogether, reflecting the fact that this was a period of inactivity. That is why September, whose Latin derivation means 'seventh', is the ninth month of the year. Martius, Maius, Quintilis (July), and October had thirty-one days. All the other months, apart from Februarius (twenty-eight days in length), had twenty-nine days. This gave the

---

The Romans chose midnight as the transition from one day to the next, but had no way of knowing when that moment occurred.

---

civic calendar a total of 355 days.

In an effort to overcome the discrepancy between the solar and the civic year, from 153 BC onwards the Romans intercalated an extra month called Mercedonius, which was twenty-seven days in length, and shortened Februarius to twenty-three or twenty-four days. We do not know on what basis they decided that any given year should be intercalary, however, and the decision, which rested with the priesthood, may have been somewhat arbitrary. Possibly the priesthood sometimes intercalated for no better purpose than to extend the term of office of a magistrate whom they favoured or were forced to favour.

By 46 BC the Roman civic calendar had fallen so far out of step with the solar calendar that no fewer than eighty days had to be intercalated. It was Julius Caesar in his capacity as Pontifex Maximus, supreme head of the Roman religious establishment, who, with the advice of a Greek astronomer called Sosigenes, took the radical step of introducing a year consisting of 365.25 days, based on the Egyptian calendar but inserting an extra day every four years between Februarius 23rd or 24th. He also determined that each month, except for Februarius, should have either thirty or thirty-one days. Februarius remained twenty-eight days long because it was sacred to the deities of the underworld,

who, it was presumed, would not have taken kindly to any alteration in their annual schedule. On Caesar's death in 44 BC, Quintilis, the fifth month of the year, was renamed Julius in his honour. Twenty years later, Sextilis, the sixth month, was renamed Augustus in honour of the first Roman emperor. Thus the names of all our months are Roman in derivation.

The Julian Calendar, which has remained in use in the West ever since, ran into slight difficulty in the first half-century after its implementation owing to the Roman tendency to count inclusively. Thus the priests were intercalating an extra day every three years instead of four. In AD 8 the proper adjustment was made and no further changes were necessary until the sixteenth century, when it became evident that the solar year was lagging eleven days behind the calendar year as the true solar year is 365.242199, i.e. a little less than 365 and a quarter days. This was a problem for the Church, since Easter was constantly moving further from New Year's Day. In 1583 Pope Gregory XIII corrected the discrepancy by decreeing that October 4th should be followed by October 15th in that year. He also remedied the problem once and for all by determining that only century years divisible by four should be treated as leap years. (This is why 2000 will be a leap year, whereas 1900 was not).

The so-called Gregorian Calendar was not adopted in Protestant countries until much later. Its introduction into Britain in 1752 led to antipapal riots because people believed that the Pope had actually shortened their lives. Though the Greek Orthodox Church also eventually accepted it, there still exists a religious order known as the Palaiohemerologites or Old Calendarians, who adhere to the pre-Gregorian system defying the authority of the Roman Catholic Church. The Russian Orthodox Church successfully resisted its introduction until the Bolshevik Revolution of 1917.

New Year's Day is a concept that has been millennia in the making. In Athens the new year coincided with the appearance of the first moon after the summer solstice, the first day of the month called

Hekatombaion. 'Hekatombaion' derives from *hekatombê,* which means 'the sacrifice of one hundred oxen'. The sacrifice in question was performed in honour of the goddess Athena, whose birthday was celebrated on this day. It was the Romans who determined that the new year should begin in the dead of winter, although they never referred to it as New Year's Day. In earlier times their year began on the *kalends* (the first day) of Martius, when the consuls and other important magistrates assumed office and when, too, the campaigning season officially began. This is why Martius was named after Mars, the god of war and agriculture. In the middle of the first century BC the Romans decided that magistrates should begin their term of office on the *kalends* of Januarius. It seems likely that Janus, the god who personifies the door of the year and who is depicted with two heads facing in opposite directions, was in origin the protector of spatial boundaries. Only now did he become associated with the passage and recording of time.

It was also the Romans who chose midnight as the transition between one day and the next, though they had no way of calculating when that moment occurred. In the Greek world, by contrast, the calendar day began at moonrise. Roman hours, like Greek, varied according to the length of the day, being therefore longer in summer than winter. Though the Babylonians invented a twenty-four hour day based on hours of unvarying length probably some time in the second millennium BC, their system had to wait until the invention of the mechanical clock in the Middle Ages before it was generally adopted.

The seven-day week, whose origins are traceable at least as far back as the Book of Genesis written in the early first millennium BC, was not formally adopted until the reign of the Emperor Theodosius in the late-fourth century. The days themselves were named after the seven regularly moving celestial bodies that were visible to the ancients viz. the Sun, the Moon, Mars, Mercury, Jupiter, Venus and Saturn. These also happened to be the names of Roman gods, and in Britain they were replaced by the names of Anglo-Saxon gods.

Thus Dies Martis, or Mars' day, became Tiw's day, Dies Mercurii, or Mercury's day, became Woden's day, and so forth. France on the other hand retained the original Roman names (*mardi, mercredi,* etc.).

The establishment of an era date was the last element of the calendar to be set in place. Every ancient society had its own idiosyncratic system for reckoning the passage of years. When, for instance, the Greek historian Thucydides, at the beginning of his *History of the Peloponnesian War,* wanted to identify the precise year in which the war broke out, he stated that hostilities began 'fourteen years after the capture of Euboea, forty-seven years after Chryses became priestess of Hera at Argos, in the year when Aenesias was ephor at Sparta, and in the year when Pythodoros was archon (or magistrate) in Athens'. Not until the third century BC did the Greeks attempt to establish a common dating system. One such system was the sequence of Olympiads, the four-yearly intervals that marked successive celebrations of the Olympic Games, which were conventionally reckoned to have been founded in 776 BC. A more popular era date in the Greek East was 312 BC, which was when Seleucus I became king of Babylon. This was known as Year One.

The Romans never adopted an era date for official purposes, although they made some strides in this direction. Their point of departure was the year of Rome's foundation, which the first-century BC grammarian Varro placed in 753 BC. But though the letters AUC meaning '*Ab Urbe Condita*' or 'From the Foundation of Rome' occur in literary contexts frequently enough, the Romans never abandoned their practice of designating the year by the names of the two consuls in office. 44 BC, for instance, when Julius Caesar was assassinated, was 'the year when Caesar was consul for the fifth time and Mark Antony for the first time'. In the Imperial period the Romans added to the names of the consuls the numbers of years that the emperor had held tribunician power—equivalent to the date of his accession. This system was still in use at the time of the fall of the Roman Empire in the late fifth century AD.

The adoption of '*Anno Domini*', indicating the presumed year of Christ's birth, was suggested by Abbot Dionysius Exiguus in AD 525. The Orthodox churches did not adopt it until the fourteenth century, owing to disputes as to the precise date of Christ's birth which have continued to the present day. Although most historians now believe that Christ was born in or around 4 BC, there is no likelihood of an adjustment being made at this point in the name of temporal exactitude. Dates BC were not introduced until the middle of the seventeenth century. They came to enable us to travel through aeons of time at the speed of thought, and the need for them reflects the growing importance of astronomy, geology and archaeology during this period. The anomaly of referring to dates *before* the birth of Christ by an English abbreviation, and dates *after* by a Latin abbreviation, reflects the fact that English was already becoming a language in which educated people could communicate.

As the new millennium approaches, many people are increasingly beset by fears about the future. The holes in the ozone layer are growing, the four seasons are being compressed into two—due to the effects of global warming, the delicate ecological balance that supports so many varied forms of life is under threat, and, to cap it all, human spermatozoa are becoming so enfeebled in the developed world that we seem to stand in danger of perishing by propagation.

Comparable anxieties that the world's biological clock is running down and will ultimately grind to a halt have concerned the human race for millennia. We encounter them in the myth of a once Golden Age when the Earth produced spontaneously and without the intervention of man. Hesiod in *Works and Days* told his audience that they were currently living in the Age of Iron and that it would be their lot 'never to cease from labour and sorrowing by day, and dying by night'. This bleak picture may well have reflected deteriorating economic and social conditions in the Greek world. He went on to warn his audience that, if things seemed bad, they were destined to become infinitely worse, for the time was fast approaching

when infants would be born with the marks of old age upon them. Human life-span, in other words, would have so contracted that infancy and old age would be virtually indistinguishable. When that apocalyptic moment was reached, Zeus would annihilate the human race altogether. Even so, the forlorn wish which prefaces the poet's description of the Age of Iron—'O that I was not among men of the fifth race, but had either died before it or been born after it'—seems to suggest a cyclical belief that the Golden Age of Kronos would return.

Hesiod's vision of ecological decline is echoed by the first-century BC Roman poet Lucretius:

> Even now the age is so broken that the exhausted earth scarcely produces tiny creatures, although previously it produced all kinds and gave birth to the huge bodies of wild beasts. . . . We wear out our oxen and the strength of our farmers, we wear out the plough and scarcely are fed by the produce of our fields, which reluctantly yield their fruits and increase our labour. And now the old ploughman shakes his head constantly since his great labour has come to nought, and when he compares the present with the past, he frequently extols the good fortune of his father.

Like ourselves, the Romans tended to equate large periodicities with cataclysmic change. Once the solar year had been fixed at 365.25 days, they came to believe that states underwent a cycle of 365 years at the end of which they were due either for extinction or renewal. Advocates of this theory pointed out that in 390 BC, which was exactly 365 years after its foundation, Rome had barely escaped destruction at the hands of the Gauls, while in 23 BC, another 365 years later, the city had been 're-founded' by the Emperor Augustus.

In the fourth century AD, Christian writers sought to counteract the persecutions of their fellows by predicting the imminent downfall of Rome. In response to the persecutions carried out in AD 303 by the Emperor Diocletian, the Christian apologist Lactantius wrote in the *Divine Institutions*:

It is apparent that the world is destined to end immediately. The only evidence to diminish our fear is the fact that the city of Rome continues to flourish. But once this city, which is the veritable capital of the world, falls and there is nothing in its place but ruins, as the sibyls predict, who can doubt that the end will have arrived both for humanity and for the entire world?

Whatever prophecies the Christians flung at the pagans, the pagans flung back in equal measure. Towards the end of the fourth century they cited the 365-year cycle as evidence that Christianity was destined to decline 365 years after its foundation. In *De Civitate Dei* (City of God), written in the early fifth century, St Augustine of Hippo found it necessary to refute this claim by pointing to the growth in the number of Christian converts over the thirty-year period following the supposed fulfilment of the prophecy. The sack of Rome by the Visigothic leader Alaric in AD 410 gave an opportunity for the Christians to turn the tables on the pagans yet again. In the prologue to his *Commentary on the Book of Ezekiel*, written shortly after this event, St Jerome venomously declared, 'The flame of the world has been extinguished and in the destruction of a single city, the whole human race has perished!'

It is these vague but incandescent embers of our Classical heritage that continue to haunt us as our own millennium draws to its close. Millennarianist fears represent more than a faint echo from a distant anxiety-ridden world, although there is no agreement as to whether we should be preparing for Armageddon, a planetary catastrophe, a shift in the earth's axis, the Last Judgement, or the thousand years of peace ushered in by the Age of Aquarius. The beginning of the present millennium produced a similar atmosphere of uncertainty. The comet which appeared in 1066, the year of the Norman Conquest, was thought to predict the end of the world though, given the pattern of life in the Middle Ages, not everyone would have been aware that they had recently entered a new millennium.

For a vision of the impending apocalypse, nothing can beat the awesome prognostications of the first-century AD philosopher Seneca. His magnificently chilling description from a work called *Natural Questions* anticipates modern forecasts of the kind of 'nuclear winter' that is destined to follow in the wake of an atomic holocaust:

It takes an age to establish cities, an hour to destroy them. A forest grows for a long time, but becomes ashes in a moment. Any deviation by nature from the existing state of the universe is enough for the destruction of mankind. At first excessive rain falls. There is no sunshine, the sky is gloomy with clouds, and there is continuous mist, and from the moisture a thick fog which no winds will ever dry out. Next there is a blight on the crops, a withering of fields of standing grain. There is suffering from famine, and recourse is had to the diet of ancient times. After the clouds have massed more and more, and the accumulated snows of centuries have melted, a torrent which has rolled down from the highest mountains carries off forests that are unable to cling fast, and tears boulders free from their loosened structures. Finally the torrent drags along cities and peoples who are forced back to their city walls, uncertain whether they should complain of cave-in or shipwreck. Meanwhile the rains continue, the sky becomes heavier and what was formerly a cloud is now black night, and a night that is dreadful and terrible with flashes of awful illumination. The remnants of the human race cling to whatever peaks are highest. As if this were not enough, winter will hold strange months, summer will be prohibited, and all the stars will have their heat repressed....

Most prophecies about the end of the world suggest that once the Earth has been destroyed, it will return to its former condition. This hope is present in the Hesiodic Myth of Ages and was central to Stoic philosophy. There is even a faint echo of the cyclical in the claim made by the author of the *Book of the Revelation of St John the Divine,* that once Christ's government of a thousand years has passed, Satan will again briefly hold sway, although in this case it takes the form of a return to our diabolical, rather than paradisiacal, past. So if the world does come to an end, let us none the less take comfort from the fact that we will no doubt meet again, even though we don't know where and don't know when. And let's just hope that the sun will be shining, as Dame Vera Lynn confidently predicts.

FOR FURTHER READING

A. Aveni, *Empires of Time.* (Basic Books, 1989); E.R. Dodds, *The Ancient Concept of Progress.* (Clarendon Press, 1979); R. Heilbroner, *Visions of the Future.* (Oxford University Press, 1995); A.T. Mann, *Millennium Prophecies* (Element, 1995); A.K. Michels, *The Calendar of the Roman Republic* (Princeton, 1967); A.E. Samuel, *Greek and Roman Chronology,* (1972).

Robert Garland is Roy D. and Margaret B. Wooster Professor of the Classics at Colgate University, New York, and the author of Daily Life of the Ancient Greeks (Greenwood Press, 1998).

Unit Selections

Key Points to Consider

❖ What is the purpose of religion in human life?

❖ Why is there concern about the historical aspects of the various religions? What difference can it make?

❖ Why do people of one religion often mistrust people of another religion?

❖ On what points are the major religions alike and different? How do they treat life after death? What do they say about relations to government? How have they treated women?

❖ Why is it difficult to study religion in a scientific manner?

 **Links** ## www.dushkin.com/online/

These sites are annotated on pages 4 and 5.

At the present time there are about 1.9 billion Christians, 1.1 billion Muslims, 747 million Hindus, 353 million Buddhists, 15 million Jews, and 6 million Confucians in the world. Most people profess some sort of religion. Although it is often difficult to ascribe religious motivation to people and events, the world religions, nonetheless, provide a moral foundation for human interaction. In some instances the role of religion is obvious, such as in the conflict between Jews and Muslims in Israel, Protestants and Catholics in Ireland, and Muslims and Hindus in India. In other situations the role of religion is subtle, but in any historical analysis religious motivation should not be ignored.

The great religions all developed in premodern times, and since they began a long time ago there are unsolved historical questions. In the story of their development, however, there are common themes—the relationship of one person to another and the relationship of people to a greater entity. Religion permeates the history of India, and T. R. Sundaram in "Ancient Jewel" outlines the significant religious ideas of Indian civilization. This civilization, among the oldest in the world, created not only Hinduism but also Buddhism. The religion of Buddha, however, left India and migrated into Asia. Pico Iyer, a non-Buddhist traveler, sought to measure the influence of the religion in "Buddha in the Round," and found that it was important in places even where Buddhists were in a minority. A compassion for the misery of the human condition has a universal appeal.

The search for historical data about the religious founders has gone on, but this has proven offensive to some believers. The Koran, the basic sacred text of Islam, is considered unchanged by orthodox followers. Yet, comparisons with earlier versions, as noted by Toby Lester in "What Is the Koran?" reveals changes. This is disturbing. Historical research on the Dead Sea Scrolls, however, has brought to light the oldest version of the Old Testament and some new information. Jeffery Sheler explains this in "The Reason God Tested Abraham." The research seems to have enriched the Old Testament rather than have diminished it.

Interestingly, three major religions—Christianity, Islam, Judaism—look upon Jerusalem as a holy city. The Christians have the Crucifixion and Resurrection, the Jews the Temple and the Wailing Wall, the Muslims the Dome of the Rock from which Muhammad is believed to have ascended into heaven. "The Dome of the Rock: Jerusalem's Epicenter" by Walid Khalidi explains the importance of this site as a point where humanity is joined to God. Even though Islam and Christianity emerge from the same background of the Middle East, they are much different in regard to government. Jesus

advocated a separate church with his advice to give to Caesar what belonged to Caesar. Under Islam, as Bernard Lewis explains, there was no separation of church and state.

Christianity has endured, nonetheless, for 2,000 years, spread around the world, and has influenced art, culture, and politics, especially in the West. The religion gave hope for salvation to individuals and gave greater protection to women, who were valued as part of God's flock. In its early years Christian teachings of charity and belief in salvation brought church members greater health and longer life because believers were willing to risk their lives to nurse the sick in time of illness.

Confucius, in comparison to the other leaders, was much less concerned about spirituality. He was vitally involved with the relationships between people and with the government. His thought from the fifth century B.C.E. endures as an influence in Chinese thinking. Jonathan Spence, a fine Chinese scholar, comments on why Confucius is worthy of study.

Comparisons between faiths are not easy. Yet, spiritual matters have long been of interest to humankind and they cannot be lightly dismissed or cynically disregarded in the study of world history. Even in nations that profess religious freedom and emphasize the separation of religion from government, such as the United States, religion has a permeating influence. Therefore, in evaluating any nation or society, this dimension of human existence demands consideration.

Ancient Jewel

From early Greece to the modern civil rights movement, Indian thought and philosophy have had a wide-ranging influence on Western culture.

T. R. (Joe) Sundaram

T. R. (Joe) Sundaram is the owner of an engineering research firm in Columbia, Maryland, and has written extensively on Indian history, culture, and science.

The very word *India* conjures up exotic images in one's mind. Yet this name for the south Asian subcontinent is of Western making, mediated by the Persians and the Arabs. The name used in ancient Sanskrit texts is *Bharat* (for the land of Bharatha, a legendary king), which is also the official name of the modern republic. Other familiar Western words such as *Hindu, caste,* and *curry* are also totally foreign to India. The general knowledge that exists in the West about India, its early history, philosophy, and culture is, at best, superficial. Nevertheless, since it would be impossible in a brief article to do justice to even one of these topics, I shall provide a brief, accurate glimpse into each.

India covers about 1.2 million square miles and is home to a population of 895 million; in comparison, the United States covers 3.6 million square miles and has 258 million residents. Thus, the population density of India is nearly 10 times that of the United States. (The size of classical India—which includes mod-

ern-day India, Pakistan, Bangladesh, and parts of Afghanistan—is about two-thirds that of the continental United States.)

But statistics about India can be misleading. For example, while only about one-quarter of the population is "literate," able to read and write, this has to be viewed in light of the strong oral traditions present in India since antiquity. Therefore, while a "literate" American may often be unaware of the collective name of the first 10 amendments to the U.S. Constitution, an "illiterate" Indian peasant would be aware of the history of his ancestors from antiquity to the present day.

Not only is India one of the oldest civilizations in the world, being more than 6,000 years old, but also it may be the oldest continuing civilization in existence; that is, one without any major "gaps" in its history. As the renowned historian A. L. Basham has pointed out,

Until the advent of archeologists, the peasant of Egypt or Iraq had no knowledge of the culture of his forefathers, and it is doubtful whether his Greek counterpart had any but the vaguest ideas about the glory of Periclean Athens. In each case there had been an almost complete break with

the past. On the other hand, the earliest Europeans to visit India found a culture fully conscious of its own antiquity.

India is a land of many ancient "living" cities, such as, for example, Varanasi. Even at sites like Delhi, many successive cities have been built over thousands of years. Among old buried cities that have been unearthed in modern times by archaeologists are Mohenjo-Daro and Harappa.

Of these cities, the renowned archaeologist Sir John Marshall writes that they establish the existence

in the fourth and third millennium B.C., of a highly developed city life; and the presence in many houses, of wells and bathrooms as well as an elaborate drainage system, betoken a social condition of the citizens at least equal to that found in Sumer, and superior to that prevailing in contemporary Babylonia and Egypt.

Thus, India was the "jewel of the world" long before the Greek and Roman civilizations.

Nor was classical India isolated from developing civilizations in other parts of the world. Clay seals from Mohenjo-Daro have been found in Babylonia and

This article originally appeared in *The World & I,* October 1996, pp. 24-31. Reprinted by permission of *The World & I,* a publication of The Washington Times Corporation. © 1996.

Continuous civilization: Excavations at Mohenjo-Daro and Harappa reveal well-planned towns and a sophisticated urban culture dating back to 2500 B.C.

Embassy of India

vice versa. Ancient Indian artifacts such as beads and bangles have been found in many parts of the Middle East and Africa. India and Indian culture were known to the Greeks even before the time of Alexander the Great. The Greek historian Herodotus wrote extensively about India during the sixth century B.C. Also, during this period many Greeks, including Pythagoras, are known to have traveled to India.

Sixth century B.C. was a period of great religious and philosophical upheaval in India. Hinduism was already an established, "old" religion, and reform movements were beginning to appear, such as one by a prince known as

---

Crucible of Learning

- *India's may be the oldest continuing civilization in existence.*

- *To avoid misunderstanding India, it is essential to appreciate three central tenets of Indian thinking: assimilating ideas and experiences, a belief in cycles, and the coexistence of opposites.*

- *India has made numerous contributions to contemporary Western understanding of mathematics, science, and philosophy.*

Siddhartha Gautama, who later came to be known as the Buddha. The religion that was founded based on his teachings spread not only throughout Asia but also to many parts of the world, including Greece, and it helped spread Indian culture in the process.

In Alexander the Great's campaign to conquer the world, his ultimate goal was India; he died without achieving that objective. When Seleucus Nicator, Alexander's successor, tried to follow in Alexander's footsteps, he was soundly defeated by Indian emperor Chandragupta Maurya. A peace treaty was signed between the two, and Seleucus sent an ambassador, Megasthenes, to the court of Chandragupta. Megasthenes sent glowing reports back to Greece about India, and he pronounced Indian culture to be equal or superior to his own, a high compliment indeed, since Greece was then near its zenith.

For the next 1,500 years or so, India—rich in material wealth, scientific knowledge, and spiritual wisdom—enjoyed the reputation of being at the pinnacle of world civilizations. Arab writers of the Middle Ages routinely referred to mathematics as *hindsat*, the "Indian science."

And as is well known now, it was Columbus' desire to reach India that led to the discovery of America. Indeed, the explorer died thinking that he had discovered a new sea route to India, while he had merely landed on a Caribbean island. Columbus' mistake also led to the mislabeling of the natives of the land as "Indians," a label that survived even after the mistake had been discovered.

THE UPANISHADS

Indian philosophy is almost as old as Indian civilization, and its zenith was reached nearly 3,000 years ago with the compilation, by unknown sages, of 108 ancient philosophical texts known as the Upanishads. These texts reflect even older wisdom, which was passed down from generation to generation through oral transmission. A Western commentator has remarked that in the Upanishads the Indian mind moved from cosmology to psychology, and that while most other contemporary civilizations were still asking the question "What am I?" the Indian mind was already asking, "Who am I?"

When translations of the Upanishads first became available in the West in the nineteenth century, the impact on European philosophers such as Goethe and Schopenhauer and on American writers such as Emerson and Whitman was profound. "In the whole world," wrote

Schopenhauer emotionally, "there is no study as beneficial and as elevating as the Upanishads." Emerson wrote poems based on the texts.

One of the principal underlying themes in the Upanishads is the quest for a "personal reality." This quest began with the conviction that the limitations of our sensory perceptions give us an imperfect model to comprehend the real world around us; this is known as the concept of *maya*. Since individual perceptions can be different, different people can also have different "realities."

For example, a happy event for one individual may be an unhappy one for another. Recognition and perfection of our personal reality is the quintessential goal of Indian philosophy and is also the basic principle behind yoga. Indeed, the literal meaning of the Sanskrit word *yoga* is "union," and the union that is sought is not with any external entity but with one's self. This is, of course, also the principal tenet of modern psychoanalysis.

From a Western perspective, to avoid misunderstanding India in general, and Indian philosophy in particular, it is essential to appreciate three central tenets of the Indian way of thinking. These are:

Assimilation. In the Indian way of thinking, new experiences and ideas never replace old ones but are simply absorbed into, and made a part of, old experiences. Although some have characterized such thinking as static, in reality such thinking is both dynamic and conservative, since old experiences are preserved and new experiences are continually accumulated.

Belief in cycles. Another central tenet of the Indian character is the belief that all changes in the world take place through cycles, there being cycles superimposed on other cycles, cycles within cycles, and so on. Inherent in the concept of cycles is alternation, and the Upanishads speak of the two alternating states of all things being "potentiality" and "expression."

Acceptance of the coexistence of opposites. Early Western readers of the Upanishads were puzzled by the apparent inherent ability of the Indian mind to accept the coexistence of seemingly diametrically opposite concepts. Belief in, and acceptance of, contradictory ideas is a natural part of the Indian way of life, and the logical complement to the tenets already mentioned. It is an indisputable fact that birth (creation) must necessarily be eventually followed by death (destruction). Creation and destruction are inseparable alternations. Even concepts such as "good" and "evil" are complementary, as each of us may have within us the most lofty and divine qualities and at the same time the basest qualities. We ourselves and the whole world can be whatever we want to make of them.

These three tenets are responsible for the amazing continuity of the Indian civilization, its reverence for the elderly, and the acceptance of the aging process without a morbid fear of death.

Ironically, the culture that taught of the need to renounce materialistic desires also produced some of the most pleasurable things in life. The intricacies and highly developed nature of Indian art, music, dance, and cuisine are examples. And the Kama Sutra is perhaps the oldest, and best known, manual on the pleasures of love and sex.

FROM PYTHAGORAS TO KING

Throughout history, India's contributions to the Western world have been considerable, albeit during the Middle Ages they were often felt only indirectly, having been mediated by the Middle Eastern cultures.

After the early contacts between Greece and India in the sixth and fifth centuries B.C., many concepts that had been in use in India centuries earlier made their appearance in Greek literature, although no source was ever ac-

A terra-cotta toy cow: Ancient Indian civilizations featured highly talented artisans and craftsmen.

Embassy of India

knowledged. For example, consider the so-called Pythagorean theorem of a right triangle and the Pythagorean school's theory of the "transmigration of souls"; the former was in use in India (for temple construction) centuries earlier, and the latter is merely "reincarnation," a concept of Vedic antiquity. There was also a flourishing trade between the Roman Empire and the kingdoms in southern India, through which not only Indian goods but also ideas made their journey westward.

During the Middle Ages, the Arabs translated many classical Indian works into Arabic, and the ideas contained in them eventually made their way to Europe. A principal mission of the "House of Wisdom" that was established by the caliph in Baghdad in the eighth century was the translation of Indian works.

Among the major Indian ideas that entered Europe through the Arabs are the mathematical concept of zero (for which there was no equivalent in Greek or Roman mathematics) and the modern numerical system we use today. Until the twelfth century, Europe was shackled by the unwieldy Roman numerals. The famous French mathematician Laplace has written: "It is India that gave us the ingenious method of expressing all numbers by ten symbols, each receiving a value of position as well as an absolute value, a profound and important idea which appears so simple to us now that we ignore its true merit."

India's contributions to other areas of science and mathematics were equally important. The seventh-century Syrian astronomer Severus Sebokht wrote that "the subtle theories" of Indian astronomers were "even more ingenious than those of the Greeks and the Babylonians."

The scientific approach permeated other aspects of Indian life as well. For example, classical Indian music has a highly mathematical structure, based on divisions of musical scales into tones and microtones.

In modern times, Indian music has had a considerable influence on Western music. Starting in the 1960s, the famous Indian sitar virtuoso Ravi Shankar popularized sitar music in the West, and now the melodic strains of the sitar, as well

Indian music has influenced Western artists, particularly in modern times. The beat of the tabla can be heard in pop music ranging from the Beatles to Michael Jackson.

Khorrum Omer/The World & I

as the beat of the Indian drum known as tabla, can be heard in the works of many pop-music artists, ranging from the Beatles to Michael Jackson. The movies of the Indian filmmaker Satyajit Ray have also made a significant impact on the West.

The contributions of many modern Indian scientists have been important to the overall development of Western science. The mathematical genius Srinivasa Ramanujan, who died in 1920, has been called "the greatest mathematician of the century" and "the man who knew infinity." The discovery by the Nobel Prize–winning Indian physicist Chandrasekhara Venkata Raman of the effect (which bears his name) by which light diffusing through a transparent material changes in wavelength has revolutionized laser technology. The theoretical predictions by the Nobel Prize-winning astrophysicist Subrahmanyan Chandrasekhar on the life and death of white-dwarf stars led to the concept of "black holes."

In the literary area, the poetry of Nobel laureate Rabindranath Tagore and the philosophical interpretations of the scholar (and a former president of India) Sarvepalli Radhakrishnan have inspired the West. Albert Einstein was one of the admirers of the former and corresponded with him on the meaning of "truth."

In terms of our daily dietary habits, many vegetables such as cucumber, eggplant, okra, squash, carrots, many types of beans, and lentils were first domesticated in India. Rice, sugarcane, and tea, as well as fruits such as bananas and oranges, are of Indian origin. The name *orange* is derived from the Sanskrit word *narangi*. Chicken and cattle were also first domesticated in India, albeit the latter for milk production and not for meat consumption. Cotton was first domesticated in India. The process of dying fabrics also was invented in India. Indian fabrics (both cotton and silk) have been world renowned for their quality since antiquity. The game of

Melodic inspiration: Performing traditional dance and music in Orissa.

Khorrum Omer/The World & I

chess was invented in India, and the name itself derives from the Sanskrit name Chaturanga.

India's most popular modern exports have been yoga and meditation. Hatha yoga, the exercise system that is a part of yoga, is now taught widely in America, in institutions ranging from colleges to hospitals. Many scientific studies on the beneficial effects of yoga practice are now under way. A similar state of affairs is true of Indian meditation techniques, which people under stress use for mental relaxation.

Finally the Rev. Martin Luther King, Jr., repeatedly acknowledged his debt to Mahatma Gandhi for the technique of nonviolent civil disobedience, which he used in the civil rights movement. For all India's material contributions to the world, it is its spiritual legacy that has had the widest impact. The ancient sages who wrote the Upanishads would have been pleased.

ADDITIONAL READING

A. L. Basham, *The Wonder That Was India,* Grove Press, New York, 1959.
——, *Ancient India: Land of Mystery,* Time-Life Books, Alexandria, Virginia, 1994.
Will Durant, *the Story of Civilization: Part I, Our Oriental Heritage,* Simon and Schuster, New York, 1954.

Buddha in the Round

A whirlwind tour of the territory conducted by a fellow traveler who has crisscrossed the vast, pluralistic, marvelously visible yet metaphysical Republic that is Buddhism today

By Pico Iyer

A little more than a decade ago, captivated by images as vital and haunting as the ones included here, I decided to take myself off to the ancient Japanese capital of Kyoto, to live for a year in a Zen temple. I wasn't a practicing Buddhist, and I knew next to nothing about what Buddhism meant, but I'd been calmed and quietly transported by the poems I'd read of the 18th-century solitary Issa, the sutras fluttering in the background of Kurosawa movies, and, especially, the clarifying elegance of all things associated with the Zen aesthetic: the empty room, the raked-sand garden, the lightning slash of bold calligraphy.

I took a bus to Los Angeles, therefore, and then a plane to Seoul, another plane to Tokyo, another bus across town, another plane, a bus, and then a taxi, and I found myself standing outside a small temple in the back streets of Kyoto in the falling dusk. A young, shaven-headed monk pulled open a heavy door and told me that I was welcome to stay, for 3,000 yen ($25) a night, with breakfast overlooking the rock garden included. Around us on the little lane were carp-pond teahouses, four-story pagodas, temples from the time of Shakespeare.

I made myself comfortable in my small, bare room, and from where I sat could see a peacock spire, soothsayers' homes, the maples turning red and gold against the eastern hills, and all the exquisite exactingness of the only wood-and-shoji area left in bustling Japan.

Next morning, at first light, I awoke to the sound of clappers from next door and murmured chants, incense seeping into my room as a solemn gong resounded.

The main appointments of the temple, though, were vehicles, great and small—bicycles, mopeds, motor scooters, and full-blown Kawasakis, 40 or more of them stashed in every corner of the quiet compound. My first morning, as I looked out upon the garden, the young monk suddenly approached, pedaling furiously a baby-blue tricycle, Donald Duck on its mudguard, his pale face spherical beneath his bobble cap, and recited to me the names of all the American cities he'd visited; later, his elder came up to me and silently passed over a sheaf of snapshots from his holiday in Europe. At night, when I went out in search of high enlightenment, I found the two of them sitting at a low table, cheering on the Hanshin Tigers on TV, and calling out, "Catch you later!" with a warmth no doubt encouraged by the empty beer bottles all around.

The monks with whom I'd found myself were kind, hospitable, and self-effacing to a fault; my only real complaint against them was that they were human, flesh and blood, not at all like the bodiless spirits I'd imagined. And much as the wooden stick, or kyosaku shocks Zen students out of sleep, their Goofy mugs and Honda Hurricanes nicely slapped me out of my romantic reveries.

A little later, when I spent a few nights in one of the Five Great Temples of Kyoto, I was to learn, even more forcibly, that Zen has precious little to do with contemplating nature and composing depthless haiku, and everything to do with sweeping leaves and cooking noodles, polishing the temple's hard floors on one's knees and chopping wood at dawn in a bootcamp hierarchy perilously close to that of the English boarding schools in which I'd put in far too many years.

So, inevitably, I turned tail and fled into the hubbub of a modern Japanese metropolis—and instantly found Buddhism all around: in the simple attentiveness of a shop-girl in the Takashimaya department store, bowing to her customers as (traditionally) to the Buddha nature within them; in the mother in McDonald's, teaching her small son to pour his sister's Coke for her; in the salaryman maintaining a pose of stoic calm as he's told of his father's death while the cherry blossoms and fireflies and posters of James Dean all around speak of life's impermanence.

It was a good lesson, and one I could never have learned had I stayed at home in California, musing on Kawabata novels and the snowfalls of Hiroshige (though, in fact, I could have learned it if only I had got in my car and driven down to the Zen center in the dark mountains behind Los Angeles, where later I would watch 30 Western students, all in black, walk barefoot through a

Reprinted from *Civilization*, December 1998/January 1999, pp. 44–49. From the book *Buddha: The Living Way* by Pico Iyer. © 1998 by Pico Iyer. Published by Random House, Inc. Reprinted by permission of the author.

The monks with whom I'd found myself were kind, hospitable, and self-effacing to a fault; my only real complaint against them was that they were human, flesh and blood, not at all like the bodiless spirits I imagined

freezing night of stars, endure seven days and winter nights of meditation without sleep, and gather each morning at 2:00 A.M., in an unheated hall, to chant the Heart Sutra before listening to an 89-year-old Zen master from Japan tell them how he'd come to America to teach people to laugh).

Yet it is a lesson that every step one takes in modern Asia reinforces as one sees that the silent common thread linking half the world together is not an exotic thing, on a pedestal, and swathed in incense (though it can be that, too, now and then), but rather a homespun reality as everywhere as air: a fact of life enacted in the Bolim Buddhist Department Store along the busy streets of downtown Seoul, in the eyes of the Nepalese stupas following Californian backpackers into lasagna joints, in the crush and confusion of crazy Bangkok, where, in the midst of belching trucks, glitzy shopping malls, and winking girlie bars, suddenly you will see a flash of gold—a monk in his saffron robe, waiting for a bus. I remember my first day in Rangoon, many years ago, going to the Sule Pagoda at the heart of town and finding, to my surprise, that the towering golden stupa really was the heart of town, a combination marketplace, bulletin board, schoolroom, and civic center where gossips clucked and boys eyed girls and toddlers chanted and half the population came to pass the night, barefoot on its marble floor.

And when first I set foot in Tibet, 12 years ago, it felt as if I were stepping into a whole universe that shook and spun with the pulse of Buddhism. Buddhas were painted on rock faces and cliff tops, and stones were piled up to form homemade shrines, while prayer flags carried thoughts unceasingly into the blue, blue heavens. In the great temples and monasteries of Lhasa, even after 26 years of brutal Chinese occupation, I could hardly move for the wizened old women and young exiles from Delhi and wild bandits in red-tasseled hats crowding in to spin prayer wheels, perform ritual three-part prostrations, and gather, with tears in their eyes, before photos of the exiled Dalai Lama on the altars of small chambers lit only by flickering butter lamps. Buddhism for them clearly had little to do with texts; it was as immediate as this hospital, that court of law, this breath.

Anyone who travels through Asia today, in fact, travels through a web of Buddhist images, rites, and, most important, values, and to a remarkable degree it is those moments that lodge inside the heart. For myself, I can remember taking an extended holiday from a little cubicle in Rockefeller Center and riding on the back of a farmer's motorbike to see the delicate stone Buddhas sedate in the 13th-century Thai capital of Sukhothai; or climbing for three hours, alone on a winter's day, to visit the Taktsang temple, or Tiger's Nest, which clung impossibly to the side of a cliff in rural Bhutan. I remember visiting the 29 caves of Ajanta, in central India, where Buddhas lie in shelters along a wild and crescent-shaped ravine, and seeing the gray Austin, in the lovely Vietnamese imperial city of Hue, preserved to recall the monk who had driven to Saigon to immolate himself in 1963. Most of all, in the 3,000-temple plains of Pagan, in Rangoon, in Bangkok, and everywhere, I remember the long, silent lines of monks and nuns, begging bowls extended, walking from hut to hut in the dawn.

Nowadays, those same unchanging images greet us in Samye Ling in Scotland (where Western monks undertake ten-year training courses), and on Canal Street in New York, or through that Thai

monk in Wimbledon, or this red-robed nun from Düsseldorf. Suddenly, many of us can go around the world to Buddhist lands long inaccessible to us (Mustang, Sikkim, Tuva), and suddenly, too, they can come to us—to that Tibetan restaurant on the rue Saint-Jacques, or thanks to those monks transcribing ancient texts onto computers in medieval Thimphu. When my parents were young, fewer than 2,000 Westerners had set foot in Tibet in all its history, and the Dalai Lama was a figure almost out of legend; today, the 14th Dalai Lama, Tenzin Gyatso, seems a part of the neighborhood almost, laughing with rabbis in New York and conferring with Green Party activists in Berlin, playing with reindeer, tapping into the Internet, and addressing crowds of 20,000 in concert halls usually reserved for pop stars. When, last year, I asked the Dalai Lama about the fate of Buddhism, he told me, with typical serenity and optimism, that the teachings' life span was predicted to extend for at least a couple of millennia more.

Buddhism has been known in the West, of course, ever since Marco Polo first brought back reports of the Buddha's life, and Henry David Thoreau produced the first English translation (via the French) of parts of the classic Lotus Sutra. It's been as intrinsic to the culture as Chinese temples in San Francisco and Sanskrit scholars in the British Museum. Yet recently, its presence has dramatically intensified, as the latest Cambodian and Vietnamese immigrants have built temples in Orange County and Louisiana, while more and more Westerners travel East to study philosophies long unavailable to them. Buddhism, which took on new forms and accents as it passed to Laos, and Mongolia, and Sri Lanka, is now developing its latest face, in what could be called Western Buddhism, a practice with its own festivals and pilgrimage sites in Vermont and rural France.

The Buddha looks out at us today from the paintings of Odilon Redon, and speaks to us in the pages of Jack Kerouac; he sits next to that bottle of perfume in a fashion ad shot by Irving Penn, and presides over a spirit house in that trendy new restaurant in Holly-

In Tibet, I felt as if I were stepping into a whole universe that shook and spun with the pulse of Buddhism. Buddhas were painted on rock faces and cliff tops, and stones were piled up to form homemade shrines, while prayer flags carried thoughts unceasingly into the blue, blue heavens

wood. He walks in the shoes of Keanu Reeves (whom once I saw stepping through the streets of 14th-century Nepal, acting as the Buddha in the movie *Little Buddha*), and he appears on new birth certificates every day (even I, though Hindu born, was given, as many Indians are, the first name of the Buddha, Siddharth). The single greatest development of the 20th century, the historian Arnold Toynbee once wrote, might prove to be the spread of Buddhism around the world.

Perhaps the greatest testimony to the versatility and practicality of Buddhism, in fact, is that it has long been central to cultures by no means predominately Buddhist. Often, at dawn, I've driven out to see the volcanic stone Buddhas of the great ninth-century mandala mountain of Borobudur, in Java, emerging from the jungle in the world's largest Islamic nation; one snowy night in the foothills of the Himalayas, I watched maroon-robed monks with yellow-crested hats blow long horns from the rooftop of a temple to mark the Tibetan New Year in India, home to 800 million Hindus. Some of the greatest Buddhist monuments surviving are the colossal 150-foot figures of Bamian, in Afghanistan, home now of an Islamic revolution, and the paintings and statues of Dunhuang, in what is technically Communist China. Even relatively secular Hong Kong boasts a temple with 12,800 Buddhas and, on Lan Tau Island, the tallest outdoor seated Buddha in the world, 70 feet high.

As Christmas Humphreys (whose name alone brings home the same point, a British judge named after Christ's day of birth, serving as one of our foremost explicators of Buddhism) once wrote of Buddhism, with typical matter-of-factness, "To describe it is as difficult as describing London."

I AM NOT, AS I SAY, A BUDDHIST, AND I leave to scholars the business of thrashing out what Buddhism really "means." But as a traveler through Buddhist countries—a tourist in Buddhism, so to speak—I have often been humbled and moved by what strikes me as the simple core at the heart of its teaching: that the central fact of life is suffering, and the central purpose of life is easing that suffering, in our own lives and those of others. One cause of delusion is desire, and it is rooted in another, the illusion of a separate self; release comes with the clear, unflinching understanding of a reality that mocks such passing trifles.

Of all philosophies, Buddhism is one of the most reasonable—in the sense that it extols reason and holds to nothing that cannot stand up to reason; the present Dalai Lama, for example, enjoys nothing so much as meeting with physicists and psychologists, and learning about how the latest scientific discoveries can sharpen and refine his thinking. That profoundly empirical, open-ended quality has prompted some people to argue that Buddhism is not a religion at all—certainly, talk of "God" is not essential to it—but rather a branch of moral philosophy, or even (as Tibetans call it) a "science of mind." I think of it as, most usefully, a kind of practical training for our lives (and so our deaths), from which we can gain as we do from our tai chi sessions or daily workouts in the gym.

It is this very down-to-earthness, and even skepticism, that has doubtless helped the current of thought to find a home in so many different cultures, adapting to countries founded around Confucianism, Hinduism, Shintoism, the Tibetan folk religion of Bön, and, now, the Information Highway. It is a philosophy that asks questions as much as it provides answers (when the Buddha was asked about metaphysical issues, tradition tells us, he said nothing), and those who meet the Dalai Lama are often taken aback to find that he's more eager to draw wisdom out of them, whoever they may be, than to lay down truths. Nothing at all, he always tells his startled followers—not the teachings of Buddha, not the words of the Dalai Lama, not religion itself—should be taken on trust. Devotion has its place, but it is most meaningful when confirmed by rigor.

The heart of Buddhism, then, which sometimes can get lost in philosophy and festivals and headlines, is compassion—and if you truly believe that I am as much a part of you as your own arm or toe, it only stands to reason that you will try to take care of me, and of that tree over there, and of that AIDS patient too. "The whole purpose of Zen," one Zen master in Kyoto once told me, "is not in the going away from the world but in the coming back"—even all those years of meditating in a silent zendo have meaning only if they can be brought into the suffering of the moment. A buddha, really, is someone who sees, and awakens, the buddha nature inside you.

From the book BUDDHA The Living Way *with photographs by deForest Trimingham copyright © 1998 and an essay by Pico Iyer copyright © 1998. Published by Random House, Inc.*

What Is the Koran?

Researchers with a variety of academic and theological interests are proposing controversial theories about the Koran and Islamic history, and are striving to reinterpret Islam for the modern world. This is, as one scholar puts it, a "sensitive business"

By Toby Lester

IN 1972, during the restoration of the Great Mosque of Sana'a, in Yemen, laborers working in a loft between the structure's inner and outer roofs stumbled across a remarkable gravesite, although they did not realize it at the time. Their ignorance was excusable: mosques do not normally house graves, and this site contained no tombstones, no human remains, no funereal jewelry. It contained nothing more, in fact, than an unappealing mash of old parchment and paper documents—damaged books and individual pages of Arabic text, fused together by centuries of rain and dampness, gnawed into over the years by rats and insects. Intent on completing the task at hand, the laborers gathered up the manuscripts, pressed them into some twenty potato sacks, and set them aside on the staircase of one of the mosque's minarets, where they were locked away—and where they would probably have been forgotten once again, were it not for Qadhi Isma'il al-Akwa', then the president of the Yemeni Antiquities Authority, who realized the potential importance of the find.

Al-Akwa' sought international assistance in examining and preserving the fragments, and in 1979 managed to interest a visiting German scholar, who in turn persuaded the German government to organize and fund a restoration project. Soon after the project began, it became clear that the hoard was a fabulous example of what is sometimes referred to as a "paper grave"—in this case the resting place for, among other things, tens of thousands of fragments from close to a thousand different parchment codices of the Koran, the Muslim holy scripture. In some pious Muslim circles it is held that worn-out or damaged copies of the Koran must be removed from circulation; hence the idea of a grave, which both preserves the sanctity of the texts being laid to rest and ensures that only complete and unblemished editions of the scripture will be read.

Some of the parchment pages in the Yemeni hoard seemed to date back to the seventh and eighth centuries A.D., or Islam's first two centuries—they were fragments, in other words, of perhaps the oldest Korans in existence. What's more, some of these fragments revealed small but intriguing aberrations from the standard Koranic text. Such aberrations, though not surprising to textual historians, are troublingly at odds with the orthodox Muslim belief that the Koran as it has reached us today is quite simply the perfect, timeless, and unchanging Word of God.

The mainly secular effort to reinterpret the Koran—in part based on textual evidence such as that provided by the Yemeni fragments—is disturbing and offensive to many Muslims, just as attempts to reinterpret the Bible and the life of Jesus are disturbing and offensive to many conservative Christians. Nevertheless, there are scholars, Muslims among them, who feel that such an effort, which amounts essentially to placing the Koran in history, will provide fuel for an Islamic revival of sorts—a reappropriation of tradition, a going forward by looking back. Thus far confined to scholarly argument, this sort of thinking can be nonetheless very powerful and—as the histories of the Renaissance and the Reformation demonstrate—can lead to major social change. The Koran, after all, is currently the world's most ideologically influential text.

LOOKING AT THE FRAGMENTS

THE first person to spend a significant amount of time examining the Yemeni fragments, in 1981, was Gerd-R. Puin, a specialist in Arabic calligraphy and Koranic paleography based at Saarland University, in Saarbrücken, Germany. Puin, who had been sent by the German government to organize and oversee the restoration project, recognized the antiquity of some of the parchment fragments, and his preliminary inspection also revealed unconventional verse orderings, minor textual variations, and rare styles of orthography and artistic embellishment. Enticing, too, were the sheets of the scripture

The effort to reinterpret the Koran, thus far confined to scholarly argument, could lead to major social change. The Koran, after all, is currently the world's most ideologically influential text.

written in the rare and early Hijazi Arabic script: pieces of the earliest Korans known to exist, they were also palimpsests—versions very clearly written over even earlier, washed-off versions. What the Yemeni Korans seemed to suggest, Puin began to feel, was an *evolving* text rather than simply the Word of God as revealed in its entirety to the Prophet Muhammad in the seventh century A.D.

Since the early 1980s more than 15,000 sheets of the Yemeni Korans have painstakingly been flattened, cleaned, treated, sorted, and assembled; they now sit ("preserved for another thousand years," Puin says) in Yemen's House of Manuscripts, awaiting detailed examination. That is something the Yemeni authorities have seemed reluctant to allow, however. "They want to keep this thing low-profile, as we do too, although for different reasons," Puin explains. "They don't want attention drawn to the fact that there are Germans and others working on the Korans. They don't want it made public that there is work being done *at all*, since the Muslim position is that everything that needs to be said about the Koran's history was said a thousand years ago."

To date just two scholars have been granted extensive access to the Yemeni fragments: Puin and his colleague H.-C. Graf von Bothmer, an Islamic-art historian also based at Saarland University. Puin and Von Bothmer have published only a few tantalizingly brief articles in scholarly publications on what they have discovered in the Yemani fragments. They have been reluctant to publish partly because until recently they were more concerned with sorting and classifying the fragments than with systematically examining them, and partly because they felt that the Yemeni authorities, if they realized the possible implications of the discovery, might refuse

them further access. Von Bothmer, however, in 1997 finished taking more than 35,000 microfilm pictures of the fragments, and has recently brought the pictures back to Germany. This means that soon Von Bothmer, Puin, and other scholars will finally have a chance to scrutinize the texts and to publish their findings freely—a prospect that thrills Puin. "So many Muslims have this belief that everything between the two covers of the Koran is just God's unaltered word," he says. "They like to quote the textual work that shows that the Bible has a history and did not fall straight out of the sky, but until now the Koran has been out of this discussion. The only way to break through this wall is to prove that the Koran has a history too. The Sana'a fragments will help us to do this."

Puin is not alone in his enthusiasm. "The impact of the Yemeni manuscripts is still to be felt," says Andrew Rippin, a professor of religious studies at the University of Calgary, who is at the forefront of Koranic studies today. "Their variant readings and verse orders are all very significant. Everybody agrees on that. These manuscripts say that the early history of the Koranic text is much more of an open question than many have suspected: the text was less stable, and therefore had less authority, than has always been claimed."

COPYEDITING GOD

By the standards of contemporary biblical scholarship, most of the questions being posed by scholars like Puin and Rippin are rather modest; outside an Islamic context, proposing that the Koran has a history and suggesting that it can be interpreted metaphorically are not radical steps. But the Islamic context—and Muslim sensibili-

ties—cannot be ignored. "To historicize the Koran would in effect delegitimize the whole historical experience of the Muslim community," says R. Stephen Humphreys, a professor of Islamic studies at the University of California at Santa Barbara. "The Koran is the charter for the community, the document that called it into existence. And ideally—though obviously not always in reality—Islamic history has been the effort to pursue and work out the commandments of the Koran in human life. If the Koran is a historical document, then the whole Islamic struggle of fourteen centuries is effectively meaningless."

The orthodox Muslim view of the Koran as self-evidently the Word of God, perfect and inimitable in message, language, style, and form, is strikingly similar to the fundamentalist Christian notion of the Bible's "inerrancy" and "verbal inspiration" that is still common in many places today. The notion was given classic expression only a little more than a century ago by the biblical scholar John William Burgon.

> The Bible is none other than *the voice of Him that sitteth upon the Throne!* Every Book of it, every Chapter of it, every Verse of it, every word of it, every syllable of it . . . every letter of it, is the direct utterance of the Most High!

Not all the Christians think this way about the Bible, however, and in fact, as the *Encyclopaedia of Islam* (1981) points out, "the closest analogue in Christian belief to the role of the Kur'ān in Muslim belief is not the Bible, but Christ." If Christ is the Word of God made flesh, the Koran is the Word of God made text, and questioning its sanctity or authority is thus considered an outright attack on Islam—as Salman Rushdie knows all too well.

The prospect of a Muslim backlash has not deterred the critical-historical study of the Koran, as the existence of the essays in *The Origins of the Koran* (1998) demonstrate. Even in the aftermath of the Rushdie affair the work continues: In 1996 the Koranic scholar Günter Lüling wrote in *The Journal of Higher Criticism* about "the wide extent to which both the text of the Koran and the learned Islamic account of Islamic origins have been distorted, a deformation unsuspectingly accepted by Western Islamicists until now." In 1994 the journal *Jerusalem Studies in Arabic and Islam* published a posthumous study by Yehuda D. Nevo, of the Hebrew University in Jerusalem, detailing seventh- and eighth-century religious inscriptions on stones in the Negev Desert which, Nevo suggested, pose "considerable problems for the traditional Muslim account of the history of Islam." That same year, and in the same journal, Patricia Crone, a historian of early Islam currently based at the Institute for Advanced Study, in Princeton, New Jersey, published an article in which she argued that elucidating problematic passages in the Koranic text is likely to be made possible only by "abandoning the conventional account of how the Qur'an was born." And since 1991 James Bellamy, of the University of Michigan, has proposed in the *Journal of the American Oriental Society* a series of "emendations to the text of the Koran"—changes that from the orthodox Muslim perspective amount to copyediting God.

Crone is one of the most iconoclastic of these scholars. During the 1970s and 1980s she wrote and collaborated on several books—most notoriously, with Michael Cook, *Hagarism: The Making of the Islamic World* (1977)—that made radical arguments about the origins of Islam and the writing of Islamic history. Among *Hagarism*'s controversial claims were suggestions that the text of the Koran came into being later than is now believed ("There is no hard evidence for the existence of the Koran in any form before the last decade of the seventh century"); that Mecca was not the initial Islamic sanctuary ("[the evidence] points unambiguously to a sanctuary in northwest Arabia . . . Mecca was secondary"); that the Arab conquests preceded the institutionalization of Islam ("the Jewish messianic fantasy was enacted in the form of an Arab conquest of the Holy Land"); that the idea of the *hijra*, or the migration of Muhammad and his followers from Mecca to Medina in 622, may have evolved long after Muhammad died ("No seventh-century source identifies the Arab era as that of the *hijra*"); and that the term "Muslim" was not commonly used in early Islam ("There is no good reason to suppose that the bearers of this primitive identity called themselves 'Muslims' [but] sources do . . . reveal an earlier designation of the community [which] appears in Greek as 'Magaritai' in a papyrus of 642, and in Syriac as 'Mahgre' or 'Mahgraye' from as early as the 640s").

Hagarism came under immediate attack, from Muslim and non-Muslim scholars alike, for its heavy reliance on hostile sources. ("This is a book," the authors wrote, "based on what from any Muslim perspective must appear an inordinate regard for the testimony of infidel sources.") Crone and Cook have since backed away from some of its most radical propositions—such as, for example, that the Prophet Muhammad lived two years longer than the Muslim tradition claims he did, and that the historicity of his migration to Medina is questionable. But Crone has continued to challenge both Muslim and Western orthodox views of Islamic history. In *Meccan Trade and the Rise of Islam* (1987) she made a detailed argument challenging the prevailing view among Western (and some Muslim) scholars that Islam arose in response to the Arabian spice trade.

Gerd-R. Puin's current thinking about the Koran's history partakes of this contemporary revisionism. "My idea is that the Koran is a kind of cocktail of texts that were not all understood even at the time of Muhammad," he says. "Many of them may even be a hundred years older than Islam itself. Even within the Islamic traditions there is a huge body of contradictory information, including a significant Christian substrate; one can derive a whole Islamic *anti-history* from them if one wants."

Patricia Crone defends the goals of this sort of thinking. "The Koran is a scripture with a history like any other—except that we don't know this history and tend to provoke howls of protest when we study it. Nobody would mind the howls if they came from Westerners, but Westerners feel deferential when the howls come from other people: who are you to tamper with *their* legacy? But we

Islamicists are not trying to destroy anyone's faith."

Not everyone agrees with that assessment—especially since Western Koranic scholarship has traditionally taken place in the context of an openly declared hostility between Christianity and Islam. (Indeed, the broad movement in the West over the past two centuries to "explain" the East, often referred to as Orientalism, has in recent years come under fire for exhibiting similar religious and cultural biases). The Koran has seemed, for Christian and Jewish scholars particularly, to possess an aura of heresy; the nineteenth-century Orientalist William Muir, for example, contended that the Koran was one of "the most stubborn enemies of Civilisation, Liberty, and the Truth which the world has yet known." Early Soviet scholars, too, undertook an ideologically motivated study of Islam's origins, with almost missionary zeal: in the 1920s and in 1930 a Soviet publication titled *Ateist* ran a series of articles explaining the rise of Islam in Marxist-Leninist terms. In *Islam and Russia* (1956), Ann K. S. Lambton summarized much of this work, and wrote that several Soviet scholars had theorized that "the motive force of the nascent religion was supplied by the mercantile bourgeoisie of Mecca and Medina"; that a certain S. P. Tolstov had held that "Islam was a social-religious movement originating in the slave-owning, not feudal, form of Arab society"; and that N. A. Morozov had argued that "until the Crusades Islam was indistinguishable from Judaism and . . . only then did it receive its independent character, while Muhammad and the first Caliphs are mythical figures." Morozov appears to have been a particularly flamboyant theorist: Lambton wrote that he also argued, in his book *Christ* (1930), that "in the Middle Ages Islam was merely an off-shoot of Arianism evoked by a meteorological event in the Red Sea area near Mecca."

Not surprisingly, then, given the biases of much non-Islamic critical study of the Koran, Muslims are inclined to dismiss it outright. A particularly eloquent protest came in 1987, in the *Muslim World Book Review*, in a paper titled "Method Against Truth: Orientalism and

Qur'ānic Studies," by the Muslim critic S. Parvez Manzoor. Placing the origins of Western Koranic scholarship in "the polemical marshes of medieval Christianity" and describing its contemporary state as a "cul-de-sac of its own making," Manzoor orchestrated a complex and layered assault on the entire Western approach to Islam. He opened his essay in a rage.

> The Orientalist enterprise of Qur'ānic studies, whatever its other merits and services, was a project born of spite, bred in frustration and nourished by vengeance: the spite of the powerful for the powerless, the frustration of the "rational" towards the "superstitious" and the vengeance of the "orthodox" against the "non-conformist." At the greatest hour of his worldly-triumph, the Western man, coordinating the powers of the State, Church and Academia, launched his most determined assault on the citadel of Muslim faith. All the aberrant streaks of his arrogant personality—its reckless rationalism, its world-domineering phantasy and its sectarian fanaticism—joined in an unholy conspiracy to dislodge the Muslim Scripture from its firmly entrenched position as the epitome of historic authenticity and moral unassailability. The ultimate trophy that the Western man sought by his dare-devil venture was the Muslim mind itself. In order to rid the West forever of the "problem" of Islam, he reasoned, Muslim consciousness must be made to despair of the cognitive certainty of the Divine message revealed to the Prophet. Only a Muslim confounded of the historical authenticity or doctrinal autonomy of the Qur'ānic revelation would abdicate his universal mission and hence pose no challenge to the global domination of the West. Such, at least, seems to have been the tacit, if not the explicit, rationale of the Orientalist assault on the Qur'ān.

Despite such resistance, Western researchers with a variety of academic and theological interests press on, applying modern techniques of textual and historical criticism to the study of the Koran. That a substantial body of this scholarship now exists is indicated by the recent decision of the European firm Brill Publishers—a long-established publisher of such major works as *The Encyclopaedia of Islam* and *The Dead*

Sea Scrolls Study Edition—to commission the first-ever *Encyclopaedia of the Qur'an*. Jane McAuliffe, a professor of Islamic studies at the University of Toronto, and the general editor of the encyclopedia, hopes that it will function as a "rough analogue" to biblical encyclopedias and will be "a turn-of-the-millennium summative work for the state of Koranic scholarship." Articles for the first part of the encyclopedia are currently being edited and prepared for publication later this year.

The *Encyclopaedia of the Qur'an* will be a truly collaborative enterprise, carried out by Muslims and non-Muslims, and its articles will present multiple approaches to the interpretation of the Koran, some of which are likely to challenge traditional Islamic views—thus disturbing many in the Islamic world, where the time is decidedly less ripe for a revisionist study of the Koran. The plight of Nasr Abu Zaid, an unassuming Egyptian professor of Arabic who sits on the encyclopedia's advisory board, illustrates the difficulties facing Muslim scholars trying to reinterpret their tradition.

"A MACABRE FARCE"

THE Koran is a text, a *literary* text, and the only way to understand, explain, and analyze it is through a literary approach," Abu Zaid says. "This is an essential theological issue." For expressing views like this in print—in essence, for challenging the idea that the Koran must be read literally as the absolute and unchanging Word of God—Abu Zaid was in 1995 officially branded an apostate, a ruling that in 1996 was upheld by Egypt's highest court. The court then proceeded, on the grounds of an Islamic law forbidding the marriage of an apostate to a Muslim, to order Abu Zaid to divorce his wife, Ibtihal Yunis (a ruling that the shocked and happily married Yunis described at the time as coming "like a blow to the head with a brick").

Abu Zaid steadfastly maintains that he is a pious Muslim, but contends that the Koran's manifest content—for example, the often archaic laws about the

treatment of women for which Islam is infamous—is much less important than its complex, regenerative, and spiritually nourishing latent content. The orthodox Islamic view, Abu Zaid claims, is stultifying; it reduces a divine, eternal, and dynamic text to a fixed human interpretation with no more life and meaning than "a trinket . . . a talisman . . . or an ornament."

For a while Abu Zaid remained in Egypt and sought to refute the charges of apostasy, but in the face of death threats and relentless public harassment he fled with his wife from Cairo to Holland, calling the whole affair "a macabre farce." Sheikh Youssef al-Badri, the cleric whose preachings inspired much of the opposition to Abu Zaid, was exultant. "We are not terrorists; we have not used bullets or machine guns, but we have stopped an enemy of Islam from poking fun at our religion. . . . No one will even dare to think about harming Islam again."

Abu Zaid seems to have been justified in fearing for his life and fleeing: in 1992 the Egyptian journalist Farag Foda was assassinated by Islamists for his critical writings about Egypt's Muslim Brotherhood, and in 1994 the Nobel Prize—winning novelist Naguib Mahfouz was stabbed for writing, among other works, the allegorical *Children of Gabalawi* (1959)—a novel, structured like the Koran, that presents "heretical" conceptions of God and the Prophet Muhammad.

Deviating from the orthodox interpretation of the Koran, says the Algerian Mohammed Arkoun, a professor emeritus of Islamic thought at the University of Paris, is "a *very* sensitive business" with major implications. "Millions and millions of people refer to the Koran daily to explain their actions and to justify their aspirations," Arkoun says. "This scale of reference is much larger than it has ever been before."

MUHAMMAD IN THE CAVE

MECCA sits in a barren hollow between two ranges of steep hills in the west of present-day Saudi Arabia. To its immediate west lies the flat and sweltering Red Sea coast; to the east stretches the great Rub' al-Khali, or Empty Quarter—the largest continuous body of sand on the planet. The town's setting is uninviting: the earth is dry and dusty, and smolders under a relentless sun; the whole region is scoured by hot, throbbing desert winds. Although sometimes rain does not fall for years, when it does come it can be heavy, creating torrents of water that rush out of the hills and flood the basin in which the city lies. As a backdrop for divine revelation, the area is every bit as fitting as the mountains of Sinai or the wilderness of Judea.

The only real source of historical information about pre-Islamic Mecca and the circumstances of the Koran's revelation is the classical Islamic story about the religion's founding, a distillation of which follows.

In the centuries leading up to the arrival of Islam, Mecca was a local pagan sanctuary of considerable antiquity. Religious rituals revolved around the Ka'ba—a shrine, still central in Islam today, that Muslims believe was originally built by Ibrahim (known to Christians and Jews as Abraham) and his son Isma'il (Ishmael). As Mecca became increasingly prosperous in the sixth century A.D., pagan idols of varying sizes and shapes proliferated. The traditional story has it that by the early seventh century a pantheon of some 360 statues and icons surrounded the Ka'ba (inside which were found renderings of Jesus and the Virgin Mary, among other idols).

Such was the background against which the first installments of the Koran are said to have been revealed, in 610, to an affluent but disaffected merchant named Muhammad bin Abdullah. Muhammad had developed the habit of periodically withdrawing from Mecca's pagan squalor to a nearby mountain cave, where he would reflect in solitude. During one of these retreats he was visited by the Angel Gabriel—the very same angel who had announced the coming of Jesus to the Virgin Mary in Nazareth some 600 years earlier. Opening with the command "Recite!," Gabriel made it known to Muhammad that he was to serve as the Messenger of God. Subsequently, until his death,

the supposedly illiterate Muhammad received through Gabriel divine revelations in Arabic that were known as qur'an ("recitation") and that announced, initially in a highly poetic and rhetorical style, a new and uncompromising brand of monotheism known as Islam, or "submission" (to God's will). Muhammad reported these revelations verbatim to sympathetic family members and friends, who either memorized them or wrote them down.

Powerful Meccans soon began to persecute Muhammad and his small band of devoted followers, whose new faith rejected the pagan core of Meccan cultural and economic life, and as a result in 622 the group migrated some 200 miles north, to the town of Yathrib, which subsequently became known as Medina (short for Medinat al-Nabi, or City of the Prophet). (This migration, known in Islam as the hijra, is considered to mark the birth of an independent Islamic community, and 622 is thus the first year of the Islamic calendar.) In Medina, Muhammad continued to receive divine revelations, of an increasingly pragmatic and prosaic nature, and by 630 he had developed enough support in the Medinan community to attack and conquer Mecca. He spent the last two years of his life proselytizing, consolidating political power, and continuing to receive revelations.

The Islamic tradition has it that when Muhammad died, in 632, the Koranic revelations had not been gathered into a single book; they were recorded only "on palm leaves and flat stones and in the hearts of men." (This is not surprising: the oral tradition was strong and well established, and the Arabic script, which was written without the vowel markings and consonantal dots used today, served mainly as an aid to memorization.) Nor was the establishment of such a text of primary concern: the Medinan Arabs—an unlikely coalition of ex-merchants, desert nomads, and agriculturalists united in a potent new faith and inspired by the life and sayings of Prophet Muhammad—were at the time pursuing a fantastically successful series of international conquests in the name of Islam. By the 640s the Arabs possessed most of Syria, Iraq, Persia,

and Egypt, and thirty years later they were busy taking over parts of Europe, North Africa, and Central Asia.

In the early decades of the Arab conquests many members of Muhammad's coterie were killed, and with them died valuable knowledge of the Koranic revelations. Muslims at the edges of the empire began arguing over what was Koranic scripture and what was not. An army general returning from Azerbaijan expressed his fears about sectarian controversy to the Caliph 'Uthman (644–656)—the third Islamic ruler to succeed Muhammad—and is said to have entreated him to "overtake this people before they differ over the Koran the way the Jews and Christians differ over their Scripture." 'Uthman convened an editorial committee of sorts that carefully gathered the various pieces of scripture that had been memorized or written down by Muhammad's companions. The result was a standard written version of the Koran. 'Uthman ordered all incomplete and "imperfect" collections of the Koranic scripture destroyed, and the new version was quickly distributed to the major centers of the rapidly burgeoning empire.

During the next few centuries, while Islam solidified as a religious and political entity, a vast body of exegetical and historical literature evolved to explain the Koran and the rise of Islam, the most important elements of which are hadith, or the collected sayings and deeds of the Prophet Muhammad; sunna, or the body of Islamic social and legal custom; sira, or biographies of the Prophet; and tafsir, or Koranic commentary and explication. It is from these traditional sources—compiled in written form mostly from the mid eighth to the mid tenth century—that all accounts of the revelation of the Koran and the early years of Islam are ultimately derived.

"FOR PEOPLE WHO UNDERSTAND"

ROUGHLY equivalent in length to the New Testament, the Koran is divided into 114 sections, known as suras, that vary dramatically in length and form. The book's organizing principle is neither chronological nor thematic—for the most part the *suras* are arranged from beginning to end in descending order of length. Despite the unusual structure, however, what generally surprises newcomers to the Koran is the degree to which it draws on the same beliefs and stories that appear in the Bible. God (*Allah* in Arabic) rules supreme: he is the all-powerful, all-knowing, and all-merciful Being who has created the world and its creatures; he sends messages and laws through prophets to help guide human existence; and, at a time in the future known only to him, he will bring about the end of the world and the Day of Judgement. Adam, the first man, is expelled from Paradise for eating from the forbidden tree. Noah builds an ark to save a select few from a flood brought on by the wrath of God. Abraham prepares himself to sacrifice his son at God's bidding. Moses leads the Israelites out of Egypt and receives a revelation on Mount Sinai. Jesus—born of the Virgin Mary and referred to as the Messiah—works miracles, has disciples, and rises to heaven.

The Koran takes great care to stress this common monotheistic heritage, but it works equally hard to distinguish Islam from Judaism and Christianity. For example, it mentions prophets—Hud, Salih, Shu'ayb, Luqman, and others—whose origins seem exclusively Arabian, and it reminds readers that it is "A Koran in Arabic,/ For people who understand." Despite its repeated assertions to the contrary, however, the Koran is often extremely difficult for contemporary readers—even highly educated speakers of Arabic—to understand. It sometimes makes dramatic shifts in style, voice, and subject matter from verse to verse, and it assumes a familiarity with language, stories, and events that seem to have been lost even to the earliest of Muslim exegetes (typical of a text that initially evolved in an oral tradition). Its apparent inconsistencies are easy to find: God may be referred to in the first and third person in the same sentence; divergent versions of the same story are repeated at different points in the text; divine rulings occasionally contradict one another. In this last case the Koran anticipates criticism and defends itself by asserting the right to ab-rogate its own message ("God doth blot out/Or confirm what He pleaseth").

Criticism did come. As Muslims increasingly came into contact with Christians during the eighth century, the wars of conquest were accompanied by theological polemics, in which Christians and others latched on to the confusing literary state of the Koran as proof of its human origins. Muslim scholars themselves were fastidiously cataloguing the problematic aspects of the Koran—unfamiliar vocabulary, seeming omissions of text, grammatical incongruities, deviant readings, and so on. A major theological debate in fact arose within Islam in the late eighth century, pitting those who believed in the Koran as the "uncreated" and eternal Word of God against those who believed in it as created in time, like anything that isn't God himself. Under the Caliph al-Ma'mum (813–833) this latter view briefly became orthodox doctrine. It was supported by several schools of thought, including an influential one known as Mu'tazilism, that developed a complex theology based partly on a metaphorical rather than simply literal understanding of the Koran.

By the end of the tenth century the influence of Mu'utazili school had waned, for complicated political reasons, and the official doctrine had become that of *i'jaz* or the "inimitability" of the Koran. (As a result, the Koran has traditionally not been translated by Muslims for non-Arabic-speaking Muslims. Instead it is read and recited in the original by Muslims worldwide, the majority of whom do not speak Arabic. The translations that do exist are considered to be nothing more than scriptural aids and paraphrases.) The adoption of the doctrine of inimitability was a major turning point in Islamic history, and from the tenth century to this day the mainstream Muslim understanding of the Koran as the literal and uncreated Word of God has remained constant.

PSYCHOPATHIC VANDALISM?

GERD-R. Puin speaks with disdain about the traditional willingness, on the part of Muslim and Western scholars, to accept the conventional understanding of the Koran. "The Koran claims for itself that it is *'mubeen,'* or 'clear.'" he says. "But if you look at it, you will notice that every fifth sentence or so simply doesn't make sense. Many Muslims—and Orientalists—will tell you otherwise, of course, but the fact is that a fifth of the Koranic text is *just incomprehensible*. This is what has caused the traditional anxiety regarding translation. If the Koran is not comprehensible—if it can't even be understood in Arabic—then it's not translatable. People fear that. And since the Koran claims repeatedly to be clear but obviously is not—as even speakers of Arabic will tell you—there is a contradiction. Something else must be going on."

Trying to figure out that "something else" really began only in this century. "Until quite recently," Patricia Crone, the historian of early Islam, says, "everyone took it for granted that everything the Muslims claim to remember about the origin and meaning of the Koran is correct. If you drop that assumption, you have to start afresh." This is no mean feat, of course; the Koran has come down to us tightly swathed in a historical tradition that is extremely resistant to criticism and analysis. As Crone put it in *Slaves on Horses,*

> The Biblical redactors offer us sections of the Israelite tradition at different stages of crystallization, and their testimonies can accordingly be profitably compared and weighed against each other. But the Muslim tradition was the outcome, not of a slow crystallization, but of an explosion; the first compilers were not redactors, but collectors of debris whose works are strikingly devoid of overall unity; and no particular illuminations ensue from their comparison.

Not surprisingly, given the explosive expansion of early Islam and the passage of time between the religion's birth and the first systematic documenting of his history, Muhammad's world and the worlds of the historians who subsequently wrote about him were dramatically different. During Islam's first century alone a provincial band of pagan desert tribesmen became the guardians of a vast international empire of institutional monotheism that teemed with unprecedented literary and scientific activity. Many contemporary historians argue that one cannot expect Islam's stories about its own origins—particularly given the oral tradition of the early centuries—to have survived this tremendous social transformation intact. Nor can one expect a Muslim historian writing in ninth- or tenth-century Iraq to have discarded his social and intellectual background (and theological convictions) in order accurately to describe a

engaged in the critical study of the Koran today must contend with Wansbrough's two main works—*Qurānic Studies: Sources and Methods of Scriptural Interpretation* (1977) and *The Sectarian Milieu: Content and Composition of Islamic Salvation History* (1978).

Wansbrough applied an entire arsenal of what he called the "instruments and techniques" of biblical criticism—form criticism, source criticism, redaction criticism, and much more—to the Koranic text. He concluded that the Koran evolved only gradually in the seventh

cles, but many Muslims understandably have found them deeply offensive. S. Parvez Manzoor, for example, has described the Koranic studies of Wansbrough and others as "a naked discourse of power" and "an outburst of psychopathic vandalism" But not even Manzoor argues for a retreat from the critical enterprise of Koranic studies; instead he urges Muslims to defeat the Western revisionists on the "epistemological battlefield," admitting that "sooner or later [we Muslims] will have to approach the Koran from methodological assumptions and parameters that are radically at odds with the ones consecrated by our tradition."

The Koran is a scripture with a history like any other,"
one scholar says, "except that we tend to provoke
howls of protest when we study it. But we are not
trying to destroy anyone's faith."

---

deeply unfamiliar seventh-century Arabian context. R. Stephen Humphreys, writing in *Islamic History: A Framework for Inquiry* (1988), concisely summed up the issue that historians confront in studying early Islam.

> If our goal is to comprehend the way in which Muslims of the late 2nd/8th and 3rd/9th centuries [Islamic calendar/Christian calendar] understood the origins of their society, then we are very well off indeed. But if our aim is to find out "what really happened" in terms of reliably documented answers to modern questions about the earliest decades of Islamic society, then we are in trouble.

The person who more than anyone else has shaken up Koranic studies in the past few decades is John Wansbrough, formerly of the University of London's School of Oriental and African studies. Puin is "re-reading him now" as he prepares to analyze the Yemeni fragments. Patricia Crone says that she and Michael Cook "did not say much about the Koran in *Hagarism* that was not based on Wansbrough." Other scholars are less admiring, referring to Wansbrough's work as "drastically wrongheaded," "ferociously opaque," and a "colossal self-deception." But like it or not, anybody

and eighth centuries, during a long period of oral transmission when Jewish and Christian sects were arguing volubly with one another to the north of Mecca and Medina, in which are now parts of Syria, Jordan, Israel and Iraq. The reason that no Islamic source material from the first century or so of Islam has survived, Wansbrough concluded, it that it never existed.

To Wansbrough, the Islamic tradition is an example of what is known to biblical scholars as a "salvation history": a theologically and evangelically motivated story of a religion's origins invented late in the day and projected back in time. In other words, as Wansbrough put it in *Qurānic Studies*, the canonization of the Koran—and the Islamic traditions that arose to explain it—involved the

> attribution of several, partially overlapping, collections of *logia* (exhibiting a distinctly Mosiac imprint) to the image of a Biblical prophet (modified by the material of the Muhammadan *evangelium* into an Arabian man of God) with a traditional message of salvation (modified by the influence of Rabbanic Judaism into the unmediated and finally immutable word of God).

Wansbrough's arcane theories have been contagious in certain scholarly cir-

REVISIONISM INSIDE THE ISLAMIC WORLD

Indeed, for more than a century there have been public figures in the Islamic world who have attempted the revisionist study of the Koran and Islamic history—the exiled Egyptian professor Nasr Abu Zaid is not unique. Perhaps Abu Zaid's most famous predecessor was the prominent Egyptian government minister, university professor, and writer Taha Hussein. A determined modernist, Hussein in the early 1920s devoted himself to the study of pre-Islamic Arabian poetry and ended up concluding that much of that body of work had been fabricated well after the establishment of Islam in order to lend outside support to Koranic mythology. A more recent example is the Iranian journalist and diplomat Ali Dashti, who in his *Twenty Three Years: A Study of the Prophetic Career of Mohammed* (1985) repeatedly took his fellow Muslims to task for not questioning the traditional accounts of Muhammad's life, much of which he called "myth-making and miracle-mongering."

Abu Zaid also cites the enormously influential Muhammad 'Abduh as a precursor. The nineteenth-century father of Egyptian modernism, 'Abduh saw the potential for a new Islamic theology in the theories of the ninth-century Mu'tazilis. The ideas of the Mu'tazilis gained popularity in some Muslim circles early in this century (leading the important

Egyptian writer and intellectual Ahmad Amin to remark in 1936 that "the demise of Mu'tazilism was the greatest misfortune to have afflicted Muslims; they have committed a crime against themselves"). The late Pakistani scholar Fazlur Rahman carried the Mu'tazilite torch well into the present era: he spend the later years of his life, from the 1960s until his death in 1988, living and teaching in the United States, where he trained many students of Islam—both Muslims and non-Muslims— in the Mu'tazilite tradition.

Such work has not come without cost, however: Taha Hussein, like Nasr Abu Zaid, was declared an apostate in Egypt: Ali Dashti died mysteriously just after the 1979 Iranian revolution; and Fazlur Rahman was forced to leave Pakistan in the 1960s. Muslims interested in challenging orthodox doctrine must tread carefully. "I would like to get the Koran out of this prison," Abu Zaid has said of the prevailing Islamic hostility to reinterpreting the Koran for the modern age, "so that once more it becomes productive for the essence of our culture and the arts, which are being strangled in our society." Despite his many enemies in Egypt, Abu Zaid may well be making progress toward this goal: there are indications that his work is being widely, if quietly, read with interest in the Arab world. Abu Zaid says, for example, that his *The Concept of the Text* (1990)—the book largely responsible for his exile from Egypt—has gone through at least eight underground printings in Cairo and Beirut.

Another scholar with a wide readership who is committed to re-examining the Koran is Mohammed Arkoun, the Algerian professor at the University of Paris. Arkoun argued in *Lectures du Coran* (1982), for example, that "it is time [for Islam] to assume, along with all of the great cultural traditions, the modern risks of scientific knowledge," and suggested that "the problem of the divine authenticity of the Koran can serve to reactivate Islamic thought and engage it in the major debates of our age." Arkoun regrets the fact that most Muslims are unaware that a different conception of the Koran exists within their own historical tradition. What a re-examination of Islamic history offers Muslims, Arkoun and others argue, is an opportunity to challenge the Muslim orthodoxy from within, rather than having to rely on "hostile" outside sources. Arkoun, Abu Zaid, and others hope that this challenge might ultimately lead to nothing less than an Islamic renaissance.

The gulf between such academic theories and the daily practice of Islam around the world is huge, of course—the majority of Muslims today are unlikely to question the orthodox understanding of the Koran and Islamic history. Yet Islam became one of the world's great religions in part because of its openness to social change and new ideas. (Centuries ago, when Europe was mired in its feudal Dark Ages, the sages of a flourishing Islamic civilization opened an era of great scientific and philosophical discovery. The ideas of the ancient Greeks and Romans might never have been introduced to Europe were it not for the Islamic historians and philosophers who rediscovered and revived them.) Islam's own history shows that the prevailing conception of the Koran is not the only one ever to have existed, and the recent history of biblical scholarship shows that not all critical-historical studies of a holy scripture are antagonistic. They can instead be carried out with the aim of spiritual and cultural regeneration. They can, as Mohammed Arkoun puts it, demystify the text while reaffirming "the relevance of its larger intuitions."

Increasingly diverse interpretations of the Koran and Islamic history will inevitably be proposed in the coming decades, as traditional cultural distinctions between East, West, North and South continue to dissolve, as the population of the Muslim world continues to grow, as early historical sources continue to be scrutinized, and as feminism meets the Koran. With the diversity of interpretations will surely come increased fractiousness, perhaps intensified by the fact that Islam now exists in such a great variety of social and intellectual settings—Bosnia, Iran, Malaysia, Nigeria, Saudi Arabia, South Africa, the United States, and so on. More than ever before, anybody wishing to understand global affairs will need to understand Islamic civilization, in all its permutations. Surely the best way to start is with the study of the Koran—which promises in the years ahead to be at least as contentious, fascinating, and important as the study of the Bible has been in this century.

Toby Lester is the executive editor of Atlantic Unbound, the *Atlantic Monthly* Web site.

State and Society Under Islam

Bernard Lewis

Bernard Lewis is professor of Near Eastern Studies (emeritus) at Princeton University and the director of the Annenberg Research Institute in Philadelphia. Born in London, England, he received his A.B. (1936) and Ph.D. (1939) from London University. His books include The Assassins *(1967) and* The Muslim Discovery of Europe *(1982). This essay was presented in August 1989 at a conference on "Europe and Civil Society" at Castel Gandolfo in Italy under the auspices of the* Institut für die Wissenschaften vom Menschen *of Vienna, Austria.*

Christendom and Islam are in many ways sister civilizations, both drawing on the shared heritage of Jewish revelation and prophesy and Greek philosophy and science, and both nourished by the immemorial traditions of Middle Eastern antiquity. For most of their joint history, they have been locked in combat, in an endless series of attacks and counter-attacks, jihads and crusades, conquests and reconquests. But even in struggle and polemic they reveal their essential kinship and the common features which link them to each other and set them apart from the remoter civilizations of Asia.

As well as resemblances, there are, of course, profound disparities between the two, and these go beyond the obvious differences in dogma and worship. Nowhere are these differences more profound—and more obvious—than in the attitudes of these two religions, and of their authorized exponents, to the relations among government, religion, and society. The founder of Christianity bade his followers "render unto Caesar the things which are Caesar's; and unto God the things which are God's"—and for centuries Christianity grew and developed as a religion of the downtrodden, until Caesar himself became a Christian and inaugurated a series of changes by which the new faith captured the Roman Empire and—some would add—was captured by it.

The founder of Islam was his own Constantine and founded his own empire. He did not therefore create—or need to create—a church. The dichotomy of *regnum* and *sacerdotium*, so crucial in the history of Western Christendom, had no equivalent in Islam. During Muhammad's lifetime, the Muslims became at once a political and a religious community, with the Prophet as head of state. As such, he governed a place and a people, dispensed justice, collected taxes, commanded armies, waged war, and made peace. For the first generation of Muslims, whose adventures are the sacred and salvation history of Islam, there was no protracted testing by persecution, no tradition of resistance to a hostile state power. On the contrary, the state that ruled them was that of Islam, and God's approval of their cause was made clear to them in the form of victory and empire in this world.

In pagan Rome, Caesar was God. For Christians, there is a choice between God and Caesar, and endless generations of Christians have been ensnared in that choice. In Islam, there was no such choice. In the universal Islamic polity as conceived by Muslims, there is no Caesar, but only God, who is the sole sovereign and the sole source of law. Muhammad was his Prophet, who

 From *The Wilson Quarterly*, Autumn 1989, pp. 39–51. © 1989 by Bernard Lewis. Reprinted by permission of the author.

during his lifetime both taught and ruled on God's behalf. When Muhammad died in A.D. 632, his spiritual and prophetic mission, to bring God's book to man, was completed. What remained was the religious mission of spreading God's revelation until finally all the world accepted it. This was to be achieved by extending the authority and thus also the membership of the community which embraced the true faith and upheld God's law. To provide the necessary cohesion and leadership for this task, a deputy or successor of the Prophet was required. The Arabic word *khalifa*, the title by which that successor came to be known, combines the two meanings. This was the title adopted by the Prophet's father-in-law and first successor, 'Abū Bakr, whose accession to the leadership of the Islamic community marked the foundation of the great historic institution of the caliphate.

Under the caliphs, the community of Medina, where the Prophet had held sway, grew in a century into a vast empire, and Islam became a world religion. In the experience of the first Muslims, as preserved and recorded for later generations, religious belief and political power were indissolubly associated: The first sanctified the second; the second sustained the first. The late Ayatollah Khomeini once remarked that "Islam is politics or it is nothing." Not all Muslims would go that far, but most would agree that God is concerned with politics, and this belief is confirmed and sustained by the Shari'a, the Holy Law, which deals extensively with the acquisition and exercise of power, the nature of authority, the duties of ruler and subject—in a word, with what we in the West would call constitutional law and political philosophy.

In the Islamic state, as ideally conceived and as it indeed existed from medieval through to Ottoman times almost into the 19th century, there could be no conflict between Pope and Emperor; in classical Middle Eastern Islam, the two mighty powers which these two represented were one and the same, and the caliph was the embodiment of both. As a building, a place of public worship, the Muslim equivalent of the church is the mosque; as an institution, a corpo-

Islamic civilization, as it spread, accommodated and absorbed other cultures. In this 16th-century Mughal painting, Alexander the Great, wearing an Islamic turban, is shown being lowered into the sea in a glass jar.

rate body with its own hierarchy and laws, there is no church in Islam. For the same reason, there is no priesthood in the true sense of the term, and therefore no prelates or hierarchy, no councils or synods, to define orthodoxy and thus condemn heterodoxy. The ulema, the professional men of religion in the Islamic world, may perhaps be called a clergy in the sociological but certainly not in the theological sense. They receive no ordination, have no parishes, perform no sacraments. There is no priestly mediation between the worshiper and his God, and in early Islam there was no constituted ecclesiastical authority of any kind.

The primary function of the ulema—from a word meaning knowledge—is to uphold and interpret the Holy Law. From late medieval times, something like a parish clergy emerged, ministering to the needs of ordinary people in

cities and villages, but these were usually separate from and mistrusted by the ulema, and owed much more to mystical than to dogmatic Islam. In the later Islamic monarchies, in Turkey and Iran, a kind of ecclesiastical hierarchy appeared, but this had no roots in the classical Muslim tradition, and members of these hierarchies never claimed and still less exercised the powers of Christian prelates.

If one may speak of a clergy only in a limited sociological sense in the Islamic world, there is no sense at all in which one can speak of a laity. The very notion of something that is separate or even separable from religious authority, expressed in Christian languages by such terms as lay, temporal, or secular, is totally alien to Islamic thought and practice. It was not until relatively modern times that equivalents for these terms were used in Arabic. They were borrowed from the usage of Arabic-speaking Christians.

Yet, from the days of the Prophet, the Islamic society had a dual character. On the one hand it was a polity—a chieftaincy which successively became a state and an empire. At the same time, it was a religious community, founded by a Prophet and ruled by his deputies who were also his successors.

Christ was crucified, Moses died without entering the Promised Land, and the beliefs and attitudes of their religious followers are still profoundly influenced by the memory of these facts. Muhammad triumphed during his lifetime and died a conqueror and a sovereign. The resulting Muslim attitudes can only have been confirmed by the subsequent history of their religion.

In the West, barbarian but teachable invaders came to an existing state and religion, the Roman empire and the Christian church. The invaders recognized both and tried to serve their own aims and needs within the existing structures of Roman polity and Christian religion, both using the Latin language. The Muslim Arab invaders who conquered the Middle East and North Africa brought their own faith, with their own scriptures in their own language; they created their own polity, with a new set of laws, a new imperial language, and a new imperial structure, with the caliph as supreme head. This state was defined by Islam, and full membership belonged, alone, to those who professed the dominant faith.

The career of the Prophet Muhammad, in this as in all else the model which all good Muslims seek to emulate, falls into two parts. In the first, during his years in his birthplace Mecca (?570–622), he was an opponent of the reigning pagan oligarchy. In the second, after his migration from Mecca to Medina (622–632), he was the head of a state. These two phases in the Prophet's career, the one of resistance, the other of rule, are both reflected in the Qur'an, where, in different chapters, the believers are enjoined to obey God's representative and to disobey Pharaoh, the paradigm of the unjust and tyrannical

ruler. These two aspects of the prophet's life and work inspired two traditions in Islam, the one authoritarian and quietist, the other radical and activist. Both are amply reflected, on the one hand in the development of the tradition, on the other, in the unfolding of events. It was not always easy to determine who was God's representative and who was Pharaoh; many books were written, and many battles fought, in the attempt. Both tradi-

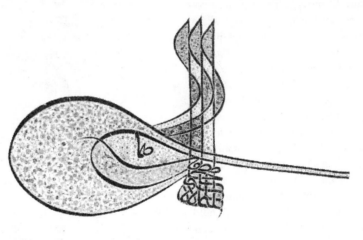

Calligraphic emblem of Süleyman I.

tions can be seen very clearly in the polemics and struggles of our own times.

Between the extremes of quietism and radicalism, there is a pervasive, widely expressed attitude of reserve, even of mistrust, of government. An example is the sharp difference, in medieval times, of popular attitudes towards the qadi, a judge, and the mufti, a jurisconsult in the Holy Law. The qadi, who was appointed by the ruler, is presented in literature and folklore as a venal, even a ridiculous figure; the mufti, established by the recognition of his colleagues and the general population, enjoyed esteem and respect. A recurring theme in biographies of pious men—of which we have hundreds of thousands—is that the hero was offered a government appointment, and refused. The offer establishes his learning and reputation, the refusal his integrity.

Under the Ottoman sultans there was an important change. The qadi gained greatly in power and authority, and even the mufti was integrated into the public chain of authority. But the old attitude of mistrust of government persisted, and

is frequently expressed in proverbs, folk tales, and even high literature.

For more than a thousand years, Islam provided the only universally acceptable set of rules and principles for the regulation of public and social life. Even during the period of maximum European influence, in the countries ruled or dominated by European imperial powers as well as in those that remained independent, Islamic political notions and attitudes remained a profound and pervasive influence.

In recent years there have been many signs that these notions and attitudes may be returning, albeit in much modified forms, to their previous dominance. There are therefore good reasons to devote a serious study to these ideas, and in particular to how they deal with the relations among government, religion, and society.

The term "civil society" has become very popular in recent years, and is used in a number of different—sometimes overlapping, sometimes conflicting—senses. It may therefore be useful to examine Islamic perceptions of civility, according to various definitions of that term.

Perhaps the primary meaning of civil, in the Middle East today, is as the converse of military; it is in this sense that civility must begin, before any other is conceivable. This has a special relevance in a place and at a time when the professional officer corps is often both the source and the instrument of power. Understood this way, Islamic society, at the time of its inception and in its early formative years, was unequivocally civil. The Prophet and the early caliphs that followed employed no professional soldiers but relied for military duties on a kind of armed, mostly voluntary militia.

It is not until the second century of the Islamic era (A.D. eighth century) that one can speak, with certitude, of a professional army. The caliph, who in early though not in later times occasionally commanded his armies, was nevertheless a civilian. So too was the wazir, who, under the caliph's authority, was in charge of all branches of the government, both civil and military. The wazir's emblem of office was an inkpot, which was carried before him on ceremonial public occasions. During the later Middle Ages, internal upheavals and external invasions brought about changes which resulted in the militarization of most Islamic regimes. This has persisted to modern times. During the late 19th and early 20th centuries, there was an interlude of civilian, more or less constitutional government, mostly on Western models. During the 1950s and after, these civilian regimes, for the most part, came to an end and were replaced by authoritarian governments under ultimate military control.

This is, however, by no means universal. In some countries, including, for example, Saudi Arabia and Morocco, traditional monarchies still maintain a traditional civilian order; in others, such as Turkey and, later, Egypt and Pakistan, the military themselves have prepared the way for a return to civilian legality. On the whole, the prospects for civilianization at the present time seem to be reasonably good.

In the more generally accepted interpretation of the term civil society, civil is opposed not to religious or to military but to government as such. So construed, the civil society is one in which the mainsprings of organization, initiative, and action come from within the society rather than from above, from the holders of authority, the wielders of power. Islamic precept, as presented by the jurists and theologians, and Islamic practice, as reflected by the historians, offer a variety of sometimes contradictory precedents.

The tradition of private charity, for example, is old and deeply rooted in Islam, and is given legal expression in the institution of *waqf*. A *waqf* is a pious endowment in mortmain, consisting of some income-producing property, the proceeds of which are dedicated to a pious purpose—the upkeep of a place of worship, a school, a bathhouse, a soup kitchen, a water fountain, and the like. The donor might be a ruler or government official; he might equally be, and very often was, a private person. Women, who in Islamic law had the right to own and dispose of property, figure prominently among founders of *waqfs,* sometimes reaching almost half the number. This is perhaps the only area in the traditional Muslim society in which they approach equality with men. By means of the institution of *waqf,* many services, which in other systems are the principal or sole responsibility of the state, are provided by private initiative. One of the major changes brought by modernizing autocrats in the 19th century was to bring the *waqfs* under state control. (Several present-day Muslim states, including Egypt, have departments or ministries of *waqfs.*)

Islamic law, unlike Roman law and its derivatives, does not recognize corporate legal persons, and there are therefore no Islamic equivalents to such Western corporate entities as the city, the monastery, or the college. Cities were mostly governed by royal officers, while convents and colleges relied on royal or private *waqfs.* There are, however, other groupings of considerable importance in traditional Muslim society. Such, for example, are the kin group—family, clan, tribe; the faith group, often linked together by common membership of a sufi fraternity; the craft group, joined in a guild; the ward or neighborhood within a city. Very often these groups overlap or even coincide, and much of the life of a Muslim city is determined by their interaction.

In the Islamic context, the independence and initiative of the civil society may best be measured not in relation to the state but in relation to religion, of which, in the Muslim perception, the state itself is a manifestation and an instrument. In this sense, the primary meaning of civil is nonreligious, and the civil society is one in which the organizing principle is something other than religion, that being a private affair of the individual. This idea received its first classical formulation in the *Letter Concerning Toleration* by the English philosopher John Locke, published in 1689. Locke's conclusion is that "neither Pagan, nor Mahometan, nor Jew, ought to be excluded from the civil rights of the commonwealth because of his religion."

The first European country which actually accorded civil rights to non-Christians was Holland, followed within a short time by England and the English colonies in North America, where extensive, though not as yet equal rights were granted to nonconformist Christians and to Jews. These examples were followed by others, and the libertarian ideas which they expressed contributed significantly to the ideologies of both the American and French Revolutions.

In time, these ideas were almost universally accepted in Western Christendom. Though few nations, other than France and the United States, accepted a formal constitutional separation of religion and the state, most of them in fact accepted secular principles. This virtually ended the earlier situation which Danish scholar Vilhelm Gronbech spoke of as "a religion which is the soul of society, the obverse of the practical, a living and real religion, the practical relationship of the people to God, soul and eternity, that manifests itself in worship and works as a life-giving power in politics and economics, in crafts and commerce, in ethics as in law. In this sense," he concludes, "the modern state has no religion."

Despite the personal devoutness of great and growing numbers of people, Gronbech is right—the Western democratic state has no religion, and most, even among the devout, see this as a merit, not a defect. They are encouraged in this belief by the example of some states in Central and Eastern Europe, yesterday and today, where the principle of unity and direction was retained but with a shift of stress—religion replaced

Muhammad the Prophet

The Prophet Muhammad (?570–632) lived only 1400 years ago. Of all the founders of major world religions, he is the closest to us in time. Yet historians have struggled to piece together a complete and accurate biography of the man who Muslims believe is the last prophet in the succession of Abraham. Scarce primary sources include the Qur'an and the *Hadith*, traditional accounts of Muhammad's words and deeds. Early biographies (8th–9th centuries)—the *Sirah* (Life) by Ibn Ishaq, the *Maghazi* (Expeditions) by Al-Waqidi, and the writings of Ibn Sa'd—also remain valuable to scholars.

The Prophet was born in Mecca, a prosperous trading town located in the western part of the Arabian Peninsula. Shortly before his birth around 570, the town's preeminent tribe, the Quraysh, appears to have gained control of the lucrative caravan trade running between Yemen and Syria. This new prosperity, according to some historians, may have created a rift between the great merchants and the lesser Quraysh "clans," undermining an older code that emphasized communal wealth and protection through kinship ties.

Muhammad, the son of a respected Quraysh family, was orphaned at six and raised, successively, by his grandfather and uncle. He himself went on to become a successful caravan merchant, and at 25 he married his employer, Khadijah, a wealthy widow (and the first of several wives). Financially secure, Muhammad turned to other, higher matters, and sometime in his late thirties he began to meditate in a hill cave outside of town. Around 610, the faithful believe, he had a vision of the archangel Gabriel, who pronounced Muhammad the "Messenger of God." To his friends and relatives and later to the entire community, Muhammad began to relate messages that he claimed came directly from God.

The central tenet of Muhammad's teachings posed a threat to the polytheistic creed of most of his fellow Arabs: He declared that there was only one good and all-powerful God. He also preached about the coming of a Day of Judgment and the existence of Heaven (the Garden) and Hell (the Fire). Islam literally means submission, and Muhammad's faith called on Muslims (those who submit) to acknowledge God's might and majesty and to accept Muhammad as the final prophet.

Muhammad's preaching was, above all, religious, but it also contained a social message that was troubling to some of Mecca's wealthier merchants. By A.D. 616, many of the Quraysh leaders had grown alarmed by the Prophet's success, and Muhammad began coming under verbal and then physical attack. By this time, too, the Prophet's reputation had begun to spread beyond Mecca. During the summer of 620, six pilgrims from Yathrib, an oasis town 250 miles north of Mecca, came to hear the Prophet preach. Impressed, they begged him to return with them to arbitrate among the rival tribes in their own community. In 622, Muhammad and some 70 of his followers moved to Yathrib; the *Hijra* (migration) marks year one of the Islamic calendar.

Established in Yathrib (which the Muslims renamed al-Madina, the city), Muhammad and his followers soon came into conflict with the pagan oligarchy in Mecca. War broke out and Muhammad's forces, though greatly outnumbered, outfought their foes. Each victory seemed proof of Allah's will, and the Islamic ranks swelled to some 10,000 fighting men. In 630, Muhammad triumphantly returned to Mecca at the head of his army; the city surrendered and many of its inhabitants converted to Islam. Muhammad now ruled as the most powerful political and religious leader in Arabia.

The Prophet, however, had little time to savor his triumph. He died a natural death in 632. Thereafter, a line of caliphs (successors), beginning with Muhammad's faithful lieutenant and father-in-law, 'Abū Bakr, spread the power and faith of Islam. Within little more than a century, Islam had expanded north as far as the Atlas Mountains, east across Persia and central Asia to the borders of India and China, and west across North Africa and into Spain.

---

by ideology, and the church by the single ruling party, with its own hierarchy, synods, inquisition, dogmas, and heresies. In such countries, it was not the state that withered away but the civil society.

In the Islamic world, the dethronement of religion as the organizing principle of society was not attempted until much later and resulted entirely from European influences. It was never really completed and is perhaps now being reversed. Certainly in Iran, organized religion has returned to something like the status which it enjoyed in the medieval world, both Christian and Islamic. Indeed, in some ways—notably in the power of the priesthood and the emergence of a political prelacy—the Iranian theocracy is closer to the Christian than to the classical Islamic model.

During the 14 centuries of Islamic history, there have been many changes. In particular, the long association, sometimes in coexistence, but more often in confrontation, with Christendom, led to the acceptance, in the later Islamic monarchies in Iran and Turkey and their successor states, of patterns of religious organization that might suggest a probably unconscious imitation of Christian ecclesiastical usage. Certainly there is nothing in the classical Islamic past that resembles the more recent offices of the chief mufti of the Ottoman empire or the grand ayatollah of Iran.

These Western influences became more powerful and more important after the French Revolution—the first great movement of ideas in Christendom which was not Christian but was even, in a sense, anti-Christian, and could therefore be considered by Muslim observers with relative detachment. Such earlier movements of ideas in Europe as the Renaissance, the Reformation, or the Enlightenment had no impact whatsoever on the Muslim world, and are virtually unnoticed in contemporary Muslim philosophical and even historical writings. The initial response to the French Revolution was much the same, and the first Muslim comments dismiss it as an internal affair of Christendom, of no interest or concern to Muslims and, more important, offering them no threat.

It was on this last point that they were soon obliged to change their minds. The dissemination of French revolutionary ideas in the Islamic world was not left to chance but was actively promoted by successive French regimes,

Qur'an

Accepted as the word of God by Muslims, the Qur'an, the holy book of Islam, remains the fundamental source of Islamic doctrine, law, thinking, and teaching. It says to its followers, "You are the best nation ever brought forth to men, bidding to honour, and forbidding dishonour, and believing in God" (III, 106).[*]

During Muhammad's life, observes historian Marshall Hodgson in *The Venture of Islam* (1974), it "served at once as the inspiration of Muslim life and the commentary on what was done under that inspiration; its message transcended any particular circumstances yet at the same time served as a running guide to the community experiences, often down to seemingly petty details." The Qur'an (literally "recitations") touches on everything from manners—"O believers, do not enter houses other than your houses until you first ask leave and salute the people thereof . . ." (XXIV, 27)—to the largest questions of spiritual import: "O believers, fear God as He should be feared, and see you do not die, save in surrender" (III, 97).

Scholars distinguish between two main parts of the Qur'an, the whole of which consists of 114 *Surahs* (chapters) of varying numbers of *Ayahs* (verses). The early *Surahs*, revealed to Muhammad while at Mecca, focus upon ethical and spiritual teachings: "Then he whose deeds weigh heavy in the Balance shall inherit a pleasing life, but he whose deeds weigh light in the Balance shall plunge in the womb of the Pit" (CI, 6). *Surahs* revealed later at Medina, however, concern social legislation and the politico-moral principles for constituting and ordering the community. Verses such as "God has promised those

of you who believe and do righteous deeds that He will surely make you successors in the land . . ." (XXIV, 54) point to a concern with the rightful rule.

According to tradition, Muhammad received the verses of the Qur'an at irregular intervals from around A.D. 610 to 632. Many of Muhammad's devout followers memorized the Qur'an, and for a time no comprehensive written collection of the

Surahs existed. After the Prophet's death, and especially after the battle of Yamamah (633), where many who knew the words by heart fell in combat, fear of losing the record of God's word spurred meticulous collection efforts. Several versions resulted. But a desire for consistency led the third caliph, 'Uthmān (ruled 644–656), to order its consolidation, producing the authoritative 'Uthmānic recension now used. 'Uthmān then had all other copies destroyed.

'Uthmān's version, compiled by a handful of learned Muslims, arranges the chapters approximately according to length (except for the opening chapter, longest first). Yet Qur'anic specialists have assembled a rough chronology and identified a handful of recurring themes. The essential message is that there is only one God, Allah, who will judge men by their earthly deeds on the Last Day. Men, therefore, should endeavor to worship God and to act generously in dealings with others.

As Islam became established during the centuries after Muhammad's death, theological and legal questions inevitably arose. What was the correct way for Muslims to pray, to live, to do business, to govern? To deal with such questions, a succession of distinguished theologians and jurists employed three methods: study of the Qur'an; consideration of the precepts and practices of the Prophet, as handed down by tradition; the use of independent reason to apply the first two to problems that arose. (Sunnis, the majority of Muslims, believed that independent reason ceased to be a valid method after the ninth century; Shiites believe that it still is.) The Qur'an remains the ultimate authority to all Muslims, but pious believers have frequently differed over points of interpretation. For example, the Shiites argue that passages on divorce allow temporary marriages for a fixed dower; the Sunnis, however, find no Qur'anic support for such temporary arrangements.

---

[*]Qur'anic quotations are from *The Koran Interpreted,* translated by A. J. Arberry (© George Allen & Unwin Ltd., 1955).

---

both by force of arms, and, much more effectively, by translation and publication. The penetration of Western ideas into the Islamic world was greatly accelerated when, from the early 19th century, Muslim students in increasing numbers were sent to institutions of higher education in France, Italy, and Britain, and later also in other countries. Many of these, on their return home, became carriers of infectious new ideas.

The revolutionaries in France had summarized their ideology in a formula of classical terseness—liberty, equality, fraternity. Some time was to pass before they, and ultimately their disciples else-

where, came to realize that the first two were mutually exclusive and the third meaningless. Of far greater effect, in the impact of Western ideas on Islam, were two related notions—neither of them originating with the French Revolution, but both of them classically formulated and actively disseminated by its leaders: namely, secularism and nationalism. The one sought to displace religion as the ultimate basis of identity, loyalty, and authority in society; the other provided an alternative.

In the new dispensation, God was to be doubly replaced, both as the source of authority and as the object of wor-

ship, by the Nation. Secularism as such had no appeal to Muslims, but an ideology of change and progress, free—as it seemed then—from any taint of a rival religion, offered attractions to 19th-century Muslims who were increasingly aware of the relatively backward and impoverished state of their own society, as contrasted with the wealth and power of Europe. Liberalism and patriotism seemed to be part of the same progressive ideology and were eagerly adopted by young Muslim intellectuals, seeking arguments to criticize and methods to change their own societies. The West European civic patriotism proved to

An illustration from a 13th-century Iraqi manuscript on the pharmaceutical uses of plants. Islamic civilization is known for its contributions to medicine and other sciences.

have limited relevance or appeal, but the ethnic nationalism of Central and Eastern Europe had greater relevance to Middle Eastern conditions, and evoked a much more powerful response. According to the old view, the Muslims are one community, subdivided into such nations as the Turks, the Arabs, the Persians, etc. But according to the new, the Arabs are a nation, subdivided into Muslims and Christians, to which some were, for a while, willing to add Jews.

For a time the idea of the secular nation, defined by country, language, culture, and descent, was dominant among the more or less Westernized minority of political activists. Beginning with the decline and fall of the old Westernized elites in the mid-20th century, and the entry into political life of more authentically popular elements, the ideal of the secular nation came under challenge and in some areas has been decisively defeated.

Nowadays, for the first time in many years, even nationalism itself is under attack and has been denounced by some Muslim writers as divisive and un-Islamic. When Arab nationalists complain that the religious fundamentalists are creating divisions between Muslim and Christian Arabs, the latter respond that the secular nationalists are creating divisions between Arabs and other Muslims and that theirs is the larger and greater offense.

The attack on secularism—seen as an attempt to undermine and supplant the Islamic way of life—has been gathering force and is now a major element in the writings of religious fundamentalists and other similar groups. For these, all the modernizing leaders—Kemal Atatürk in Turkey, the Shah in Iran, Faruq, Nasser, and Sadat alike in Egypt, the Ba'thist rulers of Syria and Iraq, and their equivalents elsewhere—are tarred with the same brush. They are all apostates who have renounced Islam and are trying to impose neo-pagan doctrines and institutions on the Muslim world. Of all the Muslim states, only one, the Turkish republic, has formally declared itself a secular state and legislated, in its constitution, the separation of religion and government. Indonesia, by far the largest Islamic state, includes belief in one God among the basic constitutional principles but does not formally establish Islam. Virtually all the others either proclaim Islam as the state religion or lay down that the laws of the state shall be based on, or inspired by, the holy law of Islam. In fact, many of them had adopted secular legislation, mostly inspired by European models, over a wide range of civil and criminal matters, and it is these laws that are now under strong attack.

This is of particular concern to the two groups which had, in law at least, benefited most from the reforms, namely women and non-Muslims. Hence the phe-nomenon, paradoxical in Western but not in Muslim eyes, that such conventionally liberal causes as equal rights for women have hitherto been espoused and enforced only by autocratic rulers like Kemal Atatürk in Turkey and Mohamed Reza Shah in Iran. For the latter, this was indeed one of the main grievances of the revolutionaries who overthrew him. It has been remedied under their rule.

Until the recent impact of Western secularist ideas, the idea of a non-religious society as something desirable or even permissible was totally alien to Islam. Other religious dispensations, namely Christianity and Judaism, were tolerable because they were earlier and superseded versions of God's revelation, of which Islam itself was the final and perfect version, and therefore lived by a form—albeit incomplete and perhaps debased—of God's law. Those who lacked even this measure of religious guidance were pagans and idolaters, and their society was evil. Any Muslim who sought to join them or imitate them was an apostate.

Some medieval Muslim jurists, confronting a new problem posed by the Christian reconquest, asked whether it was lawful for Muslims to live under non-Muslim rule, and found different answers. According to one view, they might stay, provided that the non-Muslim government allowed them to observe the Muslim religion in all its aspects and to live a full Muslim life; according to another school, no such thing was possible, and Muslims whose homeland was conquered by a non-Muslim ruler were obliged to migrate, as the Prophet did from pagan Mecca to Medina, and seek a haven in Muslim lands, until in God's good time they were able to return and restore the rule of Islam.

One of the tests of civility is surely tolerance—a willingness to coexist with those who hold and practice other beliefs. John Locke, and most other Westerners, believed that the best way to ensure this was to sever or at least to weaken the bonds between religion and state power. In the past, Muslims never professed any such belief. They did however see a certain form of tolerance as an obligation of the dominant Islamic religion. "There is no compulsion in religion" runs a much quoted verse in the Qur'an, and this was generally interpreted by Muslim jurists and rulers to authorize a limited measure of tolerance for certain specified other religious beliefs, though of course without questioning or compromising the primacy of Islam and the supremacy of the Muslims.

Does this mean that the classical Islamic state was a theocracy? In the sense that Britain today is a monarchy, the answer is certainly yes. That is to say that, in the Muslim conception, God is the true sovereign of the community, the ultimate source of authority, the sole source of legislation. In the first extant Muslim account of the British House of Commons, written by a visitor who went to England at the end of the 18th century, the writer expresses his astonishment at the fate of a people who, unlike the Muslims, did not have a divinely revealed law and were therefore reduced to the pitiable expedient of enacting their own laws. But in the sense of a state ruled by the church or by priests, Islam was not and indeed could not be a theocracy. Classical Islam had no priesthood, no prelates who might rule or even decisively influence those who did. The caliph, who was head of a governing institution that was state and church in one, was himself neither a jurist nor a theologian but a prac-

The harem, no pleasure-den, was simply where women and children lived in a Muslim house.

titioner of the arts of politics and sometimes of war. There are no popes in Islamic history and no political cardinals like Wolsey or Richelieu or Alberoni. The office of ayatollah is a creation of the 19th century; the rule of Khomeini an innovation of the 20th.

In most tests of tolerance, Islam, both in theory and in practice, compares unfavorably with the Western democracies as they have developed during the last two or three centuries, but very favorably with most other Christian and post-Christian societies and regimes. There is nothing in Islamic history to compare with the emancipation, acceptance, and integration of other-believers and non-believers in the West. But equally, there is nothing in Islamic history to compare with the Spanish expulsion of Jews and Muslims, the Inquisition, the autos-da-fé, the wars of religion, not to speak of more recent crimes of commission and acquiescence. There were occasional persecutions, but they were rare and atypical, and usually of brief duration, related to local and specific circumstances.

Within certain limits and subject to certain restrictions, Islamic governments were willing to tolerate the practice, though not the dissemination, of other revealed, monotheistic religions. They were able to pass an even severer test by tolerating divergent forms of their own. Even polytheists, though condemned by the strict letter of the law to a choice between conversion and enslavement, were in fact tolerated, as Islamic rule spread to most of India. Only the total unbeliever—the agnostic or atheist—was beyond the pale of tolerance, and even this exclusion was usually enforced only when the offense became public and scandalous. The same standard was applied to the tolerance of deviant forms of Islam.

In modern times, Islamic tolerance has been somewhat diminished. After the second Turkish siege of Vienna in 1683, Islam was a retreating force in the world, and Muslims began to feel threatened by the rise and expansion of the great Christian empires of Eastern and Western Europe. The old-easy-going tolerance, resting on an assumption not only of superior religion but also of superior power, was becoming difficult for Muslims to maintain. The threat which

Christendom now seemed to be offering to Islam was no longer merely military and political, it was beginning to shake the very structure of Muslim society. Western rulers, and, to a far greater extent, their enthusiastic Muslim disciples and imitators, brought in a whole series of reforms, almost all of them of Western origin or inspiration. These reforms increasingly affected the way Muslims lived in their countries, their cities and villages, and finally in their own homes.

These changes were rightly seen as being of Western origin or inspiration; the non-Muslim minorities, mostly Christian but also Jewish, were often seen, sometimes also rightly, as agents or instruments of these changes. The old pluralistic order, multi-denominational and polyethnic, was breaking down, and the tacit social contract on which it was based was violated on both sides. The Christian minorities, inspired by Western ideas of self-determination, were no longer prepared to accept the tolerated but inferior status accorded to them by the old order; and made new demands—sometimes for equal rights within the nation, sometimes for separate nationhood, sometimes for both at the same time. Muslim majorities, feeling threatened, became unwilling to accord even the traditional measure of tolerance.

By a sad paradox, in some of the semi-secularized nation-states of modern times, the non-Muslim minorities, while enjoying complete equality on paper, in fact have fewer opportunities and face greater dangers than under the old Islamic yet pluralistic order. The present regime in Iran, with its ruling clerics, its executions for blasphemy, its consecrated assassins, represents a new departure in Islamic history. In the present mood, a triumph of militant Islam would be unlikely to bring a return to traditional Islamic tolerance—and even that would no longer be acceptable to minority elements schooled on modern ideas of human, civil, and political rights. The emergence of some form of civil society would therefore seem to offer the best hope for decent coexistence based on mutual respect.

The Dome of The Rock: Jerusalem's Epicenter

Written By Walid Khalidi

Islam is the third great monotheistic religion of the world. Its followers, about a billion people, constitute the majority of the population in some 50 countries. Like Judaism and Christianity, Islam has rich and deep associations with the city of Jerusalem.

Islam is an Arabic word which means "submission"; in its religious context it means submission to the will of God alone. The message of Islam was delivered by the Prophet Muhammad, who was born in Makkah, in present-day Saudi Arabia, in the year 570 and died in 632. Such was the power of the divine message he preached that, within 100 years of his death in Madinah, Islam had spread across North Africa, into Spain and across the borders of France in the West, and to the borders of India and China in the East. (See *Aramco World*, November/December 1991.)

Very early in this period—in 637—the forces of Islam won Jerusalem from the Byzantine Empire, whose capital was in Constantinople, signing a treaty by which the holy city was surrendered to 'Umar ibn al-Khattab, the second caliph, or successor, of Muhammad. For the following 1280 years, except for the period between 1109 and 1187, during the Crusades, Jerusalem remained in Muslim hands: In 1917, during World War I, the British took control of the city Muslims call al-Quds, "The Holy."

To understand Jerusalem's position in Islam, we need to look at how Islam sees itself in relation to Judaism and Christianity, to which of course Jerusalem is also sacred.

Islamic doctrine states that God has, since creation, revealed His teachings repeatedly to humankind through a succession of prophets and scriptures. The first of this line was the prophet Noah, according to many Muslim scholars; others believe Adam must be considered the first. But in this line of succession, Muhammad is the last, or "seal" of the prophets, and the teachings revealed to him are the culmination of all the previous messages. Muslims believe that the Qur'an, the literal word of God revealed to Muhammad, follows the Torah and the Gospels as God's final revelation. Thus the Qur'an accords great reverence to the Hebrew prophets, patriarchs and kings who received revelations from God and are associated with Jerusalem. Similarly, Jesus Christ is revered as one of God's most dedicated messengers, and Jerusalem, as the locus of much of his teaching, is further blessed by that association.

To Islam, then, Jerusalem is sacred for many of the reasons it is sacred to Judaism and Christianity, but in addition, it is sacred for specifically Muslim reasons. The most important of these is the Prophet Muhammad's miraculous nocturnal journey, or *isra',* to *Bayt al-Maqdis,* "the house of holiness," in Jerusalem and his ascent from there to heaven—the *mi'raj.* These events are mentioned in a number of verses of the Qur'an, most clearly in the first verse of Chapter 17, titled *Al-Isra'.* Accounts of the Prophet's life supply the details. Led by the angel Gabriel, Muhammad traveled in one night from Makkah to the

site of *al-masjid al-aqsa,* "the furthest mosque," on Mount Moriah, called the Temple Mount, in Jerusalem. The site derives its name from the temples and houses of worship built there over the millennia, including the temple of the prophet Solomon, the temple of Jupiter, the Herodian temple and the al-Aqsa Mosque.

There, Muhammad led Abraham, Moses, Jesus and other prophets in prayer. Then, from a rock on the Temple Mount, Muhammad was taken by Gabriel to heaven itself, to "within two bowlengths" of the very throne of God.

The spot from which the Prophet's ascent began was sanctified in the eyes of Muslims by the *mi'raj*; the Qur'an refers to the prayer site as *al-masjid al-aqsa.* From Muhammad's journey evolved a vast body of Muslim devotional literature, some authentic and some uncanonical, that places Jerusalem at the center of Muslim beliefs concerning life beyond the grave. This literature is in circulation in all the diverse languages spoken by the world's one billion Muslims, most of whom to this day celebrate the anniversary of the *mi'raj.*

Jerusalem is also uniquely linked to one of the "pillars" of the Muslim faith, the five daily prayers. The earliest Muslims, for a time, turned toward Jerusalem to pray. A later revelation transferred the *qibla,* the direction of prayer, to Makkah, but to this day Jerusalem is known as "the first of the two *qiblas.*" And according to Muhammad's teachings, it was during the *mi'raj* that Muslims were ordered by God to pray,

Reprinted from *Aramco World*, September/October 1996, pp. 2-17. © 1996 by Aramco Services Company.

and that the number of the daily prayers was fixed at five.

The center of Muslim power shifted, through the centuries, from one great capital to the next: from Madinah to Umayyad Damascus to Abbasid Baghdad to Mamluk Cairo and to Ottoman Constantinople. But after Jerusalem became part of the Muslim state in 637, whichever dynasty was in control of that

THE NOBLE SANCTUARY

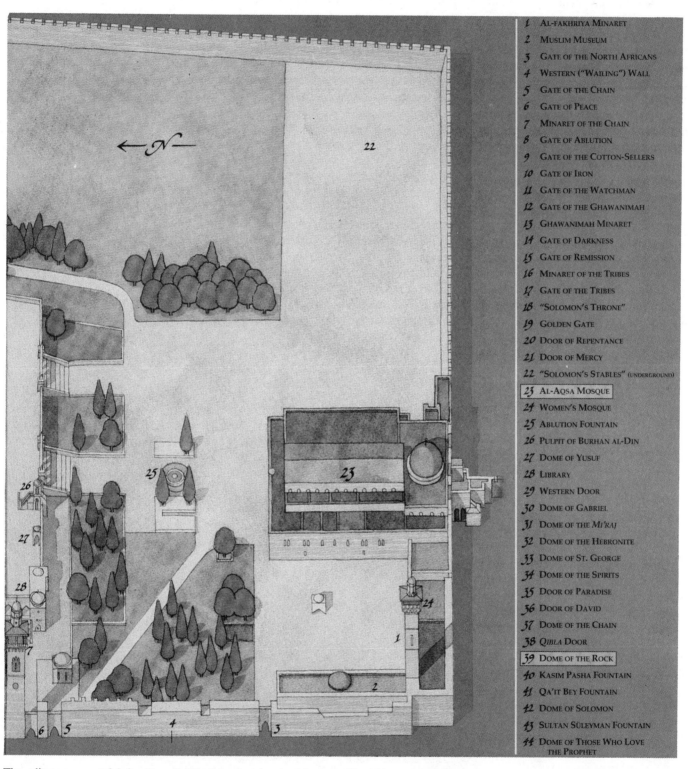

1 AL-FAKHRIYA MINARET
2 MUSLIM MUSEUM
3 GATE OF THE NORTH AFRICANS
4 WESTERN ("WAILING") WALL
5 GATE OF THE CHAIN
6 GATE OF PEACE
7 MINARET OF THE CHAIN
8 GATE OF ABLUTION
9 GATE OF THE COTTON-SELLERS
10 GATE OF IRON
11 GATE OF THE WATCHMAN
12 GATE OF THE GHAWANIMAH
13 GHAWANIMAH MINARET
14 GATE OF DARKNESS
15 GATE OF REMISSION
16 MINARET OF THE TRIBES
17 GATE OF THE TRIBES
18 "SOLOMON'S THRONE"
19 GOLDEN GATE
20 DOOR OF REPENTANCE
21 DOOR OF MERCY
22 "SOLOMON'S STABLES" (UNDERGROUND)
23 AL-AQSA MOSQUE
24 WOMEN'S MOSQUE
25 ABLUTION FOUNTAIN
26 PULPIT OF BURHAN AL-DIN
27 DOME OF YUSUF
28 LIBRARY
29 WESTERN DOOR
30 DOME OF GABRIEL
31 DOME OF THE MI'RAJ
32 DOME OF THE HEBRONITE
33 DOME OF ST. GEORGE
34 DOME OF THE SPIRITS
35 DOOR OF PARADISE
36 DOOR OF DAVID
37 DOME OF THE CHAIN
38 QIBLA DOOR
39 DOME OF THE ROCK
40 KASIM PASHA FOUNTAIN
41 QA'IT BEY FOUNTAIN
42 DOME OF SOLOMON
43 SULTAN SÜLEYMAN FOUNTAIN
44 DOME OF THOSE WHO LOVE
    THE PROPHET

The editors are grateful for the valuable help they received in compiling this map and checking it for accuracy. Thanks to architectural photographer Saïd Nuseibeh, whose book *The Dome of The Rock,* was published by Rizzoli (1996); to Jeff Spurr of the Aga Khan Program for Islamic Architecture and the Visual Collections of the Fine Arts Library at Harvard University; to Ahmad Nabal of the Aga Khan Visual Archives, Rotch Visual Collection, Massachusetts Institute of Technology; and to Dr. Walid Khalidi.

city lavished it with care and attention in the form of public monuments: mosques, colleges for the study of the Qur'an and the traditions of the Prophet, hospitals, hospices, fountains, orphanages, caravansarais, baths, convents for mystics, pools and mausolea. This is why Jerusalem's Old City, within the 16th-century walls built by the Ottoman sultan Süleyman, strikes the modern-day visitor with its predominantly Muslim character.

Caliph 'Umar personally came to Jerusalem to accept the city's surrender from the Byzantines, and visited the site of *al-masjid al-aqsa,* known to some Muslims today as *al-Haram al-Maqdisi al-Sharif,* "the Noble Sanctuary of Jerusalem," or simply *al-Haram al-Sharif.* The site lay vacant and in ruins; 'Umar ordered it cleaned, and, tradition says, took part in the work himself, carrying dirt in his own robe. When the site had been cleansed and sprinkled with scent, 'Umar and his followers prayed there, near the rough rock from which Muhammad had ascended to heaven.

Two generations later, about 691, the Umayyad caliph 'Abd al-Malik ibn Marwan's Syrian craftsmen built in the same location the earliest masterpiece of Islamic architecture, the Dome of the Rock *(Qubbat al Sakhra)*—the octagonal sanctuary, centered on the rock, whose golden dome still dominates the skyline of Old Jerusalem. 'Abd al-Malik's son al-Walid, who ruled from 705 to 715, built the second major monument, the al-Aqsa Mosque, also on the Temple Mount.

The octagonal plan of the Dome of the Rock may not have been accidental. Cyril Glassé, in his *Concise Encyclopedia of Islam,* points out that "the octagon is a step in the mathematical series going from square, symbolizing the fixity of earthly manifestation, to circle, the natural symbol for the perfection of heaven.... In traditional Islamic architecture this configuration symbolizes the link between earth ... and heaven...." Nor is it coincidence that the elegant calligraphy that encircles the structure inside and out—240 meters, or 785 feet,

of it—includes all the Qur'anic verses about the prophet Jesus. "The calligraphic inscriptions," writes Glassé, "recall the relationship between Jerusalem and Jesus ... ; and the architecture, above all the octagonal form supporting a dome, is symbolic of the ... ascent to heaven by the Prophet, and thus by man." Mount Moriah, with the Dome of the Rock at its center, is thus "the place where man, as man, is joined once more to God...."

History, tradition and symbolism intersect in this building, whose presence suffuses Jerusalem.

Dr. Walid Khalidi was educated in London and Oxford and has taught at Oxford University, the American University of Beirut and Harvard University. Since 1982, he has been a senior research fellow at Harvard's Center for Middle Eastern Studies. Members of his family have served Jerusalem as scholars, judges, diplomats and members of parliament since the late 12th century.

The reason God tested Abraham

And other revelations from a half century of Dead Sea Scrolls scholarship

By Jeffrey L. Sheler

In 1947, the year that a Bedouin shepherd stumbled upon a stash of ancient jars while exploring a rocky cave in the Judean desert, Emanuel Tov was 5 years old and living in the Netherlands. The desert find proved to be monumental: Hidden inside the jars were hundreds of brittle manuscripts, including some of the earliest known texts of the Bible and other early Jewish writings.

By the time Tov was 10, the first of the Dead Sea Scrolls had found their way into the hands of biblical scholars, who began the painstaking task of reconstructing and deciphering the documents—some of which had disintegrated into fragments the size of a dime. The work was agonizingly slow, and as the scholars labored, Tov grew up, went to college, and became a Bible professor at Hebrew University in Jerusalem. Now, at 55, he has become the leader of the scholarly team still toiling to complete the task. "It has been a long and arduous process," says Tov, "but we are near the end."

In late July, Tov and other biblical scholars from around the world will gather in Jerusalem to commemorate a half century of scroll research. In the 50 years since their discovery near the desert ruins of Qumran, the scrolls have fascinated and amazed but also stirred frustration and controversy. They reveal a Bible much more unsettled, a Judaism much more diverse, and a fledgling Christianity much more Jewish than anyone previously had imagined.

The glacial pace of publication has infuriated many scholars, who for years were excluded from examining the scrolls—a task reserved for a small cadre of experts. The delays even triggered speculation that the scrolls contained explosive material that might topple Christianity. But suspicion dissipated as the documents slowly made their way to public view. The logjam broke in 1991, when a California library released photographic images of the remaining unpublished fragments. Since then, research and publication have accelerated. Roughly 80 percent of the scrolls' content has now been published by Oxford University Press in an official series, *Discoveries in the Judean Desert.* Tov says the final volumes may be completed by the year 2000.

Biblical potpourri. The Qumran cache consists of scrolls or fragments from 800 different documents written between about 200 B.C. and A.D. 50. About 127 of them are biblical texts, including the oldest known versions of the Old Testament minus the book of Esther. The remainder are biblical commentaries, prayers, prophecies, hymns, and sectarian rules of conduct and worship.

On the whole, says Eugene Ulrich, a University of Notre Dame professor and editor of the biblical texts, the scrolls show that the Hebrew Bible "has been amazingly accurately preserved" through centuries of hand-copying. One scroll that contains a major portion of the book of Isaiah, for example, shows only 13 minor variations from the modern version.

Yet among the multiple copies of some biblical texts discovered at Qumran, scholars have found that "variant literary editions" of the Bible existed side by side. That, says Ulrich, suggests that at the time there was in Judaism no single "authorized" version. The sacred texts, he theorizes, were updated occasionally with new theological ideas or to explain changing historical circumstances. Only later, when doctrinal debates arose between Christians and Jews, did religious leaders settle on preferred editions of the Hebrew Bible.

Roughly half the Old Testament texts at Qumran contain passages that do not appear in modern translations, or they omit passages that appear in later texts. Some variations are startling. Among them:

■ A new collection of Psalms containing nine compositions not included in the traditional Bible. The texts claim King David as their author. One declares that David wrote the book "through prophecy given him by the Most High." Most scholars doubt that David actually wrote the unfamiliar Psalms. Even so, says Ulrich, it is likely the collection was accepted as a biblical book by its readers 2,000 years ago.

■ A new passage in the book of 1 Samuel that may help explain the "missing prophecy" referred to in the Nativity story that appears in the Gospel of Matthew. Matthew cites five ancient prophecies that he says were fulfilled by the birth of Jesus. Four of those appear in the traditional Hebrew Bible. The fifth prophecy—that the messiah "will be called a Nazorean"—does not. "It is clear," says Ulrich, "that Matthew was reading an edition of the biblical prophets that we don't have." The location of that prophecy remains a mystery. But Ulrich says a passage in the Qumran version of 1 Samuel contains language that "is startlingly close."

■ A new version of the book of Joshua that portrays the invading Israelites building an altar to the Lord immediately after crossing the Jordan River at Gilgal. In the traditional Bible, the Israelites erect the altar far to the north on Mount Ebal and then inexplicably abandon it and return to the south. Scroll scholars now think the traditional passage may have been edited. The Qumran version, says Ulrich, "makes

much more sense" and is corroborated by the Jewish historian Josephus.

■ A provocative rewrite of the story of Abraham's near sacrifice of his son Isaac. In the traditional Bible, God commands Abraham to sacrifice Isaac. At the last second, an angel stays Abraham's knife and points to a ram trapped in a thicket as a substitute sacrifice. The biblical tale, says James VanderKam, a scroll editor and professor at the University of Notre Dame, has always posed a difficult theological question: How could God tempt Abraham to slay his son? The Qumran text, says VanderKam, attempts to "soften the blow of God's action" by introducing a Satan figure, called Mastemah or "prince of malevolence," who goads God into the test. God thus does not originate the evil but merely countenances it and permits Abraham to prove his faithfulness.

Mystery authors. Some corrections based on the Qumran texts already have been incorporated into the latest editions of the Bible. But other issues still divide scholars. One is the nature and identity of the people who wrote the documents and hid them from Roman invaders in the caves near Qumran. The strongest theory is still that the scrolls belonged to a zealous sect of ascetic Jews known as Essenes, who withdrew to the desert to await an apocalyptic messiah. But some scholars now think the scrolls may

have been transported from Jerusalem shortly before the Roman invasion. If that is true, says Hershel Shanks, editor of the *Biblical Archaeology Review,* the diversity of views contained in the scrolls suggests that "mainstream Judaism" of the era "was much more pluralistic" than scholars previously had thought.

While no Christian writings were discovered in the Qumran caves, the scrolls have shed important new light on the religious milieu that gave rise to Christianity. Some texts contain themes and images that closely parallel those in the New Testament. References in some fragments to the "Son of God," the "Son of the Most High," and to the spiritual dichotomy between the powers of darkness and light, for example, indicate that those ideas—long thought to be of Christian or even Greek origin—were present in Judaism before Christianity arrived on the scene. "Early Christianity, we learn, was not a hybrid of Judaism and Hellenism," write authors Michael Wise, Martin Abegg, and Edward Cook in *The Dead Sea Scrolls: A New Translation.* "It was rooted in the native soil of Palestine."

After a half century of study, that may prove to be the most important finding of Emanuel Tov and his colleagues. The scrolls of Qumran are a powerful reminder of the shared heritage of these two faiths.

2000 Years of Jesus

For believers, he is the hinge of history. But even by secular standards, Jesus is the dominant figure of Western culture. How Christian ideas shaped the modern world—for good and, sometimes, for ill.

By Kenneth L. Woodward

Historians did not record his birth. Nor, for 30 years, did anyone pay him much heed. A Jew from the Galilean hill country with a reputation for teaching and healing, he showed up at the age of 33 in Jerusalem during Passover. In three years, he was arrested, tried and convicted of treason, then executed like the commonest of criminals. His followers said that God raised him from the dead. Except among those who believed in him, the event passed without notice.

Two thousand years later, the centuries themselves are measured from the birth of Jesus of Nazareth. At the end of this year, calendars in India and China, like those in Europe, America and the Middle East, will register the dawn of the third millennium. It is a convention, of course: a fiction and function of Western cultural hegemony that allows the birth of Jesus to number the days for Christians and non-Chris-

tians alike. For Christians, Jesus is the hinge on which the door of history swings, the point at which eternity in-

---

LAMB OF GOD

For every time and place, we reimagine and reimage Jesus," says Thomas Lucas, professor of fine arts at the University of San Francisco. But some imagery—such as the agony of crucifixion, a symbol of the redemptive power of suffering—has had special resonance over the last two millennia.

---

tersects with time, the Savior who redeems time by drawing all things to himself. As the second millennium draws to a close, nearly a third of the

world's population claims to be his followers.

But by any secular standard, Jesus is also the dominant figure of Western culture. Like the millennium itself, much of what we now think of as Western ideas, inventions and values finds its source or inspiration in the religion that worships God in his name. Art and science, the self and society, politics and economics, marriage and the family, right and wrong, body and soul—all have been touched and often radically transformed by Christian influence. Seldom all at once, of course—and not always for the better. The same Jesus who preached peace was used to justify the Crusades and the Inquisition. The same gospel he proclaimed has underwritten both democracy and the divine right of kings. Often persecuted—even today—Christians have frequently persecuted others, including other Christians. As Pope John Paul II

MIRACLE WORKER

One of the most important functions of religious art throughout the ages has been to bring Jesus' story alive for the many unlettered believers who would never hold a Bible in their own hands. Depictions of miracles like the healing of the sick, the raising of the dead and the story of the loaves and fishes are a reminder of the transformative power with which God endowed his son—and the compassion that first endeared him to humanity.

---

has repeatedly insisted, Christians cannot welcome the third millennium without repenting of their own sins.

This millennial moment invites historical reflection: how has Christianity shaped the way we think about God, about ourselves, about how individuals ought to live and the way that societies are to be organized? As scholars have long realized, there was little in the teachings *of* Jesus that cannot be found in the Hebrew Scriptures he expounded. From this angle, says theologian Krister Stendahl of Harvard Divinity School, "Christianity became a Judaism for the Gentiles." But the New Testament is primarily Scripture *about* Jesus—the Risen Christ as Lord. This message was something altogether new. Like a supernova, the initial impact of Christianity on the ancient Greco-Roman world produced shock waves that continued to register long after the Roman Empire disappeared.

A NEW CONCEPTION OF GOD

THE FIRST CHRISTIANS WERE JEWS WHO preached in the name of Jesus. But Jesus wasn't all that they preached. As Jewish

monotheists, they believed in one God—the father to whom Jesus was obedient unto death. But they also worshiped Jesus as his "only begotten Son" conceived through the power of the Holy Spirit. This experience of God as three-in-one was implicit in the New Testament, but defied efforts to fit into the traditional monotheistic mold. By "asking Greek questions of Hebrew stories," says theologian David Tracy of the University of Chicago Divinity School, the early church fathers developed a doctrine of God that was—and remains—unique among world religions. "All monotheists tend to make God into a transcendent individual standing outside time and outside all relationships," Tracy observes. "Now, as in modern physics, we are coming to see that all of reality is interrelated. The doctrine of the Trinity says that even the divine reality in all its incomprehensible mystery is intrinsically relational." In short, Christianity bequeathed to Western culture a God who revealed himself definitively in the person of Jesus, and who continues to redeem the world by the work of the Holy Spirit. Time itself was

---

What is your religious preference?

PERCENT RESPONDING

62	Protestant
20	Roman Catholic
7	No religion
4	Non-Christian
3	Jewish

Do you think Jesus Christ ever actually lived?

PERCENT RESPONDING "YES"

93	Christians
68	Non-Christians

SON OF MAN

While the earliest depictions of Jesus often presented a distant, almost imperial Christ, artists later came to focus on the humanity of God's only son. "Everyone understands what a baby is about," says Professor Lucas. "There is no more vivid way of showing God's vulnerability in the person of Jesus than a tender scene of the infant in the manger."

---

transformed: where the Greeks and Romans thought of the universe as fixed and eternal, Christianity—building on the Hebrew prophets—injected into Western consciousness the notion of the future as the work of God himself.

BREAKING THE BOUNDARIES

TO A WORLD RULED BY FATE AND THE whims of capricious gods, Christianity brought the promise of everlasting life. At the core of the Christian faith was the assertion that the crucified Jesus was resurrected by God and present in the church as "the body of Christ." The message was clear: by submitting to death, Jesus had destroyed its power, thereby making eternal life available to everyone. This Christian affirmation radically changed the relationship between the living and the dead as Greeks and Romans understood it. For them, only the gods were immortal—that's what made them gods. Philosophers might achieve immortality of the soul, as Plato taught, but the view from the street was that human consciousness survived in the dim and affectless underworld of Hades. "The Resurrection is an enormous answer to the problem of death," says Notre Dame theologian John Dunne. "The idea is that the Chris-

How important is it to you that non-Christians convert to Christianity?

PERCENT RESPONDING "VERY IMPORTANT"

72	Evangelical Protestants
25	Other Protestants
17	Catholics

Do you believe that Jesus Christ rose from the dead after dying on the cross?

PERCENT RESPONDING "YES"

88	Christians
32	Non-Christians

tian goes with Christ through death to everlasting life. Death becomes an event, like birth, that is lived through."

Once death lost its power over life, life itself took on new meaning for believers. Sociologist Rodney Stark of the University of Washington sees dramatic evidence of this in the high Christian survival rates during the plagues that repeatedly hit the citizens of the ancient Roman Empire. "The Romans threw people out into the street at the first symptoms of disease, because they knew it was contagious and they were afraid of dying," says Stark. "But the Christians stayed and nursed the sick. You could only do that if you thought, 'So what if I die? I have life eternal'."

Indeed, those who were martyred for the faith were revered as saints and heavenly "friends of God" who could intercede for the faithful below. Their bones became sacred relics, their tombs

the sites of pilgrimage. Thus was the Christian cult of the saints born, a reverencing of the dead and their bodies that confounded Rome's elites. "You keep adding many corpses newly dead to the corpse [Christ] of long ago," complained Emperor Julian, a fourth-century persecutor of Christians. "You have filled the whole world with tombs and sepulchers." Eventually, churches were built over the tombs of saints (the Vatican's Basilica of St. Peter is the most famous example) and cemeteries were turned into cities.

INVERSION OF VALUES

AS THE SIGN OF THE NEW RELIGION, THE cross signified much more than Christ's victory over death. It also symbolized an inversion of accepted norms. Suffering was noble rather than merely pathetic when accepted in imitation of the crucified Christ. Forgiveness—even of one's enemies—became the sign of the true Christian. More radically, Jesus taught that in the kingdom of God the last would be first, the first last. "In the New Testament, you find Jesus more among the beggars than the rulers, the sick than the healthy, the women and children than the conquerors, the prostitutes and lepers than the holy people," says Martin Marty, director of the Public Religion Project at the University of Chicago.

Christianity also challenged prevailing notions of the virtuous life. Where Aristotle had touted prudence, justice, courage and temperance as the virtues proper to the good life, Jesus emphasized the blessedness of humility, patience and peacemaking in his crowning Sermon on the Mount. Where the Buddha taught compassion as an *attitude* of the Enlightened, Jesus demanded deeds: "In truth I tell you, in so far as you did this to one of the least of these brothers of mine, you did it to me." In Roman times, Christian compassion was manifest in special concern for widows, orphans, the aged and infirm. When Saint Lawrence, an early Christian martyr and deacon of the nascent church, was ordered by Roman authorities to reveal the church's treasures, he showed them the hungry and the sick. Twenty centuries

later, the same attitude can be seen in the work of exceptional contemporary figures (usually women) like Dorothy Day and Mother Teresa. "The idea," says Marty, is "the poor are my masters."

DISCOVERING THE INDIVIDUAL

IF, AS HAROLD BLOOM HAS LATELY ARgued, Shakespeare "invented the human," it can be said—with equal hyperbole—that Christianity "discovered" the individual. In the ancient world, individuals were recognized as members of tribes or nations or families, and conducted themselves accordingly. For Jews, this means—as now—that one's relationship with God depends upon the prior covenant he has made with Israel as his chosen people. But the Gospels are replete with scenes in which Jesus works one on one, healing this woman's sickness, forgiving that man's sins and calling each to personal conversion. He invites Jews and Gentiles alike to enter God's kingdom. "Christianity discovers individuality in the sense that it stresses personal conversion," says Bernard McGinn, professor of historical theology at the University of Chicago Divinity School. "This is a crucial contribution to Western civilization because it releases the individual from the absolute constraints of family and society."

The sense of self deepened. Prayer became more personal. As Jesus himself taught, God could be addressed as "Abba"—the equivalent of "Dad." But as the possibility of intimacy with God increased, so did the interior sense of personal unworthiness. As a moralist, Jesus had set the bar high: those who even looked on another's wife with sexual desire, he declared, committed "adultery in the heart." With the evolution of the Roman Catholic Church came the practice of personal confession and repentance. And in the Confessions of Saint Augustine (354–430), we have the first great document in the history of what Stendahl has called "the introspective conscience of the West." A towering figure whose shadow stretched

LIGHT OF THE WORLD

How do you show the power of God—the divinity of Jesus that set him apart, which made him more than a man? Many painters used an unearthly glow to remind their viewers that Jesus was indeed not of this world; even the crudest early mosaics and the darkest crucifixion scenes are suffused with a glow that shines out of the body of Christ: the light of God shining through our humanity.

across the Middle Ages and touched a tormented Martin Luther, Augustine remains to this day the father of autobiography, the first great psychologist and the author who anticipated—by a millennium and a half—the modern novel's explorations of individual self-consciousness.

REDEFINING MALE AND FEMALE

IN ROMAN AS IN JEWISH SOCIETY, WOMEN were regarded as inherently inferior to men. Husbands could divorce their wives but wives could not divorce their husbands. In rabbinic circles, only males were allowed to study the Torah. Jesus challenged these arrangements. Although he called only men to be his apostles, Jesus readily accepted women into his circle of friends and disciples. He also banned divorce, except in cases of adultery.

The early Christians heeded his example. In its initial stages, at least, the church strove to become an egalitarian society: in Christ, wrote Paul, "there is neither Jew nor Greek, slave nor free man, male or female." Although Paul's household code for Christians (Ephesians 5:22–23) called for wives to be

subordinate to their husbands, both were equally subject to God.

Christianity's appeal for women was a major reason that it grew so rapidly in competition with other religions of the Roman Empire. Then, as now, most Christians were women. The new religion offered women not only greater status and influence within the church but also more protection as wives and mothers. For one thing, the church did away with the common practice of marrying girls of 11 or 12 to much older men. The result was a stronger, "more symmetrical marriage," says sociologist Stark. For another, Christianity carried over from Jewish tradition a profound respect for marriage. Eventually, the Catholic Church made marriage a sacrament, declaring the bond between Christian husband and wife insoluble.

In an even more radical challenge to the social mores of the ancient world, the church made room for virgins—both male and female—who consecrated their lives to Christ. In this way, says McGinn, consecrated Christian virgins "broke the bonds by which families controlled the fate of their members"—especially women. Thus, Christianity made it possible for celibate females or males to claim a complete life and identity apart from marriage and procreation.

The church also protected children from the whims of tyrannical fathers. Under Roman law, fathers could and often did commit infanticide. Female babies were especially vulnerable because they were nothing but an expense. From a study of gravestones at Delphi, Stark says, we know that of 600 upperclass families, "only half a dozen raised more than one daughter." From the beginning, Christians also opposed abortion, defending both mother and child from barbarous procedures that often left women either dead or sterile.

In a less direct way, Christianity also transformed the way that masculinity was defined throughout the ancient world. In place of the dominant image of the male as warrior, Jesus counseled men to be peacemakers—to "turn the other cheek" rather than strike back. "A woman preaching that people must be patient and meek and mild would have sounded just like a woman," argues Michael Novak, who cov-

THE GLOBAL JESUS

As believers—and artists—all over the world can attest, the image and ideal of Jesus belongs to everybody. "The Christ of faith is so much bigger than his three decades in Judea at the beginning of the first millennium," says Professor Lucas. "Look at an African crucifixion scene, or a Chinese nativity. Jesus is constantly being remythologized according to the needs and longings of the times."

ers religion and public policy at the American Enterprise Institute— and, he implies, would have been dismissed by men. But to believe, as Christians did, that this was the Son of God speaking meant that Christians could never make war with a clear conscience.

OPPOSITION TO WAR

NONVIOLENCE WAS EASY TO ESPOUSE AS long as Christians had no power. As Yale church historian Jaroslav Pelikan observes, "They never imagined that Caesar might become a Christian"—which he did when Constantine converted in 312—much less that theirs would become the official religion of the Roman Empire. With establishment came the power to wage war and to stamp out heretics. From his imperial throne in Constantinople, Constantine did both as protector of the church. But in the West, as "eternal" Rome fell to invaders from the North, Augustine laid down severe restrictions if the conduct of war between states is to be considered just. Among other principles outlined in his monumental "The City of God," Augustine said that only defensive wars could be justified. They should be brief, a last resort and never for spoils or gains. The means of war should never be excessive but always proportional to its goals. Noncombatants were to be immune from harm, and once the war was over, the aim of the winners was to be peace, not revenge.

While Augustine's just-war principles have never prevented wars from happening—including those waged in Jesus' name—they have, over the centuries, at least prompted some statesmen to try to make warfare less barbarous. We are still a long way from nonviolence. "But before Christ," notes Stark, "conquerors butchered people for the hell of it."

Ironically, once Christianity was identified with the state, many Christians found it more difficult to follow Christ than when they were a persecuted sect. To escape an increasingly worldly and compromised church, many Christian men and women fled to the desert (as some Jewish sects before them had done), where they could live in complete poverty, chastity and obedience. These became the basis of the Rule of Saint Benedict—"one of the most influential documents of Western civilization," according to Pelikan—which established monastic communities as places set apart for those called to fully "participate in the life of Christ."

The effects of monasticism on Western society can hardly be exaggerated. For more than a millennium, the monasteries produced saints who established the diverse forms of Christian mysticism and spirituality that are so much in revival today. The monks were also the church's reformers, calling popes to task for their worldliness and eventually becoming popes themselves. Through the example of the monks, celibacy became required of bishops in the East and, eventually, of all priests in the West.

MONKS AND MODERNITY

IT WAS THE MONKS WHO BECAME CHRIStianity's greatest missionaries, planting the church in England, Ireland and other outposts of no-longer eternal Rome. As the barbarians dismantled the empire, the monks copied and later disseminated the Latin classics, thus preserving much of the old civilization and laying the foundations of the new. They also cre-

ated music and chants, magnificent liturgies and marvelous illuminated manuscripts. In the so-called Dark Ages—a fiction created by anti-religious *philosophes* of the French Enlightenment—it was the monks who founded the first European universities in cities like Paris and Bologna. It was a Dominican friar, Thomas Aquinas, who crowned the Middle Ages with his towering synthesis of philosophy and theology, the "Summa Theologica." And it was another monk, Martin Luther, who fathered the Protestant Reformation.

One measure of Christian influence on Western culture is the extent to which innovations of the church have survived in secular form. The law is a prime example. "Much of medieval canon law has passed over—often unnoticed—into the laws of the state," says Harold Berman, professor of law emeritus at Harvard law school. "And many of the legal reforms the medieval papacy promoted command respect even seven and eight centuries later." Among them: rational trial procedures, which replaced trial by ordeal; the necessity of consent as the foundation of marriage; the need to show wrongful intent for conviction of crime, and legal protection of the poor against the rich.

The legacy of medieval "Christendom" had its darker side as well. From Christmas Day in 800, when Pope Leo III crowned Charlemagne as "Holy Roman Emperor," politics and religion were seldom separate. The results were mixed at best. Had the secular powers not defended Christianity, Europe might well be Muslim today. But the medieval Crusades to rescue the Holy Land from the Turks became excuses for plunder by conscripted thugs. Once church and state were yoked, almost any military action could be justified.

Although the New Testament contains no outline for a Christian society, medieval Christianity was one long effort to establish one. The doctrine the church preached became the doctrine the king enforced. Even Augustine had reluctantly concluded that the secular arm of society could be used to crush heresy. Acting on the premise that error has no rights, the church created the Inquisition, dispatching traveling squads

of Franciscans and Dominicans to ferret out heretics. In 1252 Pope Innocent IV allowed suspects to be tortured. The guilty were imprisoned and sometimes put to death. Two centuries later, the Spanish monarchs Ferdinand and Isabella created a separate Inquisition aimed at discovering and expelling converted Jews and Muslims who secretly

---

In the next millennium, which one of the following do you think should be organized Christianity's top priority?

PERCENT CHRISTIANS RESPONDING

38	Returning to traditional moral values
32	Spreading the faith
13	Increasing tolerance
7	Righting social ills

---

practiced their own religion. Even old women and children were tortured, and their descendants barred from universities and public office. In subsequent centuries Inquisitors expanded their list of heretics to include suspected Protestants and practitioners of witchcraft. Altogether, the Inquisition remains a monument to religious intolerance and a reminder of what can happen when church and state share total authority.

The Reformation shattered the old Christendom but also unleashed new energies. Protestants translated the Bible into vernacular languages and encouraged lay learning and initiative. From Europe, Christian missionaries dispersed to Asia, Africa and the Americas. In many cases, it was a matter of the cross following the flag—a shameless blessing of imperialism and colonialism. But there are other ways of measuring the missionaries' impact. From the 16th-century Jesuits to the 19th-century Protestants, missionaries developed written languages for many "indigenous" peoples who had none—not to mention grammars and dictionaries. In this way, Protestant and Catholic missionaries "preserved local cultures that otherwise would have been swept away by global forces," says Mark Noll, professor of history at Wheaton College. The missionaries also established countless schools and hospitals, bringing literacy and modern medicine to those that the indigenous elites ignored. "Nelson Mandela," notes Noll, " is a graduate of two missionary schools."

As the world moves toward the third millennium, Christianity seems far removed from the Jesus movement of its birth. And yet, the same gospel is being preached. Christians are still being persecuted: in the 20th century alone, there were many times more martyrs—especially under Hitler and Stalin—than all the victims of the Caesars combined. But the differences from times past are also striking. Post-Christian Europe seems spiritually exhausted. In the United States, secularism is the reigning ideology. However, there is more unity among Christians now than at any time since the Reformation. Despite the Holocaust—or perhaps because of it— "the people to whom Jesus belonged, and the people who belong to Jesus," as Pelikan puts it, are no longer spiritual enemies. Science and religion, once thought to be implacable adversaries, are beginning to talk to each other: the hubris of the Enlightenment has run its course.

Numerically, it is already clear, the future of Christianity lies with the youthful churches of Africa, the Hispanics of the Americas and—who knows?— the millions of stalwart Christians in China. Christianity already comprises the most diverse society known to humankind. But what new ideas and forms the gospel will inspire await the birth of the third millennium. Of the future, the Book of Revelation has only this to say: "Behold, I make all things new."

Live Longer, Healthier, & Better

The untold benefits of becoming a Christian in the ancient world.

by Rodney Stark

Constantine, the first Christian to rule Rome, governed for 31 years and died in bed of natural causes at a time when the average imperial reign was short and emperors' lives usually came to violent ends.

That he lived to old age illustrates a more general, if not widely known, early Christian achievement: Christians in the ancient world had longer life expectancies than did their pagan neighbors.

Modern demographers regard life expectancy as the best indicator of quality of life, so in all likelihood, Christians simply lived better lives than just about everyone else.

In fact, many pagans were attracted to the Christian faith because the church produced tangible (not only "spiritual") blessings for its adherents.

WHY CHRISTIANS LIVED LONGER

Chief among these tangibles was that, in a world entirely lacking social services, Christians were their brothers' keepers. At the end of the second century, Tertullian wrote that while pagan temples spent their donations "on feasts and drinking bouts," Christians spent theirs "to support and bury poor people, to supply the wants of boys and girls destitute of means and parents, and of old persons confined to the house."

Similarly, in a letter to the bishop of Antioch in 251, the bishop of Rome mentioned that "more than 1,500 widows and distressed persons" were in the care of his congregation. These claims concerning Christian charity were confirmed by pagan observers.

"The impious Galileans support not only their poor," complained pagan emperor Julian, "but ours as well."

The willingness of Christians to care for others was put on dramatic public display when two great plagues swept the empire, one beginning in 165 and the second in 251. Mortality rates climbed higher than 30 percent. Pagans tried to avoid all contact with the afflicted, often casting the still living into the gutters. Christians, on the other hand, nursed the sick even though some believers died doing so.

The results of these efforts were dramatic. We now know that elementary nursing—simply giving victims food and water without any drugs—will reduce mortality in epidemics by as much as two-thirds. Consequently Christians were more likely than pagans to recover—a visible benefit. Christian social services also were visible and valuable during the frequent natural and social disasters afflicting the Greco-Roman world: earthquakes, famines, floods, riots, civil wars, and invasions.

GIRL POWER

Women greatly outnumbered men among early converts. However, in the empire as a whole, men vastly outnumbered women. There were an estimated 131 men for every 100 women in Rome. The disparity was even greater elsewhere and greater still among the elite.

Widespread female infanticide had reduced the number of women in society. "If you are delivered of a child," wrote a man named Hilarion to his pregnant wife, "if it is a boy, keep it, if it is a girl discard it." Frequent abortions "entailing great risk" (in the words of Celsus) killed many women and left even more barren.

The Christian community, however, practiced neither abortion nor infanticide and thus drew to itself women.

More importantly, within the Christian community women enjoyed higher status and security than they did among their pagan neighbors. Pagan women typically were married at a young age (often before puberty) to much older men. But Christian women were older when they married and had more choice in whom, and even if, they would marry.

From *Christian History,* February 1998, pp. 28-30. © 1998 by Rodney Stark. Reprinted by permission of the author.

In addition, Christian men could not easily divorce their wives, and both genders were subject to strongly enforced rules against extramarital sex.

Christian women benefitted further from their considerable status *within* the church. We have it from the apostle Paul that women held positions of leadership, as was confirmed by Pliny the Younger, who reported to Emperor Trajan that he had tortured two young Christian women "who were called deaconesses."

URBAN SANCTUARY

Yet the early church attracted and held members of both sexes, and not just because it offered longer life and raised social standing. Christianity also offered a strong community in a disorganized, chaotic world.

Greco-Roman cities were terribly overpopulated. Antioch, for example, had a population density of about 117 inhabitants per acre—more than three times that of New York City today.

Tenement cubicles were smoky, dark, often damp, and always dirty. The smell of sweat, urine, feces, and decay permeated everything. Outside on the street, mud, open sewers, and manure lay everywhere, and even human corpses were found in the gutters. Newcomers and strangers, divided into many ethnic groups, harbored bitter antagonism that often erupted into violent riots.

For these ills, Christianity offered a unifying subculture, bridging these divisions and providing a strong sense of common identity.

To cities filled with the homeless and impoverished, Christianity offered charity and hope. To cities filled with newcomers and strangers, Christianity offered an immediate fellowship. To cities filled with orphans and widows, Christianity provided a new and expanded sense of family.

In short, Christianity offered a longer, more secure, and happier life.

THE EMOTIONAL BENEFITS OF MARTYRDOM

It seems obvious that in periods of persecution, church membership would decrease dramatically. In fact, persecutions rarely occurred, and only a tiny number of Christians were ever martyred—only "hundreds, not thousands" according to historian William H. C. Frend. Usually only bishops and other prominent figures were singled out for martyrdom. The actual threat to rank-and-file Christians was quite small.

However, the martyrdoms played a crucial role in cementing the faith of early believers. Persecution eliminated the "free-rider" problem common to many new religions. Those who stayed in the church believed strongly in the tenets of the faith because it was "expensive" to do so.

Anyone who has participated in a cause that demands great sacrifice will understand that services conducted in those early house churches must have yielded an intense, shared emotional satisfaction. Shared risk usually brings people together in powerful ways.

COMPASSION EQUATION

It was not simply the promise of salvation that motivated Christians, but the fact that they were greatly rewarded in the here and now for belonging. Thus while membership was "expensive," it was, in fact, "a bargain." Because the church asked much of its members, it followed that it gave much.

For example, because Christians were expected to aid the less fortunate, they could expect to receive such aid, and all could feel greater security against bad times. Because they were asked to nurse the sick and dying, they too would receive such nursing. Because they were asked to love others, they in turn would be loved.

In similar fashion, Christianity mitigated relations among social classes, and at the very time when the gap between rich and poor was growing. It did not preach that everyone could or should be socially or politically equal, but it did preach that all were equal in the eyes of God and that the more fortunate had a responsibility to help those in need.

GOOD THEOLOGICAL NEWS

Converts not only had to learn to act like Christians but to understand why Christians acted as they did. They had to learn that God commanded them to love one another, to be merciful, to be their brother's keeper. Indeed, they had to understand the *idea* of "divinity" in an entirely new way.

The simple phrase "For God so loved the world . . ." puzzled educated pagans, who believed, as Aristotle taught, that the gods could feel no love for mere humans. Moreover, a god of mercy was unthinkable, since classical philosophers taught that mercy was a pathological emotion, a defect of character to be outgrown and overcome.

The notion that the gods care how we treat one another would also have been dismissed as patently absurd by all sophisticated pagans.

When we examine the gods accepted by these same sophisticates, they seem trivial in contrast with "God the Father," and wicked incompetents compared to "His Son." Yet to many pagans, this new teaching was more than absurd. It was also good news.

Behind all these tangible, sociological, and intellectual motives, of course, Christians believe the Holy Spirit prodded and persuaded pagans to believe. Christian conversion, after all, is ultimately a spiritual affair. But is it too much to imagine that God perhaps used the tangible to influence the spiritual?

RODNEY STARK is professor of sociology and comparative religion at the University of Washington, and author of The Rise of Christianity: A Sociologist Reconsiders History (*Princeton University Press, 1996*).

CONFUCIUS

Confucianism, once thought to be a dead doctrine, has made an astonishing comeback during the past 20 years. Cited as a major force behind East Asia's economic "miracles," it is now finding a renewed following among mainland Chinese grown disillusioned with communism. Yet what exactly Confucianism means is hard to say. All the more reason, Jonathan Spence urges, to return to the man himself—and to the little we know about his life and words.

Jonathan D. Spence

Jonathan D. Spence is George B. Adams Professor of History at Yale University. His many books include The Death of Woman Wang *(1978),* The Gate of Heavenly Peace *(1981),* The Search for Modern China *(1990), and, most recently,* Chinese Roundabout *(1992).*

Across the centuries that have elapsed since he lived in northern China and lectured to a small group of followers on ethics and ritual, the ideas of Confucius have had a powerful resonance. Soon after his death in 476 B.C., a small number of these followers dedicated themselves to recording what they could remember of his teachings and to preserving the texts of history and poetry that he was alleged to have edited. In the fourth and third centuries B.C., several distinguished philosophers expanded and systematized ideas that they ascribed to him, thus deepening his reputation as a complex and serious thinker. During the centralizing and tyrannical Ch'in dynasty that ruled China between 221 and 209 B.C., the works of Confucius were slated for

destruction, on the grounds that they contained material antithetical to the obedience of people to their rulers, and many of those who prized or taught his works were brutally killed on the emperor's orders.

Despite this apparently lethal setback, Confucius's reputation was only enhanced, and during the Han dynasty (206 B.C.–A.D. 220) his ideas were further edited and expanded, this time to be used as a focused source for ideas on good government and correct social organization. Despite the pedantry and internal bickering of these self-styled followers of Confucius, his ideas slowly came to be seen as the crystallization of an inherent Chinese wisdom. Surviving the importation of Buddhist metaphysics and meditative practices from India in the third to sixth centuries A.D., and a renewed interest in both esoteric Taoist theories of the cosmos and the hardheaded political realism of rival schools of legalistically oriented thinkers, a body of texts reorganized as "Confucian," with their accumulated commentaries, became the basic source for competitive examinations for entrance into the Chinese civil service and for the

analysis of a wide spectrum of political and familial relationships: those between ruler and subject, between parents and children, and between husband and wife. In the 12th century A.D., a loose group of powerful philosophers, though differing over the details, reformulated various so-called Confucian principles to incorporate some of the more deeply held premises of Buddhism, giving in particular a dualistic structure to the Confucian belief system by separating idealist or universalist components—the inherent principles or premises, known as the *li*—from the grosser matter, or manifestations of life-in-action (the *ch'i*).

A final series of shifts took place in the last centuries of imperial China. During the 16th century elements of Confucian doctrine were deepened and altered once again by philosophers who emphasized the inherent morality of the individual and tried to overcome the dualism that they felt Confucians had erected between nature and the human emotions. In the 17th century Confucian scholars confronted the promise and challenge of newly imported scientific ideas from the West,

From *The Wilson Quarterly,* Autumn 1993, pp. 30–38. © 1993 by Jonathan D. Spence. Reprinted by permission of the author.

brought by Jesuits and other Catholic missionaries. During the following century Confucian scholars embarked on a newly formulated intellectual quest for the evidential basis of historical and moral phenomena, one that led them cumulatively to peaks of remarkable scholarship. In the 19th century these scholars began to cope with Western technology and constitutional ideas and with the development of new modes of education. But in the 20th century Confucian ideas were attacked from within and without China as contributing to China's economic backwardness, myopic approach to social change, denial of the idea of progress, resistance to science, and a generally stultified educational system.

These attacks were so devastating that as recently as 20 years ago, one would have thought that the chances of Confucius ever again becoming a major figure of study or emulation were slight indeed, in any part of the world. In Communist China, where he had been held up to ridicule or vilification since the Communist victory of 1949, his name was invoked only when mass campaigns needed a symbol of the old order to castigate, as in the "Anti-Confucius and anti-Lin Biao Campaign" of 1973–74. But in that case the real focus of the campaign was Chairman Mao's former "closest comrade-in-arms," General Lin Biao, not the discredited sage of Lu. In Taiwan, though constant lip service was paid to the enduring values of Confucianism, the doctrine that lived on under that name was slanted in content and attracted few of the brightest young minds. It was a version of Confucian belief that followed along lines first laid down by Nationalist Party ideologues during the 1930s in an attempt to boost their own prestige and give a deeper historical legitimacy to party leader Chiang Kai-Shek. Although in Taiwan as in other parts of Asia there were great scholars who continued to explore the sage's inner meaning, in many Asian schools Confucius was also invoked in support of authoritarian and hierarchical value systems. In Europe and the United States, though Confucian texts were studied in East Asian and

Oriental studies centers, they did not arouse much excitement, and the young—if they were interested in earlier Asian studies at all—were likely to be far more interested in Taoism or Buddhism.

Now, however, the revival is in full swing. Confucian study societies have sprung up inside the People's Republic of China, with government approval. In Taiwan, Confucianism is studied as a central aspect of philosophical inquiry, and so-called New Confucians are linking his ideas on conduct and the self to certain preoccupations in modern ethics. In the United States especially, many colleges now teach sophisticated and popular courses in "Confucian belief," and a distinguished stream of "Confucian" academics jet around the world as conference participants and even as consultants to foreign governments on the sage. Translations of Confucius's work, and that of his major followers, are in print with popular presses, often in variant editions. And "Confucian principles" are cited approvingly as being one of the underpinnings of the disciplined work habits and remarkable international economic success of a number of Asian states.

The renewed interest in Confucius is not the result of any rush of new information about him. There has been no newly discovered cache of intimate details about him or his family that could engage the public interest, no fresh sources that can be ascribed to him and thus deepen our sense of his achievement, or that could serve as the basis for new controversies. The scraps of information about Confucius are so slight that they barely give us an outline, let alone a profile, of the man. (The modern name Confucius is an early Western rendering of the sage's Chinese honorific name, "K'ung-fu'tsu.") We are almost certain that he was born in 551 B.C. We have a definite year of death, 479 B.C. He was born in the kingdom of Lu, one of the many small states into which China was then divided and which corresponds roughly to the area of modern Shandong province. His parents might have had aristocratic roots, but they were neither prominent nor wealthy, and though Confucius received a good education in historical and ritual matters,

his parents died when he was young, and the youth had to fend for himself. He acquired a number of skills: in clerical work, music, accounting, perhaps in charioteering and archery, and in certain "menial activities" on which we have no other details. Sometime between 507 and 497 B.C. he served in the state of Lu in an office that can be translated as "police commissioner" and that involved hearing cases and meting out punishments. Before and after that stint of service he traveled to various neighboring states, seeking posts as a diplomatic or bureaucratic adviser but meeting with little success. Because of some feud he was, for a time, in mortal danger, but he handled himself with calmness and courage. He married and had one son and two daughters. His son predeceased him, but not before producing an heir. One of his daughters married a student of Confucius who had served time in jail. Confucius approved the match because he believed that the young man had in fact done no wrong. During his later years Confucius was a teacher of what we might now call ethics, ritual, and philosophy; the names of 35 of his students have come down to us.

To compound the problems caused by this paucity of biographical information, we have nothing that we can be completely sure was written by Confucius himself. What we do have is a record of what some of his disciples and students—or their students—said that he said. Usually translated as *The Analects of Confucius,* this collection is brief, aphoristic, and enigmatic. But the *Analects*, despite the problem of indirect transmission, remain our crucial source on Confucius's beliefs, actions, and personality. Not surprisingly, scholars disagree on how to interpret many passages and how much to believe in the authenticity of the different parts of this text. The best and perhaps the only gauges of authenticity are internal consistency, tone, and coherence. One can also look at the construction of each book—there are 20 in all, each running about five pages in English translation—and search for obvious distortions and later additions. The last five of the books, for example, have lengthy sections that present Confucius either as a butt to the Taoists or as an uncritical transmitter of doctrines with which he can be shown in earlier chapters to have disagreed. It is a fairly safe assumption that these were added to the original text by persons with a special cause to plead. Other books give disproportionate space to Confucius's praise of a particular student whom we know from other passages that he rather disliked. Perhaps in such cases we are witnessing attempts to correct the record by later followers of the student concerned. There does not seem to be any political censorship; indeed, one of the mysteries of the later uses of Confucianism concerns the way that the original text as we now have it has been preserved for two millennia even though it seems quite obviously to contradict the ideological uses to which it was being put. Interpretation and commentary, that is to say, carried more weight with readers than did the original words.

Given the bewildering array of philosophical and political arguments that Confucianism has been called on to support, and given, in particular, the generally held belief that Confucius was a strict believer in hierarchy and the values of absolute obedience to superiors, and that he lacked flexibility and imagination, it is an intriguing task to read the *Analects* with open eyes and without any presuppositions drawn from later interpretative attempts. What was, in fact, the central message of the man Confucius himself?

Personally, almost two and a half millennia after his death, I find that Confucius is still especially valuable to us because of the strength of his humanity, his general decency, and the fervor of his belief in the importance of culture and the act of learning. He emphatically did not feel that he had any monopoly on truth. Rather, he was convinced that learning is a perpetual process that demands flexibility, imagination, and tenacity. He scolded students who would not get up in the morning, just as he scolded those who were unctuous or complacent. He said that he had no interest in trying to teach those who did not have the curiosity to follow up on a philosophical argument or a logical sequence of ideas after he had given them an initial prod in the right direction. He let his students argue among themselves—or with him—and praised those who were able to make moral decisions that might benefit humankind in general. But at the same time he adamantly refused to talk about the forces of heaven or to speculate on the nature of the afterlife, since there was so much that he did not know about life on this Earth that he was convinced such speculations would be idle.

It is clear that Confucius derived great pleasure from life. Once, one of his students could not think what to say to an influential official who had asked what sort of a person Confucius really was. Hearing of the incident, Confucius gently chided his student with these words: "Why did you not simply say something to this effect: He is the sort of man who forgets to eat when he tries to solve a problem that has been driving him to distraction, who is so full of joy that he forgets his worries and who does not notice the onset of old age?"

This brief exchange comes from *The Analects of Confucius*, book VII, section 19, and it is typical of words that Confucius left us, words through which we can in turn analyze his character.* Another example could be taken from Confucius's views concerning loyalty to the state and the value of capital punishment. In later periods of Chinese history, it was commonplace to assert that "Confucian" bureaucrats and scholars should always put their duty to the state and the dynasty they served ahead of personal and family loyalties. Chinese history is also replete with grim details of executions carried out in the name of "Confucian" ideology against those who violated the state's laws. But in the most clearly authenticated books of the *Analects* that we have, we find completely unambiguous views on these central matters of human practice and belief. What could be clearer than this?

---

*All citations of the *Analects* are from D. C. Lau's Penguin Books translation, *Confucius, The Analects*. In some cases I have made minor modifications to his translations.

The Governor of She said to Confucius, "In our village there is a man nicknamed 'Straight Body.' When his father stole a sheep, he gave evidence against him." Confucius answered, "In our village those who are straight are quite different. Fathers cover up for their sons, and sons cover up for their fathers. Straightness is to be found in such behavior." (XIII/18)

On executions, Confucius was equally unambiguous:

Chi K'ang Tzu asked Confucius about government, saying, "What would you think if, in order to move closer to those who possess the Way, I were to kill those who do not follow the Way?" Confucius answered, "In administering your government, what need is there for you to kill? Just desire the good yourself and the common people will be good. The virtue of the gentleman is like wind; the virtue of the small man is like grass. Let the wind blow over the grass and it is sure to bend." (XII/19)

If it were humanly possible, Confucius added, he would avoid the law altogether: "In hearing litigation, I am no different from any other man. But if you insist on a difference, it is, perhaps, that I try to get the parties not to resort to litigation in the first place." (XII/13) In the long run, the fully virtuous state would be forever free of violent death: "The Master said, 'How true is the saying that after a state has been ruled for a hundred years by good men it is possible to get the better of cruelty and to do away with killing.'" (XIII/11)

Since the words of Confucius have been preserved for us mainly in the form of aphorisms or snatches of dialogue—or the combination of the two—one way to find a coherent structure in his thought is to track the remarks he made to specific individuals, even if these are widely scattered throughout the *Analects*. Sometimes, of course, there is only one remark, especially in the case of those whose behavior Confucius considered beyond the pale. My favorite example here is his dismissal of Yuan Jang, allegedly once his friend: "Yuan Jang sat waiting with his legs spread wide. The Master said, 'To be neither modest nor deferential when young, to have passed on nothing worthwhile when grown up, and to refuse to die when old, that is what I call being a pest.' So saying, the Master tapped him on the shin with his stick." (XIV/43) That tapping on the shin, perhaps playful, perhaps in irritation, shows an unusual side of Confucius. Was he trying to add physical sting to his sharp words? More commonly with him, it was a laugh or a shrug that ended a potentially confrontational exchange.

With several of his students, Confucius clearly felt a deep rapport, even when they did not see eye to eye. One such student was Tzu-lu, who was more a man of action than a scholar. Confucius loved to tease Tzu-lu for his impetuosity. Thus, after telling his students that if he were on a raft that drifted out to sea, Tzu-lu would be the one to follow him, Confucius added wryly that that would be because Tzu-lu had at once more courage and less judgment than his teacher. On another occasion, when Tzu-lu asked if Confucius thought he, Tzu-lu, would make a good general, Confucius replied that he would rather not have as a general someone who would try to walk across a river or strangle a tiger with his bare hands. (V/7 and VII/11)

Different in character, but still very much his own man, was the merchant and diplomat Tzu-kung. Confucius acknowledged that Tzu-kung was shrewd and capable, and made a great profit from his business deals. He even agreed that Tzu-kung's type of intelligence was especially useful in the world of literature and thought: "Only with a man like you can one discuss the Odes. Tell such a man something and he can see its relevance to what he has not been told." (I/16) But Confucius did not like Tzu-kung's insistence on always trying to put people in a ranked order of priorities, as if they were so many objects—"For my part I have no time for such things," Confucius observed—and he was equally upset if he felt that Tzu-kung was skimping things that really mattered because of his private feelings: "Tzu-kung wanted to dispense with the practice of ritually killing a sacrificial sheep at the announcement of the new moon. The Master said, 'You love the sheep, but I love the Rites.' " (XIV/29 and III/17)

Most readers of the *Analects* feel that the student called Yen Yuan was clearly Confucius's favorite, and the one closest to the Master by behavior and inclination. Yen Yuan was poor but lived his life without complaining. He did not allow poverty to sour or interrupt his search for the Way, and his intelligence was truly piercing. As Tzu-kung, not a modest man, put it, "When he [Yen Yuan] is told one thing he understands 10. When I am told one thing I understand only two." To which Confucius sighed in agreement, "Neither of us is as good as he is." (V/9) In a similar vein, Confucius praised Yen Yuan's prudence, contrasting it with Tzu-lu's bravado. As Confucius phrased it, Yen Yuan was the kind of man who "when faced with a task, was fearful of failure," and who knew how "to stay out of sight when set aside;" furthermore, Yen Yuan was not above making mistakes, but more important, "he did not make the same mistake twice." (VII/11 and VI/3) When Yen Yuan died young, before being able to achieve his full promise, Confucius gave way to a conspicuous display of immoderate grief. When some of his students remonstrated with him for showing such "undue sorrow," Confucius's answer was brief but powerful: "If not for him for whom should I show undue sorrow?" (IX/10)

Confucius lived to a fine old age, and not even regret over the loss of his favorite student and his own son could blunt the pleasures he felt at his own mounting experience and the attainment of something that might be approaching wisdom. He did not boast about the knowledge he had acquired—indeed he thought he was lucky to have got as far as he had. As he put it once to Tzu-lu: "Shall I tell you what it is to know? To say you know when you know, and to say you do not know when you do not, that is knowledge." (II/17) His own greatest ambition, as he once told Yen Yuan and Tzu-lu jointly, was "to bring peace to the old, to have trust in my friends, and to cherish the young." (V/26) On another occasion he went even further, telling his followers, "It is fitting that we hold the young in awe. How do we know that the generations

to come will not be the equal of the present?" (IX/23) In the passage that is perhaps the most famous of his sayings, Confucius gave his own version of the stages of life, and it is as different as anything could be from Shakespeare's "Seven Ages of Man," with its heartrending account of man's descent into the weakness and imbecility of old age after a brief phase of youthful vigor. Whereas according to the *Analects*, the Master said, "At 15 I set my heart on learning; at 30 I took my stand; at 40 I came to be free from doubts; at 50 I understood the Decree of Heaven; at 60 my ear was attuned; at 70 I followed my heart's desire without overstepping the line." (II/4)

Certainly we should not read Confucius as though he were always right. And as we read through the *Analects* we can find Confucius revealing a fussy and sometimes impatient side. Some of his vaunted arguments seem like quibbles, and he could be punctilious to the point of prudishness. His political motivations are often obscure, and he seems to appreciate various struggling rulers' foibles less than his own. But cleared of the accumulation of unsubstantiated details and textual over-interpretations that have weighed him down across the centuries, we find to our surprise an alert, intelligent, and often very amusing man.

How then did he get the reputation that he did, one at once more austere, more pompous, harsh even, and as a reinforcer of the status quo? Strangely enough, part of the reappraisal resulted from the efforts of the man who is undeniably China's greatest historian, Ssu-ma Ch'ien, who lived from around 145 to 89 B.C., during the Han dynasty. In his life's work, a composite history of China entitled simply *Historical Records*, which was completed between 100 and 95 B.C., Ssu-ma Ch'ien aimed to integrate the histories of all China's earlier states and rulers with the steady and inexorable rise to power of the centralizing Ch'in dynasty (221–209 B.C.), and he determined to give Confucius an important role in this process. Thus Ssu-ma Ch'ien paid Confucius the ultimate accolade by placing his story in the section devoted to the ruling houses of early China, as opposed to placing him with other individual thinkers and statesmen in the 70 chapters of biographies that conclude the *Historical Records*. In the summation of Confucius's worth with which he ended his account, Ssu-ma Ch'ien gave concise and poignant expression to his homage:

> In this world there have been many people—from kings to wise men—who had a glory while they lived that ended after their death. But Confucius, though a simple commoner, has had his name transmitted for more than 10 generations; all those who study his works consider him their master. From the Son of Heaven, the princes, and the lords on down, anyone in the Central Kingdom who is dedicated to a life of learning, follows the precepts and the rules of the Master. Thus it is that we call him a true Sage.

To give substance to this judgment, Ssu-ma Ch'ien took all known accounts written over the intervening three centuries that purported to describe Confucius, following the principle that if there was no clear reason for discarding an item of biographical information, then he should include it, leaving for later generations the task of winnowing the true from the false. Thus was Confucius given courageous ancestors, his birth described in semi-miraculous terms, his own physical distinction elaborated upon. In one curious addition, Confucius's father was described as being of far greater age than the sage's mother: By one interpretation of the phrase used by Ssu-ma Ch'ien, that the marriage was "lacking in proportion," Confucius's father would have been over 64, while his mother had only recently entered puberty. Confucius's precocious interest in ritual and propriety, his great height and imposing cranial structure, the fecundity of the flocks of cattle and sheep that he supervised in one of his first official posts, his preternatural shrewdness in debate, his instinctive brilliance at interpreting unusual auguries—all of these were given documentary precision in Ssu-ma Ch'ien's account. The result is that Confucius not only emerges as a key counselor to the rulers of his native state of Lu, but the meticulousness of his scholarship and his flair for editing early texts of poetry, history, and music are presented as having attracted an ever-widening circle of hundreds or even thousands of students from his own and neighboring states.

Having constructed this formidable image of a successful Confucius, Ssu-ma Ch'ien was confronted by the need to explain the reasons for Confucius's fall from grace in Lu and for his subsequent wanderings in search of rulers worthy of his service. Being one of China's most gifted storytellers, Ssu-ma Ch'ien was up to this task, presenting a convincing scenario of the way the sagacity of Confucius's advice to the ruler of Lu made him both respected and feared by rival rulers in northern China. One of them was finally able to dislodge Confucius by sending to the ruler of Lu a gift of 24 ravishing female dancers and musicians, along with 30 magnificent teams of chariot horses. This gift so effectively distracted the ruler of Lu from his official duties—most important, it led him to forget certain key ritual sacrifices—that Confucius had no choice but to leave his court.

In various ways, some subtle, some direct, the portrait of Confucius that Ssu-ma Ch'ien wove incorporated diverse levels of narrative dealing with the unpredictability of violence. This was surely not coincidental, for the central tragedy of Ssu-ma Ch'ien's own life had been his court-ordered castration, a savage punishment inflicted on him by the Han dynasty emperor Wu-ti (r. 141–87 B.C.). Ssu-ma Ch'ien's "crime" had been to write a friend a letter in which he incautiously spoke in defense of a man unjustly punished by the same emperor. Despite this agonizing humiliation, which placed the historian in the same physical category as the venal court eunuchs he so deeply despised, Ssu-ma Ch'ien refused to commit suicide; he maintained his dignity by making his history as grand and comprehensive as possible—his presentation of Confucius being a stunning example of his dedication to craft and content. Thus he describes Confucius as a man who had the bureaucratic power to make major judicial decisions but who did so only with care and consideration of all the evidence. When Confucius acted harshly, according to Ssu-ma Ch'ien, it was only when the long-term threat to his kingdom was so strong that leniency would have been folly. This explains one shattering moment in Ssu-ma Ch'ien's biography. One rival leader was planning to overthrow the ruler of Lu, but each of his ruses was seen through and foiled by Confucius. At last, in desperation, the rival ruler ordered his acrobats and dwarfs to perform wild and obscene dances at a ritual occasion that the ruler of Lu was attending. Confucius, according to Ssu-ma Ch'ien, ordered the dwarfs killed.

In another dissimilar but equally powerful comment on violence, Ssu-ma Ch'ien showed that even the descendants of a man of Confucius's integrity could not escape Emperor Wu-ti's willful power. Thus at the very end of his long biography, before the final summation, Ssu-ma Ch'ien lists all of Confucius's direct descendants in the male line. When he comes to the 11th in line, An-kuo, the historian mentions tersely that An-kuo had died "prematurely" under the "ruling emperor." Ssu-ma Ch'ien knew—and knew that his readers knew—that An-kuo had been executed on Wu-ti's orders for involvement in an alleged court coup. The line had not, however, been stamped out, because An-kuo's wife had borne a son before her husband was killed.

Ssu-ma Ch'ien's attempt to reconstruct a convincing psychological and contextual universe for Confucius was a brilliant one, and his version was elaborated upon and glossed by scores of subsequent scholars, even as suitable pieces of the Confucian legacy were seized upon by later rulers and bureaucrats to justify some current policy decision or to prove some philosophical premise. But after more than two millennia of such accretions, it seems time to go back to the earlier and simpler version of the record and try to see for ourselves what kind of a man Confucius was. The results, I feel, in our overly ideological age, are encouraging to those who value the central premises of humane intellectual inquiry.

Unit 6

Key Points to Consider

❖ Why was it significant to break the Mayan code? How does Mayan writing compare to that of Sumer (see Unit 2)?

❖ Describe the economic and cultural importance of Timbuktu.

❖ What is the significance of Arab scholarship in world history?

❖ How did Europeans learn from the Arabs?

❖ What is the legacy of Byzantium?

❖ What was the role of warfare in the writing of the Magna Carta?

❖ Would you agree that the clock is the single most important invention of Western civilization? Why or why not?

 **Links**   # www.dushkin.com/online/

These sites are annotated on pages 4 and 5.

World historians have some difficulty with this period of time. In the history of Europe, the Middle Ages, or the medieval period, is a time of retreat after the fall of Rome. The thousand-year span covers feudalism, the growth of nation-states, the bubonic plague called the Black Death, reestablishment of long-distance trade, the domination of the Roman Catholic Church, and the emergence of Western civilization. For world historians, Western develop- ments during this period of time are important for the future, but pale in comparison to the achieve- ments of China and Islam and to the changes that people elsewhere in the world were experiencing.

In the Western Hemisphere, Mesoamerican civilization flourished, with magnificent stone cities rising out of the jungles of southern Mexico and Central America. The conquering Spanish destroyed much of the cultural information, and it is only recently that the writing of the Maya has been deciphered. Mayan civilization, however, suffered a precipitous decline 600 years before the coming of the Europeans. The deciphering of the Mayan language was an intellectual breakthrough that resulted in new interpretations about these warlike people. The Aztecs eventually came to dominate the land shortly before the onslaught of Hernán Cortés and his soldiers, who swept away this civilization with warfare and disease.

The legendary Timbuktu, an oasis trading town in the southern Sahara, was a mixture of Arab and African peoples bound together by belief in Islam. Timbuktu was not only a point of contact for African trade, but also a place of learning and a staging point for pilgrims on their way to Mecca, as Tahir Shah tells us in "The Islamic Legacy of Timbuktu."

Arab schools and scholarship carried forward the learning of the ancient Greeks, as outlined in "The Arab Roots of European Medicine." Translations from Arabic to Latin provided a classical education for Europeans, starting in the tenth century. This was a "golden age" for Islamic civilization. What is often forgotten, however, is the endurance of that portion of the eastern Roman Empire that continued as Byzantium. It lasted 1,200 years and spanned the ancient, medieval, and modern periods of Western civilization. Its influence is noted in "The Persistence of Byzantium."

Western Europe in the Middle Ages was ravaged by fierce Norse raiders who attacked the Atlantic coastline in good weather at harvest seasons. Their boats, the Viking longship, were marvels of nautical engineering at the time—fast, sleek, and easy to maneuver. At the time that their raids ceased, about 1100 C.E., Western civilization began to evolve. The Magna Carta of the thirteenth century, composed in England to grant personal liberties to the barons, became one of the great foundation stones for the civil liberties of the future. It was important for restric- ting a monarch to a rule of law rather than of whim.

In that same century the first mechanical clock, invented by an unknown genius, appeared in Europe. This key invention, as described by David Landes, changed attitudes about time and inspired further developments, such as miniaturization of parts and mass production. It led to the industrial revolution. By the fifteenth century the Europeans were ready to reach out into the world as no other civilization had done.

Cracking the Maya's Code

New light on dark history

What the discovery of the Rosetta stone did for the study of ancient Egypt, some inspired detection has done for the Maya people of Central America

ONE of the greatest intellectual achievements of our century." Thus Michael Coe of Yale University, about the deciphering of the ancient Mayan script. His exaggeration is pardonable. When the Maya's strange, pebble-like writings were rediscovered in 1839, the man who found them, John Lloyd Stephens, lamented that "No Champollion has yet brought to them the energies of his enquiring mind [Champollion had deciphered Egyptian hieroglyphics 17 years before]. Who shall read them?" It has taken 150 years to answer that question.

The Maya were the only pre-Columbus Americans to have developed a sophisticated writing system, and they covered their buildings with it. These buildings, now ruined, lie buried in the fast-eroding jungles of Mexico and Central America. The temples, with their steeply stepped sides and crests of limestone, peer down upon an ebbing sea of trees, which undulates slightly as it rolls over unearthed temples, their coats of jungle waiting to be stripped away. It is like another world—and, indeed, the largest surviving Maya city, Tikal in Guatemala, played the part of an alien fort in the film "Star Wars".

As for the people who built these places, they might indeed have come from another world. Or so the scholars who wrote about them made it appear.

According to the traditional view, the Maya were unlike any other people in the annals of mankind: they were men without war, without cities, without kings, and even without history—or rather without any interest in it (which comes to much the same thing).

5 Eb 15 Mac (October 28th 709 AD) He is letting blood ? 4 Katun Lord Shield Jaguar the captor of

Ah Ahaual

Lord of Yaxchilan

She is letting blood

Name or titles

Lady Xoc

Lady Batab

The Yaxchilan scene and its inscription

Two men were largely responsible for this. One was an American, Sylvanus Morley. He thought the limestone in the jungle was not the ruins of cities but of vacant temples, which had been inhabited only by priests and acolytes. When his "The Ancient Maya" was revised in

| balam | ba-balam | balam-ma | ba-balam-ma | ba-la-ma |

Five spellings of "balam" (jaguar): cat's head and syllable-signs

1956, the word "city" was replaced throughout by "ceremonial centre". Morley was obsessed with the Maya calendar, an extraordinarily elaborate construction with concentric cycles of hundreds and thousands of years wheeling around a 260-day period, made up of a magic number 13 and a base number 20 (the Maya counted in twenties).

The other figure was Sir Eric Thompson, an upper-class Anglican whose powerful mind and waspish, elegant pen dominated Maya studies until his death in 1975. Thompson put religion centre-stage. In his view, the Maya were star-worshippers living at peace in scattered villages, presided over by priests absorbed by astronomical calculation. The writing on the monuments, he thought, was about not kings, but gods: "I do not believe that historical events were recorded on the monuments."

That was hardly surprising: Thompson barely thought the Maya had a history at all—certainly no states or kings or wars. When evidence of cities and states appeared, he dismissed it, saying it showed only barbarian invasion: cities were not really Mayan. As for the script itself, he thought that too was unique. Unlike other writing, it did not express a language ever spoken by anyone. It was a mystical rebus invented by priests for calendrical and religious purposes, not merely unknown but unknowable.

Alas, it was all rubbish: Arcadia did not exist. Over the past decade or so, a fundamentally different way of looking at the Maya has upturned almost every assumption of the traditionalists. In the new version, the Maya created an urban civilisation. They were far from peaceful. They had a knowable history. Their collapse came about through internal political failure, not invasion or (as Thompson argued) religious upheaval. Above all, they wrote a real language—and it was the discovery of this that opened the door to

the new conclusions. As with many great changes in thinking, the transformation has come about not in a blinding flash, but gradually.

FROM OBSCURITY TO HISTORY

The first breakthrough appeared in part of the world about as far from the steamy heat of Central America as you can get: Leningrad, in 1952, where a young scholar, Yuri Knosorov, published an article in *Soviet Ethnography*.

In 1945, as a young soldier, Mr Knosorov had been present at the fall of Berlin—and had rescued a single book from the flames engulfing the city's National Library. It turned out to be an edition of three of only four surviving Mayan books. He took the tome back to Russia and seven years later announced what Thompson had always declared to be unknowable: how the words were spelled. Mr Knosorov argued that Mayan, like virtually all other early scripts (and like Japanese and Chinese), was partly pictorial and partly phonetic; the technical term is logographic. "The system of Mayan writing", he asserted, "is typically hieroglyphic, and in its principles of writing does not differ from known hieroglyphic systems." Thompson denounced this as Bolshevik propaganda.

The second step, ironically, had nothing to do with the first. In 1960, Tatiana Proskouriakoff, a Russian-American, published an article with the mind-numbing title, "Historical Implications of a Pattern of Dates at Piedras Negras". Using numbers that had already been worked out (mostly by Thompson) and repeating symbols that could only be names, she argued that sequences of names separated by intervals of time conform to human life-cycles—birth, marriage and death. In other words, the inscriptions were personal histories. Thompson had always denied this but the evidence was so compelling that he had to back down.

The third step put these two arguments together with linguistic analysis and came to a new conclusion: the script referred to a spoken language, with an identifiable grammar and syntax. By concentrating on those symbols which were not dates or names, and by looking at the structure of modern Mayan languages, Linda Schele of the University of Texas isolated Mayan verbs. Others then showed that the phonetic bit of the script was more important than had been thought: the Maya routinely wrote the same word using phonetic and pictorial signs interchangeably. This unleashed a torrent of decipherments. During the 1980s, about 80% of the hieroglyphic characters ("glyphs" in scholarly jargon) were translated and most inscriptions read. The Mayan code had been cracked.

THE MAYA EMERGE

Maurice Pope, a language expert, wrote that "decipherments are by far the most glamorous achievements of scholarship. There is a touch of magic about unknown writing." True—but the unglamorous reality is that the deciphering is only a start. What matters is understanding what the words say. By the mid-1980s, the scholars knew the script and understood the grammar and syntax. They could see what to look for. The flood-gates opened.

The Maya turn out to have created a world much older and more durable than had been realised. In the old view, their civilisation had lasted about 500 years, from 300AD until 800. It was at its height when Charlemagne was crowned as emperor of Christian Europe on Christmas Day 800 and when Muhammad was fleeing from Mecca to Medina. But the new scholars found glyphs from 200 years earlier, in 100AD, and the first cities seemed earlier still, from the 5th and 6th century BC. In other words, Maya civilisation ran from Periclean Athens to the start of medieval Europe.

This means that the Maya are emerging not as a prehistoric people but as possessors of a very familiar sort of history. As Proskouriakoff had argued, the people on the inscriptions were not priests but kings. In Copan in Honduras, writing experts first worked out the dynastic chain from the carvings, and then archaeologists discovered the bodies. In city after city, scholars reconstructed who ruled when, who his children were, what wars he fought and how he dealt with the neighbours. Like the ancient Egyptians, the Maya wrote their politics and diplomacy on their temples.

Just as important as the length of the history and its nature was the astounding detail in which it is being recovered. The Maya did not worship time but they were concerned to place political actions in their precise historical context in order to make them legitimate. The result is that scholars have worked out not only the year in which an event occurred centuries ago, but also the day and sometimes even the hour. Far from being non-historical, the records yield a chronology whose accuracy was not surpassed until the 19th century.

This onslaught of detail has made it possible to work out both what happened and also, to some extent, why. In "A Forest of Kings" (William Morrow, $17.95), Mrs Schele and David Friedel of Southern Methodist University, in Dallas, Texas, argue that kingship was the central Maya political institution. The royal monuments were not just lists but accounts of new military strategies (as at Tikal); what happens when a woman inherits the throne (as at Palenque); what happens when the succession is disputed (at Yaxchilan); how you create a new system of government after social collapse (at Chichen Itza); and so on. In "The Blood of Kings" (George Braziller, $29.95) Mrs Schele and Mary Miller, now of Yale University, argue that the principal concerns of the rulers were royal blood and bloody conquest. These were expressed literally, with scenes of the most hair-raising sacrifice and self-sacrifice carved in gruesome detail. In a series of carvings from Yaxchilan (now on display in a new gallery in the British Museum after years in its cellar), a woman kneels before her son, pulling a rope-like barbed wire through her tongue. Her son perforates his penis and threads strips of paper through it.

In yet another book, "Maya Cosmos" (William Morrow, $15) Mrs Schele and

Mr Friedel examine the system of beliefs behind such things. The Maya, they argue, looked at the world in an unusual way. They tracked their creation stories through the vast movement of the stars across the heavens, and thought that the point at which the Milky Way appeared as a vertical band in the night sky represented both the growth of the maize stalk (their staple crop) and the moment of creation.

And they thought of the world as alive. If you took something from it (by growing foods you had to give something back—and blood was your most precious fluid. The word for blood also meant God and soul and was related to the words for sun and dream. The Maya believed you could summon up sacred ancestors by shedding blood and by inducing trances (sometimes, bizarrely, with hallucinogenic enemas). But the purpose of the blood-letting ceremony at Yaxchilan was dynastic, too: because the succession was disputed, the claimants wanted to contact the first ruler to justify their titles.

THE END OF THE MAYA WORLD

At first, the new scholars thought the political arrangements of the Maya world were rather like those of ancient Greece—20 or so city states that co-existed for the most part independently of each other and without any over-arching political organisation. Of these, the biggest was Tikal, with a population of perhaps 40,000 people in the city and 500,000 in the hinterland.

But such is the pace of the change in the field that even this relatively recent theory is now being superseded. Two younger scholars, Nikolai Grube and Simon Martin, argue on the basis of newly-deciphered glyphs that most of the city-states were grouped into two loose alliances centred on Tikal and Kalakmul. The alliances were largely military, held together by payments of tribute (discovered by deciphering another new glyph) and by marriage. Mr Friedel reckons these alliances, and their wars, were a more or less permanent feature of Maya society from start to finish.

The finish is important. These alliances cast new light on what remains one of the great mysteries of the Maya world: its collapse. The Maya were not, like the Aztecs, cut down in their prime by the Spanish conquistadors. Rather, Maya civilisation collapsed of its own accord, in an astonishingly brief space of time, six centuries before the Spaniards arrived. The last dates recorded on monuments in the cities tell their own story: Copan, 820AD; Naranjo, 849AD; Caracol, 859AD; Tikal, 879AD.

Tikal was overrun not by its traditional enemies but by outsiders: portraits of moustachioed warriors start appearing there, along with foreign orange pots. What was left of the Maya world then degenerated into anarchy: the remains of defensive walls can be found thrown up hurriedly in the 9th century AD, first around large areas, then towns and lastly, in a few cases, villages and fields.

By about 1000 there is nothing. In the Copan valley and elsewhere, the population seems to have fallen by 90%. Here was a case, like Europe's Dark Ages, of a world going backwards. The Maya had been wealthy. At their height, their world was more successful than the one that exists today in the Maya area— successful as defined by the number of people able to sustain life there. The Yucatan, the green thumb sticking into the Gulf of Mexico, now has about two people per square kilometre. When the Maya kingdoms were at their height, they sustained a population 150 times greater—a density as great as that of Java today—largely thanks to a complex irrigation system now in ruins.

The Maya have been held up as an example of a society which exploited its environment beyond the possible limits. Certainly, evidence of soil erosion, drought and malnutrition exist in the late period. But so they do at other times. The new research proposes another explanation of the cataclysm: profound political failure.

In 695, the old system of alliances came unstuck when Tikal conquered Kalakmul and sacrificed its king. The first outcome was the dissolution of the Kalakmul alliance. But then, because the alliances never completely overrode the power of local kings, Tikal failed to exert any control over the extended area. The result was Balkanisation, silted canals, anarchy and collapse.

There is a coda to this story. For the most part, the scholarly revolution has wrung history out of the mute stones. But not just history. The rediscovery of the past by western scholars has coincided with a cultural revival among the modern Maya—and indeed is reinforcing it.

THE BEGINNING OF THE MAYA WORLD

That revival is partly a response to what some call the third great calamity of the Maya (after the 9th-century collapse and the arrival of the Spaniards, who destroyed those states which had revived after the 10th century). This third calamity was the counter-insurgency launched by the Guatemalan army in the 1980s in which an estimated 190,000 Maya died and 1m (from a population of 3m) were made refugees.

The Maya recovery under subsequent governments has had repercussions beyond Guatemala. In Mexico, the Zapatist rebellion—usually described as an uprising of economically desperate peasants—in fact has strong Maya roots. In both countries, the first peace accords struck between government and rebels promised the use (for the first time) of Mayan languages in schools and in government. Gary Goosen, of New York State University, has shown that some of the old beliefs outlined in "Maya Cosmos", are still held by modern Maya, particularly the all-important one that links blood, soul and sun. Suddenly, all over Central America, there are diaries using the Maya 260-day calendar; comic books use old Maya stories; even the glyphs are back in commemorative plaques.

So the Maya do, indeed, have an extremely unusual ancient civilisation. Not because it was based on star-worship or peace but because it is neither dead, like those of ancient Greece or Mesopotamia, nor living, like those of China or India. Instead, it is waking up: the old system died but its way of looking at the world still influences Mayan-speakers today. They, like the scholars, are rediscovering history.

The Islamic Legacy of Timbuktu

Written by Tahir Shah

The caravan of Sultan Mansa Musa, ruler of the Mali Empire, snaked its way through the scorching heat of the central Sahara on its long return from the 1324 pilgrimage to Makkah. Eight thousand soldiers, courtiers and servants—some say as many as 60,000—drove 15,000 camels laden with gold, perfume, salt and stores of food in a procession of unrivaled size.

Their destination was, first, the newly conquered city of Gao, on the Niger River. From there, they turned toward another metropolis just added to the Mali Empire, one surrounded by unrelenting dunes, a fabled oasis city on which Mansa Musa had longed to make his mark: Timbuktu. Thirsty and flagging under the searing sun, the caravan entered Timbuktu's ochre walls in the year 1325.

No word in English connotes remoteness more than *Timbuktu*. Thanks to the astonishing wealth that Mansa Musa had displayed on his visits to Cairo and Makkah, it also connoted riches. For eight centuries, Timbuktu captured the imaginations of both East and West, albeit for very different reasons. In 1620, the English explorer Richard Jobson wrote:

> The most flattering reports had reached Europe of the gold trade carried on at Timbuktu. The roofs of its houses were represented to be covered with plates of gold, the bottoms of the rivers to glisten with the precious metal, and the mountains had only to be excavated to yield a profusion of the metallic treasure.

Other reports said that rosewater flowed in the city's fountains and that the sultan showered each visitor with priceless gifts. Europe's greatest explorers set out to risk their lives in search of the riches of Timbuktu. Exploration and travel societies sponsored competitions, with a prize for the man who reached there by the most difficult route. In fact, most European travelers perished before they ever saw the city rise above the desert horizon, and those who did get there found that the tales they had heard had missed the point.

Muslim travelers—most notably Ibn Battuta and Hasan al-Wazan, also called Leo Africanus—were no less eager to visit the city, but for them and a host of rulers, dignitaries and scholars from Morocco to Persia, the remote city held riches of another sort: Timbuktu was the starting point for African pilgrims going on the Hajj, and a center of some of the finest—and most generously available—Islamic scholarship of the Middle Ages.

Located in today's Mali, some 12 kilometers(eight miles) north of the Niger flood-plain along the southern edge of the Sahara, Timbuktu today is little more than a sleepy, sweltering stop on the adventure-tourism trail. Most visitors fly in and out in a single afternoon; the city's days as a caravanserai and desert entrepôt are long past.

A more purposeful visit, however, has its rewards. There is much to see as one strolls about the stark streets, lin-gers, looks beyond the soft-drink stalls and engages in casual conversation here and there. Although Timbuktu has been conquered many times by many powers, absorbed into one empire after another, none ever sacked or looted it. As a result, traces of its Islamic legacy appear at almost every turn. Qur'anic inscriptions decorate doorways. The tombs of hundreds of famous scholars and revered teachers dot the town—some unremembered, some within the knowl-

---

Timbuktu was the product of an eclectic mixture of West African and Arab influences.

---

edge of local guides. Most noticeably, a handful of fabulous mosques reel upward into the brilliant African sky and constitute the anchor points of the city's plan.

Set on the Islamic world's southwestern edge, Timbuktu was the product of an eclectic mixture of West African and Arab influences that found in Islam a common denominator. Its peoples often saw themselves as the faithful pitted against the pagans lurking beyond the city's walls. Tuareg, Fulani, Berbers, Soninke and Songhoi lived side by side, in peace, bound together by their belief in God, their acceptance of the Qur'an, and their familiarity with Arabic.

Because the city lay on the periphery of the kingdoms that ruled it—and was left to its own devices by most of them—the community of Timbuktu was forced through isolation to look inward. This introspective attitude influenced all aspects of Timbuktu's society, and nowhere did this become more apparent than in its pious pursuits. Barely two centuries after being founded as a small Tuareg settlement around 1100, Timbuktu had earned its reputation as the most important Islamic center in West Africa. Its quiet rise to high regard—against enormous odds of geography and climate—is remarkable. Equally astonishing is that Timbuktu also prospered economically, seemingly beyond reason, as if to spite the adversity of its surroundings.

At its height during the mid-16th century, the city had a population of about 60,000. A prime caravan stop and center of manufacturing, it dominated West Africa in trade and exports. Al-Wazan wrote that:

> the rich king of Tombuto . . . keeps a magnificent and well furnished court. The coin of Tombuto is gold. . . . There is a most stately temple to be seen, the walls of which are made of mortared stone; and a princely palace also built by a most excellent workman of Granada. Here are many shops of craftsmen and merchants, and especially of such as weave linen and cotton cloth.

Though undergirded by its economic success, Timbuktu's key role was cultural, as a crucible of learning. The difficulty of the journey to or from Timbuktu induced pilgrims and traders alike once they got there, to spend months, even years, in the city before moving on. In time, local belief held that, by studying the Qur'an or donating generously to Timbuktu's Islamic schools, one would be assured safe passage through the surrounding desert.

A rich account of Timbuktu's history and Islamic heritage has come to us through a series of chronicles, known as *tarikhs,* written from the mid-17th through the mid-18th centuries. These texts—some plain and undeviating, others embroidered with ornate rhetoric—help us slip into the world of Timbuktu in the Middle Ages. Here we learn of its great mosques, of its ruling families, of the eminent schools of literature and learning, and of its "golden age."

Of these chronicles, none is more detailed or intricate than the *Tarikh al-Sudan,* or *History of the Sudan.* Written in 1653 by the city's most eminent scholar, 'Abd al-Rahman al-Sadi, the *tarikh* traces the history and society of Timbuktu from its founding until the time of writing. Al-Sadi's work is so reliable, and his descriptions so exact, that 250 years after it was written the French journalist Felix Dubois used it as his guidebook. "The author displays an unusual conscientiousness, never hesitating to give both versions of a doubtful event," wrote Dubois in 1897.

The two major *tarikhs* that followed al-Sadi's were essentially less ambitious updates. The first, Mahmoud Kati's *Tarikh al-Fattash,* supplements al-Sadi's work up to the early 18th century. Kati lacks the astute insight of his predecessor, but his book does contain important information on the legal and administrative heritage of Timbuktu. The anonymous *Tadhkirat al-Nisyan,* or *A Reminder to the Oblivious,* is similarly thin in detail, and it in turn brings the history up through the mid-18th century. The two latter chronicles frequently lapse into nostalgia and lament the decline of Timbuktu's fortunes.

Since its earliest beginnings, when the Tuareg would move down to the plateau each summer from the pastures of Arawan, Timbuktu has been dominated by its mosques. It is to them that the old city, with its triangular layout, owes its specific quarters—each with its unique character. Built literally of the desert itself, the adobe mosques of Timbuktu became famous throughout the Islamic world. They towered high above the sandy streets and afforded the city an impressive skyline.

The northern quarter, at the apex of the triangular city, takes its name from the Sankoré Mosque. A great, tawny, pyramidal structure laced with protruding wooden support beams, the Sankoré Mosque was the bastion of learning in Timbuktu. Its imams were regarded with unequaled respect; its school attracted the noble and the rich as students. Indeed, mentors and scholars alike are said to have flocked to Sankoré's *jam'iyyah,* or university, from as far afield as the Arabian Peninsula. Here, surrounded by the Sahara's windswept dunes, students could concentrate their minds as nowhere else. And, as Timbuktu's fame grew in the Islamic world, Sankoré became the most important center of Islamic scholarship in Africa.

The eastern corner of the city was home to the much smaller Jami' al-Suq, the Market Mosque. Like many of the less grand mosques of Timbuktu, it has fallen into disrepair, been enlarged or been rebuilt many times. The adobe construction, characteristic of sub-Saharan buildings (See *Aramco World,* November-December 1990), weakens when it rains. Each year, after the winter downpours—if they occur—many of the city's major buildings must be patched up and reinforced, but it is unexpected thunderstorms that are the dread of Timbuktu. The noted mosque Jami' al-Hana collapsed in a storm in 1771 and killed 40 people. Local legend relates that, rather than being embittered by catastrophe, the residents of Timbuktu believed that God had been so stirred by the prayers from the mosque that he had whisked the congregants up to heaven at once.

When the grand caravan of Mansa Musa arrived on that scorching day in 1325, the sultan ordered the Granadan architect and poet Abu Ishaq al-Sahili, who had traveled with him from Makkah, to build a magnificent mosque—one far larger than any the region had known—in the western corner of the city. Its name, Jingerebir, is a corruption of the Arabic *jami' al-kabir,* or "the great mosque." Five hundred years later, in 1858, the British traveler Henry Barth wrote that the mosque "by its stately appearance made a deep impression on my mind. [It] . . . includes nine naves, of different dimensions and structure."

Giant and rambling, and one of the first mosques in Africa to be built with fired-brick walls, Jingerebir at once became the central mosque of the city, and it dominates Timbuktu to this day. In times of crisis, in years when rains failed and the Niger River had risen insufficiently or not at all in its annual, life-giving flood, the people of Timbuktu gathered at Jingerebir. Within the cool shade of its walls, the imam—who often doubled as the town's ruler—would lead his congregants in prayer.

According to the *tarikhs*, Timbuktu's religious leaders, judges and officials all tended to be graduates of the city's illustrious schools. In the city where the study of Islamic principles was regarded as of supreme importance, al-Wazan found "a great store of doctors, judges, priests, and other learned men." This scholastic elite was underwritten largely by the

---

By Timbuktu's golden age, the city boasted well over 150 schools.

---

city's business class, who themselves formed a considerable part of the student body. Especially at Sankoré it was also these scholars who provided energy and direction to civil administration, commercial regulation, legislation, town planning and architectural projects—in addition to maintaining a number of superb libraries. The ranks of the city's elite were limited, however: Six families have provided two-thirds of Timbuktu's *qadis*, or judges, during the last 500 years.

By the mid-16th century—the so-called golden age of Timbuktu—the city boasted well over 150 schools, and the curricula were rigorous. The Islamic sciences formed the core of the academic syllabus, including Qur'anic interpretation (*tafsir*), the traditions of the Prophet (*hadith*); jurisprudence (*fiqh*), sources of the law (*usul*), and doctrinal theology (*tawhid*). Apart from the religious courses, students were also required to study grammar (*nahw*), literary style and rhetoric (*balaghah*), and logic (*mantiq*). Scholars focused on the way that a per-

son should behave within the context of Islamic society.

Only when religious and linguistic literacy had been achieved was a student assigned to a particular mentor. The relationship between pupil and master often grew to be a strong one, and favored students might work as *mulazama*, or private secretaries, to their teachers. As the community grew, an intellectual genealogy developed, similar to those acknowledged elsewhere in the Islamic world, that linked masters to pupils and those pupils to their own students. Strong academic and religious ties with other scholastic centers of the Middle East and North Africa linked Timbuktu to the rest of the Islamic world.

As the number of students increased, so did the fields of study available. Subjects such as history, mathematics, astronomy and cartography in time joined the wealth of courses available.

Although Timbuktu prided itself on the rigor of its teaching for even the youngest of pupils, visiting traders or travelers were encouraged to enroll while they stayed in the city. Thus many itinerant non-Muslim merchants were led to conversion in Timbuktu through encounters with Muslim scholars. Even older visitors could be assured that the city's scholastic community would educate them. Indeed, the people of Timbuktu were reputed to be so philanthropic that they would afford any visitor an education regardless of his means—maintaining that anyone who had endured the journey to their desert metropolis had earned himself a scholarship.

Likewise, those born in Timbuktu to humble families were also guaranteed their education. So great was the fervor for Islamic learning that even the tailors of Timbuktu, among other craft guilds, founded their own centers of learning where instructors oversaw both the workshop and its college. In this environment, students worked as apprentice tailors while they were also instructed in the foundations of Islamic scholarship. By the 16th century, Timbuktu is said to have had more than 26 establishments for tailor-scholars alone, many employing more than 100. Thus these

institutes also reinforced the city's role as a significant manufacturer of cloth.

At the height of the city's golden age, Timbuktu boasted not only the impressive libraries of Sankoré and the other mosques, but also a wealth of private ones. One of the greatest, containing more than 700 volumes, was left by the master scholar Hajji Ahmad bin 'Umar. His library was said to have included many of the rarest books ever written in Arabic, and he copied and annotated a considerable number of the volumes himself.

The libraries of Timbuktu grew through a regular process of hand-copying manuscripts. Scholars would visit the caravanserais and appeal to learned travelers to permit their precious volumes to be reproduced. Alternatively, they duplicated texts borrowed from their mentors' collections, studying the material as they did so.

Al-Wazan commented that "hither are brought divers manuscripts or written books, which are sold for more money than any other merchandise." As late as the close of the 19th century, Felix Dubois purchased a number of antique books in Timbuktu, including a copy of the *Divan of Kings,* a chronology of the rulers and events of the Sudan between 1656 and 1747.

Timbuktu's position as a principal staging point along the pilgrimage route to Makkah may partly explain why so many books were available. Even so, modern scholars are staggered by the sheer quantity and rarity of Arabic texts and poems proffered and composed in the city. Of the books written in Timbuktu, a number are surprising in their scope. Ahmed Baba's biographical dictionary, for example, included the lives of notables from Arabia, Egypt, Morocco and Central Asia, as well as Timbuktu itself.

Of the city's scholars, none is more lionized today than Muhammad Askia, called "Muhammad the Great," who reigned over Timbuktu for more than three decades in the late 15th and early 16th centuries. Regarded as the city's savior, it was he who wrested Timbuktu from the infamous Songhoi ruler Sunni Ali in 1493. Ali was despised as one who undermined Islam by persecuting the scholastic class, efforts that earned him uncomplimentary entries in the *tarikhs*. Under Askia, however, scholarship and Islam were again revered and supported, and a new era of stability began that led to Timbuktu's 16th-century golden age.

Like any frontier town, Timbuktu also gained strength from the melting-pot of peoples who sought to make their lives within its walls. A mixture of North and West African tribes wove their unique ways into the framework of Timbuktu's culture.

The influence of the Songhoi people, for example, extended to the calendar, where Ramadan, the holy month of fasting, was popularly known by the Songhoi word haome, which translates, literally, as "closed mouth." The end of the Ramadan fast was known similarly as *ferme,* or "open mouth." Observance of the Ramadan fast has never been easy in Timbuktu, where the desert climate much resembles that of central Arabia, but the holy month has always been taken very seriously in the city.

Like Muslims everywhere, the people of Timbuktu were united by Ramadan. As the sun scorched down, or as the flour-fine Sahara sand squalled through the streets, the faithful would gather in the mosques, protected from the desert and enveloped in the simplicity of the adobe architecture, in order to renew their faith.

During Tyibsi, as Dhu al-Hijjah, the month which follows Ramadan, was called, feasting was in order. On the 10th day of the month, as pilgrims prepared to begin the taxing journey to

---

Scholars are staggered by the quantity and rarity of the texts.

Makkah, the men of Timbuktu would gather for special prayers, and the imam of Jingerebir would sacrifice a ram. Then everyone would hurry home, for a local tradition maintained that the first man to follow the imam's sacrifice with one of his own would be the first to ride into paradise.

With desert dunes surrounding it in all directions, and trapped in a severe and perfidious climate, the fact that fabled Timbuktu rose and prospered for 800 years is remarkable. That it also became a center of scholarship so fertile that it advanced the worldwide community of Islamic learning is astonishing. But more surprising still is that Timbuktu's intellectual tradition remained largely intact generation after generation. Even during times of economic depression, caused by shifting caravan routes or spoiled crops, the community ensured that the Qur'anic academies survived.

Early in the 19th century, the young French explorer René Caille remarked that all the population of Timbuktu was apparently "able to read the Qur'an and even know it by heart." Some 66 years later, when the French colonized the region, they recorded that some two dozen key scholastic centers still flourished in Timbuktu. Continuing to teach Arabic, Qur'anic doctrine and traditional lore, the schools had altered little in 500 years.

Now, as the desert creeps slowly southward all across sub-Saharan Africa, Timbuktu stands more isolated by sand and heat than ever. At the same time, in the city that captivated both West and East, some of the richest parts of the legacy of Islam lie only just beneath the city's baked-mud surface, waiting silently to be rediscovered, and perhaps reawakened.

Tahir Shah lives in London and is the author of Beyond the Devil's Teeth: Journeys in Gondwanaland, *published by Octagon Press, as well as five other books.*

The Arab Roots of European Medicine

Wel knew he the olde Esculapius and Deyscorides and eek Rufus Olde
Ypocras, Haly and Galeyn, Serapion, Razi and Avycen, Averrois, Damascien
and Constantyn, Bernard and Gatesden and Gilbertyn.

Written by David W. Tschanz

In the "General Prologue" of *The Canterbury Tales,* Geoffrey Chaucer identifies the authorities used by his "Doctour of Physic" in the . . . lines quoted above. The list includes four Arab physicians: Jesu Haly (Ibn'Isa), Razi (Al-Razi, or Rhazes), Avycen (Ibn Sina, or Avicenna) and Averrois (Ibn Rushd, or Averroes). These four did not make Chaucer's list only to add an exotic flavor to his late-14th-century poetry. Chaucer cited them because they were regarded as among the great medical authorities of the ancient world and the European Middle Ages, physicians whose textbooks were used in European medical schools, and would be for centuries to come. First collecting, then translating, then augmenting and finally codifying the classical Greco-Roman heritage that Europe has lost, Arab physicians of the eighth to eleventh century laid the foundations of the institutions and the science of modern medicine.

After the collapse of the western Roman empire in the fifth century, Europe lost touch with much of its intellectual heritage. Of Greek science, all that remained were Pliny's *Encyclopedia* and Boethius's treatises on logic and mathematics; the Latin library was so limited that European theologians found it nearly impossible to expand their knowledge of their own scriptures.

The center of Europe's new world view became the church, which exerted profound new influences in medicine. Because Christianity emphasized compassion and care for the sick, monastic orders ran fine hospitals—but they did not function as hospitals do today. They were simply places to take seriously ill people, where they were expected to either recover or die as God willed. There were no learned physicians to attend them, only kindly monks who dispensed comfort and the sacraments, but not medicines.

Because the Christian church viewed care of the soul as far more important than care of the body, medical treatment and even physical cleanliness were little valued, and mortification of the flesh was seen as a sign of saintliness. In time, nearly all Europeans came to look upon illness as a condition caused by supernatural forces, which might take the form of diabolical possession. Hence, cures could only be effected by religious means. Every malady had a patron saint to whom prayers were directed by the patient, family, friends and the community. Upper respiratory infections were warded off by a blessing of the throat with crossed candles on the feast of Saint Blaise. Saint Roch became the patron of plague victims. Saint Nicaise was the source of protection against smallpox. Kings, regarded as divinely appointed, were believed to be able to cure scrofula and skin diseases, among other maladies, with the "royal touch."

With the study of disease and of patients neglected, licensed medicine as an independent craft virtually vanished.

Those physicians who endured were mostly connected with monasteries and abbeys. But even for them, the generally accepted goal was less to discover causes, or even to heal, than to study the writings of other physicians and comment on their work. In the middle of the seventh century, the Catholic church banned surgery by monks, because it constituted a danger to their souls. Since nearly all of the surgeons of that era were clerics, the decree effectively ended the practice of surgery in Europe.

At roughly the same time, another civilization was rising in the east. The coming of Islam, also in the seventh century (See *Aramco World,* November/December 1991), led to a hundred years of continuous geographical expansion and an unprecedented era of ferment in all branches of learning. The Arabs rapidly melded the various cultures of the Islamic domain, and Arabic—the language of the Qur'an—became the universal language. By the 10th century a single language linked peoples from the Rann of Kutch to the south of France, and Arabic became to the East what Latin and Greek had been to the West—the language of literature, the arts and sciences, and the common tongue of the educated.

Medicine was the first of the Greek sciences to be studied in depth by Islamic scholars. After Plato's Academy was closed in 529, some of its scholars found refuge at the university at Jun-

Reprinted from *Aramco World,* May/June 1997, pp. 20-31. © 1997 by Aramco Services Company.

Illuminating Europe's Dark Ages

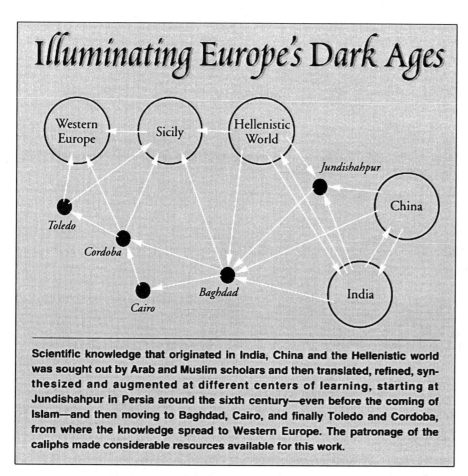

Scientific knowledge that originated in India, China and the Hellenistic world was sought out by Arab and Muslim scholars and then translated, refined, synthesized and augmented at different centers of learning, starting at Jundishahpur in Persia around the sixth century—even before the coming of Islam—and then moving to Baghdad, Cairo, and finally Toledo and Cordoba, from where the knowledge spread to Western Europe. The patronage of the caliphs made considerable resources available for this work.

DIAGRAM AND CAPTION ADAPTED FROM *THE CREST OF THE PEACOCK: NON-EUROPEAN ROOTS OF MATHEMATICS* BY GEORGE GHEVERGHESE JOSEPH (PENGUIN BOOKS/I.B. TAURIS) © 1991. USED BY PERMISSION OF PENGUIN BOOKS LTD.

dishahpur, the old Sassanid capital of Persia, which had also sheltered excommunicated Nestorian Christian scholars—among them physicians—in 431. Persia became part of the Islamic world in 636, and Arab rulers supported the medical school at Jundishahpur; for the next 200 years it was the greatest center of medical teaching in the Islamic world. There, Islamic physicians first familiarized themselves with the works of Hippocrates, Galen and other Greek physicians. At the same time, they were also exposed to the medical knowledge of Byzantium, Persia, India and China.

Recognizing the importance of translating Greek works into Arabic to make them more widely available, the Abbasid caliphs Harun al-Rashid (786–809) and his son, al-Ma'mun (813–833) established a translation bureau in Baghdad, the Bayt al-Hikmah, or House of Wisdom, and sent embassies to collect Greek scientific works in the Byzantine Empire. (See *Aramco World*, May/June 1982.) This ushered in the first era in Islamic medicine, whose effects we feel today: the period of translation and compilation.

The most important of the translators was Hunayn ibn Ishaq al-'Ibadi (809–73), who was reputed to have been paid for his manuscripts by an equal weight of gold. He and his team of translators rendered the entire body of Greek medical texts, including all the works of Galen, Oribasius, Paul of Aegin, Hippocrates and the *Materia Medica* of Dioscorides, into Arabic by the end of the ninth century. These translations established the foundations of a uniquely Arab medicine.

Muslim medical practice largely accepted Galen's premise of humors, which held that the human body was made up of the same four elements that comprise the world—earth, air, fire and water. These elements could be mixed in various proportions, and the differing mixtures gave rise to the different temperaments and "humors." When the body's humors were correctly balanced, a person was healthy. Sickness was due not to supernatural forces but to humoral imbalance, and such imbalance could be corrected by the doctor's healing arts.

Muslim physicians therefore came to look upon medicine as the science by which the dispositions of the human body could be discerned, and to see its goal as the preservation of health and, if health should be lost, assistance in recovering it. They viewed themselves as practitioners of the dual art of healing and the maintenance of health.

Even before the period of translation closed, advances were made in other health-related fields. Harun al-Rashid established the first hospital, in the modern sense of the term, at Baghdad about 805. Within a decade or two, 34 more hospitals had sprung up throughout the Islamic world, and the number grew each year.

These hospitals, or *bimaristans,* bore little resemblance to their European counterparts. The sick saw the *bimaristan* as a place where they could be treated and perhaps cured by physicians, and the physicians saw the *bimaristan* as an institution devoted to the promotion of health, the cure of disease and the expansion and dissemination of medical knowledge. Medical schools and libraries were attached to the larger hospitals, and senior physicians taught students, who were in turn expected to apply in the men's and women's wards what they had learned in the lecture hall. Hospitals set examinations for their students, and issued diplomas. By the 11th century, there were even traveling clinics, staffed by the hospitals, that brought medical care to those too distant or too sick to come to the hospitals themselves. The *bimaristan* was, in short, the cradle of Arab medicine and the prototype upon which the modern hospital is based.

Like the hospital, the institution of the pharmacy, too, was an Islamic development. Islam teaches that "God has provided a remedy for every illness," and that Muslims should search for those remedies and use them with skill and compassion. One of the first pharmacological treatises was composed by

The Caliphs' Researches

Fourteenth-century historian and political scientist Ibn Khaldun wrote about the intellectual curiosity that helped to preserve Greek learning.

When the Byantine emperors conquered Syria, the scientific works of the Greeks were still in existence. Then God brought Islam, and the Muslims won their remarkable victories, conquering the Byzantines as well as all other nations. At first, the Muslims were simple, and did not cultivate learning, but as time went on and the Muslim dynasty flourished, the Muslims developed an urban culture which surpassed that of any other nation.

They began to wish to study the various branches of philosophy, of whose existence they knew from their contact with bishops and priests among their Christian subjects. In any case, man has always had a penchant for intellectual speculation. The caliph al-Mansur therefore sent an embassy to the Byzantine emperor, asking him to send him translations of books on mathematics. The emperor sent him Euclid's *Elements* and some works on physics.

Muslim scholars studied these books, and their desire to obtain others was whetted. When al-Ma'mun, who had some scientific knowledge, assumed the caliphate, he wished to do something to further the progress of science. For that purpose, he sent ambassadors and translators to the Byzantine empire, in order to search out works on the Greek sciences and have them translated into Arabic. As a result of these efforts, a great deal of material was gathered and preserved.

Jabir ibn Hayyan (ca. 776), who is considered the father of Arab alchemy. The Arab pharmacopoeia of the time was extensive, and gave descriptions of the geographical origin, physical properties and methods of application of everything found useful in the cure of disease. Arab pharmacists, or *saydalani*, introduced a large number of new drugs to clinical practice, including senna, camphor, sandalwood, musk, myrrh, cassia, tamarind, nutmeg, cloves, aconite, ambergris and mercury. The *saydalani* also developed syrups and juleps—the words came from Arabic and Persian, respectively—and pleasant solvents such as rose water and orange-blossom water as means of administering drugs. They were familiar with the anesthetic effects of Indian hemp and henbane, both when taken in liquids and inhaled.

By the time of al-Ma'mun's caliphate, pharmacy was a profession practiced by highly skilled specialists. Pharmacists were required to pass examinations and be licensed, and were then monitored by the state. At the start of the ninth century, the first private apothecary shops opened in Baghdad. Pharmaceutical preparations were manufactured and distributed commercially, then dispensed by physicians and pharmacists in a variety of forms—ointments, pills, elixirs, confections, tinctures, suppositories and inhalants.

The blossoming of original thought in Arab medicine began as the ninth century drew to a close. The first major work appeared when Abu Bakr Muhammad ibn Zakariya Al-Razi (ca. 841–926) turned his attention to medicine.

Al-Razi, known to the West as Rhazes, was born in Persia in the town of Rayy, near Tehran. After a youth spent as a musician, mathematician and alchemist, Al-Razi went to Baghdad to take up the study of medicine at the age of 40. Completing his studies, he returned to Rayy and assumed the directorship of its hospital. His reputation

grew rapidly and within a few years he was selected to be the director of a new hospital to be built in Baghdad. He approached the question of where to put the new facility by hanging pieces of meat in various sections of the city and checking the rate at which they spoiled. He then ordered the hospital built at the site where the meat showed the least putrefaction.

Al-Razi is regarded as Islamic medicine's greatest clinician and its most original thinker. A prolific writer, he turned out some 237 books, about half of which dealt with medicine. His treatise *The Diseases of Children* has led some historians to regard him as the father of pediatrics. He was the first to identify hay fever and its cause. His work on kidney stones is still considered a classic. In addition, he was instrumental in the introduction of mercurial ointments to treat scabies. Al-Razi advocated reliance on observation rather than on received authority; he was a strong proponent of experimental medicine and the beneficial use of previously tested medicinal plants and other drugs. A leader in the fight against quacks and charlatans—and author of a book exposing their methods—he called for high professional standards for practitioners. He also insisted on continuing education

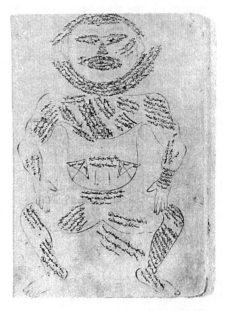

Seeds of *Silene gallica* (top left), called *hashishat al-thubban*, or *flyweed*, in Arabic, were effective in a snakebite antiodote, according to Dioscorides. Above, Persian notations detail the human muscle system in Mansur ibn Ilyas' late-14th-century Tashrih-i Badan-i Insan (The Anatomy of the Human Body).

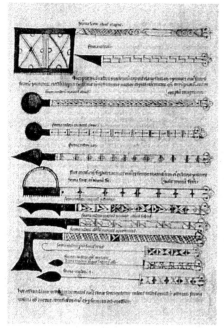

Surgical instruments are shown in detail in a 13th-century Latin translation of The Method *(above), a 30-part medical text written by Islam's greatest medieval surgeon, Abu al-Qasim, who practiced in 10th-century Córdoba.*

His most esteemed work was a medical encyclopedia in 25 books, *Al-Kitab al-Hawi,* or *The Comprehensive Work,* the *Liber Continens* of Al-Razi's later Latin translators. Al-Razi spent a lifetime collecting data for the book, which he intended as a summary of all the medical knowledge of his time, augmented by his own experience and observations. *In Al-Hawi,* Al-Razi emphasized the need for physicians to pay careful attention to what the patients' histories told them, rather than merely consulting the authorities of the past. In a series of diagnosed case histories entitled "Illustrative Accounts of Patients," Al-Razi demonstrated this important tenet. One patient, who lived in a malarial district, suffered from intermittent chills and fever that had been diagnosed as malaria, but nonetheless seemed incurable. Al-Razi was asked to examine him. Upon noting pus in the urine, he diagnosed an infected kidney, and he treated the patient successfully with diuretics.

Al-Razi's clinical skill was matched by his understanding of human nature, particularly as demonstrated in the attitudes of patients. In a series of short monographs on the doctor-patient relationship, he described principles that are still taught a millennium later: Doctors and patients need to establish a mutual bond of trust, he wrote; positive comments from doctors encourage patients, make them feel better and speed their recovery; and, he warned, changing from one doctor to another wastes patients' health, wealth and time.

for already licensed physicians. Al-Razi was the first to emphasize the value of mutual trust and consultation among skilled physicians in the treatment of patients, a rare practice at that time.

Following his term as hospital director in Baghdad, he returned to Rayy where he taught the healing arts in the local hospital, and he continued to write. His first major work was a 10 part treatise entitled *Al-Kitab al-Mansuri,* so called after the ruler of Rayy, Mansur ibn Ishaq. In it, he discussed such varied subjects as general medical theories and definitions; diet and drugs and their effect on the human body; mother and child care, skin disease, oral hygiene, climatology and the effect of the environment on health; epidemiology and toxicology.

Al-Razi also prepared *Al-Judari wa al Hasbah,* the first treatise ever written on smallpox and measles. In a masterful demonstration of clinical observation (see column at right), Al-Razi became the first to distinguish the two diseases from each other. At the same time, he provided still-valid guidelines for the sound treatment of both.

Right: Mandrake (Mandragora officinalis; al-luffah in Arabic) was described in the 10th century by Al-Biruni as a useful soporific.

Not long after Al-Razi's death, Abu'Al al-Husayn ibn 'Abd Allah ibn Sina (980–1037) was born in Bukhara, in what today is Uzbekistan. Later translators Latinized his name to Avicenna. It is hard to describe Ibn Sina in anything other than superlatives. He was to the Arab world what Aristotle was to Greece, Leonardo da Vinci to the Renaissance and Goethe to Germany. His preeminence embraced not only medicine, but also the fields of philosophy, science, music, poetry and statecraft. His contemporaries called him "the prince of physicians."

Ibn Sina's life was in fact the stuff of legend. The son of a tax collector, he

was so precocious that he had completely memorized the Qur'an by age 10. Then he studied law, mathematics, physics, and philosophy. Confronted by a difficult problem in Aristotle's *Metaphysics,* Ibn Sina re-read the book 40 times in his successful search for a solution. At 16 he turned to the study of

A Physician Observes

In Al-Judari wa al-Hasbah, *Al-Razi distinguished smallpox from measles for the first time in medical history. This passage shows his skill as a medical observer, a competence on which he placed great importance.*

The eruption of the smallpox is preceded by a continued fever, pain in the back, itching in the nose and terrors in the sleep. These are the more peculiar symptoms of its approach, especially a pain in the back with fever; then also a pricking which the patient feels all over his body; a fullness of the face, which at times comes and goes; an inflamed color, and vehement redness in both cheeks; a redness of both the eyes, heaviness of the whole body; great uneasiness, the symptoms of which are stretching and yawning; a pain in the throat and chest, with slight difficulty in breathing and cough; a dryness of the breath, thick spittle and hoarseness of the voice; pain and heaviness of the head; inquietude, nausea and anxiety; (with this difference that the inquietude, nausea and anxiety are more frequent in the measles than in the smallpox; while on the other hand, the pain in the back is more peculiar to the smallpox than to the measles;) heat of the whole body; an inflamed colon, and shining redness, and especially an intense redness of the gums.

medicine, which he said he found "not difficult." By 18, his fame as a physician was so great that he was summoned to treat the Samanid prince Nuh ibn Mansur. His success with that patient won him access to the Samanid royal library, one of the greatest of Bukhara's many storehouses of learning.

Testing New Medicines

In his voluminous writings, Ibn Sina laid out the following rules for testing the effectiveness of a new drug or medication. These principles still form the basis of modern clinical drug trials.

1 The drug must be free from any extraneous accidental quality.

2 It must be used on a simple not a composite, disease.

3 The drug must be tested with two contrary types of diseases, because sometimes a drug cures one disease by its essential qualities and another by its accidental ones.

4 The quality of the drug must correspond to the strength of the disease. For example, there are some drugs whose heat is less than the coldness of certain diseases, so that they would have no effect on them.

5 The time of action must be observed, so that essence and accident are not confused.

6 The effect of the drug must be seen to occur constantly or in many cases, for if this did not happen, it was an accidental effect.

7 The experimentation must be done with the human body, for testing a drug on a lion or a horse might not prove anything about its effect on man.

At 20, Ibn Sina was appointed court physician, and twice served as vizier, to Shams al-Dawlah, the Buyid prince of Hamadan, in western Persia. His remaining years were crowded with adventure and hard work, yet he somehow found time to write 20 books on theology, metaphysics, astronomy, philology and poetry and 20 more on medicine—including *Kitab al-Shifa'*, or *The Book of Healing*, a medical and philosophical encyclopedia.

His supreme work, however, is the monumental *Al-Qanun fi al-Tibb, The Canon of Medicine.* Over one million words long, it was nothing less than a codification of all existing medical knowledge. Summarizing the Hippocratic and Galenic traditions, describing Syro-Arab and Indo-Persian practice and including notes on his own observations, Ibn Sina strove to fit each bit of anatomy, physiology, diagnosis and treatment into its proper niche.

The Canon stressed the importance of diet and the influence of climate and environment on health. It included discussions of rabies, hydrocele, breast cancer, tumors, labor and poisons and their treatment. Ibn Sina differentiated meningitis from the meningismus of other acute diseases; and described chronic nephritis, facial paralysis, ulcer of the stomach and the various types of hepatitis and their causes. He also expounded the dilation and contraction of the pupils and their diagnostic value, described the six motor muscles of the eye and discussed the functions of the tear ducts, and he noted the contagious nature of some diseases, which he attributed to "traces" left in the air by a sick person.

The Canon also included a description of some 760 medicinal plants and the drugs that could be derived from them. At the same time Ibn Sina laid out the basic rules of clinical drug trials, principles that are still followed today. (*See box,* "Testing New Medicines".)

Not surprisingly, *The Canon* rapidly became the standard medical reference work of the Islamic world. Nizami-i Arudi of Samarkand spoke for generations of physicians when he wrote, in the early 12th century, "From him who manages the first volume [*of The Canon*], nothing will be hidden concerning the general theory and principles of medicine." *The Canon* was used as a reference, a teaching guide and a medical textbook until well into the 19th century, longer than any other medical work.

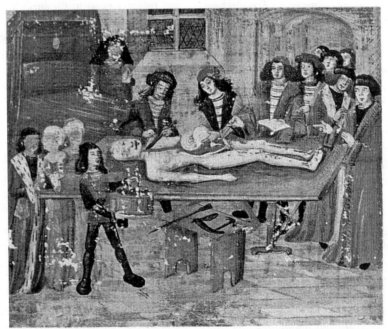

ART RESOURCE/MUSEÉ ALGER

This depiction of mandrake before flowering (top) appeared in an Arabic version of De Materia Medica *titled* Khawass al-Ashjar (The Properties of Plants), *translated in Baghdad in 1240. Above, an anatomy lesson at the medical school at Montpellier—one of Europe's earliest—from de Chauliac's 1363* Grande Chirurgie.

During the 10th century, when Arab astronomical texts were first translated in Catalonia, Europe began to reap the intellectual riches of the Arabs and, in so doing, to seek out its own classical heritage. The medical works of Galen and Hip-

Ibn Sina's *Canon* made its first appearance in Europe by the end of the 12th century, and its impact was dramatic. Copied and recopied, it quickly became the standard European medical reference work. In the last 30 years of the 15th century, just before the Euro-

University of Paris. In *The Inferno*, Dante placed Ibn Sina side by side with antiquity's two greatest physicians, Hippocrates and Galen. Roger Bacon consulted Ibn Sina to further his own inquiries into vision.

But it was not only Al-Razi and Ibn Sina who influenced Europe. Translations of more than 400 Arab authors, writing on such varied topics as ophthalmology, surgery, pharmaceuticals, child care and public health, deeply influenced the rebirth of European science.

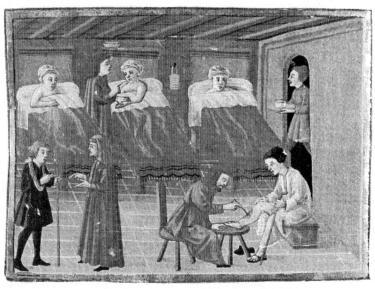

ART RESOURCE/BIBLIOTECA LAURENZIANA

At the Benedictine monastery at Monte Cassino in the 10th century, the Middle Eastern traveler Leo Africanus translated Arab medical texts and supervised a hospital run on Arab principles. Between that time and the Renaissance, European hospitals, like the one above, from an undated Italian manuscript, were increasingly modeled on the Arab bimaristan.

pocrates returned to the West by way of the Middle East and North Africa, recovered through Latin translations of what had become the Arab medical classics. Through the intellectual ferment of the Islamic present, Europe recovered some of its past.

The two main translators of classical material from Arabic into Latin were Constantinus (also known as Leo) Africanus (1020–1087), who worked at Salerno and in the cloister of Monte Cassino, and Gerard of Cremona (1140–1187), who worked in Toledo. It was no accident that both translators lived in the Arab-Christian transition zone, where the two cultures fructified each other. And it was no coincidence that Salerno, Europe's first great medical faculty of the Middle Ages, was close to Arab Sicily, nor that the second, Montpellier, was founded in 1221 in southern France, near the Andalusian border.

pean invention of printing, it was issued in 16 editions; in the century that followed more than 20 further editions were printed. From the 12th to the 17th century, its *materia medica* was the pharmacopoeia of Europe, and as late as 1537 *The Canon* was still a required textbook at the University of Vienna.

Translations of Al-Razi's *Al-Kitab al-Hawi* and other works followed rapidly. Printed while printing was still in its infancy, all of Al-Razi's works gained widespread acceptance. The ninth book of *Al-Kitab al-Mansuri* ("Concerning Diseases from the Head to the Foot") remained part of the medical curriculum at the University of Tübingen until the end of the 15th century.

Contemporary Europeans regarded Ibn Sina and Al-Razi as the greatest authorities on medical matters, and portraits of both men still adorn the great hall of the School of Medicine at the

Despite their belief in now superseded theories such as humors and miasmas, the medicine of Ibn Sina, Al-Razi and their contemporaries is the basis of much of what we take for granted today.

It was those Arab physicians who made accurate diagnoses of plague, diphtheria, leprosy, rabies, diabetes, gout, cancer and epilepsy. Ibn Sina's theory of infection by "traces" led to the introduction of quarantine as a means of limiting the spread of infectious diseases. Arab doctors laid down the principles of clinical investigation and drug trials, and they uncovered the secret of sight. They mastered operations for hernia and cataract, filled teeth with gold leaf and prescribed spectacles for defective eyesight. And they passed on rules of health, diet and hygiene that are still largely valid today.

Thus the Islamic world not only provided a slender but ultimately successful line of transmission for the medical knowledge of ancient Greece and the Hellenic world, it also corrected and enormously expanded that knowledge before passing it on to a Europe that had abandoned observation, experimentation and the very concept of earthly progress centuries before. Physicians of different languages and religions had cooperated in building a sturdy structure whose outlines are still visible in the medical practices of our own time.

David W. Tschanz lives and works in Saudi Arabia as an epidemiologist with Saudi Aramco. He holds master's degrees in both history and epidemiology, and writes about the history of medicine.

The Viking Longship

Long, Narrow Ships Packed With Warriors Helped to Make the Vikings the Dominant Power in Europe for Three Centuries, Beginning in about A.D. 800

By John R. Hale

In September 1997 Danish archaeologists discovered a Viking longship in the mud of Roskilde harbor, 40 kilometers (25 miles) west of Copenhagen. The discovery was the kind of serendipitous event that earned Viking Leif Eriksson the appellation "Leif the Lucky." Lying unsuspected next to the world-renowned Viking Ship Museum at Roskilde, the longship came to light during dredging operations to expand the harbor for the museum's fleet of historic ship replicas.

According to Ole Crumlin-Pedersen, former head of the museum, the longship must have been sunk by a storm centuries ago, then hidden by silt. Tree-ring dating of its oak planks showed that the ship had been built about A.D. 1025 during the reign of King Canute the Great, who united Denmark, Norway, southern Sweden and England in a Viking empire.

With its immense length of 35 meters, the Roskilde longship surpasses all previous longship finds. By doing so, the ship also refuted skeptical modern scholars who judged these leviathans, described in Norse sagas, to be as mythical as the dragon whose name they bore. (Longships became known generally as dragons.) The sagas had been accurate in their accounts of "great ships," the largest class of Viking warship.

The passage of a millennium has not dimmed the pride Scandinavians feel for the Viking longships. Their vital role in seaborne raiding, which is the meaning of the Norse term *viking*, assures them a prominent place in medieval history.

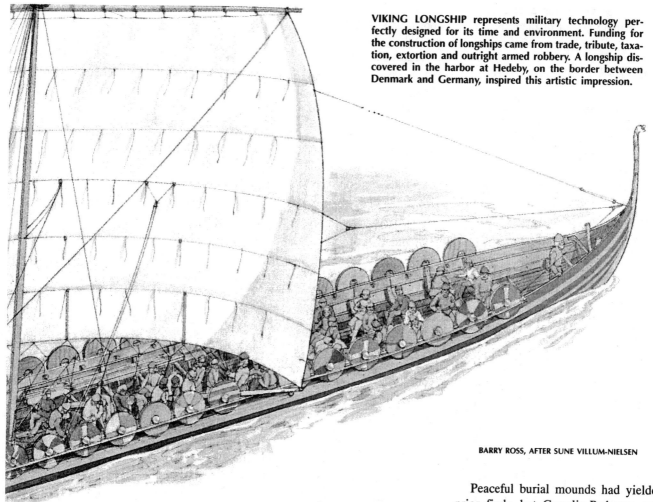

VIKING LONGSHIP represents military technology perfectly designed for its time and environment. Funding for the construction of longships came from trade, tribute, taxation, extortion and outright armed robbery. A longship discovered in the harbor at Hedeby, on the border between Denmark and Germany, inspired this artistic impression.

BARRY ROSS, AFTER SUNE VILLUM-NIELSEN

Fleets of these long, narrow ships attacked coasts from Northumberland to North Africa, carried pioneers to the British Isles and Normandy, and made the Vikings the dominant sea power in Europe from about A.D. 800 to 1100, the Viking Age.

Although finds of various Viking ships and boats have been made since 1751—most spectacularly in the royal burial mounds at Gokstad and Oseberg in Norway—the classic longship itself proved elusive until 1935, when Danish archaeologists excavated a chieftain's burial mound at Ladby. Only the shadow of a ship remained, with dark-stained soil revealing the form of the hull. Iron spirals marked the crest of the dragon's head at the prow, and seven long rows of iron rivets on either side still followed the lines of the vanished planks. The Ladby ship was much narrower than the celebrated Norwegian ships and looked quite unseaworthy: 20.6 meters long, only 3.2 wide amidships and a mere meter from the keel to the top plank. Critics dismissed as implausible the accounts in the sagas of much larger longships with the same extreme proportions.

Actual timbers of a longship were located in 1953 in Hedeby harbor, site of a prosperous Viking emporium on the German border. Although the ship was not raised, public interest ran so high that the diver who discovered it made a radio broadcast underwater; his fascinated audience included 18-year-old Ole Crumlin-Pedersen. By age 22, he had embarked on a series of finds that exploded the timid theories of the skeptics and ultimately involved him in the retrieval and study of every longship discovered since Ladby.

Peaceful burial mounds had yielded prior finds, but Crumlin-Pedersen specialized in disaster sites. Between 1957 and 1962 he was co-director of the team that recovered two longships and three other Viking ships from a blockade in a channel near Skuldelev, where desperate Danish townsfolk in the 11th century had deliberately sunk the ships to create a barricade against invaders. The bigger of the two Skuldelev longships, measuring 29 meters, met its end after making at least one successful voyage across the North Sea: its wood was Irish oak, cut about 1060 near the Viking stronghold of Dublin. Both ships in fact showed many seasons of wear, evidence that longships were more seaworthy than some scholars had thought.

In 1979 Crumlin-Pedersen fulfilled a dream of his youth by leading the excavation of the Hedeby longship. It proved to have perished as a fire ship, a vessel intentionally set ablaze as an offensive weapon, during an attack on the town in about 1000. Here, too, the wood was remarkable: local oak cut from 300-year-old trees in lengths exceeding 10 meters without a knot or blemish.

AN EVOLVED DESIGN

The five longships discovered since 1935 show the full range of the species. Small levy vessels of up to 20 rowing benches (Ladby and the little Skuldelev warship) were maintained by local communities for royal service, to answer the call whenever the king sent around the symbolic war arrow. Standard longships of up to 30 rowing benches (Hedeby and the big Skuldelev warship) were the pride of Viking earls and kings, displaying craftsmanship of superb quality. The "great ships" of more than 30 rowing benches (Roskilde) appear only in the dynastic wars of the late Viking Age.

These finds reveal that Viking shipwrights, in quest of the ultimate raiding machine, created the most extreme of all traditional ship designs. The length-to-breadth ratio, greater than 6:1, and a rapierlike 11.4:1 in the Hedeby longship, combined with the shallow draft to allow longships to land on any beach and penetrate virtually any waterway in Europe. With speed as a goal, whether under oars or sail, expert shipwrights achieved strength through resilience and lightness. They pared the planking to a thickness of two centimeters—a finger's breadth—and trimmed every sliver of excess wood from the rib frames. Yet this drive for technical perfection produced a masterpiece of beauty as well, above all in the noble curves of stem and stern. A court bard sang the praises of King Harald Hardruler's dragon: "As Norsemen row the serpent, the riveted [ship], down the icy stream, it is like a sight of eagle's wings." Plato may have denied the existence of ideal forms in this world, but Plato never saw a Viking ship.

The longship's perfect mating of design, structure and material derives neither from a single creative genius nor even a single age. Rather these vessels represent the culmination of 6,000 years of technical evolution.

The primeval ancestors appear to be Stone Age dugout canoes, the earliest

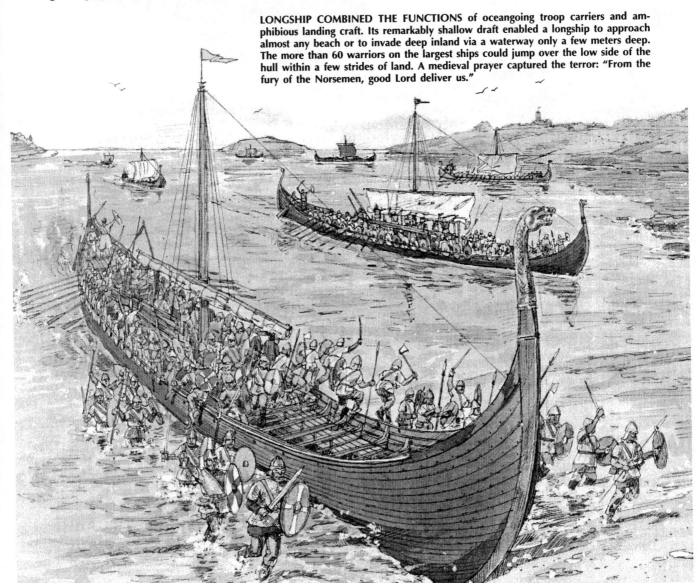

LONGSHIP COMBINED THE FUNCTIONS of oceangoing troop carriers and amphibious landing craft. Its remarkably shallow draft enabled a longship to approach almost any beach or to invade deep inland via a waterway only a few meters deep. The more than 60 warriors on the largest ships could jump over the low side of the hull within a few strides of land. A medieval prayer captured the terror: "From the fury of the Norsemen, good Lord deliver us."

BARRY ROSS

LONGSHIP FINDS appear on map as white dots. Boats ancestral to longships were found at sites marked with black dots.

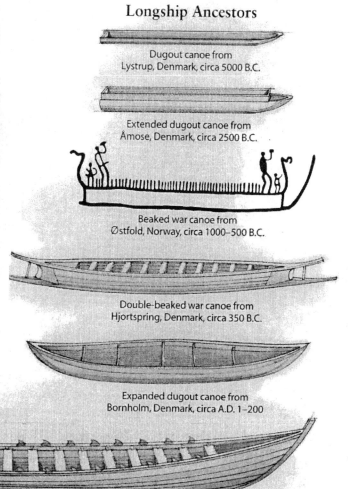

Longship Ancestors

Dugout canoe from Lystrup, Denmark, circa 5000 B.C.

Extended dugout canoe from Åmose, Denmark, circa 2500 B.C.

Beaked war canoe from Østfold, Norway, circa 1000–500 B.C.

Double-beaked war canoe from Hjortspring, Denmark, circa 350 B.C.

Expanded dugout canoe from Bornholm, Denmark, circa A.D. 1–200

Oared warship from Nydam, Denmark, circa A.D. 300

Oared warship with keel and fixed side rudder from Kvalsund, Norway, circa A.D. 700

BARRY ROSS; BRYAN CHRISTIE, AFTER A TRACING BY SVERRE MARSTRANDER (beaked war canoe)

dating to about 5000 B.C., which have been found at many coastal sites in Denmark. Using flint tools, boatwrights sculpted logs of soft, durable linden wood to an even thickness of two centimeters. As in all dugouts, the shell itself provided structural integrity, a true exoskeleton. The canoes reached lengths of 10 meters and seem to have been paddled out to sea for cod fishing, whaling and raiding expeditions. Some canoes later served as coffins. The creators of dugouts bequeathed to their successors

the ideal of light, open vessels with shallow draft and a long, narrow hull.

About 3000 B.C., boatbuilders along the Åmose River in Denmark began to bore a row of holes along the upper edges of their dugout canoes. They could than secure the lower edge of a plank, with matching holes, to the top of the dugout with cords of sinew or fiber. The resulting overlap marked the birth of the distinctive northern European construction technique known as lapstrake, a strake being a line of plank-

ing. The added plank improved seaworthiness by increasing the extended dugout's "freeboard," the distance between the waterline and the hull's top. Axes of Danish flint found far to the north in Norway and Sweden bear witness to the adventures of these Stone Age voyagers.

During the Bronze Age (2000 to 500 B.C.), the watercraft of Scandinavia took on some of the appearance of the future Viking ship, including high posts at each end crowned with spirals or animal heads. Some of these heads are certainly serpents or dragons, and dragons are depicted hovering over boats in Bronze Age art. The warriors manning these boats often wore the horned helmets that have come to symbolize the caricature Viking of opera or cartoons. In fact, such headgear was quite out of fashion by the true Viking Age.

The designs on Bronze Age metalwork and rock carvings show boats with a beak at the prow. Although unfamiliar in European watercraft, the same structure could be found in the early 20th century on extended dugouts with sewn plank sides in Siberia, central Africa and the South Pacific. The beak was in fact the projecting tip of the dugout underbody. With a curved branch attached, it acted as a cutwater to protect the vulnerable stem where the planking closed off the forepart of the hull. Eventually, the wooden cutwater of the Bronze Age Scandinavian design would coalesce with the ornamented end post to form the great curved prow of the Viking ship.

The beak became the prominent feature of war canoes at the beginning of the Iron Age (500 B.C. to A.D. 400), a time of severe climatic and economic stress in northern Europe. Too high and too flimsy to serve as a ram, the beak must have been preserved by boatbuilders because it protected and stabilized the hull. Shipwrights deemed the beak valuable enough to include it at both ends, creating, in the Iron Age, the first truly double-ended design.

A bog near Hjortspring, Denmark, yielded an early Iron Age canoe—complete with paddles, weapons and other gear—built in about 350 B.C. With its symmetric beaks and large steering paddles at each end, the Hjortspring boat could have reversed directions without turning. Such adaptability might mean the difference between life and death when encountering enemies in a narrow fjord or pushing off after a raid on a hostile shore. For the next 1,500 years, all Scandinavian warships would maintain the double-ended design of the Hjortspring boat, even after the fixing of rudder, mast and sails had irrevocably distinguished the bow from the stern. The trait was unique: even the Romans,

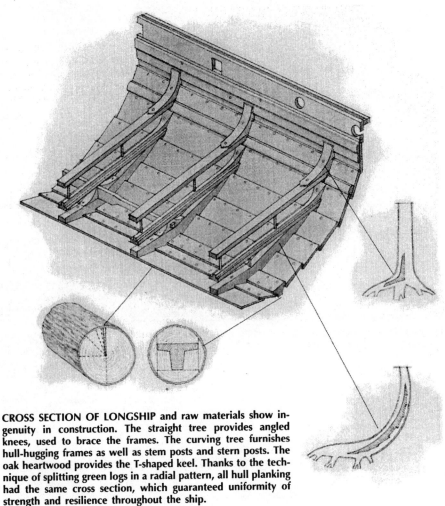

CROSS SECTION OF LONGSHIP and raw materials show ingenuity in construction. The straight tree provides angled knees, used to brace the frames. The curving tree furnishes hull-hugging frames as well as stem posts and stern posts. The oak heartwood provides the T-shaped keel. Thanks to the technique of splitting green logs in a radial pattern, all hull planking had the same cross section, which guaranteed uniformity of strength and resilience throughout the ship.

who left little commentary on Scandinavia, felt compelled to mention the double-ended boats.

Some Stone Age features still survived in the Hjortspring boat, such as the use of linden for the hull and the stitching of the lapstrake planks with fiber cords. But the dugout underbody almost disappeared, trimmed down to a narrow bottom plank bent in a gentle curve—a step toward the Viking keel. The elevated ends kept the vessel drier as it breasted oncoming waves, whereas the deeper midsection improved handling during turns. (Future shipwrights inherited this curve. Viking ships had keels 30 centimeters deeper amidships than at the ends, a refinement almost as subtle as the entasis of the Parthenon's columns but adopted for function rather than appearance.)

The 20 warriors who paddled the Hjortspring canoe sat in pairs on intricate frames of linden, ash and hazel. The 90-centimeter interval between frames allowed each paddler ample room. As this spacing became standardized, Scandinavians began to compute the length of a vessel by counting the "rooms" between its frames or benches. Coupled with the narrow bottom plank, the widely spaced frames allowed the hull remarkable flexibility; as in the ancestral dugout, the shell, rather than any rib structures, conferred strength. The lithe hull enabled the Hjortspring canoe, like later Viking ships, to snake its way through the water like a living creature.

INNOVATIONS IN DESIGN

In the later Iron Age, thanks to an act of technological crossbreeding, the complicated end structures of the Hjortspring canoe dropped out of the evolutionary line in favor of a far more elegant and simple solution to the problem of closing off the end of a hull. According to Crumlin-Pedersen, the innovation came from the expanded dugout canoe, a type that appears for the first time in Iron Age graves on the Danish island of Bornholm. Worldwide, makers of dugout canoes at times have been confronted with tree trunks too slender for a simple dugout. Independently, they worked out techniques for making a tubelike hollow in the log with an open slit on top, hewing the wood as thin as possible and then gradually expanding the sides by applying heat and inserting longer and longer stretchers. As the sides flared outward, the ends would draw upward into symmetric, curved points: the inspiration for the graceful design of the future Viking ship.

A vessel found at Nydam, north of Hedeby, is the earliest surviving offspring of the cross between the design of the expanded dugout and the lapstrake construction of the Hjortspring canoe. The late Iron Age Nydam vessel, built about A.D. 300, marks a fresh start on many counts. The planks, ribs and end posts were oak; clenched iron nails supplanted the stitches of earlier times; and the crew sat backward and propelled the vessel with long oars looped to rowlocks on the top strake. Most important, the five broad strakes on each side extended all the way to the low curving stem posts and stern posts, thus establishing the classic Viking prow structure.

An even more revolutionary change appeared about 700, just a century before the first important Viking raids. A ship from Kvalsund in western Norway sported an embryonic keel; the ever narrowing bottom plank finally acquired verticality with a T-shaped cross section. A fixed side rudder, the descendant of the steering paddle held over the side of earlier canoes, further stabilized the ship by projecting below the hull to prevent side slipping, like a modern centerboard. Thinner strakes, now eight in number, would make possible the more complex curves of the longships. The hardy Scandinavians stoically accepted the extra leaking around all these new seams. A Norse law regarded a boat unseaworthy if it needed bailing thrice in two days. (The crew could still choose to assume the risk.)

The Kvalsund ship's keel and side rudder heralded the arrival of leading performers in the drama of ship evolution that remained mysteriously in the wings until the dawn of the Viking Age: the mast and sail. Gravestone art on the Swedish island of Gotland began to depict ships with sails by 700, although the earliest physical remains of a mast come from a royal ship built in about 815 and buried at Oseberg in about 835. By then, the sail had been evolving for over four millennia, and Celtic sailing ships had been plying the seas near Scandinavia since the time of Caesar. Norwegian archaeologist Arne Emil Christensen, the greatest authority on early Viking ships and the introduction of the sail, speculates that resistance to sailing may have been less technical than cultural: tough men row. Elder Vikings at the time "must have scorned the young," Christensen writes. He imagines them deriding their sons, "who were too lazy to row as we did, and want to be blown across the sea." In the long run, however, the advantages offered by the sail prevailed.

A pole, or spar, on the deck connected to a lower corner of the sail. Moving the spar angled the sail, which allowed the ship to tack into the wind. Rowing had carried the immediate ancestors of the Vikings east to Russia and west as far as the British Isles, but with the sail, the explosive career of the Vikings truly started. And the sail dictated most of the final steps of Viking ship evolution, including deeper keels, broader hulls and higher sides. The Viking longships, the direct descendants of the Stone Age canoes, soon found themselves surrounded by a family of related ship types that took advantage of the evolutionary potential to be found in the mast and sail. New designs proliferated, like Darwin's finches in the Galápagos, to fill every available environmental niche. Many of the newcomers were specialized sailing ships built for trade, exploration and colonization, such as the famous knorrs—stout ships with deep holds that carried Vikings across the Atlantic to America. As funeral vessels, these various ships and boats transported pagan Vikings on their final voyage;

where ships could not go, in this world or the next, Vikings did not venture.

Small boats of Viking design would persist for centuries as cargo craft or church boats in such remote regions as the isles of western Norway or the Swedish lakes. But after 1100, the humble, flat-bottomed Hanseatic cog became the forebear of the next great line of sailing ships, including even the flagships of Scandinavian monarchs. The Viking longship, designed for raiding, could not compete in a world of fortified port cities, organized naval warfare and kings who demanded the pomp and comfort of a cabin when on board. The last naval levy of Viking warships was called out in 1429 and defeated by seven cogs. The dragon had retreated into the realm of legend.

REPLICATING THE DESIGN

From Captain Magnus Andersen's *Viking* of 1893 (a replica of the Gokstad ship from Norway), a long line of reconstructions has shown the astounding seaworthiness and resilience of Viking trading ships and sailing ships. Could replicas do the same for the longship?

In 1963 Danish boy scouts built a replica of the Ladby ship. Observing that the warships depicted on the 11th-century Bayeux tapestry were used as horse transports, the young mariners wanted to see if horses could really clamber on board from a beach. Such a capability would have provided a motive for retaining the low freeboard throughout the Viking Age. The sea trials of the Ladby ship were a complete success, with horses, scouts and hull all performing well. The ship proved surprisingly swift and handy on the open sea, again vindicating the skill and ingenuity of the Viking shipwrights.

After the recovery of the Skuldelev ships in 1962, the Viking Ship Museum was built at Roskilde to house the remains and provide a center for study and reconstruction. In 1991 the Roskilde team built *Helge Ask*, an exact replica of the smaller (17-meter) Skuldelev longship and saw its predatory power in action. Even with only half the crew of 24 at the oars, the ship easily outrowed a replica of the smaller, broader trading ship, also found at Skuldelev (*Roar Ege*). The longship also outsailed the trader, with a working speed approaching eight knots.

Although the trading ship performed better tacking into the wind, *Helge Ask*'s crew could make up the difference by quickly lowering sail and rowing. Crumlin-Pedersen calculates that the longship could overtake its prey in any conditions short of an outright gale. The sagas include an account of this capability: A Viking named Gauti Tófason overtook four Danish knorrs in his longship. He was on the verge of capturing a fifth when a storm blew up, allowing his prey to escape.

In the past century more than 30 Viking ships have been reconstructed, and a host of neo-Vikings maintains and operates many of these replicas. At Roskilde, the guild of the *Helge Ask* takes the ship on sea trials and cruises in summer, hauls it overland to test portage accounts, repairs it during winter—and reports it all on the World Wide Web. A millennium after the building of the original longships, the rough, expansive vigor of the Vikings is seaborne again.

The AUTHOR

JOHN R. HALE, archaeologist and director of Liberal Studies at the University of Louisville, has conducted fieldwork in Scandinavia, Britain, Portugal, Greece and the Ohio River Valley. In the course of his doctoral research at the University of Cambridge, he studied boat designs found in Bronze Age Scandinavian art. He recognized that the vessels, commonly thought to be skin boats, were in fact wooden craft directly ancestral to the Viking longships. An oarsman himself, Hale has also reconstructed the rowing techniques used on the ancient Greek trireme (see the author's article in *Scientific American*, May 1996).

FURTHER READING

THE VIKING SHIPS. A. W. Brøgger and Haakon Shetelig. Twayne Publishers, New York, 1971, and C. Hurst, London, 1971.

PLANK-BUILT IN THE BRONZE AGE. John R. Hale in *Antiquity*, Vol. 54, No. 211, pages 118–126; 1980.

SAILING INTO THE PAST: PROCEEDINGS OF THE INTERNATIONAL SEMINAR ON REPLICAS OF ANCIENT AND MEDIEVAL VESSELS. Edited by Ole Crumlin-Pedersen and Max Vinner. Viking Ship Museum, Roskilde, 1986.

THE EARLIEST SHIPS: THE EVOLUTION OF BOATS INTO SHIPS. Edited by Robert Gardiner and Arne Emil Christensen. Naval Institute Press, Annapolis, 1996.

VIKING-AGE SHIPS AND SHIPBUILDING IN HEDEBY/HAITHABU AND SCHLESWIG. Ole Crumlin-Pedersen. Viking Ship Museum, Roskilde and Provincial Museum of Archaeology, Schleswig, 1997.

The Persistence of Byzantium

Longevity alone makes Byzantium remarkable. Lasting almost 1,200 years, it outlived all of the other great empires. More impressive than mere age are the reach and influence of its civilization. Russians, Serbs, Bulgarians, and others owe to Byzantium, in varying degrees, their Christianity, their literacy, and the beginnings of their art, literature, and architecture. Yet for all that, the Byzantine Empire has been slighted or misconstrued, even by some notable historians. To see the Byzantine record clearly, our author argues, is to understand not only a once and great power but a civilizing force that continues to shape the contemporary world.

By Warren Treadgold

For a civilization so distant in time and place from our own, Byzantium interests a surprising number of Americans. The *Glory of Byzantium* exhibition at the Metropolitan Museum in New York in the spring of 1997 enjoyed even greater critical and popular success than its predecessor on early Byzantine art, *The Age of Spirituality.* Reviewers have praised recent books on Byzantium by Viscount Norwich and Peter Brown, as well as the three-volume *Oxford Dictionary of Byzantium.* Some earlier histories of Byzantium remain both classics and best-sellers, from Edward Gibbon's *De-*

WARREN TREADGOLD, *a former Wilson Center Fellow, is Professor of Late Ancient and Byzantine History at Saint Louis University. His most recent books are* Byzantium and Its Army *(1995),* A History of the Byzantine State and Society *(1997), and* A Concise History of Byzantium *(forthcoming).*

cline and Fall of the Roman Empire to the many works of Sir Steven Runciman. Even some of the Byzantines themselves are being read, with six titles in the Penguin Classics series led by that perennial favorite, Procopius's *Secret History.* Beyond artistic and literary interest, many Americans are curious about the larger cultural influence of Byzantine civilization on a part of the world that extends from Russia to Ethiopia and includes much of the Balkan region and the eastern Mediterranean basin.

No doubt, as the popularity of the *Secret History* suggests, Byzantine plots, murders, luxury, decadence, and intrigue explain some of this interest. But the contemporary image of Byzantium is more positive than that. Besides its obvious beauty, Byzantine art combines the traditional with the abstract and the spiritual with the luxurious, implying a society, that was at once stable and imaginative, religious and civilized. This art reflects the fact that Byzantine civi-

lization joined a multiplicity of cultures into a harmonious and self-confident whole. Byzantium lives on, above all, in the Eastern Orthodox Church, whose devotion, rituals, and mysticism appeal to many Christians who find such things lacking in Protestantism and too hard-edged in Roman Catholicism.

None of the contemporary perceptions of Byzantine civilization is wholly wrong, and, except for those emphasizing scandal, most are mostly right. Yet, for us, Byzantine civilization remains a curious compound of the familiar and the alien. It was certainly a part of Western civilization, but very much its own part, and different from Western Europe and America. Spanning the ancient, medieval, and modern worlds, it was the successor of the Roman Empire and contributed to the rise of the Italian Renaissance, but its culture was distinct from the cultures of both.

Such differences continue to give rise to misconceptions about the Byzantine

From *The Wilson Quarterly,* Autumn 1998, pp. 66-71. © 1998 by Warren Treadgold. Reprinted by permission of the author.

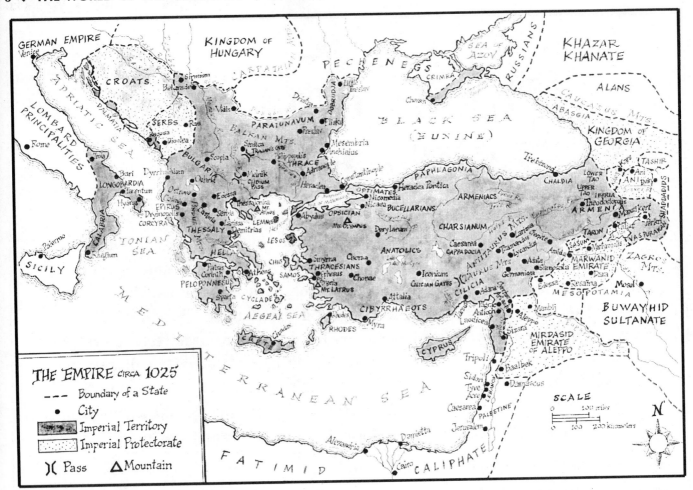

world. Norman Davies, in his recent *Europe: A History* (1996), provides a fairly typical nonspecialist's description:

> The state and the church were fused into one indivisible whole.... This "Caesaropapism" had no equal in the West, where secular rule and papal authority had never been joined. The imperial court was the hub of a vast centralized administration run by an army of bureaucrats.... The despotic nature of the state machine was self-evident in its oriental ceremonies. "Byzantium" became a byword for total subservience, secretiveness, and intrigue.... The Byzantine state practiced unremitting paternalism in social and economic affairs. Trade was controlled by state officials, who exacted a straight 10 percent tax on all exports and imports.

Except for the 10 percent duty, which was less onerous and intrusive than most modern tariffs, almost all of this is greatly exaggerated.

In terms of basic material conditions, Byzantium was a typical preindustrial society, like the earlier Roman Empire or today's Ethiopia. By our standards, it was rural, backward, and poor. Around nine-tenths of the Byzantines were illiterate peasants living in villages and engaged in subsistence farming. Again by our standards, Byzantine cities (like all medieval cities) were small and squalid, with narrow, winding streets, ramshackle houses, and populations seldom exceeding 30,000. Probably the only cities ever to pass 100,000 were Alexandria and Antioch up to the sixth century A.D., and the capital, Constantinople, which might have approached 400,000 for brief periods in the sixth and 12th centuries but was usually less than half that size. Though it boasted a broad boulevard for parades and a few palaces and churches built as showpieces by the emperors, most of Constantinople resembled a collection of small towns separated by

fields—an ensemble that would hardly count as a great metropolis today.

Nevertheless, by medieval standards, and in some respects by ancient ones as well, Byzantium was an advanced society. Its cities were larger, its literacy rates higher, and its economy more monetarized and diversified than those of medieval Western Europe, at least up to the 13th century. By comparison with most ancient empires, including Rome, Byzantium was well governed. Our ideas of "Byzantine bureaucracy" to the contrary, Byzantium was blessed with a cadre of officials that was generally efficient, well educated, well paid, and relatively small in number—perhaps 2,500 in the central bureaucracy toward the beginning of the empire's history, and around 600 by the ninth century.

The notion of despotic rule is also a caricature. Although a Byzantine emperor had no formal checks on his power, he had to be ac-

Portrait of a City

In *The Journey of Louis VII to the East,* Odo of Deuil, a French monk and chronicler, and Louis VII's chaplain for the Second Crusade, paints a vivid picture of the imperial city of Constantinople, where the Crusaders spent the winter of 1148 on their ill-fated journey to the Holy Land.

Constantinople, the glory of the Greeks, rich in renown and richer still in possessions, is laid out in a triangle shaped like a ships sail. In its inner angle stand Santa Sophia and Constantinople's Palace, in which there is a chapel that is revered for its exceedingly holy relics. Moreover, Constantinople is girt on two sides by the sea; when approaching the city we had the Arm of St. George on the right and on the left a certain estuary, which, after branching from the Arm, flows on for about four miles. In that place the Palace of Blachernae, although having foundations laid on low ground, achieves eminence through excellent construction and elegance and, because of its surroundings on three sides, affords its inhabitants the triple pleasure of looking out upon sea, fields, and city. Its exterior is of almost matchless beauty, but its interior surpasses anything that I can say about it. Throughout it is decorated elaborately with gold and a great variety of colors, and the floor is marble, paved with cunning workmanship; and I do not know whether the exquisite art or the exceedingly valuable stuffs endows it with the more beauty or value. The third side of the city's triangle includes fields, but it is fortified by towers and a double wall which extends for about two miles from the sea to the palace. This wall is not strong, and it possesses no lofty towers; but the city puts its trust, I think, in the size of its population and the long period of peace which it has enjoyed. Below the walls lies open land,

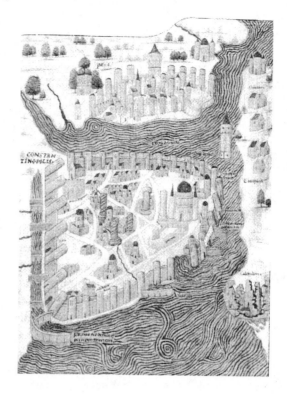

cultivated by plough and hoe, which contains gardens that furnish the citizens all kinds of vegetables. From the outside underground conduits flow in, bringing the city an abundance of sweet water.

The city itself is squalid and fetid and in many places harmed by permanent darkness, for the wealthy overshadow the streets with buildings and leave these dirty, dark places to the poor and to travelers; there murders and robberies and other crimes which love the darkness are committed. Moreover, since the people live lawlessly in this city, which has as many lords as rich men and almost as many

thieves as poor men, a criminal knows neither fear nor shame, because crime is not punished by law and never entirely comes to light. In every respect she exceeds moderation; for, just as she surpasses other cities in wealth, so, too, does she surpass them in vice. Also, she possesses many churches unequal to Santa Sophia in size but equal to it in beauty, which are to be marveled at for their beauty and their many saintly relics. Those who had the opportunity entered these places, some to see the sights and others to worship faithfully.

claimed by the people and crowned by the patriarch of Constantinople at his accession, and he defied their wishes at his peril. The few emperors who showed signs of tyrannical behavior, such as Andronicus I Comnenus (r. 1183–85), were promptly overthrown. Byzantium never endured a Nero, a Hitler, or an Idi Amin. The closest thing it had to a Henry VIII was the emperor Constantine V (r. 741–75), who in an effort to impose the beliefs of the iconoclasts on a recalcitrant church and people not only destroyed religious

images but purged the ecclesiastical hierarchy and confiscated monastic property. Although several attempts to overthrow him failed, a church council declared iconoclasm a heresy 12 years after his death, and Constantine went down in history with the epithet Copronymus, which we translate delicately as "Name of Dung." The common modern view that Byzantine emperors had power over the Eastern Church comparable to that of popes in the West—"Caesaropapism"—is an exaggeration.

In fact, the church had profound reservations about almost every emperor and his courtiers. In contrast to the Western Church, which has traditionally accepted that sometimes a greater good can justify acts that would otherwise be sinful—including the waging of war—the Eastern Church has insisted that such acts can never be fully excused. Despite awkward attempts at accommodation, such as blinding political opponents instead of executing them, emperors were always falling short of the church's moral standards. Among Byzantine emperors, the only one to be widely recognized as a saint was Constantine I, who, by delaying his baptism until he was on his deathbed, supposedly gained absolution from his sins. The only emperors in Byzantine scenes of the last judgment are those burning in hell. The modern idea that the Byzantines idolized their rulers is far from the truth.

Another widespread misconception about Byzantium is that anyone in Byzantine times ever called it "Byzantium." Because it was simply the eastern part of the Roman Empire, separated from the western part through a peaceful administrative division in A.D. 285, the people we call "Byzantines" always called themselves Romans, and their empire the Roman Empire. Byzantium was the insignificant town Constantine I (r. 306–37) chose as the site of his greatly expanded city of Constantinople, after which only archaizing stylists referred to it as Byzantium. The name "Byzantine" was first used for the empire by Renaissance scholars, who hesitated to call it "Roman" because it had not included Rome and found "Constantinopolitan" cumbersome. This modern habit of calling the Eastern Roman Empire by the obsolete name of its principal city is a bit like calling the United States "New Amsterdam." Odd though the choice of name may be, the empire did become different enough to warrant renaming it. Because the division between East and West roughly fit the dividing line in the Roman Empire between Greek and Latin cultures, the Eastern Empire on its own soon shed its Latin veneer, became a mainly Greek state, grew overwhelmingly Christian, and long outlived the Western Empire.

Byzantium's longevity was, in fact, unique. The historical rule for ancient empires had been that after a few centuries of prosperity they declined and disintegrated, usually soon after suffering their first major military defeats. This pattern held for the Assyrian Empire, the Neo-Babylonian Empire, the Achaemenid Persian Empire, the Parthian Empire, the Sassanid Persian Empire, the

Arab Caliphate, and the Western Roman Empire. But the Byzantine Empire lasted almost 1,200 years.

Byzantium naturally had its ups and downs. As Gibbon saw, over the very long run the trend was down: the empire fell in the end. Yet the pattern was far more complex than a simple decline and fall. Because Byzantium suffered most of its losses during sudden catastrophes and made most of its gains during periods of steady expansion, it was more often expanding than contracting. Again and again it survived its defeats, usually outlasting the enemies who had defeated it.

The story begins in the third century A.D., a time of crisis for the Roman Empire. Various German tribes devastated the empire's European provinces, the Sassanid Persians overran most of the Asian provinces, and the rebellious Roman ally, Palmyra, briefly took over the Asian lands and Egypt. The commanders of the armies that fought these invaders repeatedly seized the imperial throne for themselves. Between 211 and 284, the Germans killed one emperor, the Persians captured another, a third died in a disastrous epidemic, and the remaining 23 emperors were either certainly or probably killed by Romans, in most cases after reigning for less than two years. Diocletian, who seized the throne in 284 as the latest in a series of military strongmen, seemed to have no better chance than his predecessors of dying in bed or of righting the foundering Roman state.

But the half-educated Diocletian showed remarkable political insight. Realizing that the task of keeping invaders and rebels at bay was too big for one man, he chose a deputy, his friend Maximian, and gave him the title of emperor and the western half of the empire, with a separate army and administration. Diocletian's portion in the East consisted of the Balkans, Anatolia, Syria, and Egypt. Because he kept a separate government in the East and strengthened its army and expanded its bureaucracy, Diocletian can be considered the real founder of the Byzantine Empire, though his favorite residence was at Nicomedia, about 50 miles from the city of Byzantium, and his administration traveled so much that it really had no set capital.

His enlarged government succeeded in stabilizing the empire, and he reigned for 21 years before retiring voluntarily.

A pagan of the traditional Greco-Roman kind, Diocletian had thousands of Christians killed or maimed in an effort to suppress their faith—ultimately to no avail. Christianity became the empire's favored religion under the charismatic Constantine I, who took power as a Western emperor in 306, a year after Diocletian's abdication, and finished conquering the domain of the Eastern emperor Licinius in 324. Though Constantine ruled both East and West, he administered them through different officials and through his sons, who were to inherit their portions at his death. His new city of Constantinople grew steadily, and by the end of the fourth century it was recognizably a capital, the usual seat of the emperor and his government. Constantine's new official religion also prospered, and within a century of his accession Christians had grown from a small minority to a large majority in both East and West.

Between them, Diocletian and Constantine set Byzantium on a promising course, even if they did so partly by accident. While Diocletian divided the empire mainly for military and administrative reasons, the Greek East happened to form a natural geographical, cultural, and economic unit. Although Constantine's conversion seems to have been the result of a somewhat confused religious conviction—at first he appears not to have realized that it required him to repudiate paganism entirely—Christianity gave the empire more cohesiveness than the ill-assorted cults we call paganism could ever have done. Constantine seems to have been inspired to refound Byzantium as Constantinople merely because he had defeated his rival Licinius nearby, but the site happened to be well located at a junction of trade routes, on a splendidly defensible peninsula on the straits dividing the Balkans from Anatolia.

During its first 300 years, Byzantium usually prospered. From the late fourth to the late fifth century it lost some territory to the Persians, Huns, and Germans, but by 500 Byzantium had driven out its invaders and held almost all the lands Diocletian had taken for his portion of the Roman Empire in 285. The empire was already thriving before the ambitious Justinian I (r. 527–65) showed what it could do if it tried. Justinian built an array of public structures in Constantinople, of which his great Church of the Holy Wisdom (Saint Sophia) is only the most famous and extraordinary. He deserves some credit for a flowering of art, much of which he paid for, and of scholarship, to which he contributed his great codification of Roman law. Most impressively, if not most lastingly, he dispatched expeditions that won back from the Germans the richest parts of the former Western Roman Empire in Italy, Dalmatia, northern Africa, and southern Spain.

Justinian's achievements were the more remarkable because he finished them in the teeth of the worst epidemic the Western world had known, a bubonic plague that reached the empire from Ethiopia in 541 and killed up to a third of its people. Yet because the plague kept returning at intervals of roughly 15 years right up to the mid-eighth century, Byzantium grew weaker and was thrown on the defensive.

After 602, when the first successful rebellion in three centuries of Byzantine history overthrew the emperor Maurice, the Persians were emboldened to invade Syria and Egypt and the Avars to overrun the Balkans. By 626, Constantinople was besieged and the empire was in mortal danger. The emperor Heraclius (r. 610–41) averted disaster by invading the Persian homeland, which forced the Persians to evacuate Egypt and Syria. But barely five years after Heraclius's victory, with the Balkans unreclaimed and Byzantium still exhausted, the Arabs invaded. After seizing Syria and Egypt and conquering the Persian Empire outright, they seemed poised to deal a similar fate to Byzantium.

At this point, according to historical precedent, Byzantium should have been doomed. The younger, more vigorous Arab Caliphate held about 10 times as much land as the

Byzantines, with at least five times as many people and an army to match. The newly Muslim Arabs embraced the doctrine of holy war (jihad), which held that those who died fighting for the faith went straight to heaven; by contrast, the Byzantine Church required a soldier who killed an enemy in battle to do penance for three years before receiving Communion again. Yet Byzantium stopped the Arabs and outlived their state by hundreds of years.

How did the Byzantines do this? Historians still disagree, but most think one answer was a change in military organization. Heraclius's grandson Constans II (r. 641–68) seems to have reorganized the army, previously a regularly paid professional force, into largely self-supporting divisions known as "themes"—army groups settled in districts (also called themes) where they held grants of farmland, probably taken from the vast imperial estates that disappeared around this time. Although some historians doubt that the troops received lands this early (none of the scanty sources records the distribution at any date), the grants were evidently given when the empire could no longer afford to pay its troops a living wage, and that was very probably during Constans's reign.

While Constans's main motive was doubtless to save money, by the same sort of lucky accident that made Diocletian's and Constantine's reforms so beneficial, the themes turned out to put up a stiffer defense than the old army, once the soldiers were stationed all over the empire and were fighting to defend their own lands. The themes helped contain not only the Arabs but the rising new power of the Bulgars in the Balkans. Thus Byzantium held out until the middle of the eighth century, when the plague finally abated and the Arabs started to fight among themselves.

The Byzantines then made a remarkable recovery, again without precedent for so ancient a state. During the next 300 years the empire almost doubled in size, recapturing many of its lost lands to the east and all its lost lands to the north, where it annexed the Bulgarian

Empire outright. The final push was the work of three great conquerors, the emperors Nicephorus II Phocas (r. 963–69), John I Tzimisces (r. 969–76), and Basil II the Bulgar-Slayer (r. 976–1025). Byzantine power, wealth, and culture grew to such proportions that the pagan Bulgars, Serbs, and Russians spontaneously requested conversion to Byzantine Christianity. Similarly, the Bulgars and many Armenians and Georgians accepted direct Byzantine rule even though Basil II would have permitted them to become Byzantine clients.

The Byzantines themselves halted their expansion at Basil's death, though they showed every sign of being able to continue it. The weakened Arab states of southern Syria, through which John I had marched at will, could scarcely have prevented a Byzantine conquest. Even the Arabs of Egypt would have been hard put to resist the Byzantines. But the Byzantine reconquest in the east ended approximately where Christians ceased to be a majority. While southern Syria and Egypt had strong Christian minorities—much stronger than today—the Byzantines disliked ruling Muslims, whom in the lands already conquered they had given a choice between conversion and expulsion. Few Muslims chose conversion, and the Byzantines had no use for empty land.

Basking in the afterglow of Basil II's victories, the Bulgar-Slayer's successors misspent their revenues and let the army and navy decay. As a result, the Byzantines were unprepared for the arrival of the Seljuk Turks from Central Asia. At the Battle of Manzikert in 1071, the Turks scattered the atrophied Byzantine army, and within 10 years they had overrun Byzantine Anatolia. The Byzantines appealed to Pope Urban II, and received the unexpected response of the First Crusade.

With help from the Crusaders, Byzantium took back most of the plains along the Anatolian coast. This was much the richest part of the peninsula, but it was hard to defend while the Turks held the interior. Throughout the 12th century, as the emperors relied more on diplomacy than on rebuilding their army, Byzantium was rich but militarily weak, a dangerous combination. Though the Turks missed their chance, some opportunistic Westerners took it. The knights of the Fourth Crusade turned from attacking the Turks to backing the claim to the Byzantine throne of the pretender Alexius IV. The Crusaders captured Constantinople for Alexius, but when they failed to receive their promised payment they seized the city for themselves in 1204.

After the loss of Constantinople, unconquered Byzantines continued to hold more than half of what had been their empire, divided among several squabbling successor states. Gradually one of these, known to us as the Empire of Nicaea after its temporary capital, gained the upper hand, and recovered Constantinople in 1261. From that date we begin to call the empire Byzantium again, and for a time it seemed to recover much of its former power, though some Byzantine splinter principalities remained independent. But soon the restored empire repeated the mistake of the previous century by skimping on defense. This gave another chance to the Turks, who, led by the energetic Ottoman dynasty, occupied most Byzantine holdings in Anatolia by 1305.

Byzantium still seemed to have a future as a Balkan power. Even after crippling itself in a civil war between 1341 and 1347, it might have revived, if the next year the plague had not returned, after an absence of 600 years. Spread largely by ship, the disease hit the Byzantines on the coasts much harder than their Turkish and Slavic neighbors inland. This was one blow too many. Only the walls of Constantinople and occasional help from Western Europeans allowed the sad remnant of the empire to hold out for another century. Constantinople finally fell to the Ottoman Turks in 1453, and the Ottomans took the last tiny Byzantine splinter, the Empire of Trebizond, in 1461.

Almost up to the end, Byzantine history shows a pattern of sudden reverses followed by long recoveries, each of which brought Byzantium back a little short of where it had been before the preceding setback. The reason for the in-

completeness of these recoveries was more often a lack of interest than a lack of strength. The Byzantines wanted to retake recently lost lands, which they believed were rightfully theirs. The church, for all its reservations about warfare, sometimes contributed ecclesiastical treasures to such efforts, on the ground that they were being used to rescue captured Christians. But the longer a country had been lost to Byzantium, the less the Byzantines wanted to reclaim it. They were not even strongly driven to convert others to Christianity, unless the others asked to be converted. With a high opinion of their empire and church, the Byzantines were usually content to keep both of them as they were, or had been not long before.

This attitude served the former subjects of Byzantium well under the Turks, and helped Byzantine civilization survive the fall of the Byzantine state. Even before the Fourth Crusade, many people who lived outside Byzantine territory spoke Greek and acknowledged the primacy of the patriarch of Constantinople. After the fall of Constantinople, the Turkish sultans appointed patriarchs, as the emperor had done before them. The Russians never came under Ottoman rule, and considered themselves heirs of Byzantium. They, like the Bulgarians, the Serbs, and others, owed Byzantium their Christianity and literacy, and the beginnings of their literature, art, and architecture. Like the Greeks, the Russians dreamed of driving the Turks from Constantinople, which had a large Christian minority until the early 20th century. When the Ottoman Empire fell apart after World War I, the Greeks tried to reclaim something like the borders of Byzantium in 1203. But a Greek invasion of Anatolia ended with a Turkish victory in 1922.

Ever since a population exchange in 1923 removed most of the Greeks from Turkey, few people have spoken Greek outside Greece and Cyprus. Yet a patriarch of Constantinople remains in Turkish Istanbul as head of the Eastern Orthodox Church. Eastern Orthodoxy remains the majority faith not only in Greece and Cyprus but

in Russia, Bulgaria, Yugoslavia, Macedonia, Romania, Ukraine, Moldova, Georgia, and Belarus. Eastern Orthodox Christians remain significant minorities in Albania, Syria, and Lebanon—and in the United States, Canada, and Australia. Most Armenians and many Egyptians and Ethiopians remain Eastern Christians without formally belonging to Eastern Orthodoxy. All of these groups have inherited much of their culture from Byzantium. It is mainly people who are not Eastern Christians whom Byzantium still perplexes.

As it happens, some works on Byzantium have increased this perplexity by giving a confusing and misleading picture. The objects in the *Glory of Byzantium* exhibition speak for themselves, and a number of treatments of the subject are balanced and accurate, including those by Runciman and the *Oxford Dictionary of Byzantium* (1991). Although some historians, from Gibbon in the 18th century to Romilly Jenkins in the 20th, have disliked Byzantium, that dislike did not necessarily lead to errors in itself; usually what they disliked most was Byzantine Christianity, and they were right that Byzantium was profoundly Christian, like it or not. Probably the main reason for distortion in more recent work has been not bias against Byzantium but well-meant misconceptions of it.

Sometimes the aim has been to reach a wide audience by playing up the exotic and playing down its context. So Lord Norwich in his three-volume *Byzantium* (1989, 1992, 1996)—which some have taken for an academic history despite his frank disclaimers—has compiled a collection of partly legendary anecdotes about the Byzantine court while almost completely ignoring social, economic, and cultural history. Accordingly, he leaves the impression that plots and intrigue were typical of Byzantine civilization, which they were not—certainly no more so than they were of other great imperial courts. The occasional ruthlessness of the Byzantine court mainly reflects the jaundiced view the Byzantine Church took toward politics, which led some politicians to despair of combining moral behavior with public life and to see a deathbed repentance as their only hope of salvation. When in political difficulty, such emperors and courtiers ventured to commit acts that would have been unthinkable for the mass of Byzantines whom Norwich neglects.

A more serious source of historical distortion is the attempt to connect Byzantium with modern (or postmodern) academic fashions, which are poorly suited to understanding a deeply religious and traditional society. Most notable is the insistence of Peter Brown, in such books as *The Body and Society* (1988) and *Power and Persuasion in Late Antiquity* (1992), that Byzantine religion was mostly about sexuality, anxiety, and power, a view that owes much less to Byzantine sources than to the poststructuralism of Michel Foucault. Particularly jarring is the view of Brown and other poststructuralists that the Byzantines' idealization of virginity showed an obsession with sexuality.

In another work, *Christianity and the Rhetoric of Empire* (1991), Averil Cameron explains the poststructuralist approach to Byzantine Christianity:

> The sign system of Christianity . . . [formed] around the body itself, and especially the mechanics and avoidance of carnal knowledge and procreation. Paradoxically, in the context of the discourse of abstinence, the true knowledge at which the signs pointed was defined in terms of desire. . . . Now *eros,* desire, also occupies the center of poststructuralist poetics and is often seen as a key to theories of the subject. Whereas in modern intellectual circles Christian discourse is rarely acceptable as such, ironically *eros,* the discourse of desire, has filled the space left vacant.

Yet beyond a reasonable doubt, the Byzantines were guilty of the charge against which poststructuralists defend them: they were less interested in sex than we are, and more interested in God.

The Byzantines regarded sex much as we regard smoking or overeating: many did it, but nobody really approved of it. They agreed that virginity was better even than a faithful marriage, not because sex was important but because it

was unimportant—a distraction from God, who was transcendently important. Some Byzantine moralists advised the widowed that concubinage was better than remarriage, because asking God to bless serial monogamy was blasphemous, and blasphemy was worse than fornication. Contrasting real Byzantine attitudes with poststructuralist thinking shows (as Cameron hints) how sexuality has taken the place of religion for some of us. Those who think that sexual fulfillment is the greatest good and God is an illusion may well be baffled by people who thought that God was the greatest good and sexual fulfillment an illusion.

Some of Brown's other ideas are similarly anachronistic. Brown sees Byzantine holy men as protopsychiatrists who treated patients for "moral hypochondria" by counseling them. What his sources rather show is monks who worked miracles, mostly to relieve physical or material distress, and treated people suffering from what we would call mental illness not by counseling but by exorcism. Today, however, many find psychiatry far easier to understand than a belief in miracles, exorcism, or God.

Byzantium is also a frustrating subject for those who adopt the modern view that all that matters, or has ever mattered, is race, class, and gender. Like other ancient and medieval peoples, the Byzantines had no idea of race in the modern sense, and to them black skin was like red hair, merely an uncommon physical characteristic. Practically all Byzantines, including their few slaves, were what we would call white. They may be called multiethnic in the sense that, along with the ethnically mixed people we call Greeks, they included Armenians, Slavs, Syrians, Egyptians, Albanians, and others. Sometimes we can find groups of Armenians or Syrians in Greek-speaking territory who helped each other in various ways. But we can also find groups of Greeks from the same town or region who helped each other. Moreover, in a generation or two, the Armenians, Syrians, and others who migrated to Greek-speaking areas forgot their own languages, intermarried with Greeks, and became indistinguishable from them. Byzantium was far less a

multicultural society. than it was a melting pot.

A few Byzantine theological disputes did correspond roughly to ethnic or linguistic divisions. The most obvious case is Monophysitism, the belief that Christ has a single nature rather than different divine and human natures, which became the majority faith in Egypt but not elsewhere. Yet it cannot properly be called an ethnic or linguistic movement, because Egyptian Monophysites included speakers of both Greek and Coptic (the native Egyptian language). It might be called a regional movement, except that the originator of Monophysitism had been a Greek monk in Constantinople, and at first Monophysites could be found all over the empire. They were common in northern Syria but rare in southern Syria, though both parts of Syria had Syriac-speaking majorities and Greek-speaking minorities.

The apparent explanation for the geographical split in Syria over Monophysitism is that most Christians followed their religious leaders. The church in northern Syria was subject to the patriarch of Antioch, who, like the patriarch of Alexandria in Egypt, came to favor Monophysitism; the church in southern Syria was under the patriarch of Jerusalem, who, like the patriarch of Constantinople, came to oppose Monophysitism. At a certain point these views took root among the local Christian population, and even when the emperor appointed patriarchs of the opposite persuasion, the people refused to change. Because the ecclesiastical jurisdictions were regional, the theological dispute can be mistaken for a regional one—or, by further confusion, an ethnic one. In reality, even though many Byzantines spoke mutually incomprehensible languages, ethnic consciousness was very weak in the empire, as in most premodern societies.

Byzantine class consciousness was somewhat stronger. Although Byzantium never had any hereditary titles of nobility, most Byzantines had some idea of where they belonged in the social hierarchy, based on their wealth or profession. This was particularly true of the group at the top, whose members often held appointments in the army or civil service with clearly graded ranks and salaries. By the 11th century, Byzantium did develop a loosely defined aristocracy, though most of its families were not very old and it remained open to new members, including Turks and Western Europeans. What can confuse modern historians is that this class awareness almost never resulted in a sense of class solidarity.

For example, most historians have seen the late 11th century as the beginning of a period of rule by the landed aristocracy. At this time the dynasty of the Comneni seized power, and the Comneni were indeed landed aristocrats. But the Comneni took over just as the Byzantines were losing the region where aristocrats held most of their land—the interior of Anatolia—and the Comneni made no serious attempt to retake either the region or the estates. Moreover, under the Comneni the highest positions in the government and army were monopolized by members or relatives of the Comnenus family itself. Most of the aristocracy was excluded from political or military power, and aristocrats often joined rebellions against the Comneni. When one of these rebellions finally succeeded, the aristocracy was left even weaker and more divided than before.

The explanation of these seemingly paradoxical facts is that Byzantine aristocrats had almost no feeling that they shared common interests as a class. The Comneni saw other aristocrats as rivals to be kept down, while the other aristocrats saw the Comneni as a clique indifferent or hostile to their interests. Both perceptions were pretty much correct. The rebels who brought down the Comneni, moreover, came from all levels of society and had nothing in common but dislike of the reigning emperor, Andronicus I Comnenus. The aristocracy was riven by family rivalries, and Byzantines cared far less about their class than about their family. The common modern assumption that aristocrats would favor each other out of class loyalty seems unsupported by any Byzantine source.

As for gender differences, in Byzantium, as in any traditional society, sex roles were more distinct than in today's America. Byzantine women had somewhat wider opportunities than women in most premodern societies, though, and no fewer than women in much of Africa and Asia today. Unlike classical Greece, where women were denied any independent role in politics or culture, Byzantium shared the more liberal attitudes of Rome and archaic or Hellenistic Greece. The emphasis that Byzantine Christianity put on morality and orthodoxy also allowed women to gain recognition as nuns, abbesses, and eventually saints. Two Byzantine empresses, Irene and Theodora, were revered as saints for their crucial parts in condemning iconoclasm, in 787 and 843 respectively. They and other empresses became the real rulers of the empire as regents for their underage sons, and three empresses—Irene (r. 797–802), Zoe (r. 1042), and another Theodora (r. 1055–56)—reigned without sharing the throne with an emperor. Emperors often gave their wives considerable prominence; the most famous example is Justinian's consort, yet another Theodora. Byzantium also had a few notable women writers, including the poet Cassia and the historian Anna Comnena.

Like Byzantine aristocrats, however, Byzantine women showed scarcely any signs of solidarity as a group. Neither Irene (a determined and skillful politician of the type of Margaret Thatcher or Indira Gandhi) nor any other empress made a serious effort to promote other women. The attitude shared by almost all Byzantines of either sex seems to have been that women, though capable of taking part in public life, were poorly suited to it. If dynastic accidents put a woman in power, she was better than a civil war, but not as good as a legitimate male heir. Many Byzantines believed that women in their private roles were not inferior to men, and every Byzantine had to admit that female saints were spiritually and morally superior to ordinary males. (That Theodora—"gift of God"—was a favorite Byzantine name for girls is hardly a sign of misogyny.) But practically no Byzantines, male or female, seem to have felt that women as

a group were being deprived of their due, or that their role in society ought to be expanded or changed in any way.

In Byzantium, as in nearly all premodern societies, not only were race, class, and gender not matters of ideology, but ideology itself barely existed in the modern sense. Byzantines occasionally showed patriotism, but it was emotional and not ideological—patriotism rather than nationalism. In part it was loyalty to the state, though most of the opinions the Byzantines expressed about their government were complaints about taxes and corruption. The Byzantines felt some loyalty to their emperors, though usually when an emperor was overthrown that loyalty went automatically to his successor. Most of all, the Byzantines felt loyalty to their state religion, Christianity. Their army's victory cry was not a patriotic slogan but "The Cross has conquered!"

This lack of ideology has long been hard for modern scholars to grasp. For instance, most have looked for an ideological significance in the Byzantines' two factions, the Blues and the Greens, whose official function was to organize sports and theatrical events, mainly chariot races and performances in which women took off their clothes. The Blues and Greens also cheered on their own performers and teams, and sometimes fought each other in the stands or rioted in the streets. Persistent modern efforts to define the Blues and Greens as representatives of political, social, or religious groups have so conspicuously failed that they seem to have been abandoned. Now, however, without trying to distinguish Blues from Greens, Peter Brown has depicted their spectacles as solemn patriotic ceremonies. Yet such a generalization seems indefensible after Alan Cameron has shown in two meticulous and persuasive books, *Porphyrius the Charioteer* (1973) and *Circus Factions* (1976), that the Blues and Greens were interested primarily in sports and shows, secondarily in hooliganism, and not at all in ideology.

If the Byzantines were so unlike us Americans—or at least unlike the way modern scholars think we should be—why should we care about them today? One answer is that we should care even about people who are unlike us, including Russians, Greeks, Serbs, and others who continue the Byzantine tradition and with whom we still need to deal. Another answer is that in some ways the Byzantines did resemble some of us, and in a few ways were a bit like the most up-to-date of us. Let us take up these points in turn.

What difference has the Byzantine heritage made in the dozen or so countries where it remains strongest? At first glance, Russia, Greece, Yugoslavia, Armenia, and the rest look just as nationalistic as any other countries, indeed more so. Several of them have recently fought wars with their neighbors, inspired by rhetoric that seems to us ultranationalistic. On closer inspection, however, we should note that their sharpest conflicts have been not with other Eastern Orthodox nations but with countries or peoples that do not share their Eastern Orthodox background.

Thus, Orthodox Serbs have fought Muslim Bosniacs and Kosovars and Catholic Croats, Orthodox Russians have fought Muslim Chechnyans, Orthodox Georgians have fought Muslim Abkhazians, and eastern Christian Armenians have fought Muslim Azeris. Orthodox Greeks remain distrustful of Muslim Turks, as was made evident by the passion shown on both sides in a recent dispute over an uninhabited islet in the Aegean Sea. Since 1974 a cease-fire line has divided Cyprus between an Orthodox Greek majority and a Muslim Turkish minority, and all attempts at reconciliation have failed. Also within national boundaries, tensions persist between Orthodox Bulgarians and a Muslim Turkish minority, between Orthodox Romanians and a Catholic or Protestant Hungarian minority, and between Orthodox Macedonians and a Muslim Albanian minority.

Although there have been some cases of Orthodox fighting Orthodox—Moldovans and Russians in Transnistria, and Balkan states on different sides in the Balkan Wars and the two world wars—many more of the recent conflicts have been between different religious groups than between different ethnic groups. Most Bulgarian "Turks" speak Bulgarian, and Bosniacs and Croats speak the same language as Serbs, which used to be called Serbo-Croatian. Greeks, Russians, and Romanians have all shown obvious sympathy for their fellow Orthodox Serbs, whom most of the rest of the world, regardless of religion, has blamed for aggression against the Muslim Bosniacs and Catholic Croats.

By the same token, the heirs of Byzantium seem scarcely nationalistic at all. Romanians, for example, have only the most tepid interest in unification with Moldova, a Romanian-majority statelet that Romania lost in 1940 for no better legal or moral reason than the Molotov-Ribbentrop Pact. The Bulgarians care even less about annexing Macedonia, which was part of medieval Bulgaria and whose residents still speak a language barely different from Bulgarian. Greek Cypriots, in their struggle with Turkish Cypriots, have largely forgotten the cause of unification of Cyprus with Greece.

Similarly, Russians have shown little enthusiasm for reincorporating Belarus, even though its president says he wants the reincorporation, or Ukraine, where a strong minority wants the same. Yet both Belarus and Ukraine were part of Russia through most of its history and speak languages quite close to Russian, and two of the three stripes of the Russian flag stand for Belarus and Ukraine. One would expect any true Russian nationalist to want both of them back more than anything else. But the people we call Russian nationalists care more about denouncing Catholics, Protestants, and Jews within Russia proper. In all of this, modern national boundaries seem to matter less than the transnational solidarity of the old Byzantine melting pot.

This bond is more complex than a shared devotion to the Eastern Orthodox faith, even though the fall of communism has brought a modest Orthodox revival in Eastern Europe. Though church practices had differed slightly in the eastern and western parts of the Roman Empire even before the third century, none of the differences was of obvious importance, and scarcely anyone made an issue of them until the 11th century. The usual date given for the schism between Eastern Orthodoxy and Roman Catholicism is 1054, but all that occurred then was the excommunication of Patriarch Michael Cerularius by three legates sent to Constantinople by Pope Leo IX (who by that time was dead), and the patriarch's retaliatory excommunication of the legates.

Personal animosities aside, the main issue at the time was the patriarch's objection to western (and Armenian) Christians' long-standing use of unleavened bread in the eucharist. Yet the personal animosities really were the main issue, as each side defended its dignity jealously and took offense easily. That this petty quarrel was allowed to become a schism shows a growing xenophobia on both sides that led to still more hostility during the Crusades, culminating in the brutal conquest of Constantinople by the misdirected Fourth Crusade.

Once the schism had begun, theologians found reasons for it. The authority of the pope eventually became an issue, but in the 11th century it was a minor matter, since papal claims were no more extensive than they had long been, and the Eastern Church recognized most of them. True, some Eastern Christians objected that the original version of the Nicene Creed, still used by Easterners, says simply that the Holy Spirit proceeds from God the Father, while the Western version adds "and the Son" (in Latin, *filioque*). But this difference had no real consequences for religious belief and had caused no schism for centuries. Even in medieval times, the main Orthodox criticism of the *filioque* was the reasonable one that the western part of the church had no right to add to the creed without consulting the eastern part.

As this objection and the matter of the Fourth Crusade might suggest, much of the reason for Eastern Orthodox distrust of Muslims and Western Christians is a lingering and not wholly unjustified sense of grievance. To Eastern Christians, with their traditional reluctance to engage in aggressive warfare or vigorous evangelization, differing Western and Muslim attitudes toward Orthodoxy can look like unprovoked hostility. After all, no predominantly Eastern Orthodox armies have ever marched into Mecca, Baghdad, Paris, or London. But both Muslim and Western Christian armies have conquered Constantinople, Jerusalem, Alexandria, and Antioch, and none of those great Byzantine cities is in Orthodox hands today. Except for the Russians, all the Orthodox peoples were under foreign rule until the 19th century, and even the Russians suffered severely from invasions by Western Christian powers in the Napoleonic and First and Second World Wars.

By comparison with almost all western Christian countries, almost all Eastern Christian countries are impoverished today, and not even Russia is a truly great power any longer. Only Greece has been accepted into the North Atlantic Treaty Organization and the European Union, both of which regard it as something of a problem member. Americans and Western Europeans still harbor more serious reservations about Orthodox countries than about Western Christian countries with a communist past, such as Poland, Hungary, the Czech Republic, Slovenia, and Estonia. None of the formerly communist Orthodox countries has yet made as good an economic recovery as any of those, or has yet established quite as stable a democracy. In the Balkans and the Caucasus much can be blamed on the combined heritage of some five centuries of Turkish rule and communism, but the question remains whether Byzantium might also be to blame.

Probably a little, at least as far as democracy is concerned. Though Byzantine emperors were no more absolute in their rule than Louis XIV, Frederick the Great, Mussolini, or Franco, Byzantium was a somewhat less pluralistic society than late medieval or modern France, Germany, Italy, or Spain. Church leaders were a bit less independent of the government in Byzantium than in Roman Catholic countries—though more so than in Protestant ones. The Byzantine aristocracy was more fractious than Western European aristocracies, and so more easily manipulated. Byzantium,

with a Senate that was merely a group of officials appointed by the emperor, had no representative body like the British Parliament or the French Estates-General, and no independent or nearly independent cities such as those in Italy or Germany. Probably most important, the general Byzantine disapproval of politics—the result of uncompromising Eastern Orthodox morality—kept many people from taking part in public life and discouraged some who did from trying to act responsibly.

Yet, as a hindrance to the development of democracy in Eastern Orthodox states, only the distrust of politics was nearly as important an influence as years of Turkish autocracy or communist dictatorship. Both of these periods reinforced the traditional Byzantine feeling that decent men should avoid political life. Both also deprived the Orthodox, who in Byzantine times had at least as strong a legal tradition as Western Europeans, of the chance to develop in modern times a rule of law comparable to that of Western Europe.

Many of the character traits of the empire's modern successor states have little to do with Byzantium. Russian autocracy antedated Russia's conversion to Orthodoxy, and, if anything, was Scandinavian in origin. In any case, Greece and Cyprus, the only Orthodox countries to be spared communist dictatorship, have as good a democratic record since their independence as Spain or Germany. And Orthodox Romania and Bulgaria are currently more democratic than Catholic Slovakia or Croatia.

Byzantine influence may also have been slightly unfavorable to the growth of capitalism, which shows some correlation with democracy. Byzantine merchants, while probably richer than their Western counterparts until the Renaissance, were less independent than Italian or German merchants because the Byzantine government was stronger—though Byzantine emperors taxed and regulated trade scarcely more than French or English kings did. In Byzantium landholders were richer and more powerful than merchants, but the same was true

in most of Western Europe until the French Revolution. The Byzantine Church was often suspicious that merchants might be exploiting the poor, but so was the Catholic Church in Western Europe. Ottoman and communist influences have surely harmed Eastern European business more than Byzantine influence has, and in the 20th century Greek and Armenian businessmen have been no less enterprising than Westerners. If the business climate is now worse in Romania or Bulgaria than in Hungary or Poland, the main reasons are probably that the old indiscriminate distrust of politicians has led to a resigned tolerance of government corruption, and that the lingering eastern distrust of Westerners applies to foreign investment.

How much, then, do the Byzantines and their heirs resemble some or all of us Americans? First and most obviously, around five million Americans belong to Eastern Orthodox churches that officially hold the same doctrines that the Byzantine Church did. Most other American Christians accept the dogmas defined by the first six ecumenical councils, which were held by Byzantine emperors on Byzantine territory, and use the Nicene Creed (though usually adding the *filioque*). Roman Catholics also accept the Byzantines' seventh ecumenical council, which endorsed the use of religious images, and share the Orthodox prohibition of married bishops and of the ordination of women. The Orthodox resemble Protestants in ordaining married men (though the Orthodox prohibit marriage after ordination) and in permitting remarriage after divorce (though the Orthodox strongly disapprove of divorce and impose a lifetime limit of three marriages).

American pacifists would sympathize with the Byzantine argument that killing an enemy soldier in battle is a sin, but would be puzzled by the fact that Byzantine soldiers went ahead and killed and then did their penance. This is an instance of a more comprehensive Byzantine and Orthodox attitude alien to Catholic and Protestant thinking: that sinful actions are sometimes allowable or even necessary, but still sinful. Such a denial that ends could justify means was the main reason Byzantines judged politicians so harshly. Though compatible with the Christian doctrine of original sin, this idea may well go back to the ancient Greeks, who felt that Orestes had to kill Clytemnestra because she had murdered his father but still blamed him because she was his mother.

Although some of these attitudes may appear primitive, Byzantine culture can also seem strangely modern. One reason for the success of the *Glory of Byzantium* exhibition is doubtless that Byzantine art is often abstract, more concerned with emotions and ideas than with realism. Because much of it is formulaic, employing set religious images and repetitive patterns, it puts a high value on technique, just as modern artists do. Byzantine literature and scholarship are again more concerned with style than with mundane reality, and often attain a virtually postmodern level of incomprehensibility and self-indulgence.

All of these characteristics reflect the fact that most of Byzantine art and literature was produced for an elite—the small fraction of Byzantines who had the money to pay for art, or the education to read literature, even though most of the best artists and some of the best writers came from humble backgrounds. While some Byzantine art and literature of a more popular kind has survived, most of it religious, even lower-class Byzantines considered it inferior, meant for people lacking the education or wealth to enjoy the best. In its cultural divide Byzantium somewhat resembled our own society, where most serious art, literature, and scholarship is intended for an elite, and most of what the population at large watches or reads (some of it religious) makes no pretense to literary or artistic value. Yet many other places and times have shown no comparable divide between elite and popular culture. Ancient Greeks of every sort, including the illiterate, listened to the poems of Homer, the tragedies of Sophocles, and the comedies of Aristophanes. A cross section of English society flocked to Shakespeare's plays and, with the rise of mass literacy, read Dickens's novels. But today, American efforts to bring together elite and popular cultures are largely limited to some professors' offering courses on television shows and other products of the entertainment industry at the expense of supposedly elitist works, including those from other countries. Like us, the Byzantines made few efforts to bridge their culture gap and were particularly indifferent to foreign cultures.

Byzantium, like the United States of today, was both a state and a world of its own, a great power with a diverse but largely self-contained economy and culture. Both Byzantium and America deserve comparison not to England, France, or Germany, but to all of Western Europe, or to all of today's Eastern Orthodox countries. Like the contemporary United States, Byzantium felt even more self-sufficient than it was. Such a feeling can lead a society to think that the diversity at home is all the diversity there could possibly be, and such thinking can lead that society either to ignore the outside world or—in the case of the better educated—to picture the outside world too much in one's own image.

Thus, educated Byzantines often saw Islam simply as a particularly aberrant Christian heresy, and thought of Western Europe as a poorer, weaker, and more ignorant version of Byzantium. So some educated Americans have believed in a democratic Soviet Union, a feminist Third World, a Bosnia ready to implement the Dayton accords, or a Byzantium more interested in sexuality than in spirituality. Such misunderstandings of outsiders can lead to unpleasant surprises, such as the Arab, Crusader, and Turkish invasions of Byzantium, or the Bosnian crisis so mishandled by the United States. Today's Eastern Orthodox countries remain at something of a political and economic disadvantage because they have inherited some of this myopia from the Byzantines.

Yet this weakness of Byzantium was in most respects a result of its strengths. If Byzantium had a strong sense of superiority over its neighbors, it usually did surpass them in wealth, political and military organization, literacy, and scientific and philosophical knowledge. Even in the 14th and 15th centuries, Byzantine scholars who arrived in Italy were greeted as the bearers of a superior culture, with more to teach the West than to learn from it. Even so, some Byzantines were already beginning to learn Latin and to translate Latin literature, and if the empire had survived, there is every reason to believe that it would have participated in the scientific discoveries of the Renaissance. While Byzantium's complacency and lack of aggressiveness may have contributed to its fall after 1,168 years, that was nonetheless more than five times as long as the United States has lasted so far.

The Making of Magna Carta

Ruth I Mills

On 15th June, 1215, at Runnymede, between Windsor and Staines by the river Thames, King John of England sealed a document called 'The Articles of the Barons'. The charter between the King and his subjects had a life of only about ten weeks and it was a later version that bore the name—Magna Carta—by which they both became known to history.

John was the youngest of the four surviving sons of King Henry II of England and his Queen, Eleanor of Aquitaine, and as such he had not been expected to rule. One by one, however, his brothers died—Henry, Geoffrey, and, finally in 1199, King Richard perished while fighting on the Continent.

Richard had been an exceptional warrior and had joined the 3rd Crusade to the Holy Land but while there he quarrelled with his French and German allies and made a treaty with his enemy, Saladin. On his way back to England he had been captured by the Archduke of Austria and held for ransom by the Emperor of Germany.

During Richard's absence, from 1190 until 1194, John had tried to persuade the barons to support him in an effort to seize the throne. The rebellion failed when Richard returned from captivity to quell the uprising, but when the King died, John gained by lawful succession the crown he had been unable to wrest from his brother. Those barons who had

King John ratifying Magna Carta at Runnymede (The Mansell Collection)

resisted John's rule now feared retribution. They fortified their castles in anticipation of John's wrath, but the influential Earl of Pembroke, William Marshal, persuaded them to pledge fealty to the new King.

From *British Heritage*, October/November 1990, pp. 41–44. ©1990 by Cowles Magazines, Inc. Reprinted by permission of *British Heritage*, P.O. Box 8200, Harrisburg, PA 17105–8200.

Above: Pope Innocent III, who reigned from 1198 to 1216 (The Mansell Collection).
Below: King John, Innocent's nemesis and later his vassal (The Mansell Collection).

Widows were deprived of rightful inheritances.

On 12th July, 1205, Hubert Walter, the Archbishop of Canterbury, died, bringing the King into conflict with the Church as well. John, as every English King before him, named a successor. Simultaneously, the Canterbury monks, by Canon Law, nominated their own successor. John's envoy and the monks went to Rome to present their choices to Pope Innocent III, but he rejected them both. During December, 1206, he prevailed upon the Canterbury monks to elect Cardinal Stephen Langton, an Englishman born at Langton-by-Wragby, Lincolnshire.

John refused to accept Langton and forced him into exile in France. Pope Innocent retaliated by laying an interdict on England on 23rd March, 1208. English churches were closed and all clerical services were suspended except for baptisms and confession for the dying. Many bishops and monks, fearing John's wrath, fled to France.

In 1209 Innocent realized that John was not repentant and, determined to employ harsher measures, he ordered King John's excommunication. The edict was not announced in England un-

Under John's command, the barons defended their Norman and Angevin castles against the French. According to the French, John had forfeited the right to his French lands by supposedly murdering the son of the Duke of Brittany (who had been a contender for the British throne) and marrying the already-engaged Isabelle of Angoulême. Unfortunately, the barons met with little success and by 1204 the last of the castles had fallen to the enemy. The frustrated barons claimed that John was a poor leader, disinclined toward fighting and inept at it. John accused them of acting irresponsibly after many of them had turned their castles over to the French without a fight.

The cost of John's campaigns in France and his exhorbitant lifestyle, in addition to unpaid bills stemming from Richard's crusade and ransom, swelled England's debts. When John demanded that his barons pay higher taxes, many refused, saying that they had no more to give. The King grew ever more insistent. He imposed fees for the preservation of the 'King's peace', exacted huge fines for trivial offences, increased inheritance and dowry charges

and demanded that castles be turned over to him. He took barons' sons as hostage and murdered them whenever his demands were not met.

til 30th August, 1211, because most of the clerics remaining in England were either sympathetic towards the King or afraid of incurring his anger.

During the excommunicate years John's actions became even more extreme. Rumours of his cruelty were rampant. The barons kept silent, not knowing who among them were John's spies. Secretly, though, they took heart in the prophesy announced by a hermit, Peter of Wakefield, in the spring of 1212: 'Within the year King John will lose his crown to one pleasant in God's sight.'

At first John laughed, but when he discovered that his subjects believed the prophecy he became enraged. John imprisoned the hermit and his son and awaited the outcome of the prediction. Frightened that this might presage a French invasion or a baronial uprising, and seeking now to reconcile himself with the Pope and thereby win his support, John sent an envoy to Rome to say that Stephen Langton was welcome in England.

Innocent no longer trusted John, however, and he sent an envoy to France commanding King Phillip to invade England in a 'holy war'. Unknown to Phillip, Innocent's envoy then continued to England, where, in January 1213, he told John that his choices were to irrevocably accept Langton or suffer invasion.

King John was now afraid he would lose all and not only repeated his willingness to accept Langton but also gifted the Kingdoms of England and Ireland to Pope Innocent who, with his successors, would serve as Lord of these lands in perpetuity. The Pope accepted the offer and on Ascension Day, 1212, John was still the ruler of England, even though he was technically now only a vassal of the Pope. The hermit's prophecy had not come true. Tied to horses' tails, Peter and his son were dragged to the gallows and hanged.

At Winchester on 20th July, 1213, Archbishop Stephen Langton removed the excommunication from King John, who swore that he'd act justly toward his subjects. Many barons scoffed. The King's promises, they said, were worthless. Within days John ordered military service for another continental campaign, but many barons refused to go.

Langton realized that a serious break between the King and his subjects was impending and, serving in the Archbishop of Canterbury's traditional rôle as church primate and first adviser to the King, he sought for a surer way of reaching agreement than through another verbal promise. At a meeting with several barons at St Paul's on 25th August, 1213, Langton promised them his support provided they acted legally—by means of a charter. He showed them the King Henry I Coronation Charter, considered 'ancient custom that is just', which promised that the excesses of King William Rufus's reign would not be repeated. That charter, Langton explained, could serve as the precedent for a new charter, one fair to baron, merchant, peasant and King, according to the 'laws of nature's God'—justice.

In May 1214 John was defeated in his attempts to recover the lands he had lost to the French, and, blaming his failures on the barons' lethargy, he again requested that they pay the expenses of his campaigns. He closeted himself with his advisers, whom the barons called 'evil counselors'. The barons met together as well, to sharpen their fighting skills and demand to be heard.

Aware that the malcontents' numbers were growing, John agreed to a meeting in London on the day of the Feast of the Epiphany, 6th January, 1215. There the barons, dressed in battle gear, exacted a promise from John that he would hear their proposal for redress of grievances during Easter week.

During that spring Marshal and Langton acted as intermediaries. At the Easter meeting, John refused to consider draft after draft of the barons' statement of redress whilst complaining to England's Lord, Pope Innocent, about the barons' intransigence. On Ash Wednesday, 1215, John declared himself a holy crusader, thus ensuring by Canon Law that no one could take or destroy his property.

The longer King John delayed, the less the barons trusted Langton's sincerity. At last they decided that force was the only avenue open to them. Assisted by peasants, barons began assaulting Royal castles at the end of April. On 17th May the residents of London

opened the city gates to the insurgents and by 6th June, John asked for a truce. He ordered the barons to compose another statement of redress of grievances and granted many of the demands he had previously refused.

Finally, both sides to the argument met at Runnymede on 15th June, 1215. The recalcitrants promised they'd pledge fealty to John were he to seal 'The Articles of the Barons'. After minor details of the charter were worked out, John affixed his seal and 'The Articles of the Barons' became the law of the land. Sixteen years of turmoil seemed over.

Instead, horrendous events took place that rocked the Nation. First the barons refused to pledge fealty to King John and retained their private armies. Threatened with excommunication, they finally disbanded, but once back home, they fortified their castles and prepared for war. On 16th August, word reached England that Pope Innocent, in defence of his crusader-vassal, had issued an order on 18th June for Langton to excommunicate each dissenting baron. Then, on 24th August, the supreme blow came: Pope Innocent, Lord of England, had annulled the charter of liberties.

Langton, however, defied the Pope and refused to excommunicate the barons. He had urged them to seek a charter and knew the Pope had been misinformed. Planning to attend the Lateran Council in Rome, he decided to arrive early and explain the barons' position to Pope Innocent. As Langton embarked, the Pope's envoy suspended him from his see.

The barons now realized that Langton had worked on their behalf and had sacrificed his own position for them. He had failed to establish a charter, but every baron knew St Augustine's dictum: 'When all else fails, war is justified.' They were determined to succeed where Langton had not by defeating John in battle and dividing up the Kingdom amongst themselves. But, not having been actively engaged in warfare for a decade, the rebels were no match for John's supporting barons and mercenaries. From the autumn of 1215 until the spring of 1216, John's forces prevailed. By May the insurgents controlled only London and a few castles.

Meanwhile, in Rome, Pope Innocent refused to heed Langton's pleas. If not for the intervention of his fellow cardinals, the Archbishop would have been expelled from his post. Forbidden by the Pope to return to England, Langton went again into exile in France in January 1216.

In May 1216, the war in England took on a new dimension. Prince Louis of France invaded John's domain at the barons' invitation, in return for a promise of the British throne should he succeed. At the same time, several barons who had been loyal to John deserted him. Louis and his troops easily restored castle after castle to the rebellious barons, while John raced frantically about the Kingdom, doing whatever he could to preserve his lands. His last trip, on 9th October, took him to the Lincolnshire tidal flats where, supposedly, his treasure was lost in quicksand. Ten days later the King died of dysentery. His 10-year-old son became King Henry III.

John's death marked a drastic reversal of the political climate. Many barons who'd opposed John deserted Louis and pledged fealty to King Henry. William Marshal became Regent to the young King and took command of the Royal Army. Within the year Louis was expelled from England. By then Pope Innocent had died and been replaced by Pope Honorious III, who had respected Langton's position.

One of the Marshal's first acts as Regent was to revise the barons' charter, deleting certain offensive clauses and those pertaining to Royal forests. The remaining clauses, those ensuring personal liberties, became the Great Charter, Magna Carta, sealed 12th November, 1216, by the Regent.

During the ensuing years of Henry's reign and that of his son, King Edward I, Magna Carta was further revised and reconfirmed many times and in 1297 it became a part of the Revised Statutes. Almost a century in the making, Magna Carta now stands as a beacon, for under its medieval concerns are found timeless ethical principles that Stephen Langton called the 'laws of nature's God'.

CLOCKS
REVOLUTION
IN   TIME

Ancient Clepsydra

The question to ask is: Why clocks? Who needs them? After all, nature is the great time-giver, and all of us without exception, live by nature's clock. Night follows day; day, night; and each year brings its succession of seasons. These cycles are imprinted on just about every living being in what are called circadian ('about a day') and circannual biological rhythms. They are stamped in our flesh and blood; they persist even when we are cut off from time cues; they mark us as earthlings.

These biological rhythms are matched by societal work patterns: day is for labour, night for repose, and the round of seasons is a sequence of warmth and cold, planting and harvest, life and death.

Into this natural cycle, which all people have experienced as a divine providence, the artificial clock enters as an intruder.

David Landes

WHEN IN THE LATE SIXTEENTH century Portuguese traders and Christian missionaries sought entry into China, they were thwarted by a kind of permanent quarantine. Chinese officials correctly perceived these foreigners as potential subversives, bringing with them the threat of political interference, material seduction, and spiritual corruption. The ban was not lifted for decades, and then only because Matteo Ricci and his Jesuit mission brought with them knowledge

and instruments that the Celestial Court coveted. In particular, they brought chiming clocks, which the Chinese received as a wondrous device. By the time Ricci, after numerous advances and retreats, finally secured permission from the court eunuchs and other officials to proceed to Peking and present himself to the throne, the emperor could hardly wait. 'Where', he called, 'are the self-ringing bells?' And later, when the dowager empress showed an interest in her son's favourite clock, the emperor

had the bell disconnected so that she would be disappointed. He could not have refused to give it to her, had she asked for it; but neither would he give it up, so he found this devious way to reconcile filial piety with personal gratification.

The use of these clocks as a ticket of entry is evidence of the great advance European timekeeping had made over Chinese horology. It had not always been thus. The Chinese had always been much concerned to track the stars for astrological and horoscopic purposes. For the emperor, the conjunctions of the heavenly bodies were an indispensable guide to action, public and private—to making war and peace, to sowing and reaping, to conceiving an heir with the empress or coupling with a concubine. To facilitate the calculations required, court mechanicians of the Sung dynasty (tenth and eleventh centuries) built a series of remarkable clock-driven astraria, designed to track and display the apparent movements of the stars. The clock mechanism that drove the display was hydraulic—a water clock (clepsydra) linked to a bucket wheel. As each bucket filled, it activated a release mechanism that allowed the big drive wheel to turn and bring the next bucket into position. The water clock in itself was no more accurate than such devices can be; but in combination with the wheel, it could be adjusted to keep time within a minute or two a day. By way of comparison, the ordinary drip or flow water clocks then in use in Europe probably varied by a half-hour or more.

These astronomical clocks marked a culmination. The greatest of them, that built by Su Sung at the end of the eleventh century, was also the last of the series. When invasion and war forced the court to flee, the clock was lost and its secret as well. From this high point of achievement, Chinese timekeeping retrogressed to simpler, less accurate instruments, so that when the Jesuits arrived some five hundred years later with their mechanical clocks, they found only objects that confirmed their comfortable sense of technological, and by implication moral, superiority.

Meanwhile European timekeeping made a quantum leap by moving from hydraulic to mechanical devices. The new clocks, which took the form of weight-driven automated bells, made their appearance around 1280. We don't know where—England possibly, or Italy—and we don't know who invented them. What we do know is that the gain was immense and that the new clocks very rapidly swept the older clepsydras aside. Since these first mechanical clocks were notoriously inaccurate, varying an hour or more a day, and unreliable, breaking down frequently and

needing major overhauls every few years, one can only infer that water clocks left even more to be desired. The great advantage of the mechanical clock lay in its relative immunity to temperature change, whereas the drip or flow of the water clock varied with the seasons while frost would halt it altogether (the temperature did not have to go down to freezing to increase viscosity and slow the rate). In the poorly heated buildings of northern Europe, especially at night, this was a near-fatal impairment. Dirt was another enemy. No water is pure, and deposits would gradually choke the narrow opening. The instructions for use of a thirteenth-century water clock installed in the Abbey of Villers (near Brussels) make it clear that no one expected much of these devices: the sacristan was to adjust it daily by the sun, as it fell on the abbey windows; and if the day was cloudy, why then it was automatically ten o'clock at the end of the morning mass.

Why Europe should have succeeded in effecting this transition to a superior technology and China not is an important historical question. Anyone who looked at the horological world of the eleventh or twelfth century would have surely predicted the opposite result. (He would have also expected Islam to surpass Europe in this domain.) The Chinese failure—if failure is the right word—cannot be sought in material circumstances. The Chinese were as troubled and inconvenienced by the limitations of the water clock as were the Europeans; it can get very cold in Peking. (The Chinese tried substituting mercury or sand for water, but mercury kills and neither behaves very well over time.) Instead the explanation must be sought in the character and purposes of Chinese timekeeping. It was, in its higher forms, a monopoly of the imperial court, as much an attribute of sovereignty as the right to coin money. In this instance, dominion over time and

A monastic water-driven wheel clock of thirteenth-century Europe. The mechanism is hard to make out, but the picture suggests that water-driven wheel clocks of the Chinese type were used (or at least known) in Europe before the advent of the weight-driven wheel-clock.

Manuscript illustrations from the fifteenth century show the metaphorical importance clocks had in a medieval application of the concept of time. The goddess Attemprance, half-figure in a cloud, grasps a clock with hanging bells in both hands; large bell above. A French manuscript illustration of the late fifteenth century.

Manuscript illustration of 1450 showing a huge, intricate clock, standing on earth, but with its open and visible wheel-work and dial and bell in heaven. The four traditional symbols of the evangelists are shown on the four corners of the dial. The goddess Attemprance, resting on the clouds, is winding the clock.

taken as special projects, the work of a team assembled for the occasion. Each of these machines was a *tour de force*, and each built on earlier models, researched in the archives by way of preparation. There was, then, no continuous process of construction and emendation; no multiplicity of private initiatives; no dynamic of continuing improvement. Instead we have these occasional peak moments of achievement, highly fragile, vulnerable to political hostility and adventitious violence, easily buried and forgotten once the team of builders had dissolved or died.

Outside these rarefied circles, the Chinese people had little interest in time measurement for its own sake. Most of them were peasants, and peasants have no need of clocks. They wake with the animals in the morning, watch the shadows shorten and lengthen as the sun crosses the sky, and go to bed once night falls—because they are tired, illumination is costly and they must get up very early. They are not unaware of the passage of time, but they do not have to measure it. Time measurement is an urban concern, and in medieval China the authorities provided time signals (drums, trumpets) in the cities to mark the passage of the hours and warn the residents of such things as the closing of the gates to the separate quarters or neighbourhoods. But such noises could not easily be used to order the daily round of activities, for the Chinese did not number the hours sequentially; rather they named them, so that auditory

calendar was a major aspect of power, for it laid the cognitive foundation for imperial decisions in every area of political and economic life. So much was this the case that each emperor began by proclaiming his own calendar, often different from that of his predecessor;

by so doing, he affirmed his legitimacy and identity.

Timekeeping instruments were therefore reserved to the court and certain of its officials; there was no civilian clock trade. Such great astronomical clocks as were built for the throne were under-

signals transmitted limited information. Such as they were, they sufficed, for the organisation of work created no need for closer or continuous timing. The typical work unit was the household shop, comprising master, assistants, and apprentices. The day started at dawn, when the youngest or newest apprentice woke to make the fire and wake the rest; and work continued until night imposed its interruption. This mode of production set no artificial *clocktime* limited to labour; nature fixed the bounds.

In contrast, medieval Europe did have a constituency concerned to track and use time. This was the Christian church, especially those monastic orders that followed the rule of Benedict. This rule, which was defined in the sixth century, became over time the standard of monachal discipline in western Europe. The aim of the rule was to ensure that the entire day be ordered and devoted to the service of God—to pray above all, but also to work, which was defined as another kind of prayer. The daily prayer offices numbered seven (later eight), six

(later seven) in the daytime and one at night. The institution of a nocturnal office was peculiar to Christianity and sharply differentiated it from the other monotheistic religions. It went back to the prayer vigils conducted by the earliest Christians in imminent expectation of the *parousia*, or second coming. It was these vigils that were later merged with the morning prayer to constitute the canonical hour known as matins.

The obligation to rise to prayer in the dark imposed a special condition on Christian worship. Whereas Jews (and later Muslims) set their times of prayer by natural events (morning, afternoon, and evening) that do not require the use of an artificial timekeeper, Christians needed some kind of alarm to wake to matins. In the cities of the Roman empire, the night watch could give the signal. In medieval Europe such municipal services had long disappeared, and most abbeys were located in rural areas. Each house, then, had to find its own way to satisfy the requirement, usually by means of an alarm device linked to a

water clock. This would rouse the waker, usually the sacristan, who would then ring the bells that called the others to prayer. Most house rules—for although the principal was general, there was little uniformity in the details of practice—enjoined the sacristan to be scrupulous in his performance of this duty, for his neglect imperilled the salvation of his brethren (and the larger church) as well as his own. 'Nothing, therefore, shall be put before the Divine Office', says the Rule.

To the ordinary monk, getting up in the dark of the night was perhaps the hardest aspect of monastic discipline. Indeed the practical meaning of 'reforming' a house meant first and foremost the imposition (reimposition) of this duty. The sleepyheads were prodded out of bed and urged to the offices; they were also prodded during service lest they fail in their obligations. Where the flesh was weak, temptation lurked. Raoul Glaber (early eleventh century) tells the tale of a demon who successfully seduced a monk by holding the lure of sweet sleep:

A sketch of a clock tower by Villard de Honnecourt, circa 1225–1250. An early example of a chiming clock tower which kept equal hours and provided regular signals—a constraint for worker and employer alike.

As for you, I wonder why you so scrupulously jump out of bed as soon as you hear the bell, when you could stay resting even unto the third bell . . . but know that every year Christ empties hell of sinners and brings them to heaven, so without worry you can give yourself to all the voluptuousness of the flesh. . . .

The same Glaber confesses to two occasions when he himself woke late and saw a demon, 'come to do business with the laggards'. And Peter the Venerable, Abbot of Cluny in the twelfth century, tells the story of Brother Alger, who woke thinking he had heard the bell ring for nocturns. Looking around, he thought he saw the other beds empty, so he drew on his sandals, threw on his cloak, and hastened to the chapel. There he was puzzled not to hear the sound of voices lifted in prayer. Now he hurried back to the dormitory, where he found all the other monks fast asleep. And then he understood: this was all a temptation of the devil, who had awakened him at the wrong time, so that when the bell for nocturns really rang, he would sleep through it.

These, I suggest, are what we now know as anxiety dreams. They clearly reflect the degree to which time-consciousness and discipline had become internalised. Missing matins was a serious matter, so serious that it has been immortalised for us by perhaps the best known of children's songs:

Frère Jacques, Frère Jacques,
Dormez-vous? dormez-vous?
Sonnez les matines, sonnez les matines,
Ding, dang, dong; ding, dang, dong.

We know far less than we should like about monastic horology in the Middle Ages, and such information as we have is confused by the use of the general term *(h)orologium* for any and all kinds of timekeeper. It seems clear, however, that the century or two preceding the appearance of the mechanical clock saw important improvements in technique and a growing emphasis on the details of the monastic time service. The enhanced temporal consciousness may be related to the revival of monastic life after the millennium and in particular to the needs of the Cistercian order—that economic empire with its agricultural, mining, and industrial enterprises, its ever-turning water wheels, its large labour force of lay brethren, its place in the forefront of European technology.

One of the innovations of this period seems to have been the combination clepsydra/mechanical alarm. This worked as follows: when the water in the recipient vessel reached an appropriate height, it tripped a weight-driven escape wheel, so called because it meshed with pallets that alternately blocked and released it (allowed it to escape). This stop-go motion in turn imparted a to-and-fro oscillation to the rod or *verge* holding the pallets; hence the name *verge escapement*. Attach a small hammer to the end of the verge, and it could ring a bell. Put an oscillating cross bar on the end, and you had a controller for a clock.

The first clocks were probably alarms converted in this manner. The very name *clock* meant bell, and these were essentially machines to sound the passing hours. Their use entailed a drastic change in the character of European timekeeping. Because the mechanical clock beat at a more or less uniform rate, it sounded equal-length hours—what later came to be known as mean (average) time. But the standard of medieval Europe was the sun, and the hours were natural, equal fractions of the day and night. Thus as days got longer, daylight hours lengthened and night hours shrank; and vice versa. These seasonally variable hours (often called temporal hours) were easily measured by the water clock; all one had to do was change the scale with the seasons. But an automated bell was another story: changing the times of ringing to take account of changing hours would have been a difficult and time-consuming task. So Europeans learned a new time standard in which the sun rose and set at different hours as the days passed. This seems natural enough to us, but it must have come as a shock at first. (Some places chose to start their day at sunrise, which took care of one end of the problem, though not the other).

In effect the new clock offered a rival time standard in competition with the older church time. It was not only the hours that differed; it was the signals also. The old water clocks did not sound public, tower bells. They told the time for the bell ringer, who usually rang, not the unequal, temporal hours, but the hours of prayer, the so-called canonical hours. These were not equally spaced and did not lend themselves to the kind of calculation we take for granted: how long since? how long until? It was equal hours that made this possible and thereby contributed significantly to the growing numeracy of the urban population. Insofar as the medieval church resisted the new time standard, it gave over an important symbol of authority to the secular power. Where once people punctuated their day by such marks as sext, none, and vespers, now they thought in terms of hours and, very soon, minutes.

The transition from church time to lay time was at once sign and consequence of the rise of a new, urban social order. The new machines appealed from the start to the rich and powerful, who made them the preferred object of conspicuous consumption. No court, no

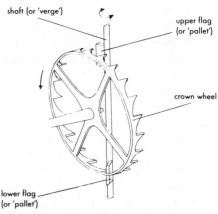

Diagram illustrating the 'verge' escapement. An escapement is the mechanism which could control and slow down the speed at which the weights of a clock dropped. The 'verge' escapement is the earliest surviving form.

prince would be without one. But far more important in the long run was the rapid acceptance of the new instrument in cities and towns, which had long learned to regulate many aspects of civil life by bells—bells to signal the opening and closing of markets, waking bells and work bells, drinking and curfew bells, bells for opening and closing of gates, assembly and alarms. In this regard, the medieval city was a secular version of the cloister, prepared by habit and need to use the clock as a superior instrument of time discipline and management.

The pressure for time signals was especially strong in those cities that were engaged in textile manufacture—the first and greatest of medieval industries. There the definition of working time was crucial to the profitability of enterprise and the prosperity of the commune. The textile industry was the first to go over to large-scale production for export, hence the first to overflow the traditional workshop and engage a dispersed work force. Some of these workers—the *ciompi* in Florence, the 'blue nails' (stained by dye) in Flanders—were true proletarians, owning none of the instruments of production, selling only their labour power. They streamed early every morning into the dye shops and fulling mills, where the high consumption of energy for heating the vats and driving the hammers encouraged concentration in large units. Other branches of the manufacture could be conducted in the rooms and cottages of the workers: employers liked this so-called putting out because it shifted much of the burden of overhead costs to the employee, who was paid by the piece rather than by time; and the workers preferred it to the time discipline and supervision of the large shops. They could in principle start and stop at will, for who was to tell them what to do in their own home?

The bells would tell them. Where there was textile manufacture, there were work bells, which inevitably gave rise to conflict. Part of the problem was implicit in the effort to impose time discipline on home workers. In principle, payment by the piece should have taken care of the matter, with workers responding to wage incentives. In fact, the home workers were content to earn what they felt they needed, and in time of keen demand, employers found it impossible to get them to do more, for higher pay only reduced the amount of work required to satisfy these needs. The effort to bring the constraints of the manufactory into the rooms and cottages of spinners and weavers made the very use of bells a focus of resentment.

Meanwhile in the fulling mills and dyeshops the bells posed a different kind of problem, especially when they were controlled by the employer. Consider the nature of the wage contract: the worker was paid by the day, and the day was bounded by these time signals. The employer had an interest in getting a full day's work for the wages he paid; and the worker in giving no more time than he was paid for. The question inevitably arose how the worker could know whether bell time was honest time. How could he trust even the municipal bells when the town council was dominated by representatives of the employers?

Under the circumstances, workers in some places sought to silence the *werkclocke*: at Therouanne in 1367 the dean and chapter promised 'workers, fullers, and other mechanics' to silence 'forever the workers' bell in order that no scandal or conflict be born in city and church as a result of the ringing of a bell of this type'. Such efforts to eliminate time signals never achieved success: as soon suppress the system of wage labour. Be-

The clockmaker at work, from a sixteenth-century wood engraving.

sides, once the work day was defined in temporal rather than natural terms, workers as well as employers had an interest in defining and somehow signalling the boundaries. Time measurement here was a two-edged sword: it gave the employer bounds to fill, and to the worker bounds to work. The alternative was the open-ended working day, as Chrétien de Troyes observed of the silk weavers of Lyons in the twelfth century:

> ... nous sommes en grand'misère,
> Mais s'enrichit de nos salaires
> Celui pour qui nous travaillons.
>
> Des nuits grand partie nous veillons
> Et tout le jour pour y gagner
> ... we are in great misery,
> The man who gets rich on our wages
> Is the man we worked for.
> We're up a good part of the night
> And work all day to make our way....

It was not the work bells as such, then, that were resented and mistrusted, but the people who controlled them; and

it is here that the chiming tower clock made its greatest contribution. It kept equal hours and provided regular signals, at first on the hour, later on at the halves or quarters, and these necessarily limited the opportunities for abuse. With the appearance of the dial (from the word for day), of course, it was possible for all interested parties to verify the time on a continuous basis.

The early turret clocks were very expensive, even when simple. Wrought iron and brass needed repeated hammering, hence much labour and much fuel. The casting of the bells was a precarious operation. The placement of the mechanism usually entailed major structural alterations. The construction and installation of a tower clock might take months if not years. Teams of craftsmen and labourers had to be assembled on the site and there lodged and boarded. Subsequent maintenance required the attendance of a resident technician, repeated visits by specialised artists, and an endless flow of replacement parts.

These costs increased substantially as soon as one went beyond simple time-keepers to astronomical clocks and/or automata. The medieval accounts show this process clearly: the sums paid to painters and woodcarvers bear witness to the growing importance of the clock as spectacle as well as time signal. The hourly parade of saints and patriarchs; the ponderous strokes of the hammer-wielding *jaquemarts*; the angel turning with the sun; the rooster crowing at sunrise; the lunar disc waxing and waning with the moon—and all these movements and sounds offered lessons in theology and astronomy to the upgrazing multitude that gathered to watch and wonder at what man had wrought. They hourly pageant was an imitation of divine creation; the mechanism, a miniaturisation of heaven and earth. As a result, the show clock was to the new secular, urbanising world of the later Middle Ages what the cathedrals had been to the still worshipful world of the high Middle Ages: a combination of a sacrifice and affirmation, the embodiment of the highest skills and artistry, a symbol of prowess and source of pride. It was also a source of income—the lay analogue to the religious relics that were so potent an attraction to medieval travellers. When Philip the Bold of Burgundy defeated the Flemish burghers at Rosebecke in 1382 and wanted to punish those proud and troublesome clothiers, he could do no worse (or better) than seize the belfry clock at Courtrai and take it off to his capital at Dijon.

These public clocks, moreover, were only the top of the market. They are the ones that history knows best, but we know only a fraction of what was made. In this regard, the records are misleading: they have preserved the memory of a spotty, biased selection and largely omitted the smaller domestic clocks made to private order. As a result, it was long thought that the first mechanical clocks were turret clocks, and that the smaller domestic models were the much later product of advances in miniaturisation. Yet there was no technical impediment to making chamber clocks once the verge escapement had been invented. Indeed, since the mechanical clock is a development of the timer

alarm, itself made to chamber size, small may well have preceded big.

Whichever came first, the one logically implied the other, so that we may fairly assume that both types of clock were known and made from the start. In the event, the first literary allusion to a mechanical clock refers to domestic timepieces. This goes back to the late thirteenth century, in Jean de Meung's additional verse to *Le roman de la rose*. Jean, a romantic poet of curiously worldly interest, attributes to his Pygmalion a fair array of chamber clocks:

Et puis faire sonner ses orloges
Par ses salles et par ses loges
A roues trop subtillement
De pardurable mouvement.

And then through halls and chambers,
Made his clock chime
By wheels of such cunning
Ever turning through time.

By the end of the fourteenth century, hundreds of clocks were turning in western Europe. A new profession of horologers had emerged, competing for custom and seeking severally to improve their product. There could be no surer guarantee of cumulative technical advance. Few inventions in history have ever made their way with such ease. Everyone seems to have welcomed the clock, even those workers who toiled to its rules, for they much preferred it to arbitrary bells. *Summe necessarium pro omni statu hominum* was the way Galvano Fiamma, chronicler of Milan, put it when he proudly marked the erection in 1333 (?) of a clock that not only struck the hours but signalled each one by the number of peals. And this in turn recalls an earlier inscription on a clock installed in 1314 on the bridge at Caen:

Je ferai les heures ouir
Pour le commun peuple rejouir.

I shall give the hours voice
To make the common folk rejoice.

Even the poets liked the new clocks. That is the most astonishing aspect of these early years of mechanical horology, for no group is by instinct and sensibility so suspicious of technical innovation. Here, moreover, was an in-

vention that carried with it the seeds of control, order, self-restraint—all virtues (or vices) inimical to the free, spontaneous imagination and contemplation so prized by creative artists. Yet it would be anachronistic to impute these ideals to the thirteenth and fourteenth centuries; they came much later. The medieval ideal was one of sobriety and control, along with due respect for worthy models. Besides, it was surely too soon to understand the potential of the new device for forming the persona as well as dictating the terms of life and work. Instead, the availability of this new knowledge gave all a sense of power, of enhanced efficiency and potential, of ownership of a new a valuable asset, whereas we, living by the clock, see ignorance of or indifference to time as a release from constraint and a gain in freedom. Everything depends, I suppose, on where one is coming from. In any event, the early celebrators of the clock were no mere poetasters: thus Dante Alighieri, who sang in his *Paradise* (Canto X) the praises of the 'glorious wheel' moving and returning 'voice to voice in timbre and sweetness'—*tin tin sonando con si dolce nota* (almost surely a reference to a chamber clock, unless Dante had a tin ear), therein echoing the pleasure that Jean de Meung's Pygmalion took in his chiming clocks a generation earlier. And a half-century later we have Jean Froissart, poet but more famous as historian, composer of 'love ditties', among them *L'horloge amoureuse* (1369):

> . . . The clock is, when you think about it,
> A very beautiful and remarkable instrument,
> And it's also pleasant and useful,
> Because night and day it tells us the hours
> By the subtlety of its mechanism
> Even when there is no sun.
> Hence all the more reason to prize one's machine,
> Because other instruments can't do this
> However artfully and precisely they may be made
> Hence do we hold him for valiant and wise
> Who first invented this device
> And with his knowledge undertook and made
> A thing so noble and of such great pride.

The invention and diffusion of the mechanical clock had momentous consequences for European technology, culture, and society—comparable in their significance to the effects of the later invention of movable type and printing. For one thing, the clock could be miniaturised and, once small enough, moved about. For this, a new power source was needed, which took the form of a coiled spring, releasing energy as it unwound. This came in during the fifteenth century and gave rise to a new generation of small domestic clocks and, by the early sixteenth, to the watch, that is, a clock small enough to be worn on the person. Domestic clocks and, even more, the watch were the basis of the private, internalised time discipline that characterises modern personality and civilisation—for better or worse. Without this discipline, we could not operate the numerous and complex activities required to make our society go. (We could, no doubt, have recourse to public signals, as in the army. But that would mean a very different kind of collectivity).

For another thing, the mechanical clock was susceptible of great improvement in accuracy, even in its smaller form. This potential lay in its revolutionary principle of time measurement. Whereas earlier instruments had relied on some continuous movement—of shadow (the sundial) or fluid (the clepsydra)—to track the passage of time, the mechanical clock marked time by means of an oscillating controller. This took the form of a bar or wheel swinging to and fro. The swings (pulses or beats) could then be counted and converted to time units—hours, minutes, and eventually sub-minutes. To the ancients who invented the sundial and water clock, a continuous controller on what we would not call the analogue principle seemed only logical, for it was an imitation of time itself, always passing. But in the long run, its possibilities for improvement were limited not only by the inherent flaws of sunlight (no use at night or in cloudy weather) and flowing liquids, but by the difficulty of sustaining and even, continuously moving display. Time measurement by beats or pulses, on the other hand—the digital principle—had no bounds of accuracy. All that was needed was an even, countable frequency. The oscillating controller of the first medieval clocks usually beat double-seconds. Frequency was decidedly uneven, hence the large variation in rate. It took almost four hundred years to invent a vastly superior controller in the form of the pendulum, which in its seconds-beating form could keep time within less than a minute a day. Today, of course, new controllers have been invented in the form of vibrating quartz crystals (hundreds of thousands or even millions of beats per second), which vary less than a minute a year; and atomic resonators (billions of vibrations per second), which take thousands of years to gain or lose a second. These gains in precision have been an important impetus to scientific inquiry; indeed, almost all of them came about because scientists needed better time-keeping instruments. How else to study process and rates of changes?

Finally, the clock with its regularity came to stand as the model for all other machines—the machine of machines, the essence of man's best work in the image of God; and clock-making became the school for all other mechanical arts. No one has said it better than Lewis Mumford in *Technics and Civilization*:

> The clock, not the steam engine, is the key-machine of the modern industrial age . . . In its relationship to determinable quantities of energy, to standardization, to automatic action, and finally to its own special product, accurate timing, the clock has been the foremost machine in modern technics; and at each period it has remained in the lead: it marks a perfection toward which other machines aspire.

All of this was there in germ in the oscillating controllers of the first mechanical clocks. The builders of those clocks did not know what they had wrought. That the clock was invented in Europe and remained a European monopoly for some five hundred years, and that Europe then built a civilisation organised around the measurement of time;—these were critical factors in the differentiation of West from Rest and the definition of modernity.

FOR FURTHER READING

David S. Landes, *Revolution in Time: Clocks and the Making of the Modern World* is published by Harvard University Press; on January, 16th at £17. Ernest von Bassermann-Jordan, *The Book of Old Clocks and Watches* (4th ed., revised by Hans von Bertele; New York: Crown, 1964); Eric Bruton, *The History of Clocks and Watches* (New York: Rizzoli, 1979); Carlo Cipolla, *Clocks and Culture, 1300–1700* (New York: Walker, 1967); Jacques Le Goff, *Time, Work, and Culture in the Middle Ages* (University of Chicago Press, 1980); Lewis Mumford, *Technics and Civilization* (New York: Harcourt, Brace, 1934); Joseph Needham, Wang Ling, and Derek J. de Solla Price, *Heavenly Clockwork: The Great Astronomical Clocks of Medieval China* (Cambridge University Press, 1960); also articles in *Antiquarian Horology*, the journal of the Antiquarian Horological Society of Great Britain.

Unit Selections

Key Points to Consider

❖ Why were people in the Middle East and Europe so limited in their knowledge of the world in the year 1000?

❖ Was Columbus representative of his world, or was he unique?

❖ If Columbus had not sailed to the West, do you think someone else would have done it? Explain.

❖ Considering what you have read about historiography, how should historians treat Columbus?

❖ Did the massive death of Native Americans mean genocide, as some critics say about the coming of Europeans to the New World?

❖ Why were spices so important as a trade item?

❖ What was the significance of Magellan's voyage? What does it mean in respect to Western civilization and the world?

 **Links**   **www.dushkin.com/online/**

These sites are annotated on pages 4 and 5.

It can be argued that the most important event in the formation of the modern world is the industrial revolution. In that case, perhaps, textbooks should divide at that point. A date of 1800 could roughly mark the start not only of the industrial revolution, but also of the liberal political revolts in France and the United States. Yet, 1500 is the time of the Reformation, the Renaissance, and the great global explorations of the West. This is the start of the Western domination of the world that continues into the present. Therefore, most world historians accept 1500 as a suitable breaking point for teaching purposes. So it is with the two volumes of *Annual Editions: World History*.

At the year 1000, the educated people of Europe and the Middle East, though they might have known about their own locale, knew very little about the larger world. They did the best they could with limited information, as David Lindberg writes, but their maps were grossly misleading. It might have been the Chinese who led the way in exploration, however, if it had not been for indifference, internal economic problems, and, perhaps, arrogance. Zheng He, a court eunuch and Muslim, led a powerful fleet westward in the fifteenth century, but his discoveries were left unexploited by the Chinese government, which shortly ordered the admiral to remain at home.

The abdication of world exploration by the Chinese was a fortuitous turn for Europeans. The Portuguese sailed down the western coast of Africa and found a water route to India, and the Spanish sponsored Christopher Columbus for his fateful voyages westward across the "ocean sea." But, poor Columbus! During the quincentenary of his voyage he was vilified by Native Americans, environmentalists, humanists, and others. One hundred years earlier in 1892, there had been a great fair organized in his honor in Chicago, and Columbus was regarded as a hero. If nothing else, these events prove the truth of the statement that every generation rewrites history to suit itself. A summary of the various interpretations is included in "Columbus and the Labyrinth of History" by John Noble Wilford.

Contact with diseases such as smallpox brought to the New World by the Europeans had devastating effects upon the Native Americans, who had no immunity. No one knows how many died, as Lewis Lord points out, but it amounted to a human catastrophe. Columbus and the other explorers were driven by a desire, not to kill natives, but to reach the fabled spice islands of Southeast Asia. "A Taste of Adventure" captures the lasting attraction of spices that have inspired global trade for as much as 4,600 years. The spices provided an economic incentive, but there was also sheer adventure, as seen in the voyage of Magellan. This circumnavigation proved, once and for all, that the Earth was round. It was a remarkable accomplishment but at a high cost in lives.

Columbus and the other intrepid European explorers who were sailing out around the globe had an effect in the New World, but China still dominated the Far East and Islam controlled the Middle East. Through their explorations, however, Europeans were able to bypass the Middle East to open up trade lanes that marked the beginning of a global shift of commerce. Time and technology were on the side of the West.

Images of Earth in the Year 1000

One thousand years ago, people imagined a far different Earth than we do. Here's what people believed about the planet at the beginning of the millennium.

All illustrations from *The Beginings of Western Science*

In the Middle Ages, people in Europe and the Islamic world conceived of their universe as a cozy place created by a providential God, as seen in this 13th-century illustration of the architect of the cosmos.

By David C. Lindberg
University of Wisconsin—Madison

We who live at the end of the 20th century conceive Earth to be an insignificant speck of rock and water orbiting an insignificant star in an incomprehensibly vast universe. Our forebears of a thousand years ago had a very different opinion, viewing Earth as the centerpiece of a far smaller and cozier cosmos, placed there by a providential God. The contrast between these views is dramatic, and it raises the question to which this essay will be devoted: What did learned people in Christian Europe, in the Islamic world, and in Jewish communities scattered throughout Christendom and Islam know or believe about Earth and its inhabitants in the year 1000?

Knowledge throughout the Middle Ages (roughly A.D. 450–1450) was powerfully shaped by Greek ideas, particularly those of Plato and Aristotle (both fourth century B.C.). The latter definitively mapped the cosmos and defined Earth as its central object—a position from which it was not to be dislodged until the 16th and 17th centuries. But what fixes Earth in this central position? Aristotle argued simply that

From *Earth*, December 1996, pp. 26–29. © 1996 by Kalmbach Publishing Company. Reprinted by permission.

the heavy elements of which Earth is composed move by their very nature toward the center of the universe and collect there in a spherical mass. In effect, the center of the cosmos, which coincides with Earth's center, is "down" relative to all other points.

The claim that medieval people conceived of Earth as a globe may come as a surprise, because it contradicts the claim, now a staple of high school history texts, that they universally regarded Earth as flat. The truth is that Earth was conceived of as a globe by almost every person after Aristotle known to have addressed the issue. Therefore it makes sense that Christians and Jews, who were among the vast majority of people who knew Earth was round, did not allow statements in the Bible seeming to affirm Earth's flatness to overrule either the authority of Aristotle or the testimony of the senses, such as the curved shadow of Earth during a lunar eclipse.

In the Aristotelian scheme that dominated medieval thought, the terrestrial region consisted of Earth and its atmosphere, the latter extending from the surface of Earth to the inner surface of the lunar sphere. The ingredients of this terrestrial region were the four elements: earth, water, air and fire. It was understood that all real substances are composites of two or more of the four elements combined in various proportions. For example, solid or earthy stuff is composed primarily of the element earth and liquids primarily of water.

Earth's atmosphere was held to consist principally of air and fire. These were separated in the ideal case into distinct spherical shells; but in the real world, Aristotle argued, air and fire undergo considerable mixing. Meteorological phenomena in the atmosphere were of great interest to medieval people. Lightning, thunder, rain, snow, rainbows, comets and shooting stars (the latter two judged, like the others, to be meteorological) were all studied and theorized about. Indeed, before the end of the Middle Ages, a correct theory of the rainbow—involving refractions and internal reflections within individual raindrops—had appeared.

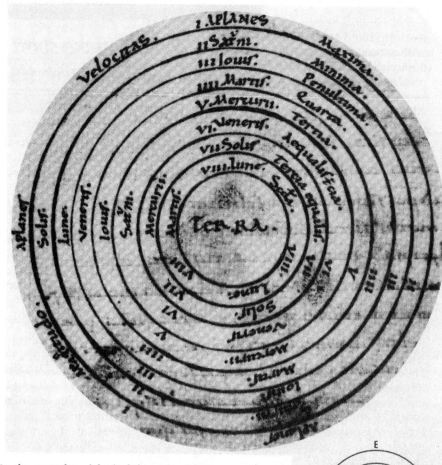

In the cosmology inherited from the Greek philosophers, Earth lay at the center of the universe and was surrounded by a series of nested spheres carrying the other planets.

Knowledge of Earth's crust in the year 1000 was limited but not insignificant. The globe was typically divided into five climatic zones—the torrid zone straddling the equator, and temperate and frigid zones running in an east-west direction on both sides of the equator. The terrestrial land mass was divided into three continents—Europe, Asia and Africa—surrounded by ocean. This conception was often represented schematically in what are known as T-O maps. These consist of a circle representing the known world, with an inscribed **T** representing the major bodies of water (the Mediterranean Sea and the Nile and Don Rivers) that separate the known world into its three continents. (East is at the top in the accompanying illustration.)

Geographical knowledge of a more local sort frequently took the form of coastal surveys listing cities, rivers, mountains and other topographical features in the order in which they would

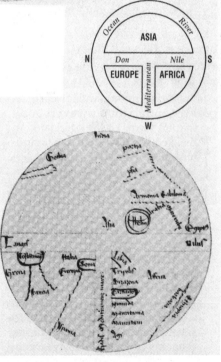

A T-O map is a schematic rendering of Earth's major continents and bodies of water developed by medieval cartographers. More realistic maps based on mathematical coordinate systems were invented in antiquity by Ptolemy and others, but they were lost during the Middle Ages and did not make a reappearance until the 15th century.

be encountered by a traveler. Of course, medieval people had good knowledge of their native region; and despite the absence during the Middle Ages of anything analogous to our road maps, pilgrims, crusaders and merchants traveled great distances without getting lost.

The principal agents of geological change were judged to be erosion, sedimentation and subterranean winds blowing through hollow cavities in Earth's interior. Such winds were invoked to explain earthquakes, volcanoes and the uplift of the crust that produces mountains. In keeping with Aristotle, the educated medieval person believed that minerals were formed by "exhalations" (something like vapors) arising within Earth's interior—dry exhalations giving rise to rocks, moist exhalations to the various metals.

Medieval people had ample practical knowledge of the oceans in their vicinity—how to catch the fish that inhabited it and how to employ the oceans for coastal transportation—but little theoretical knowledge of their origins or nature. As for the geography of the oceans, a common belief in the year 1000 held that the inhabited portion of the terrestrial globe was encircled by a continuous ocean. Oceanic tides were explained either by astrological influence emanating from the moon or by ocean currents colliding and rebounding at Earth's poles.

Medieval people of the year 1000 also focused considerable attention on the living inhabitants of Earth. It was understood by everybody that all forms of life originated in the creative activity of an omnipotent God. However, this did not forbid subsequent change in living things or even the emergence of forms of life hitherto unknown. Indeed, in an influential theory, the fourth-century Christian scholar Augustine argued that God created all forms of life in the beginning, although some as seeds that would germinate and flower subsequently.

Knowledge of plants existed in several forms. Given the agrarian economy of the Middle Ages, people had an intimate, practical, firsthand knowledge of local flora. Some of this practical botanical knowledge could be found in

> *It is easy to make sport of medieval ideas. Or, if we prefer, we can ransack the Middle Ages for anticipations of modern ideas. But we waste our time by proceeding along either of those courses.*

herbals oriented toward medical purposes. One such herbal, written by Dioscorides during the first century, contained descriptions of some 900 plant, animal and mineral products alleged to have therapeutic value. There was also a tradition of what might be called "theoretical botany" in the medieval world. This grew out of a treatise, *On Plants* (falsely attributed to Aristotle), known in Islam by the year 1000 and somewhat later in Christendom.

Knowledge of animal life followed much the same pattern. Local fauna, including domesticated animals, were well-known. "It could hardly be otherwise," the British literary scholar C. S. Lewis wrote, "in a society where everyone who could be was a horseman, hunter, and hawker, and everyone else a trapper, fisher, cowman, shepherd, swineherd, goose-girl, henwife, or beekeeper." There was also a body of theoretical literature emanating primarily from Aristotle, dealing with questions of animal anatomy, physiology and behavior.

Situated alongside these practical and theoretical bodies of zoological knowledge was a genre of literature that has attracted much modern attention: the medieval bestiary. Bestiaries are collections of animals lore and mythology— some factual, some fanciful—arranged in short entries by animal name. These works have been widely misinterpreted as attempts (unsuccessful) to write modern zoological manuals. But the authors had no such intention. Bestiaries were meant to instruct

and entertain, and their authors would have been astonished to learn that their success was to be judged by the standards of a 20th-century scientific textbook.

Medieval knowledge of the human race is too large a topic to be delved into here, but there were other forms of life deemed high on the "scale of being." Many medieval people of the year 1000 believed that distant lands were populated by monstrous races. *Natural History,* written by the first-century Roman author Pliny the Elder, was one of the principal sources for such beliefs. In this work Pliny describes the cannibal Scythians, the sexually promiscuous Garamantes, the naked Gamphasantes and the headless Blemmyae, whose mouth and eyes are attached to their chests. It is difficult to know how widespread was belief in fairies, nymphs, elves, satyrs, centaurs and the like—elusive creatures encountered not in scholarly literature and (presumably) not in the field, but in literary sources. However, it appears that skepticism among the educated was not total. And to round

Medieval knowledge of plants was rooted in the practical, especially medical, uses of plants. This page from a medieval herbal describes couch grass (top), sword lily and rosemary.

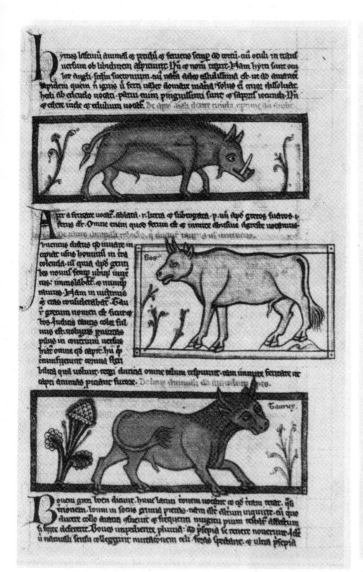

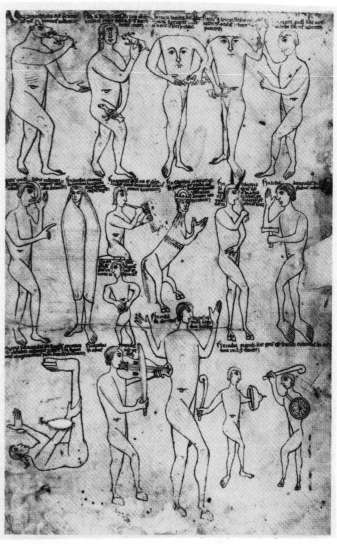

Medieval bestiaries, widely misunderstood as early zoological textbooks, were actually collections of animal lore and mythology meant to instruct and entertain. This page from an early 13th-centiury bestiary depicts a boar (top), an ox and a bull.

Among the ancient texts available to Medieval scholars was *Natural History*, a compendium of 20,000 facts about the world compiled by the first-century Roman author Pliny the Elder. This page from his book depicts the "monstrous" races of men thought to inhabit parts of the world. (above)

out the population of Earth and its atmosphere, angels and demons, inhabiting the aerial regions, were universally believed to exist.

What are we to make of these medieval beliefs? It is easy to make sport of medieval ideas—the central Earth, the four elements, bestiaries, centaurs and angels. Or, if we prefer, we can ransack the Middle Ages for anticipations of modern ideas and applaud the medieval genius for "discovering" the sphericity of Earth and the refractions and reflections that give rise to the rainbow. But we waste

our time by proceeding along either of those courses. In both, we would be judging medieval knowledge by modern criteria, imagining that people who preceded us by a thousand years were answering, or trying to answer, modern questions on the basis of modern evidence. If we want to engage in a useful quest, we would do well to judge medieval people and their achievements within the context of the Middle Ages—recognizing that they struggled with all the resources at their disposal, just as we do, to survive in and make sense of the world in which they lived.

David C. Lindberg is Hilldale Professor of the History of Science at the University of Wisconsin-Madison. He is a distinguished historian of medieval science and has published several books on the subject, including influential studies of medieval optics and visual theory. Professor Lindberg is past-president of the History of Science Society and has been a Guggenheim Fellow and a visiting member of the Institute for Advanced Study in Princeton. In 1994 he won the Watson Davis Prize of the History of Science Society for his book, The Beginnings of Western Science (University of Chicago Press, 1992).

Columbus and the Labyrinth of History

Every generation creates the Columbus it needs. As the Quincentenary of his 1492 voyage approaches, observers are torn between celebrating a brave visionary and condemning the first representative of an age of imperial exploitation. Here Pulitzer Prize-winning journalist John Noble Wilford explores the various Columbus legends and discovers, beneath them, a very human figure and an adventure unprecedented in boldness.

John Noble Wilford

John Noble Wilford has been a science correspondent for the New York Times *since 1965. Twice winner of the Pulitzer Prize, Wilford is the author of* The Mapmakers *(1981),* The Riddle of the Dinosaur *(1985),* Mars Beckons *(1990), and* Mysterious History of Columbus *(1991).*

History has not been the same since Christopher Columbus. Neither has he been the same throughout history.

During the five centuries since his epochal voyage of 1492, Columbus has been many things to many people: the protean symbol of the adventuring human spirit, the lone hero defying both the odds and entrenched thinking to change the world; the first modern man or a lucky adventurer blinded by medieval mysticism; an icon of Western faith in progress or an object of scorn for his failings of leadership and intellect; a man virtually deified at one time and roundly vilified today for his part in the initiation of an international slave trade and European imperialism. We hardly know the real Columbus. Such, it seems, is the fate of historical figures whose deeds reverberate through time.

The Columbus story surely confirms the axiom that all works of history are interim reports. What people did in the past is not preserved in amber, a moment captured and immutable through the ages. Each generation looks back and, drawing from its own experiences, presumes to find patterns that illuminate both past and present. This is natural and proper. A succeeding generation can ask questions of the past that those in the past never asked themselves. Columbus could not know that he had ushered in what we call the Age of Discovery, with all its implications, any more than we can know what two world wars, nuclear weapons, the collapse of colonial empires, the end of the Cold War, and the beginning of space travel will mean for people centuries from now. Perceptions change, and so does our understanding of the past.

Accordingly, the image of Columbus has changed through the years, sometimes as a result of new information, more often because of changes in the lenses through which we view him. Once a beneficiary of this phenomenon, Columbus in times of reigning optimism has been exalted as a mythic hero. Now, with the approach of the Quincentennial, he has fallen victim to a more self-critical society, one prone to hero-bashing and historical pessimism.

As recently as 1974, Samuel Eliot Morison, the biographer of Columbus, concluded one of his books with a paean to European influence on America: "To the people of the New World, pagans expecting short and brutish lives, void of hope for any future, had come the Christian vision of a merciful God and a glorious heaven." It is hard to conceive of those words being written today. In a forward to the 1983 edition of Morison's *Admiral of the Ocean Sea: A Life of Christopher Columbus,* British historian David Beers Quinn criticizes Morison for ignoring or dismissing Columbus's failings. Columbus, Quinn writes, "cannot be detached from the imperialist exploitation of his discoveries and must be made to take some share of responsibility for the brutal exploitation of the islands and mainlands he found."

From *The Wilson Quarterly,* Autumn 1991, pp. 66–86. © 1991 by John Noble Wilford. Reprinted by permission of the author. ·

By and large, this new perspective has produced a more realistic, demythologized version of the Columbus story. The temptation, though, is to swing too far in the other direction, rewriting history as we wish it would have been or judging people wholly by anachronistic political standards. This has happened all too often regarding Columbus, producing myth and propaganda in the guise of history.

All the more reason for us to sift through the romantic inventions and enduring misconceptions that have clouded the real Columbus and to recognize that so much of the man we celebrate or condemn is our own creation. He is the embodiment of our running dialogue about the human potential for good and evil.

Some of the facts about Columbus—who he was and what he did—are beyond serious dispute. This mariner of humble and obscure origins was possessed of an idea that became an obsession. He proposed to sail west across the uncharted ocean to the fabled shores of the Indies, the lands of gold and spices celebrated in the tales of Marco Polo and the goal of an increasingly expansionist Europe in the 15th century. The Portuguese had sought a route around the tip of Africa. Some Florentine cosmographers had pondered the prospect of a westward sea route. But Columbus was apparently the first with the stubborn courage to stake his life on the execution of such a daring scheme.

After years pleading his case before the courts of Portugal and Spain, dismissed as a hopeless visionary or a tiresomely boastful nuisance, Columbus finally won the reluctant support of Ferdinand and Isabella. At the little Andalusian port of Palos de la Frontera, he raised a fleet of three ships and enlisted some 90 seamen. Whatever the sailors' trepidations or their opinion of Columbus when he arrived at Palos, their destiny was to share with him a voyage "by which route," Columbus wrote in the prologue to his journal, "we do not know for certain anyone previously has passed."

Columbus was never more in command of himself and his destiny than on that day, August 3, 1492, when he weighed anchor at Palos. He was a consummate mariner, as all his contemporaries agreed and historians have not contradicted, and here he was doing what he did best and so sure of his success. Of course, he never made it to the Indies, as head-shaking savants had predicted, then or on any of his three subsequent voyages. His landfall came half a world short of them, on an unprepossessing island inhabited by naked people with no knowledge whatsoever of Marco Polo's Great Khan.

On the morning of October 12, Columbus and his captains, together with their most trusted functionaries, clambered into armed launches and headed for the sandy beach and green trees. They carried the flags of the Christian monarchs of Spain. A solemn Columbus, without so much as a thought that it was anything but his to take, proclaimed possession of the island for the king and for the queen. Columbus and his officers then dropped to their knees in prayer.

It did not escape Columbus that these islanders "go around as naked as their mothers bore them; and the women also." This was not prurience but culture shock. Columbus was generally admiring in his initial descriptions of the people. They were "guileless and generous." Bringing cotton, parrots, and javelins to trade, they paddled out to Columbus's ships in their dugouts, each made from a single tree and so long that they held 40 men; the West Indian term for these dugouts was *canoa*—and thus a New-World word entered European speech. Columbus was pleased to note that they had no firearms. When he had shown them some swords, "they took them by the edge and through ignorance cut themselves." "They should be good and intelligent servants," he concluded, "for I see that they say very quickly everything that is said to them; and I believed they would become Christians very easily, for it seemed to me that they had no religion." Columbus the anthropologist had his priorities.

Unfortunately, we have no record of the first impressions that the people Columbus called Indians had of the Europeans. What did they think of these white men with beards? Their sailing ships and their weapons that belched smoke? Their Christian God and their inordinate interest in gold and a place beyond the horizon called the Indies? We will never know. They could not put their feelings into writing; they had no writing. And the encounter itself doomed them. Within a generation or two, they became extinct, mainly through exposure to European diseases, and so could not pass on by word of mouth stories about the moment white men entered their lives.

Columbus made certain by his words and actions that his discovery would not be lost to history. On the homeward voyage, after visiting a string of other islands and more people, he composed a letter to the court of Ferdinand and Isabella in which he announced his discovery. He had made good his boast to one and all. He may have harbored some disappointment in not reaching the Asian mainland, but he had sailed across the Ocean Sea and found lands and peoples unknown to Europeans. And he wanted the court to read about it in his own words, especially since this justified his own claim to the titles and wealth due him pursuant to the deal he had struck with the court.

The letter Columbus wrote was also his bid for a place in history. He understood that the achievement would go for naught unless the news got back to others. To explore (the word, in one version of its etymology, comes from the Latin "to cry out") is to search out and exclaim discovery. Simply reaching a new land does not in itself constitute a discovery. It must be announced and then recorded in history so that the discovery can be acted upon.

Others besides the indigenous people preceded Columbus in finding parts of America. This is no longer an issue of consuming dispute in Columbian studies. Almost certainly the Norse under Leif Ericson landed at some northern islands and established a short-lived settlement at Newfoundland. Ericson and others may have reached America, but they failed to discover it. For nothing came of their deeds. Columbus, in writing the letter, was making sure his deeds

'Gardens the Most Beautiful I Ever Saw'

The following account of October 10–13, 1492, is taken from Columbus's **Diario,** *as abstracted by Bartolomé de las Casas and adapted by William Carlos Williams.*

Wednesday, 59 leagues, W. S. W., but counted no more than 44. Here the people could endure no longer. All now complained about the length of the voyage. But I cheered them as best I could, giving them good hopes of the advantages they might gain by it. Roused to madness by their fear, the captains declared they were going back but I told them then, that however much they might complain, I had to go to the Indies and they along with me, and that I would go until I found them, with the help of our Lord. And so for a time it passed but now all was in great danger from the men.

Thursday, 11th of October. The course was W. S. W. More sea [spilling over the deck] than there had been during the whole of the voyage. Sandpipers and a green reed near the ship. And for this I gave thanks to God as it was a sure sign of land. Those of the Pinta saw a cane and a pole, and they took up another small pole which appeared to be worked with iron; also another bit of cane, a land plant, and a small board. The crew of the caravel Niña also saw signs of land, and a small plant covered with berries.

. . . I admonished the men to keep a good lookout on the forecastle and to watch well for land and to him who should first cry out that he had seen land I would give a silk doublet besides the other rewards promised by the Sovereigns which were 10,000 *maravedis* to him who should first see it. Two hours past midnight, the moon having risen at eleven o'clock and then shining brightly in the sky, being in its third quarter, a sailor named Rodrigo de Triana sighted the land at a distance of about two leagues. At once I ordered them to shorten sail and we lay under the mainsail without the bonnets, hove to waiting for daylight.

On Friday, the 12th of October, we anchored before the land and made ready to go on shore. Presently we saw naked people on the beach. I went ashore in the armed boat and took the royal standard, and Martin Alonzo and Vincent Yañez, his brother, who was captain of the *Niña.* And we saw the trees very green, and much water and fruits of diverse kinds. Presently many of the inhabitants assembled. I gave to some red caps and glass beads to put round their necks, and many other things of little value. They came to the ship's boats afterward, where we were, swimming and bringing us parrots, cotton threads in skeins, darts—what they had, with good will. As naked as their mothers bore them, and so the women, though I did not see more than one young girl. All I saw were youths, well made with very handsome bodies and very good countenances. Their hair short and coarse, almost like the hairs of a horse's tail. They paint themselves some black, some white, others red and others of what color they can find. Some paint the faces and others paint the whole body, some only round the eyes and others only on the nose. They are themselves neither black nor white.

On Saturday, as dawn broke, many of these people came to the beach, all youths. Their legs are very straight, all in one line, and no belly. They came to the ship in canoes, made out of the

---

would have consequences and his achievement would enter history.

The letter eventually reached the court in Barcelona and had the desired effect. The king and queen received Columbus with pomp and listened to his story with genuine interest and pleasure. They instructed him to return to the new-found lands with a larger fleet including soldiers and settlers. America had entered world history, though Columbus insisted to his dying day that he had reached the Indies.

This familiar story of Columbus has been embellished to create an enduring popular legend. Some of the tales (though not all of them) have been laid to rest through historical research.

Columbus did not, for example, have to prove that the world was round: All educated people in Europe at the time accepted this as a given. Isabella did not have to pawn her jewels to raise money for the expedition; though the Crown, following its wars against the Moors, was strapped for cash, the financial adviser Luis de Santangel arranged a loan from the ample coffers of the state police and from some Italian merchant bankers. And Columbus did not set sail with a crew of hardened criminals. Only four men, accused of murdering a town crier, took advantage of a promised amnesty, and even they were seasoned mariners and acquitted themselves well on the voyage.

More troublesome for historians have been certain other mysteries and controversies.

Where, for example, did the first landfall occur? We know it was a small island the inhabitants called Guanahani and Columbus christened San Salvador. It was in the Bahamas or thereabouts, far from the Asian mainland he was seeking, but which island? No fewer than nine different possible islands have been identified from the few ambiguous clues in Columbus's journal. The site favored by most experts is the Bahamian island once called Watling's but renamed San Salvador in 1924 to help solidify its claim.

Did Columbus really come from Genoa? Nearly every European nation has at one time or another laid some claim to him. Was he Jewish? Such conjecture originated in the 19th century and was promoted in 1940 in Salvadore de Madriaga's vivid biography, *Christopher Columbus.* But the evidence is circumstantial. Records in Genoa indicate that, whatever his more remote ancestry, Columbus's family had been Christian for several generations.

When and how in the mists of his rootless life did Columbus conceive of his audacious plan? Was it sheer inspiration bolstered by rational research? Or did he come into some secret knowledge? Was he really seeking the Indies? How was he finally able to win royal backing? What were his ships like?—no caravel wreck from that period has ever been recovered. Scholars and amateur sleuths have spent lifetimes trying to resolve these questions, usually without notable success.

trunk of a tree, all in one piece, and wonderfully worked, propelled with a paddle like a baker's shovel, and go at marvelous speed.

Bright green trees, the whole land so green that it is a pleasure to look on it. Gardens of the most beautiful trees I ever saw. Later I came upon one man in a canoe going from one island to another. He had a little of their bread, about the size of a fist, a calabash of water, a piece of brown earth, powdered then kneaded, and some dried leaves which must be a thing highly valued by them for they bartered with it at San Salvador. He also had with him a native basket. The women wore in front of their bodies a small piece of cotton cloth. I saw many trees very unlike those of our country. Branches growing in different ways and all from one trunk; one twig is one form and another is a different shape and so unlike that it is the greatest wonder of the world to see the diversity; thus one branch has leaves like those of a cane, and others like those of a mastic tree; and on a single tree there are five different kinds. The fish so unlike ours that it is wonderful. Some are the shape of dories and of the finest colors, so bright that there is not a man who would not be astounded, and would not take great delight in seeing them. There are also whales. I saw no beasts on land save parrots and lizards.

On shore I sent the people for water, some with arms, and others with casks; and as it was some little distance I waited two hours for them.

During that time I walked among the trees, which was the most beautiful thing which I had ever seen. . . .

Part of the problem lies with the passage of time. Although the record of Columbus by contemporaries is more substantial than that of any other 15th-century explorer, surviving accounts are often difficult to assess from this distance. Whose version is to be trusted: The letters of Peter Martyr, the courtier in Spain who never ventured to the New World? The biography by Hernando Columbus, the devoted son protective of his father's fame? The history of the New World by Bartolomé de las Casas (1474–1566), the Dominican friar and champion of the Indians who never missed a chance to condemn the brutality of the early explorers and colonists? Even the few extant writings of Columbus himself, who could be vague, contradictory and self-serving?

Hero worship has further distorted history. We want—or used to want—our heroes to be larger than life. The result can be a caricature, a plaster saint inviting iconoclasts to step forward with their own images, which can also ignore the complexity of human reality.

We are left, therefore, with enough material to mold the Columbus we choose to extol or excoriate, but not enough ever to feel sure we truly know the man.

Nothing better illustrates history's changing images of Columbus than the succession of portraits of him that have appeared over the centuries. They show a man of many faces—handsome and stalwart, heavy and stolid, shadowed and vaguely sinister. Artistic interpretation, like history, changes with the times.

Yet, there should be little confusion over the man's physical appearance. His son Hernando, who should have known, said he was "a well-built man of more than average stature, the face long, the cheeks somewhat high, his body neither fat nor lean. He had an aquiline nose and light colored eyes; his complexion too was light and tending to be red. In youth his hair was blond, but when he reached the age of 30 it all turned white."

The son went on to describe his father's character: "In eating and drinking, and in the adornment of his person, he was very moderate and modest," Hernando wrote. "He was affable in conversation with strangers and very pleasant to the members of his household, though with a certain gravity. He was so strict in matters of religion that for fasting and saying prayers he might have been taken for a member of a religious order."

Hernando may be guilty of some exaggeration. Columbus could not be too gentle and modest if he were to promote his vision before skeptical courts and if he could control a crew of rough seamen who suspected they might be headed to their deaths. He could be harsh in meting out punishment to seamen and in ordering punitive raids against Indian villages. Like others of that time, and to this day, he presumably saw no contradiction between his behavior and his religious beliefs. By all accounts Columbus was a demonstrably pious man. Late in life, his writings portrayed a mind filled with mysticism and a belief in his divine mission to carry Christianity to all people and prepare them for the impending end of the world.

Of this mysticism, Hernando has nothing to say. He is also frustratingly reticent or misleading about the genesis of his father's consuming dream and even about his origins. Columbus himself chose to reveal very little about his early life.

Every verifiable historical document, however, indicates that Columbus was born in Genoa, which was an independent city-state (the lesser rival to Venice) whose ships traded throughout the entire Mediterranean world. He was probably born in 1451, and both his father Domenico and his father's father were wool weavers; his mother, Susanna Fontanarossa, was a weaver's daughter. Christopher was probably their eldest child. Bartholomew, the chart-maker who would share many of Columbus's adventures, was a year or two younger. The other children who grew to adulthood were a sister named Bianchetta and a brother Giacomo, better known by the Spanish equivalent, Diego, who joined Christopher on the second voyage. All in all, the Columbuses of Genoa were fruitful and humble tradespeople— and nothing for a young man to be ashamed of.

At a "tender age," as Columbus once wrote, he cast his lot with those who go to sea. At first, he probably made short voyages as a crewman, and then longer ones on trading ships to the Genoese colony of Chios in the Aegean Sea. But even more crucial to Columbus's development than his ancestry or his birthplace was the timing of his birth. He was born two years before the fall of Constantinople, Christendom's eastern capital, to the Ottoman Turks in 1453. Young Columbus was to grow up hearing about the scourge of Islam, the blockage of regular trade routes to the spices of the East, and the parlous times for Christianity. Priests and popes were calling for a new crusade to recapture Constantinople and Jerusalem. All of this could have nourished the dreams of a great adventure in an ambitious young man with nautical experience.

The most significant mystery about Columbus concerns how he came up with his idea for sailing west to the Indies. As in everything else, Columbus's own words on the subject obfuscate more than elucidate. It was his practice, writes the Italian historian Paolo Emilio Taviani, "never to tell everything to everyone, to say one thing to one man, something else to another, to reveal only portions of his arguments, clues, and evidence accumulated over the years in his mind." Perhaps Columbus told so many partial stories in so many different versions that, as Morison suspects, he himself could no longer remember the origins of his idea.

In all probability he formulated the idea in Portugal sometime between 1476 and 1481. Columbus had come to Portugal quite literally by accident. When the Genoese fleet he had shipped with was attacked and destroyed in the summer of 1476, Columbus was washed ashore at the Portuguese town of Lagos. He made his way to Lisbon, where the talk of seagoing exploration was everywhere. He heard stories of westering seamen who found islands far out in the ocean and saw maps sprinkled with mythical islands. On voyages north perhaps so far as Iceland and south along the coast of Africa, he gained a taste for Atlantic sailing. There may even be something to the story of the unknown pilot from whom Columbus supposedly obtained secret knowledge of lands across the ocean. But as far as anyone can be sure—and volumes have been written on the subject—there was no sudden revelation, no blinding flash of inspiration.

Nor did Columbus derive his plan from a careful reading of scholars. He was not then, and never became, a man who read to learn; he read to gather support for what he already thought to be true. His familiarity with the travel accounts of Marco Polo and the *Travels of Sir John Mandeville,* a 14th-century collection of travelers' tales from around the world, did not so much inform his concept as inflame a mind already stoked with the dry tinder of desire. From other sources—from a recent Latin translation of Claudius Ptolemy's second-century *Geography,* which described many Southeast Asian spice islands, to Pierre d'Ailly's *Imago Mundi,* a compendium of contemporary knowledge about the world which argued that the Western Sea was not very wide— Columbus made some calculations of global distances. Like d'Ailly, he conveniently managed to constrict the unknown he proposed to challenge, grossly underestimating the distance from Europe to Japan. Had he unwittingly deceived himself? Or had he deliberately contrived calculations to deceive those he looked to for support? All that can be said with assurance is that Columbus was by then a man consumed by an enthusiasm that willed away obstacles and brooked no doubt.

His marriage in Portugal may have indirectly contributed to his growing conviction. In 1479, he wed Felipa Perestrello de Moniz, a daughter of lesser nobility. Her widowed mother showed Columbus the journals and maps left by her husband, who had sailed for Prince Henry the Navigator. From the papers of Bartolomeo Perestrello and other Portuguese seamen, Columbus concluded, his son Hernando wrote, "for certain that there were many lands West of the Canary Islands and Cape Verde, and that it was possible to sail to, and discover them." The social position of his wife's family also smoothed the way for Columbus's introduction to the court of Portugal's King John II.

When Columbus finally laid out his plan before John II, probably in 1483 or 1484, the court cosmographers, a Portuguese historian wrote, "considered the words of Christovae Colom as vain, simply founded on imagination, or things like that Isle Cypango of Marco Polo."

Columbus refused to accept rejection. By this time, his wife had died, and in 1485 he took their son, Diego, and left Portugal for Palos, across the border in Spain. Tradition has it that Columbus and little Diego, penniless and hungry, got off the ship and trudged along a dusty road to the Franciscan monastery of La Rabida. He knocked at the portal to beg for water and bread. If the legend is true, the father may have been taking the son there to be a boarding student, freeing himself to pursue his dream.

Though a secretive man and often portrayed as a loner, Columbus must not have been without charm, even charisma. He had insinuated himself into the influential society of Lisbon and would do so again in Spain. "Columbus's ability to thrust himself into the circles of the great was one of the most remarkable things about him," writes Harvard historian John H. Parry. It was also in his character that he seldom acknowledged the help of others.

At La Rabida, Columbus won the friendship and confidence of a Franciscan official knowledgeable in cosmography and through him gained introductions to wealthy patrons and eventually his first audience with Ferdinand and Isabella. They referred his proposal to a commission of learned men at the University of Salamanca. Washington Irving, in his fanciful biography, has the commissioners saying that the "rotundity of the earth was as yet a matter of mere speculation." Many of them no doubt deserved Irving's condemnation as a "mass of inert bigotry," but they were right (and Columbus wrong) in their judgment that Asia could not be reached by ships sailing west. They recommended that the monarchs reject the venture.

Columbus was nothing if not persistent. With a modest retainer from the court, he continued to solicit support from influential courtiers. While in Cordoba, waiting for some sign of royal encouragement, he met Beatriz Enriquez de Arana, a peasant woman, and they became lovers. In August 1488 she gave birth to an illegitimate son, Hernando. (They never married, and sometime after his first voyage, they drifted apart. He likely felt a peasant woman was beneath his station.)

Through another friar at La Rabida, Columbus gained other audiences with the monarchs in 1491 and again in early 1492, just after the Moorish capital of Granada fell to the Christian forces. He had been led to believe that, after the burden of the prolonged war was lifted, the queen especially might be disposed to give her approval. Some writers have let themselves imagine that Isabella saw more in Columbus than an insistent supplicant. Such speculation of a sexual relationship between the two, Taviani says, is "a sheer fairy-tale, rejected by all historians."

Nothing seemed to change with the fall of Granada. Columbus was turned away, this time with an air of finality. Behind the scenes, however, Luis de Santangel, the chief financial adviser, interceded with assurances to the queen that financing the expedition need not be an insurmountable obstacle. No one knows why the king and queen finally relented. They might have been persuaded by the argument that they had little to lose and much to gain if this importunate foreigner just happened to be on to something.

After his first voyage, when he was the toast of Barcelona, Columbus supposedly faced down his first critics. At a banquet, some noblemen insisted that if Columbus had not undertaken the enterprise, someone else, a Spaniard and not a foreigner, would have made the same discovery. At this, Columbus called for an egg and had it placed on the table. "Gentlemen," he was reported to have said, pointing to the egg, "you make it stand here, not with crumbs, salt, etc. (for anyone knows how to do it with meal or sand), but naked and without anything at all, as I will, who was the first to discover the Indies." When it was Columbus's turn, he crushed one end of the egg and had no trouble making it stand up on the table.

The anecdote has proved irresistible to historians and storytellers to illustrate the singular role of Columbus in history. But it never happened—one more Columbian myth. The story was not only apocryphal, Morison points out, but it "had already done duty in several Italian biographies of other characters."

In reality, Columbus would not so easily put down the critics who dogged him the rest of his life—and through history. If only he had stopped with the first voyage, the echo of those fanfares in Barcelona might not have faded so fast.

A fleet of 17 ships, carrying some 1,200 people, left Cadiz in the autumn of 1493 with instructions to establish a permanent settlement on the island of Hispaniola. There, near the present city of Puerto Plata in the Dominican Republic, Columbus built a fort, church,

and house for what would be his colonial capital, La Isabela. The experiment was disastrous. The site had no real harbor, insufficient rainfall, and little vegetation. Sickness and dissension brought work to a standstill and the colony to the point of starvation. Expeditions into the mountains failed to find any rich lodes of gold. As Las Casas wrote, they "spread terror among the Indians in order to show them how strong and powerful the Christians were." Bloody warfare ensued.

With little gold to show for his efforts, Columbus ordered a shipment of Taino Indians to be sold as slaves in Spain. The best that can be said in defense of Columbus is that he was now a desperate man. His power to rule La Isabela was waning. His visions of wealth were fading. He feared that his influence back in Spain would be irreparably diminished by critical reports from recalcitrant officers who had returned to Spain. And he had failed again to find a mainland. His desperation was such that he forced all his crew to sign a declaration that, at Cuba, they had indeed reached the mainland of Cathay. Sick and discouraged, he sailed home in 1496.

The third voyage did nothing to restore his reputation. Departing from Seville in May 1498, he steered a southerly course and reached an island off the northeastern coast of South America, which he named Trinidad, for the Holy Trinity. A few days later, he saw a coastline to the south. Columbus recognized that the tremendous volume of fresh water flowing from the Orinoco River was evidence of a large land, but he failed to appreciate that this might be a continent or to pursue his investigations. Instead, his mind drifted into speculation that the river must originate in the Earthly Paradise. Bound to medieval thinking, the man who showed the way across the ocean lost his chance to have the New World bear his name. The honor would soon go to a man with a more open-minded perspective, Amerigo Vespucci, who on his second voyage of exploration (1501–2) concluded that the South American landmass was not Asia but a new continent.

Columbus turned his back on South America and sailed to Santo Domingo

Columbus disgraced, 1500. Charged with malfeasance as governor of Hispaniola, Columbus returned to Spain a prisoner in chains.

to attend to the colony there. He found that his brothers, Bartholomew and Diego, had lost control. Some of the colonists had mutinied, and the crown had dispatched a new governor empowered to do anything necessary to restore order. It was then that Columbus was arrested, stripped of his titles, and sent back in irons to Spain in October 1500.

It was an ignominious end to Columbus's authority and to his fame in his lifetime. The crown eventually restored his titles, but never again was he allowed to serve as viceroy. The monarchs now were under no illusions about Columbus. He had failed as a colonial administrator, and they had strong doubts about the validity of his claims to have reached the Indies.

Columbus was given permission for one final voyage, which lasted from 1502 to 1504. He was specifically barred from returning to Santo Domingo. Instead, he explored the coast of Central America and attempted without success to establish a settlement in Panama.

Historians cite the last voyage as one of his many "missed opportunities." With luck and more persistence, Columbus might have stumbled upon the Maya civilization or the Pacific Ocean. As it was, he barely made it back to Spain. He was marooned a year on Jamaica, where he wrote a pathetic letter to the monarchs. "I implore Your Highnesses' pardon," he wrote. "I am ruined as I have said. Hitherto I have wept for others; now have pity upon me, Heaven, and weep for me, earth! I came to Your Highnesses with honest purpose and sincere zeal, and I do not lie. I humbly beg Your Highnesses that, if it please God to remove me hence, you will aid me to go to Rome and on other pilgrimages."

Columbus in his last years was a dispirited man who felt himself to be misunderstood and unappreciated. He sought to define himself in a remarkable manuscript now known as *Libro de las profecías,* or *The Book of Prophecies.* Between the third and fourth voyages, Columbus collected passages of biblical scriptures and the words of a wide range of classical and medieval authors. According to his own description, this was a notebook "of sources, statements, opinions and prophecies on the subject of the recovery of God's Holy City and Mount Zion, and on the discovery and evangelization of the islands of the Indies and of all other peoples and nations."

The document reveals the depth and passion of Columbus's belief that he had a special relationship with God and was acting as the agent of God's scheme for history. He marshaled evidence from the prophecies of the Bible to show that his recent discoveries were only the prelude to the realization of a greater destiny. It was as if he saw his role as being not unlike John the Baptist's in relation to Christ. The wealth from his voyages and discoveries had given the king and queen of Spain the means to recover the Holy Land for Christendom, and thereby he had set the stage for the grandiose climax of Christian history, the salvation of all the world's peoples and their gathering at Zion on the eve of the end of time.

Most historians who studied the document have tended to dismiss it as the product of his troubled and possibly senile mind. His other writings at the time sometimes betrayed a mind verging on paranoia. Delno C. West, a historian who has recently translated the *Book of Prophecies,* suspects that historians were "reluctant to admit that the first American hero was influenced by prophetic ideas." If the book indeed reflects Columbus's thinking even before 1492, it undermines the popular image of Columbus as a man of the modern age who applied reason in conceiving his venture. It exposes him as a person thoroughly mired in the medieval world, obsessed with eschatology, and driven by a supposed call from God to carry out a mission of apocalyptic dimensions.

West contends that this spirituality, which fed Columbus's apocalyptic view of history, lay at the heart of the man and shaped his actions. Rather than some map or unknown pilot's tale, this may have been the "secret knowledge" that inspired Columbus. Certainly, without his unwavering belief in himself and his destiny, Columbus might not have sustained the single-minded persistence it took to win support for the enterprise and to see it through. "The Lord purposed that there should be something clearly miraculous in this matter of the voyage to the Indies," Columbus wrote in the *Prophecies,* "so as to encourage me and others in the . . . Household of God." Beginning in 1493, he began signing nearly all of his letters and documents *Christoferens,* a Latinization of his given name that means "Christbearer."

Columbus's Mysterious Signature

In 1498, Columbus instructed all of his heirs to continue to "sign with my signature which I now employ which is an X with an S over it and an M with a Roman A over it and over them an S and then a Greek Y with an S over it, preserving the relation of the lines and the points." At the top, thus, is the letter S between two dots. On the palindromic second row are the letter S A S, also preceded, separated, and ended with dots. The third row has the letters X M and a Greek Y, without dots. Below that is the final signature, Xpo Ferens, a Greco-Latin form of his given name.

To this day no one can decipher the meaning Columbus had in mind, but it almost certainly bears on his religious outlook. The simplest explanations hold that the letters stand for seven words. It has been suggested that the four letters stand for "Servus Sum Altissimi Salvatoris," for "Servant I Am of the Most High Savior." The three letters of the third line could be an invocation to Christ Jesus and Mary, or to Christ, Mary, and Joseph. Another proposed solution is that the seven letters are the initials for "Spiritus Sanctus Altissimi Salvator Xristus Maria Yesus."

John Fleming, a medievalist at Princeton University, believes he has cracked the code, finding it to be an "acrostic of considerable complexity committed to a more or less learned and hermetic mystical the-ology." Columbus, he concludes, was borrowing from two medieval traditions in formal signatures, that of the church worthies, like St. Francis, who devised intricate crucigrams, and that of the church mariners who often included in their craft marks anchors, masts, fishhooks, and so forth. For his signature, Fleming says, Co-

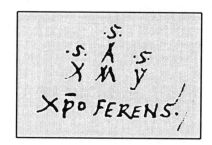

lumbus seems to have combined religious and nautical symbolism. The unifying idea is the medieval association of the Virgin Mary with Stella Maris, the indispensable navigational star also known as Polaris, or the North Star. The first cross bar stands for StellA MariS. The vertical "mast" stands for "Stella Ave Maris," after the vesper hymn *"Ave, stella maris."* By design, the structure represents both a Christian cross and a ship's mast. The line X M Y may have one meaning, *"Jesus cum Maris sit nobis in via"* (an invocation with which Columbus opened much of his writing), with the Y representing the fork in the road and the symbolism for his having chosen the hard way to destiny's fulfillment. Fleming suggests a double meaning. The X and Y at either end of the bottom line could also stand for "Christophorus," his name and destiny, and "Jacobus," for "St. James," whose feast day and Christopher's are the same and who is, not incidentally, the patron saint of Spain, Santiago—Sant Yago.

Fleming's cryptographic skills have uncovered other clues in the signature to Columbus's "religious imagination." But, for understanding Columbus the mystical discoverer, Fleming draws insight from his associations with Mary, Christopher, and Santiago. He writes: "In Columbus's heavenly city, the Virgin Mary stands ever firm between her two Christ-bearing guards, Christophorus on the one hand, San Yago the Moorslayer on the other. And in the larger meaning of these two saints, both celebrated by the Roman church on a single day, which was of course Columbus's name-day, we may see adumbrated much of the glory, and much of the tragedy, of the European encounter with the New World."

From The Mysterious History of Columbus, *copyright © 1991 by Alfred A. Knopf. Reprinted by permission of the publisher.*

New attention to the spiritual side of Columbus does not, however, necessarily bring this complex man into focus. Images of a superstitious spiritualist and the modern explorer must be superimposed to produce a stereoscopic picture of Columbus, revealing the depth and heights of the mental terrain through which he traveled as he found America and then lost his way in failure, self-pity, and a fog of mysticism.

Columbus was probably no more than 55 years old when he died on May 20, 1506, in Valladolid, Spain. But he was much older in body and in tormented mind. His last voyages had left him crippled with arthritis and weak from fever. He was reduced to a sad figure, spending his last years in disgrace while stubbornly pressing his claims for the restoration of titles and the wealth due him.

Contrary to legend, he was neither destitute nor alone at the end. His two sons were with him, in a comfortable home. We cannot be sure of the traditional story, that he died believing he had reached the Indies. He never gave explicit expression to any recognition that he had found something other than Asia. All the evidence, though, suggests that he died unsatisfied.

His death went unheralded. There was no public ceremony of mourning and no recorded expressions of grief at the royal court. The man who rose from obscurity died in obscurity. His remains have been moved so many times over the centuries, from Spain to the New World and presumably back again, that no one is sure of his final resting place.

In the first century after his voyages, Columbus languished in the backwaters of history. His reputation suffered from his many failures as a colonial governor. The 1519–1522 Magellan circumnavigation left no doubt about the magnitude of Columbus's error in thinking he had reached the Indies. Conquering explorers such as Cortes and Pizarro won greater immediate fame by their dazzling exploits against the Aztecs and Incas. Cartographers saw fit to name the New World after Vespucci, not Columbus. Books of general history scarcely mentioned Columbus or ignored him altogether.

Within 50 years of Columbus's death, Bartolomé de las Casas, the Dominican bishop who extolled and defended the Indians, produced the first revisionist history. In his *History of the Indies,* Las

Casas wrote eloquently of the atrocities committed against the Indians. To sail to the islands Columbus had discovered, Las Casas wrote, one needed only to follow the floating corpses of Indians that marked the way. His accounts of torture and killings documented the so-called Black Legend of Spanish cruelty that was seized upon by the English, Dutch, and French to fan the fires of national rivalries and religious hatreds.

As the Age of Discovery flourished during the late 16th century, Columbus began to be rescued from oblivion. He was celebrated in poetry and plays, especially in Italy and later in Spain. A glimmer of history's future hero could be seen in a popular play by Lope de Vega in 1614. In *The New World Discovered by Christopher Columbus,* he portrayed Columbus as a dreamer up against the establishment, a man of singular purpose who triumphed, the embodiment of that spirit driving humans to explore and discover.

It was in the New World, though, that Columbus would be transformed almost beyond human recognition into an icon.

By the late 17th century, people in the British colonies of North America were beginning to think of themselves as Americans and sought to define themselves in their own terms and symbols. Samuel Sewell, a Boston judge, suggested that the new lands should rightfully be named for Columbus, "the magnanimous hero . . . who was manifestly appointed by God to be the Finder out of these lands." The idea took root. In time, writers and orators used the name "Columbia" as a poetic name for America. Joel Barlow's poem *The Vision of Columbus,* appearing in 1787, has an aged Columbus lamenting his fate until he is visited by an angel who transports him to the New World to see what his discovery had brought to pass. There he could glimpse the "fruits of his cares and children of his toil."

Indeed, the young republic was busy planning the 300th anniversary of the landfall, in October 1792, when it named its new national capital the District of Columbia—perhaps to appease those who demanded that the entire country be designated Columbia. Next to George Washington, Columbus was

the nation's most exalted hero. In him the new nation without its own history and mythology found a hero from the distant past, one seemingly free of association with the European colonial powers and Old-World tyranny. Americans invoked Columbus, the solitary individual who had challenged the unknown, as they contemplated the dangers and promise of their own wilderness frontier. "Instead of ravaging the newly found countries," Washington Irving wrote in his 1828 biography, Columbus "sought to colonize and cultivate them, to civilize the natives."

This would be the Columbus Americans knew and honored throughout the 19th and into the present century. With the influx of millions of immigrants after the Civil War, he was even made to assume the role of ethnic hero. In response to adverse Protestant attitudes and to affirm their own Americanism, Irish Catholic immigrants organized the Knights of Columbus in 1882. The fraternity's literature described Columbus as "a prophet and a seer" and an inspiration to each knight to become "a better Catholic and a better citizen." Catholics in both America and Europe launched a campaign to canonize Columbus on the grounds that he had brought the "Christian faith to half the world." The movement failed not because of Columbus's brutal treatment of Indians but mainly because of the son he had sired out of wedlock.

Columbus's reputation was never higher than on the 400th anniversary of his first voyage. There were parades and fireworks, the naming of streets and dedicating of monuments. The World's Columbian Exposition in Chicago, with its lavish displays of modern technology, was less a commemoration of the past than the self-confident celebration of a future that Americans were eager to shape and enjoy. Americans ascribed to Columbus all the human virtues that were most prized in that time of geographic and industrial expansion, heady optimism, and unquestioning belief in progress. A century before, Columbus had been the symbol of American promise; now he was the symbol of American success.

The 20th century has dispelled much of that. We have a new Columbus for a

new age. He is the creation of generations that have known devastating world wars, the struggle against imperialism, and economic expansion that ravages nature without necessarily satisfying basic human needs. In this view, the Age of Discovery initiated by Columbus was not the bright dawning of a glorious epoch but an invasion, a conquest and Columbus himself less a symbol of progress than of oppression.

Columbus scholarship has changed. More historians are writing books from the standpoint of the Indians. They are examining the consequences—the exchange of plants and animals between continents, the spread of deadly diseases, the swift decline of the indigenous Americans in the face of European inroads. The Quincentennial happens to come at a time of bitter debate among Americans over racism, sexism, imperialism, Eurocentrism, and other "isms." Kirkpatrick Sale's 1990 book about Columbus said it all in its title, *The Conquest of Paradise.*

Was Columbus a great man, or merely an agent of a great accomplishment, or perhaps not a very admirable man at all? His standing in history has varied whenever posterity reevaluated the consequences of Europe's discovery of America. Ultimately, Columbus's reputation in history is judged in relation to the place that is accorded America in history.

Europeans took a long time appreciating their discovery. Columbus and succeeding explorers looked upon the islands and mainland as an inconvenience, the barrier standing in their way to Asia that must be breached or circumnavigated.

As early as Peter Martyr, Europeans tried to assimilate the new lands into what they already knew or thought, rejecting the utter newness of the discovery. This was, after all, during the Renaissance, a period of rediscovering the past while reaching out to new horizons. And so the peoples of the New World were described in terms of the Renaissance-ancient image of the "noble savage," living in what classical writers had described as the innocent "Golden Age." The inhabitants of the New

1991: Cerebration, Not Celebration

It was in 1982 that I first became aware that the 500th anniversary of Columbus's 1492 Voyage of Discovery was a minefield, where the prudent celebrant stepped lightly and guardedly.

To my long-time friend Ramon, in an institute attached to the foreign ministry in Madrid, I said on the telephone one day that year, "Ramon, here at Florida we're beginning to get interested in the Columbus Discovery Quincentenary."

"Why do you say Columbus?" he responded. "He was an Italian mercenary. It was Spain that discovered America, not Columbus."

"But, Ramon," I protested, "we can't celebrate 1492 in the United States without mentioning Columbus."

"In your country," he lectured me, "Columbus Day is an Italian holiday. But the ships, the crews, the money were all Spanish. Columbus was a hired hand."

"But—"

"So when Cape Canaveral space center holds its 100th anniversary, are you going to call it the Werner von Braun celebration?"

I was grateful to Ramon for alerting me, in his way, to the sensitive character of this anniversary. Soon afterwards I learned that "Discovery," too, is a term freighted with ethnic and cultural contentions, as many descendants of the native peoples in the Americas argue against its Eurocentric and paternalistic coloring. "We were already here," they reminded me. And they were here so long ago, 10 to 25,000 years the anthropologists say. I was left to wonder, which was the Old World and which was the New?

As the past ten years have shown, the Spanish-Italian tension has softened, but the European-Native American disjunction has hardened, as historians, epidemiologists, moralists, romanticists, and native spokespersons have clashed over the benefits, if any, that European entrance onto the American stage brought the societies of both worlds, particularly this one.

Certainly huge numbers of indigenous people died as a result of the collision: some, it is true, from the sword, but by far the majority from the Europeans' unwitting introduction of pathogens—smallpox, measles, tuberculosis, the plague—to which the native peoples had no immunities. Recognizing the dimensions of that calamity, many Westerners acknowledge that there is little to celebrate. In Spain, where a 500th Year Worlds' Fair will open in Seville, many of that country's intellectuals are decrying what they call a 15th- and 16th-century *genocidio*.

In the margins of the debate, native descendants and their advocates are publicizing a long list of grievances against the Caucasians who abused their liberties, expropriated their lands, and despoiled an environmental paradise. On July 17–21, 1990, some 400 Indian people, including a delegation from the United States, met in Quito, Ecuador, to plan public protests against 500 years of European "invasion" and "oppression." Even before that, the first sign of reaction in the United States had already come when, in December 1989, representatives of the American Indian Movement, supported by a group of university students, began picketing the "First Encounters" archaeology exhibition mounted by the Florida Museum of Natural History as it traveled from Gainesville to Tampa, Atlanta, and Dallas. (In Tampa, their presence was welcomed because it boosted paid attendance.) In 1992, a loose confederation of North American Indian groups will picket in all U.S. cities where the Columbus replica ships will dock. They seek, one of their leaders told me, "not confrontation but media attention to present-day Native American problems."

African Americans also remind their fellow citizens that the events of 1492 and afterwards gave rise to the slave trade. And Jews appropriately notice that 1492 was the year when they were forcibly expelled from their Spanish homeland. In a counter-counteraction in all this Quincentenary skirmishing, however, the National Endowment for the Humanities decided not to fund a proposed television documentary about the early contact period because, reportedly, it was too biased against the Europeans. (Spain, by contrast, is acting uncommonly large-minded: It has agreed to fund the Smithsonian-Carlos Fuentes television production, "The Buried Mirror," a show that is highly critical of Spain's colonial practices.)

It is this "politically correct" dynamic that, most likely, will keep 1992 from being quite the exuberant and careless celebration that the Bicentennial was in 1976.

Anglo-Saxon and Celtic Americans felt comfortable with the Bicentennial because it reinforced their ethnic and cultural givens (Plymouth Rock, Virginia, Washington, Jefferson, the English language, Northern European immigration, etc.). Today, nervous about what is happening to "their" country and learning that citizens of Hispanic origins are projected soon to be the largest U.S. minority, the old line white majority may not be enthusiastic about celebrating the 500th coming of the Hispanics—especially since they sense no continuing need for Columbus as a unifying principle or symbol.

What is likely to happen in 1992? Occasional public celebrations and observances will be produced by civic, ethnic, and cultural bodies. Reproductions of Columbus's ships will arrive in various ports from Spain. Tall ships may parade in New York harbor. Fireworks will explode here and there. People will view two television mini-series and read countless ambivalent newspaper stories.

The Federal Quincentenary Jubilee Commission that was appointed to superintend our exultations is in disarray, its chairman forced out on a charge of mishandling funds, its coffers empty of federal dollars, its principal private donor, Texaco, pulling the plug. Some states, and numerous individual cities (especially those named after Columbus, 63 at last count), have plans for observances, large or small. Florida which has the best reasons, geographically and temporally, to do something, has no state-wide plans, two commissions having collapsed and a third now being stripped of its funds.

But now the good news: In anticipation of the 500th anniversary an enormous amount of intellectual activity has occurred, in the form of archival discoveries, archaeological excavations, museum and library exhibitions, conferences, and publications. Some 30 new and upcoming adult titles have been enumerated by *Publishers Weekly*. Over 100 exhibitions and conferences have been counted by the National Endowment for the Humanities. This remarkable efflorescence of original research and scholarship will leave a lasting legacy of understanding and good. On the twin principles that cerebration is more valuable than celebration and that correcting one paragraph in our children's schoolbooks is worth more than a half-million dollars worth of fireworks exploded over Biscayne Bay, 1992 should be the best 1492 anniversary ever.

—*Michael Gannon*

Michael Gannon is Director of the Institute for Early Contact Period Studies at the University of Florida.

World, Martyr wrote, "seem to live in that golden world of which old writers speak so much, wherein men lived simply and innocently without enforcement of laws, without quarreling, judges and libels, content only to satisfy nature, without further vexation for knowledge of things to come."

The innocence of the indigenous Americans was more imagined than real. To one degree or another, they knew warfare, brutality, slavery, human sacrifice, and cannibalism. Columbus did not, as charged, "introduce" slavery to the New World; the practice existed there before his arrival, though his shipments of Tainos to Spain presaged a transoceanic traffic in slaves unprecedented in history.

This idealized image of people living in nature persisted until it was too late to learn who the Americans really were and, accepting them for what they were, to find a way to live and let live. Disease and conquest wiped out the people and their cultures. In their place Europeans had begun to "invent" America, as the Mexican historian Edmundo O'Gorman contends, in their own image and for their own purposes. They had set upon a course, writes historian Alfred W. Crosby, of creating "Neo-Europes." This was the America that took its place in world history.

In the 18th century, however, European intellectuals did engage in a searching reappraisal. A scientific movement, encouraged by the French naturalist Georges-Louis Leclerc de Buffon (1707–1788), spread the idea that America was somehow inferior to the Old World. As evidence, Buffon offered denigrating comparisons between the "ridiculous" tapir and the elephant, the llama and the camel, and the "cowardly" puma and the noble lion. Moreover, Old-World animals introduced there fared poorly, declining in health and size, with the sole exception of the pig. It was Buffon's thesis that America suffered an arrested development because of a humid climate, which he attributed to its relatively late emergence from the waters of the Biblical flood.

Buffon's ideas enjoyed a vogue throughout the 18th century and inspired more extreme arguments about "America's weakness." Not only were the animals inferior, so were the Americans, and even Europeans who settled there soon degenerated.

Unlike the proud patriots in colonial and post-Revolutionary North America, European intellectuals began expressing strong reservations about the benefits of the American discovery. There was no gainsaying its importance. Few disputed the opinion of Adam Smith: "The discovery of America, and that of a passage to the East Indies by the Cape of Good Hope, are the two greatest and most important events recorded in the history of mankind."

But there were negative assessments, not unlike today's. The anti-imperialist Samuel Johnson (1709–1784) wrote: "The Europeans have scarcely visited any coast but to gratify avarice, and extend corruption; to arrogate dominion without rights, and practice cruelty without incentive." He was also one of the first to make an unflattering connection between the conquest of America and its original conqueror. Columbus, Johnson said, had to travel "from court to court, scorned and repulsed as a wild projector, an idle promiser of kingdoms in the clouds: nor has any part of the world had reason to rejoice that he found at last reception and employment."

The French philosopher Abbé Guillaume-Thomas Raynal (1713–1796) challenged others to consider the following questions: Has the discovery of America been useful or harmful to mankind? If useful, how can its usefulness be magnified? If harmful, how can the harm be ameliorated? He offered a prize for the essay that would best answer those questions.

The respondents whose essays have survived were evenly divided between optimists and pessimists. Although "Europe is indebted to the New World for a few conveniences, and a few luxuries," Raynal himself observed, these were "so cruelly obtained, so unequally distributed, and so obstinately disputed" that they may not justify the costs. In conclusion, the abbé asked, if we had it to do over again, would we still want to discover the way to America and India? "Is it to be imagined," Raynal speculated, "that there exists a being infernal enough to answer this question in the affirmative?"

Pangs of guilt and expressions of moral outrage were futile, however; nothing stayed the momentum of European expansion in America. Most of the immigrants had never heard of the "American weakness" or read the intellectuals who idealized or despised the Indians or deplored Europe's blood-stained seizure of the lands. By the millions—particularly after the introduction of the steamship and on through World War I—immigrants flocked to a promised land where people could make something of themselves and prepare a better life for their children. There had been nothing quite like this in history. This was reflected in the image of Columbia. Little wonder that Columbus's standing in history was never higher than it was when the achievements and promise of America seemed so bright and were extravagantly proclaimed at home and abroad.

The "primary factor behind our [current] reassessment of the encounter," Crosby writes, "is a general reassessment of the role of rapid change, even catastrophe, in human history, and even the history of the earth and of the universe." The earlier faith in progress was founded on a Western belief that change came gradually and almost invariably for the better. In 19th-century science, the uniformitarian geology of Charles Lyell and the evolutionary theory of Charles Darwin were widely accepted because they seemed to confirm the idea of progress: The present world and its inhabitants were the products not of global disasters and multiple creations but of slow and steady change.

By contrast, Crosby observes, the 20th century has experienced the two worst wars in history, genocide, the invention of more ominous means of destruction, revolutions and the collapse of empires, rampant population growth, and the threat of ecological disaster. Catastrophism, not steady progress, is the modern paradigm. Even the universe was born, many scientists now believe, in one explosive moment—the Big Bang.

"The rapidity and magnitude of change in our century," Crosby concludes, "has prepared us to ask different questions about the encounter than the older schools of scientists and scholars asked."

If Abbé Raynal held his essay contest today, the pessimists might outnumber the optimists. Indeed, almost everything about Columbus and the discovery of America has become controversial.

And perhaps the greatest controversy of all is whether or not to celebrate the Quincentennial. The critics who advocate not celebrating it are correct, if to celebrate perpetuates a view of the encounter that ignores the terrible toll. This must be acknowledged and memorialized in the hope that nothing like it is ever repeated. Even so, it would be unhistorical to ignore the more salutary consequences. The New World, for example, changed Europe through new ideas, new resources, and new models of political and social life that would spread through the world. William H. McNeill is one of many historians who believe this led to the Enlightenment of the 18th century and thus to the philosophical, political, and scientific foundations of modern Western civilization. It should not be overlooked that this is the kind of society that encourages and tolerates the revisionists who condemn its many unforgivable transgressions in the New World.

Of course, attributing so much to any one historical development makes some historians uneasy. In cautioning against the "presentism" in much historical interpretations, Herbert Butterfield recalled "the schoolboy who, writing on the results of Columbus's discovery of America, enumerated amongst other things the execution of Charles I, the war of the Spanish Succession and the French Revolution." No one will ever know what the world and subsequent events would have been like if the discovery had not been made, or if it had not occurred until much later. But the impact of that discovery can hardly be underestimated. And it did start with Christopher Columbus.

That brings up another issue central to the Quincentenary debates: Columbus's responsibility for all that followed. It must be remembered who he was—not who we wish he had been. He was a European Christian of the 15th century sailing for the crown of Spain. There can be no expiation, only understanding. His single-mindedness and boldness, as well as the magnitude of his achievement, give him heroic standing. Others did not have Columbus's bold idea to sail across the unknown ocean, or if they did, they never acted upon it. Columbus did. In so many other respects, he failed to rise above his milieu and set a more worthy example, and so ended up a tragic figure. But he does not deserve to bear alone the blame for the consequences of his audacious act.

We must resist the temptation to shift blame for our behavior to someone dead and gone. Mario Vargas Llosa, the Peruvian novelist, finds little to admire in the early Spanish conquerors but recognizes the dangers inherent in transferring to them an inordinate share of the blame for modern America.

"Why have the post-colonial republics of the Americas—republics that might have been expected to have deeper and broader notions of liberty, equality, and fraternity—failed so miserably to improve the lives of their Indian citizens?" Vargas Llosa asks. "Immense opportunities brought by the civilization that discovered and conquered America have been beneficial only to a minority, sometimes a very small one; whereas the great majority managed to have only a negative share of the conquest.... One of our worst defects, our best fictions, is to believe that our miseries have been imposed on us from abroad, that others, for example, the conquistadores, have always been responsible for our problems.... Did they really do it? We did it; we are the conquistadores."

People have choices, but they do not always choose well. One wishes Columbus had acquitted himself more nobly, in the full knowledge that, even if he had, others who came after would have almost surely squandered the opportunity presented to them to make a truly fresh start in human history—a new world in more than the geographic sense. But wishes, yesterday's self-congratulation or today's self-flagellation, are not history.

Columbus's failings, as well as his ambitions and courage, are beyond historical doubt—and are all too human. The mythic Columbus of our creation is something else. His destiny, it seems, is to serve as a barometer of our self-confidence, our hopes and aspirations, our faith in progress, and the capacity of humans to create a more just society.

How Many People Were Here Before Columbus?

One of the few certainties: The Indian populations of North and South America suffered a catastrophic collapse after 1492

By Lewis Lord

George Catlin, the 19th-century artist, revered the American Indians—"a numerous and noble race of HUMAN BEINGS," he called them, "fast passing to extinction." In the 1830s, he traveled among four dozen tribes to paint nearly 600 portraits and scenes of Indian life; most now hang in the Smithsonian. During his visits, his hosts extolled the blissful age before the settlers came, a time when tribes were much larger. "The Indians of North America," Catlin would speculate in his diary, "were 16 millions in numbers, and sent that number of daily prayers to the Almighty."

Few contemporaries agreed with Catlin's lofty estimate of the Indian population before contact with the white man. "Twaddle about imaginary millions," scoffed one Smithsonian expert, reflecting the prevailing view that Indians were too incompetent to have ever reached large numbers. Alexis de Tocqueville's cheery assertion that America before Columbus was an "empty continent . . . awaiting its inhabitants" was endorsed by no less than the U.S. Census Bureau, which in 1894 warned against accepting Indian "legends" as facts. "Investigation shows," the bureau said, "that the aboriginal population within the present United States at the beginning of the Columbian period could not have exceeded much over 500,000."

A century later the question remains far from settled. But modern scholarship tends to side with the painter. Some experts believe that perhaps 10 million people lived above the Rio Grande in 1492—twice as many as may have inhabited the British Isles at that time. The population of the Western Hemisphere may have exceeded 15th-century Europe's 70 million.

Driving the higher estimates is the relatively new view that most of America's Indians were wiped out by smallpox, measles, and other Old World diseases that swept across the hemisphere far faster than the Europeans that brought them. "Population decay was catastrophic," concluded historian William McNeill in his 1976 book, *Plagues and Peoples.*

But that still leaves unsolved the question of how many Indians inhabited the continent when the first Europeans arrived. No one, in fact, knows how many people lived *anywhere* in those days, except for perhaps a city or two in Europe. The first national censuses occurred centuries later: 1749 in Sweden, 1790 in the fledgling United States, 1801 in France and Britain; it was 1953 when China took a complete count.

George Catlin's means of counting Indians—the guesstimate—was the only method in his day. It was the same method the Census Bureau used in 1894 when it haughtily dismissed his idea that millions of Indians once inhabited the country.

The expert whose figures would dominate scholarly thought for the first

half of this century, Smithsonian ethnologist James Mooney, did his share of guessing, too. Mooney pored through historical documents for accounts of tribal populations made by soldiers, missionaries, and others. But he suspected that his sources routinely exaggerated—soldiers to paint their conquests as more heroic, missionaries to pad their tallies of souls saved. So he often took the lowest count he could find and, to be safe, reduced it. His ultimate tribe-by-tribe estimate, published in 1928, showed an Indian population of 1,150,000 north of the Rio Grande.

Mooney was estimating the population not in 1492 but in periods that followed initial contacts with white men—including encounters in the American West as late as the 19th century. The common assumption in his day was that the Indians the whites came upon were probably as numerous as the Indians of 1492. That's what anthropologist Alfred Kroe-

ber believed in 1934 when he produced an estimate of the entire hemisphere's pre-Columbian population that dominated academic thought into the 1960s. Kroeber took Mooney's tally, shrank it a bit, and extrapolated the figures to the rest of North and South America. With a map and a device called a planimeter, he measured off various cultural areas and assigned each a population density. For the eastern United States, he averaged fewer than 1 person per square mile. For the many regions below the Rio Grande—the lands of the Incas and Aztecs and others that obviously had been much more populous—he assigned much higher densities. He multiplied the densities by the square miles in each region and concluded that 8.4 million people inhabited the Americas in 1492. They were neatly divided: 4.2 million in North America and 4.2 million in South America and the Caribbean.

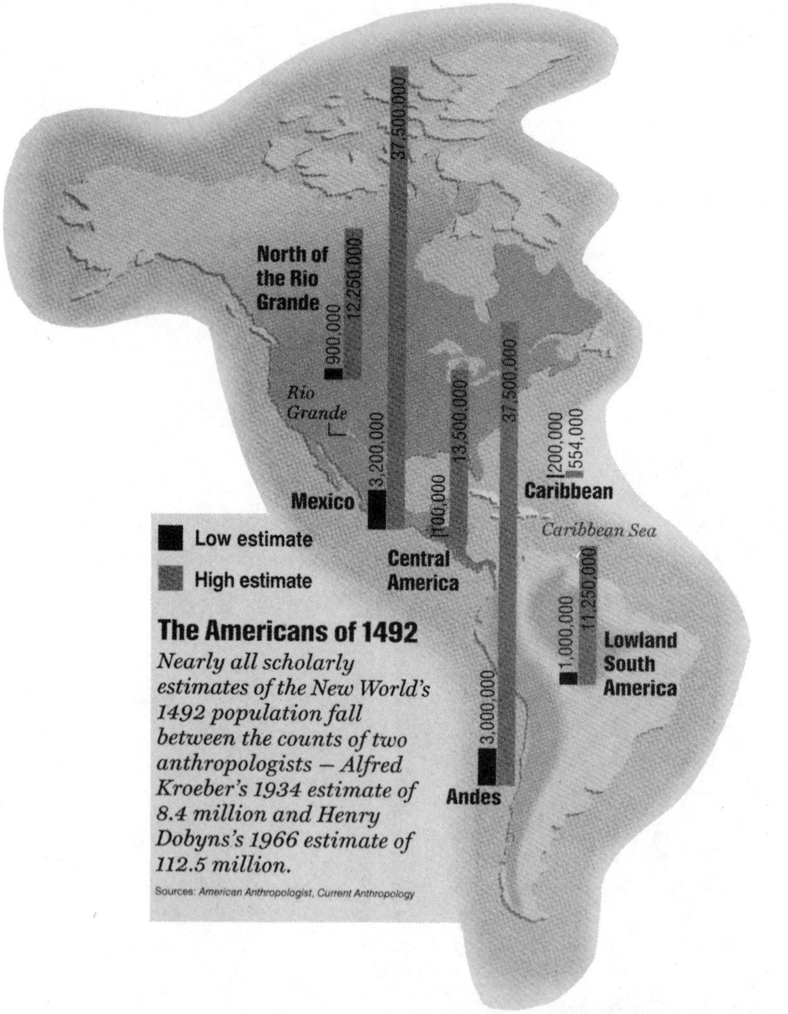

Canoe count. No one since Kroeber has made an estimate so low. In the past 40 years, scholars have sifted through thousands of volumes—from 16th-century Spanish reports of baptisms, marriages, and tax collections in Mexico to 17th-century accounts of epidemics in New England. Where the data failed to provide direct answers, the experts devised ingenious ways to draw inferences from them. Explorers, for instance, rarely estimated total populations; they tended to report only the number of warriors. Scholars now multiply the warrior counts by a correction factor such as 5 to come up with a total that includes women, children, and old men. Multiples likewise are applied to baptisms, Indian buildings, even canoes and acres of beans and corn. Archaeological sites containing heaps of oyster shells have been used to estimate how many oysters were eaten—and thus how many Indians ate them.

By the 1960s, scholars were concluding that just one spot—central Mexico—once had three times as many Indians as Kroeber had estimated in the whole hemisphere.

The highest estimate ever, made in 1966, was supported by a provocative theory. Anthropologist Henry Dobyns argued that disease reduced the Indian population by 95 percent or more throughout the hemisphere—a "depopulation ratio" that, he said, has commonly occurred even in modern times when epidemics strike peoples with no immunity. Dobyns took Indian populations at their nadirs—their lowest levels—and multiplied the numbers by 20 or 25. In America above the Rio Grande, for instance, the Indian population hit bottom early in this century when census figures reported 490,000; by Dobyns's calculation that means between 9.8 million and 12.2 million Indians once inhabited what's now the United States and Canada. For the hemisphere, he estimated a 1492 population of 90 million to 112.5 million.

Critics suspect Dobyns assumed too much. Epidemics, they say, were probably not as frequent or lethal as he claimed. Dobyns, who retired without revising his count, agrees that his method is simplistic; he proposed it "for

North of the Rio Grande

37,500,000
12,250,000
900,000

Rio Grande

Mexico 3,200,000

700,000
13,500,000

Central America

Caribbean 1,200,000
554,000

Caribbean Sea

37,500,000

■ Low estimate
▨ High estimate

The Americans of 1492
Nearly all scholarly estimates of the New World's 1492 population fall between the counts of two anthropologists — Alfred Kroeber's 1934 estimate of 8.4 million and Henry Dobyns's 1966 estimate of 112.5 million.

Sources: American Anthropologist, Current Anthropology

1,000,000
1,250,000

Lowland South America

Andes 3,000,000

GRAPHIC BY STEPHEN ROUNTREE—USN&WR

lack of something better," he says, and localized studies, if thorough, can be more accurate. A colleague's on-the-scene research in Peru, for instance, convinced Dobyns that his Inca empire estimate of 30 million to 37 million Indians was perhaps 20 million too high. But in the 31 years since his *Current Anthropology* article, Dobyns has measured other regional populations with tools that other scholars use—warrior counts, food availability, and the like—and "fairly consistently" found that his 1966 assumptions were too low. He now believes that Florida in 1492 had perhaps 700,000 Indians—several times what he concluded in 1966. His article estimated the Caribbean's 1492 population at a half million; he now agrees with other scholars that it was 5 million or more.

How close will scholars ever come to the real numbers? A recent effort by geographer William Denevan to reconcile the many conflicting estimates, by using the best findings of various scholars, concludes that 54 million people inhabited the Americas in 1492, including 3.8 million above the Rio Grande. But how meaningful such numbers are is the question. With decades of careful research, historian Woodrow Borah once predicted, scholars eventually may produce an estimate with a margin of error of 30 to 50 percent. "If I had to pick the most unanswerable question in the world to get into heaven, that would be a good choice," says David Henige, a historian at the University of Wisconsin–Madison and author of the forthcoming book *Numbers From Nowhere.* "It is absolutely impossible to answer. Yet people have written tens of thousands of pages on it."

Even if the absolute total is forever unknowable, there are other numbers that tell a haunting tale. In the 1960s, a Berkeley geographer, Carl Sauer, cited evidence of a 1496 census that Columbus's brother Bartholomew ordered for tax purposes on Hispaniola (now Haiti and the Dominican Republic). The Spanish counted 1.1 million Indians. Since that sum covered only Hispaniola's Spanish-controlled half and excluded children, Sauer concluded that 3 million Indians once inhabited the island. But a generation after 1492, a Spanish resident reported Hispaniola's Indian population had shrunk below 11,000.

The island's collapse was only a preview. By 1650, records suggest that only 6 million Indians remained in all of North America, South America, and the Caribbean. Subtract 6 million from even a conservative estimate of the 1492 population—like Denevan's consensus count of 54 million—and one dreadful conclusion is inescapable: The 150 years after Columbus's arrival brought a toll on human life in this hemisphere comparable to all of the world's losses in World War II.

A Taste of Adventure

Kerala, India, and the Molucca Islands, Indonesia

The history of spices is the history of trade

SOON after dawn on May 21st 1498, Vasco da Gama and his crew arrived at Calicut after the first direct sea voyage from Europe to Asia. If history's modern age has a beginning, this is it. Europe's ignorance of, and isolation from, the cosmopolitan intellectual and commercial life of Asia were ended forever. With ships, weaponry and a willingness to use them both, the countries of Europe were about to colonise the rest of the world. To support this expansion, its merchant classes would invent new forms of commercial credit and the first great corporations, vital parts of capitalism's operating system, and spread their trading networks across the seven seas. And what did the men shout as they came ashore? "For Christ and spices!"

The proselytising part turned out to be disappointingly unnecessary: there were already plenty of Christians living on the Malabar coast, following the arrival of a Syrian contingent many centuries earlier. But as far as spice went, Da Gama and his crew were right on the money. Then, as now, Calicut was a gateway to the world's greatest pepper-growing region—indeed this was why the Syrians had moved there in the first place. As such it was at the heart of the spice trade, a network of sea routes and entrepots in the making for millennia: the world economy's oldest, deepest, most aromatic roots.

For thousands of years before Da Gama and hundreds of years afterwards, the secret of the spice trade was simple: great demand and highly controlled supply. Some of that control was enforced through political power or contrived through mercantile guile. Some was simply a gift from the gods of climate and botany. Legend has it that, before leaving, Da Gama dared to ask the zamorin of Calicut whether he could take a pepper stalk with him for replanting. His courtiers were outraged, but the potentate stayed calm. "You can take our pepper, but you will never be able to take our rains." He knew how important the region's unusual twin monsoon, both phases of which bring heavy rain, was to its fickle crop. To this day, though regions elsewhere grow pepper, Kerala reigns supreme in its quality, dominating the high end of the market.

If those vital downpours have not washed away what passes for the road, a few days travel into Kerala's rolling Western Ghats, where waterfalls roar and herds of wild elephants loom from soft mist, brings you to the ancestral home of *Piper nigrum*. High up in the middle of nowhere, Iddicki produces the finest pepper in the world, its peppercorns always dark and heavy, bursting with flavour. Its vines wind their way around almost every tree in sight, climbing ten metres or more into the sky.

After such a journey you might expect Iddicki to be a sleepy backwater. In its own idyllic way, though, it is a boomtown worthy of the Wild West. Fancy jeeps clog the narrow streets; shops overflow with the latest necessities of rural life, like washing machines and stereos. Giant satellite dishes shove their expensive snouts at the heavens from every other house. One of the world's largest stashes of gold is in rural India, and to judge by its glittering jewellery shops this town has considerably more than its fair share. "Black gold," explains one pepper farmer with a broad grin, is fetching top prices on the world market.

And what did the men shout as they came ashore? "For Christ and spices!"

Until you talk to them about that world market, Iddicki's residents seem much like farmers anywhere else in the developing world—scraping a living at the margins of the market economy. Thomas Thomas, one of the several hundred thousand smallholders who grow Kerala's pepper, is a good example. A humble man of the earth, he speaks softly and still wears his *dhothi*, a traditional loincloth, when he tills his soil. But with a little prompting he will give you an analysis of the pepper market sophisticated enough to make a Chicago commodities trader blush: current prices, the direction of the futures market, the costs versus benefits of holding stocks. A local spice dealer explains over a feast of fiery snapper and spiced tapioca at his spacious bungalow that "there is full price-discovery in this market." The farmers who sell their crops to him (for resale at the big market in Jewtown, which has replaced Calicut as the hub of Kerala's pepper trade) do so with the latest New York and Rotterdam prices in hand. One particularly sharp farmer, he moans, is cutting out the middlemen altogether and shipping his stocks directly to Europe.

The global aspect of the dealer's trade is nothing new. As far back as 2600 BC, there are records of the Egyptians feeding spices obtained from Asia to labourers building the great pyramid of Cheops, to give them strength. Archeological evidence suggests that cloves were quite popular in Syria not long after, despite the fact that, like nutmeg and mace, they came only from the spice islands of what is now Indonesia. Long before the 6th century BC, when Confucius advocated the use of ginger, the Chinese were obtaining spices from the tropics. Europe imported them before Rome was founded.

Today spices are chiefly flavourings for food, but a hundred other uses have contributed to the demand through history. In ancient Egypt cassia and cinnamon fetched a high price because they were essential for embalming; so too were anise, marjoram and cumin, used to rinse out the innards of the worthy dead. Hammurabi's legal code, which called for severe punishment of sloppy or unsuccessful surgeons, did much to encourage the use of medicinal spices in Sumeria.

Particularly in Europe, though, food came to matter most. Spices preserve, and they also make the poorly preserved palatable, masking the appetite-killing stench of decay. After bad harvests and in cold winters the only thing that kept starvation at bay was heavily salted meat—with pepper. And there was never enough of it. Thus pepper began the association with gold it still has in the streets of Iddicki, often at a one-to-one exchange rate. In order to call off their siege of Rome in 408 AD, the Visigoths demanded a bounty in gold, silver and pepper. In the Middle Ages plague added to the demand for medicinal spices; a German price table from the 14th century sets the value of a pound of nutmeg at seven fat oxen. At the same

time "peppercorn rents" were a serious way of doing business. When the *Mary Rose,* an English ship that sank in 1545, was raised from the ocean floor in the 1980s, nearly every sailor was found with a bunch of peppercorns on his person—the most portable store of value available.

The great beneficiaries of Europe's need were the Arabs. Spices could change hands a dozen times between their source and Europe, soaring in value with each transaction, and the Arabs were the greatest of the middlemen. Keen to keep it that way, they did everything possible to confuse consumers about the spices' origins. As early as the 5th century BC an Arab cover story fooled Herodotus into believing that cinnamon was found only on a mountain range somewhere in Arabia. The spices were jealously guarded by vicious birds of prey, he wrote, which made their nests of the stuff on steep mountain slopes. Arabs would leave out large chunks of fresh donkey meat for the birds to take back to their nests, which would crash to the ground under the weight. The brave Arabs then grabbed the nests, from under the talons of their previous owners.

Not everyone was fooled. In the 1st century AD the Roman historian Pliny grew concerned at the way the empire's gold flowed ever to the east, and set out to expose the truth and undercut the Arab monopolists who he reckoned to be selling pepper at prices a hundred times what they paid for it in India. It did not help that the gluttonous Romans were, in the words of Frederic Rosengarten, a spice historian, "the most extravagant users of aromatics in history". They used spices in every imaginable combination for their foods, wines and fragrances. Legionaries headed off to battle wearing perfume. The rich slept on pillows of saffron in the belief that it would cure hangovers.

Resentment against the Arab stranglehold had led Rome to launch an invasion of Arabia in 24 BC, an ill-fated expedition that ended in humiliation. But where military means failed, market intelligence prevailed. In 40 AD, Hip-

palus, a Greek merchant, discovered something the Arabs had long tried to obscure: that the monsoons which nourish India's pepper vines reverse direction mid-year, and that trips from Egypt's Red Sea coast to India and back could thus be shorter and safer than the empire had imagined. Roman trade with India boomed: the Arab monopoly broke.

Early in the 7th century, an obscure spice merchant named Muhammad reestablished Arab dominance of the spice trade by introducing an aggressive, expansionary Islam to the world. When the muslims took Alexandria in 641 AD, they killed the trade which had long flourished between Rome and India. As they tightened their grip on the business over the next few centuries, prices in Europe rose dramatically. During the Middle Ages, spices became a luxury that only a few in Europe could afford. This was bad news for the poor and good news for Venice. Its shrewd merchants struck a deal with the Arabs that made them the trade's preferred—indeed almost exclusive—European distributors. Even during the crusades, the relationship bought wealth to all concerned.

The rest of Europe did not care at all for the Muslim Curtain, as the Islamic empire separating west from east came to be called, or for the Venetians. The final blow came in 1453 when the Ottoman Turks took Constantinople, shutting down the small overland trade that had previously evaded the Arab-Venetian monopoly. The Egyptians, gatekeepers of the trade with Venice, felt confident enough to impose a tariff amounting to a third of the value of spices passing through their fingers.

Salvation for the palates and exchequers of Europe's kings lay in finding a sea route to the Indies. In particular, the hunt was on for Malacca, the most important entrepôt in the spice trade and the fabled gateway to the Spice Islands. Spain and Portugal financed dozens of exploration parties in its general direction; half would never make it back home. The rationale for this expense and danger was simple: "He who is lord of Malacca has his hand on the throat of Venice."

It was as part of Portugal's *Drang nach Osten* that Vasco da Gama rounded Africa's Cape of Good Hope to reach India in 1498. As waves of Portuguese explorers returned to Lisbon with their loads of spices, the Venetians and the Egyptians were stunned: the price of pepper in Lisbon fell to one-fifth that in Venice.

"He who is lord of Malacca has his hand on the throat of Venice"

The Spaniards, too, were less than happy. They had sent Christopher Columbus to find a route to the Indies via the west, but he had failed, hitting upon the previously unknown Americas instead. In his zeal to convince his paymasters and himself that he had succeeded, he named the new world's natives as Indians and their sacred *chiles* "red" pepper—two unpardonable obfuscations that have confused people to this day.

Pope Alexander IV was drafted in to keep the two expansionist powers apart; the result was the treaty of Tordesillas, which granted all discoveries west of a mid-Atlantic meridian to Spain, and those east of it to Portugal. But the Spanish clung to the possibility of a western end-run to the Spice Islands, and financed Ferdinand Magellan on what would become the first circumnavigation of the earth. Magellan himself was killed in the Philippines, but his sidekick, Sebastian del Cano, completed the momentous journey—with a landfall at the Spice Islands en route. In 1522 his *Victoria* returned to Europe with a tonne of spices on board. The king awarded him a coat of arms embellished with two cinnamon sticks, three nutmegs and twelve cloves.

But the Portuguese had pipped Spain to the post. They had captured the vibrant free-trading port of Malacca, in what is now Malaysia, in 1511. Using the intelligence they gathered there, they made it to the promised land: the tiny Banda Islands, the world's only source of nutmeg and mace, which they

reached the following year. Nutmeg is the pit of the nutmeg tree's fruit, and mace, which commanded and still commands a higher price, is the delicate red aril which comes between the pit and the fruit's husky exterior. Chaucer extolled "nutemuge put in ale . . ." and it remains an essential part of Coca-Cola's secret formula.

After filling their holds, the Portuguese began their return. One ship ran aground, stranding its crew on a remote island. Hearing of a strange race of white men in his parts, the sultan of Ternate, the most powerful of the clove isles, sent for them—and so the Europeans found the last secret source of spice.

Look out from the expansive verandah of the sultan's palace in Ternate and one of history's great microcosms lies before you. Dominating one side is Gamalama, the island's temperamental volcano. Opposite it stands its equally fickle twin on the island of Tidore. The two spits of land, not a mile apart, are now almost unknown beyond their immediate vicinity. But five centuries ago their names were uttered with breathless excitement across Europe as their rulers, ancient rivals, played the new great powers off against each other with promises of limitless wealth.

Dark, husky aromas swirl through the palace as incense made specially of local spices finds its way into the thick tropical air. The place is overflowing with gifts from distant customers: priceless Chinese vases, exquisitely carved Indian daggers, fine Venetian glassware, all of them evidence of the influence these rulers once wielded. Ask politely, and you might be allowed to gaze— from a respectful distance, and only after much ceremony—at the sultan's magical crown, its hundred sparkling gemstones hanging heavy like ripe peaches. You are not the first impressionable tourist here. Francis Drake gushed about the palace, especially its 400-strong harem. And it seems that it's still good to be the king: one of the gifts on display is an enormous modern settee, helpfully labelled "Lazy chair: for the sultan to take naps."

For much of the 16th century, Spain and Portugal tried to win control of the

trade in cloves that made such a lifestyle possible. This meant entangling themselves in the long-running rivalry between the rulers of the two islands, who were in-laws. The European powers would build alliances and forts in one place and then the other, only to find themselves kicked out or caught up in endless intrigues and feuds. After decades of this Machiavellian palaver the Portuguese emerged as the top European player in the clove market, but they never really made it a monopoly. Indeed, they allowed the Dutch, who were growing increasingly anxious for a piece of the action, to be their chief distributors in the north and west of Europe. After Spain gobbled up Portugal in 1580, though, the trade changed again. The Spanish tightened control of the market to which they now had exclusive access, cutting the Dutch out of the picture and raising prices across the continent.

Convinced that they had to find a way to control the source of the spices, the Dutch got their act together. In 1602 they formed the Dutch East India Company (the *Vereenigde Oost-Indische Compagnie*, VOC), an association of merchants meant to reduce competition, share risk and realise economies of scale. Other European countries also formed East India companies—everyone from Portugal to Sweden to Austria had a go—but none was ever as successful in the spice trade as the VOC. By 1670 it was the richest corporation in the world, paying its shareholders an annual dividend of 40% on their investment despite financing 50,000 employees, 30,000 fighting men and 200 ships, many of them armed. The secret of this success was simple. They had no scruples whatsoever.

The VOC's first conquest was the Banda archipelago. Unlike the sultans of the clove islands, who relished the attention lavished upon them by their European suitors and the opportunities for mischief that came with it, the fiercely independent Islamic merchants of the Bandas had never allowed Spain or Portugal to build forts on their islands: they insisted on their freedom to trade with all nations. This independence proved their undoing, since it

Hot Chile

"Oh Blessed Incomparable Chile, ruler of all things . . . I give thee thanks for my digestive health, I give thee thanks for my very life!" Thus the Transcendental Capsaicinophilic Society, one of the worrying number of cults devoted to *capsicum*: chiles or "red" pepper.

If it sounds as if they are on drugs then so, in a way, they are. Paul Bosland of the Chile Pepper Institute in New Mexico reckons they and all chileheads are high on endorphins, painkillers released by the body to block the sting of the capsaicin which gives chiles their bite.

The addicts are spread all over the world. Travelling on the back of the European spice trade, America's chiles have since colonised every corner of the earth so thoroughly that everyone thinks they have always been around.

Even the top man at the Indian Spices Board refuses to accept that chiles are an import, pulling dubious sanskrit references from the Vedas to bolster his point. His clinching argument? "Indians can go months without touching black pepper, but not a day goes by that we don't eat chile peppers."

This is fast becoming true everywhere else, too. Americans' consumption of chile has doubled over the past two decades; they now use the spice in almost everything. Salsa now outsells ketchup as America's top condiment. But black pepper still gets all the glory as the world's most important traded spice. Unlike its fickle namesake, red pepper grows like mad all over the place. So though there may be a great demand for it, no one makes much money out of trading it.

Climb through the dense, aromatic forests that cover the steep slopes of Ternate's volcano, and you will find this living testament to the ultimate futility of monopoly. Nearly 40 metres tall and over 4 metres round, Afo is the world's oldest clove tree, planted in defiance of the Dutch ban nearly four centuries ago. Despite the VOC's extreme precautions, Afo's sister seedlings, stolen in 1770 by an intrepid Frenchman (curiously, named Poivre), ended up flourishing on the Seychelles, Réunion and especially Zanzibar, which later became the world's largest producer of cloves. By the end of the 18th century the emergence of these rivals had broken the Dutch monopoly for good.

By that time the VOC was already a hollow mockery of its original ghastly self. As early as the end of the 17th century, careful analysis of the books shows that its volume of trade was reducing every year. Even a monopoly so ruthlessly enforced could not help but leak, and the VOC's overheads were huge—tens of thousands of employees, garrisons, warships. Decades of easy rents had created a corrupt and inefficient beast. By 1735, dwindling spice income had been overtaken by textiles in the company's profit column. In 1799, the most vicious robber baron of them all met its final end. The VOC went bankrupt.

The demise of the VOC was not just a pleasing comeuppance. It was evidence that, in just two centuries, Europeans had changed the spice trade forever. The spices that were once limited to tiny islands in hidden archipelagoes were being grown around the world and in large quantities. Trade routes that spanned oceans were becoming commonplace and, as such, competitive. The Dutch did their best to buck the trend, destroying their stocks so blatantly that, according to one observer, the streets of Amsterdam were "flooded with nutmeg butter". But it was all in vain. Spices were no longer that hard to come by. Monopolies gave way to markets.

Those markets remained rich in romance; the allure of the trade, its role as a cultural crossroads, its many rival players, its uncertainties and its opportunities for smuggling (even relatively

encouraged the VOC to put the nutmeg trade first on its order of business.

For a taste of Banda's romance nothing beats a trip to Run, an explosion of nutmeg trees in the middle of a turquoise sea. Reaching it after a night aboard ship is a magical experience; scores of dolphins dart about your bow-wave as the first glints of sunrise streak across the sky. It feels much as it must have done when English adventurers first claimed the place, making it the country's first colony anywhere. Not much of a colony, it must be said: the island is so small that even a modest fishing vessel can come ashore only at

---

The secret of this success was simple. The Dutch had no scruples whatsoever

---

high tide. Yet this seemingly insignificant toe-hold in nutmeg-land so exercised the Dutch that they traded away a promising young colony on the other side of the world to secure it. That island was New Amsterdam, now better known as Manhattan.

The purchase of Run demonstrates the VOC's persistence; it does not do jus-

tice to the company's cruelty (normally, but not exclusively, meted out to non-Europeans). Its most successful head, Jan Pieterszoon Coen, had earlier convinced the reluctant Bandanese of his firm's God-given right to monopolise the nutmeg trade in a more typical style: he had had every single male over the age of fifteen that he could get his hands on butchered. Coen brought in Japanese mercenaries to torture, quarter and decapitate village leaders, displaying their heads on long poles. The population of the isles was 15,000 before the VOC arrived; 15 years later it was 600.

When they turned to the clove trade the Dutch had no time for the squabbling politics of Ternate and Tidore. The VOC uprooted all the Sultans' clove trees and concentrated production on Ambon, an island where its grip was tight. By 1681, it had destroyed three-quarters of all nutmeg trees in unwanted areas and reorganised farming into plantations. It imposed the death penalty on anyone caught growing, stealing or possessing nutmeg or clove plants without authorisation. It drenched every nutmeg with lime before export, to ensure that not one fertile seed escaped its clutches. Yet high on its hillside Afo lives to tell its tale.

cheap spices carry a lot of value for a given weight) kept the spice bazaars of Kerala, Ambon and Rotterdam fascinating. And lucrative, too; though no one could control the overall flow of spice any more, information could still be rushed ahead fast enough—or sequestered behind long enough—for people in the know to make a killing. Now, though, the information itself has started to flow freely. "There just aren't so many secrets any more," reflects a spice trader in Rotterdam. "The farmers in Vietnam are walking around with mobile phones. They know the market price as soon as I do."

Such traders are now caught in a trap. Their space for bargaining and trade, opened up with the end of monopoly production, is being hemmed in by ever more powerful purchasers—the food giants and spice multinationals. In an age of free-flowing information these buyers can bypass the markets and go directly to the source. From Jewtown, still the key pepper entrepot, to Rotterdam, London and New York, the main international markets, spice traders are a dying breed. One industry veteran reckons that only a fifth of the trading concerns that flourished 30 years ago are still in business.

Their problems stem from men like Al Goetze. Meet him in his office near Baltimore, at the staid headquarters of McCormick, the world's largest spice firm, and his conservative suit and dry manner might lead you to mistake him for a stuffy corporate type. But to his admiring colleagues he is "a modern day Marco Polo."

Procurement managers at food-processing firms were once content to purchase spices through brokers, never leaving the comfort of their air-conditioned offices. Mr Goetze hits the road. He and his men have travelled to nearly every country on earth that grows spices, again and again. McCormick has set up joint-ventures or wholly owned subsidiaries in over a dozen key spice-producing countries in recent years.

Once the reason for going to the source was price. Now, Mr Goetze says, quality is what matters. Both American and European regulators, prompted by increasing consumer awareness of food safety, have been cracking down hard on impurities. Mr Goetze points to an unlikely assortment of objects in a display case: stones, rusty nails, giant cockroaches, plastic beach sandals. All were crammed into bursting burlap bags and sold to McCormick with its spice. Big processing firms and marketers, frightened that such stuff—or, worse, microscopic impurities that come with it—might make it to the dinner plates of litigious customers, are going straight to the source to clean things up.

Alfons van Gulick, the head of Rotterdam's Man Producten, the world's biggest and most influential spice-trading firm, is understandably unimpressed: "McCormick should stick to polishing its brand and selling, rather

---

Stones, rusty nails, giant cockroaches, plastic beach sandals, all crammed into bursting burlap bags and sold with the spice

---

than telling countries how to produce spice." But the people for whose products McCormick and Man Producten compete have an interest in Mr Goetze's strategy. The Indian Spices Board is already helping members improve standards and obtain seals of approval such as ISO certification. The hope is that, over time, producers can go downstream and capture more of the fat margins that come with the "value-added" processing now done in rich countries.

Industry analysts are sceptical about vertical integration. In other commodities it has not been much of a success. Cutting out the middleman may pose

unexpected problems for conservative multinationals, unfamiliar with the culture and risks involved in going upstream. And then there is volatility, on which middlemen thrive and which farmers and multinationals dislike. Asked whether the trade has lost its mystery, one animated trader replies "Mystery? I experience it every day when I try to figure out what is going on with prices in this market!"

Producers hate this, and have made various attempts to iron out the market's ups and downs. The International Pepper Community—which includes India, Indonesia and Brazil among its members—has tried for decades to form a producers' cartel to boost prices, without any success. Price fixing by vanilla growers in Madagascar succeeded for a while, but then Uganda flooded the market with cheaper beans. Indonesia and Grenada, the top producers of nutmeg, managed to boost prices for a few years by limiting supply, but cheating quickly scuppered the arrangement. Quiet talks are underway between top cardamom producers in India and Guatemala, who produce nearly all the world's output, to restrict supply; it may work for a while, but not for long.

Every decade or so, an ambitious individual trader tries to do with money what the producers cannot do by agreement. To corner the pepper market would offer huge riches, and so people regularly have a go. Half a century ago, it was an Armenian; a decade ago, an American. Now it appears that a shadowy Indonesian tycoon may be making a play for at least the white pepper market. But history teaches that such grandiose efforts at monopoly face an uphill struggle. And though it may be possible to milk them for a while, the modern day economics of the trade ensure that they cannot last. The spice trade, once the stuff of legends, has become a market much like any other. And a taste of luxury beyond the dreams of almost every human in history is available to almost everyone, almost everywhere.

After Dire Straits, An Agonizing Haul Across the Pacific

It was only a generation after Columbus that Magellan's tiny fleet sailed west, via his strait, then on around the world

Simon Winchester

Simon Winchester is the author of eight books that combine history and travel, including The Pacific *(Hutchinson), from which this article was adapted.*

Balboa found the ocean. Then, in their droves, explorers emerged to circle and probe and colonize it, but first, in that most daring of all endeavors, to cross it.

No one could be sure how wide it was. No one could be sure where lay the Terra Australis Incognita, which Ptolemy had postulated and which Mercator would argue was a necessary balance for a spherical world—without it the whole planet might simply topple over, to be lost among the stars. No one knew the weather or the currents or the winds. But one small certainty spurred the would-be circumnavigators onward. It was that the Spice Islands, the Moluccas, lay at the farthest side of whatever might lie beyond the waters, pacific or unpacific, that Balboa had discovered.

Traders buying nutmegs and cloves from Arabian merchants had known about the Spice Islands for centuries; in the 1200s Marco Polo knew roughly where they were, for he saw junk traffic in the ports of North China loaded with spices and manned by crews who had come from the south. In 1511 a Portuguese expedition led by Antonio d'Abreu actually discovered them by moving eastward, after passing the tip of Africa, to Malacca, thence down the strait and past the immense island of Borneo to the confused archipelago where nearly all known spices grew in wild profusion. To reach their goal, d'Abreu's men had gone halfway round the world from Europe to the Orient.

The geographical fact they established was of great political and imperial importance. Since 1494, when the Treaty of Tordesillas was signed, all of the unknown world to the east of an imaginary line that had been drawn 370 leagues west of the Cape Verde Islands would belong to Portugal. Everything to the west of that line would belong to Spain. So far as the Atlantic and the Indian oceans were concerned, there was no problem; but what about the other side of the world? Conquest, squatter's rights, annexation, force majeure—these cruder tools of geopolitics might well dictate its eventual position. Thus the Moluccas, if discovered by going eastward around the globe, would belong to Portugal—at least by the logic of some explorers. But the Moluccas claimed by a party going westward might belong to Spain. So while d'Abreu and his colleagues went off eastward, even braver or more foolhardy men, carrying the banner of Castile, were determined to discover—heroically and, as it turned out for many of them, fatally—the way to reach this same Orient by traveling westward across the vast unknown.

There is thus a nice irony in the fact that the man who undertook the seminal voyage, and did so in the name of Spain, was in fact Portuguese. He was born Fernao de Magalhaes, and the Portuguese—"He is ours," they insist—rarely care to acknowledge that he renounced his citizenship after a row, pledged his allegiance to King Charles I (later to be-

From *Smithsonian magazine*, April 1991, pp. 84-90, 92, 94-95. Originally "The Strait—and Dire Straits—of Magellan" from *Pacific Rising* by Simon Winchester. © 1991 by Simon Winchester. Reprinted by permission of the Sterling Lord Literistic, Inc.

come Emperor Charles V) and was given a new name: Hernando de Magallanes. The English-speaking world, which reveres him quite as much as does Iberia, knows him as Ferdinand Magellan.

He set off on September 20, 1519, with a royal mandate to search for a passage to El Mar del Sur, and thus to determine for certain that the Spice Islands were within the Spanish domains. He had not the foggiest notion of how far he might have to travel. For all Magellan's 237 men in their five little ships knew, Balboa's Panama and the northern coast of South America, which Columbus had sighted in 1498 on his third voyage, might be the equatorial portions of a continent extending without a break to the Antarctic pole, making the southern sea they sought quite unreachable from the west. Johann Schöner's globe of the world, then the best known, placed Japan a few hundred miles off Mexico. The historian Lópex de Gómara asserts that Magellan always insisted that the Moluccas were "no great distance from Panama and the Gulf of San Miguel, which Vasco Núñez de Balboa discovered." Magellan would rapidly discover precisely what "no great distance" was to mean.

The five vessels that would soon make history—the *Victoria*, the *Trinidada* (the *Trinidad*), the *San Antonio*, the *Concepción* and the *Santiago*—were small, the largest being 120 tons, and hopelessly unseaworthy. ("I would not care to sail to the Canaries in such crates," wrote the Portuguese consul in Seville, with obvious pleasure. "Their ribs are soft as butter.")

They set sail from the Guadalquivir River under the proud corporate title of the Armada de Molucca, amply armed but hopelessly provisioned, with crews composed of men of nine different nationalities including a lone Englishman. There was one Moluccan slave, Enrique, who would act as an interpreter if the crossing was accomplished. There was a journalist, too, Antonio Francesca Pigafetta, who may also have been a Venetian spy. In any case, Pigafetta's diaries remained the source for all future accounts of the voyage; he had joined the ships, he said, because he was "desirous of sailing with the expedition so

that I might see the wonders of the world."

The sorry tales of sodomy and mutiny, of yardarm justice and abrupt changes of command, and of all the other trials that attended the armada on its path south and west across the Atlantic do not belong here. The truly important phase of the journey starts on February 3, 1520, when the vessels left their anchorage near today's Montevideo and headed south. No charts or sailing directions existed then. The sailors were passing unknown coasts, and confronting increasingly terrifying seas and temperatures that dropped steadily, day by day.

They began to see penguins—"ducks without wings," they called them, *patos sin alas*—and "sea-wolves," or seals. Seeking a way to the Pacific, they explored every indentation in the coast off which they sailed, and with depressing regularity each indentation—even though some were extremely capacious and tempted the navigators to believe that they might be the longed-for straits—proved to be a cul-de-sac. They spent much of the winter, from Palm Sunday until late August, in the center of a chilly and miserable bay at what is now Puerto San Julian. The winter was made doubly wretched by an appalling mutiny and the consequent executions and maroonings that Captain-General Magellan ordered; by the wrecking of the *Santiago*, which he had sent on a depth-sounding expedition; and by the realization of the dreadful damage done to the remaining ships by the chomping of those plank-gourmets of the seas, teredo worms.

But one important discovery was made at Puerto San Julian: these southern plains were inhabited by enormous nomadic shepherds who herded not sheep, but little wild llamas known as guanacos, and who dressed in their skins. Magellan captured a number of these immense people—one pair by the cruel trick of showing them leg-irons and insisting that the proper way to carry the shackles was to allow them to be locked around their ankles. Magellan's men also liked the giants' tricks: one, who stayed aboard only a week but allowed himself to be called Juan and

learned some biblical phrases, caught and ate all the rats and mice on board, to the pleasure of the cook and the entertainment of the men. Magellan called these men "*patagones*"—"big feet"; the land in which he found them has been known ever since as Patagonia.

By late August the fleet set sail again. Two men had been left behind, marooned for mutiny by Magellan's orders. They had a supply of wine and hardtack, guns and shot, but when other, later expeditions entered the bay, no trace of them was found. They may have been killed by the giants; they may have starved to death. All that the men of the armada remembered were their pitiful wails echoing over the still waters as the ships sailed out of the bay into the open sea, and then south.

By the time the flotilla had reached 50 degrees south latitude (not far from the Falkland Islands), the men were restive. Their artless plea now was: If the expedition wanted to reach the Spice Islands, why not turn east toward them and pass below the Cape of Good Hope, as others had? Magellan, sensible enough to know this would make a nonsense of the whole plan to render the Spice Islands Spanish, refused. But he promised that if no strait was found by the time they had eaten up another 25 degrees of latitude, he would turn east as they wished. The murmurs stilled. The Captain-General clearly had no idea of the utter impossibility of navigating at 75 degrees south latitude, for on that longitudinal track his ships would get stuck fast in the thick ice of what is now the Weddell Sea, hemmed in by the yet unimagined continent and the unendurable cold of the Antarctic.

THE CAPTAIN-GENERAL SIGHTS A VIRGIN CAPE

On October 21, 1520, Magellan sighted a headland to starboard. Cabo Virjenes, which today is equipped with a lighthouse that flashes a powerful beam and a radio direction beacon, is an important navigation point on the South American coast. It marks, as Magellan was soon to discover, the eastern end of the strait that bears his name—the tortuous entrance, at long last, to the Pacific.

Ranges of immense, snow-covered mountains crowded into view; there could be, Magellan must have thought, no possible exit. Still, he ordered the *San Antonio* and the *Concepción* into the headwaters of the bay—only to be horrified when he saw them being swept into a huge maelstrom of surf and spindrift by unsuspected currents and winds. But he had no time to dwell on such miseries, for an immense storm broke over his own ship, the *Trinidad*, as well as the *Victoria*, alongside. Men were hurled overboard. One vessel was dismasted; the other nearly turned turtle several times. The storm went on and on and on. When relief finally came to the exhausted crews, the only recourse, it seemed, was to turn tail and head for home. The expedition was over, an abject failure.

Yet just at that moment (one occasionally suspects that the mythmakers have been at work on the story) the lookout sighted sails on the western horizon. They were indeed what they could only have been: the two scouting vessels had returned. Not shattered and aground, they were safe and sound. The joy Magellan must have felt at realizing his men were still alive was, however, as nothing when, as the *San Antonio* and the *Concepción* drew closer, he saw their yardarms hung with bunting, music being played, and the crews dancing and singing.

As an account of the long voyage puts it, "Suddenly, they saw a narrow passage, like the mouth of a river, ahead of them in the surf, and they managed to steer into it. Driven on by wind and tide they raced through this passage and into a wide lake. Still driven by the storm they were carried west for some hours into another narrow passage, though now the current had reversed, so what appeared to be a great ebb tide came rushing towards them. They debouched from this second straight into a broad body of water which stretched as far as the eye could see toward the setting sun. . . ."

By tasting the water and finding it salty, and then making sure that both the ebb tides and flood tides were of equal strength (tests that argued against this body of water being a river), the captains of the scout ships realized they had, indeed, discovered the way through. Magellan, believing that his ultimate goal was within his grasp, brushed aside the persistent doubter's view that he should, despite the discovery, turn back *eastward* for the Moluccas. "Though we have nothing to eat but the leather wrapping from our masts," he declared, "we shall go on!"

The Strait of Magellan is as darkly beautiful as it is useful. Before I first visited the strait I supposed, wrongly, that since its latitude to the south is more or less the same distance from the Equator as Maine's latitude is to the north, the coastline would also be vaguely similar. But it is much starker, more hostile, more grand. Heading west, as Magellan did, the land begins flat, and wind reduces such trees as there are to stunted survivors. Even today the strait is not an easy place for sailing vessels: " . . . both difficult and dangerous, because of incomplete surveys, the lack of aids to navigation, the great distance between anchorages, the strong current, and the narrow limits for the maneuvering of vessels," says the pilot manual.

"A CARGO OF FALSEHOOD AGAINST MAGELLAN"

For Magellan and his men it was a nightmare. The currents were treacherous. Unexpected winds, now known as williwaws, flashed down steep cliffs, threatening to drive the little fleet onto the rocks. He lost another ship; though he did not know it at the time, the *San Antonio* had turned tail and was heading back to Spain, "bearing a cargo of falsehood against Magellan." She also took away supplies vital for all of the fleet—one-third of the armada's biscuits, one-third of its meat and two-thirds of its currants, chickpeas and figs. The men began begging to turn back.

Days passed. Finally, on November 28, 1520, *Trinidad, Victoria* and *Concepción* passed beyond the horrors of the strait, and sailed westward into an evening that became, suddenly, magically serene. We are told that "the iron-willed Admiral" broke down and cried. Then he assembled his men on deck. Pedro de Valderrama, the *Trinidad's* priest, stood on the poop deck and called down on the crew of all three remaining vessels the blessing of Our Lady of Victory. The men sang hymns. The gunners fired broadsides. And Magellan proudly unfurled the flag of Castile.

"We are about to stand into an ocean where no ship has ever sailed before," Magellan is said to have cried (though it has to be emphasized that there is no hard evidence that he did so). "May the ocean be always as calm and benevolent as it is today. In this hope I name it the Mar Pacifico." And just in case it was not Magellan who first uttered the name, then perhaps it was Pigafetta: "We debouched from that strait," he later wrote, "engulfing ourselves in the Pacific Sea."

THE EUROPEAN DAWN BREAKS ON THE PACIFIC

The concept of the Pacific Ocean, the greatest physical unit on Earth, had been born. Balboa had seen it. D'Abreu had ventured onto its western edges. Magellan had reached its eastern periphery. Now it was up to the explorers to try to comprehend the enormity of their discovery. But before they could do that, Magellan had to sail across it. This was his determined aim, and the aim of those who sponsored his venture.

So the Captain-General ordered the sails set to carry the shrunken, but now at long last triumphant, armada northward. He thought it might take three or four days to reach the Spice Islands. It was a savage underestimate—a tragically optimistic forecast, based quite probably on the terrible inability of long-distance navigators to calculate longitude (an inability that insured that not a single estimate then available to Magellan was even 80 percent of the true size of the ocean).

Not that anyone suspected tragedy as they breezed to the north of Cape Desado. Far from it. Once the armada had reached the lower southern latitudes, the winds began to blow balmily and unceasingly from the southeast. They were trade winds, just like those well known in the southern Atlantic and Indian oceans, and they were pleasantly warm. Their effect produced nothing but splendid sailing: no undue swells, no angry squalls, no cyclonic outbursts. Just endless days and nights of leisured running before a steady, powerful breeze. "Well was it named Pacific," wrote Pigafetta later, confirming his master's choice of name, "for during this period we met with no storms."

And for weeks and weeks, simply by wafting before the winds with sails unchanged, the fleet managed to miss every single one of the islands with which the Pacific Ocean is littered. Magellan's course, sedulously recorded by his pilot, Francisco Albo, shows him—almost uncannily—leading his vessels past the Juan Fernández Islands, past Sala y Gómez and Easter islands, past Pitcairn, Ducie, Oeno and Henderson and, indeed, past everything else. His astrolabe, his crude speed recorder, his hourglass (a watchkeeper would be flogged for holding it against his chest, since to warm it made the sand flow faster, the hour pass more quickly, the watch be more rapidly over) served Magellan admirably: he plotted the likely course to the Spice Islands, and his ships took him there, more or less.

Any deviation could have caused disaster. Had he strayed just 3 degrees north of Albo's recorded track, he would have hit the Marquesas; 3 degrees south, he would have come to Tahiti. He was a hundred miles off Bikini Atoll. He passed within half a day's sailing of razor-sharp coral reefs—thundering surfs, huge spikes and lances that would have ruined his ships forever. At this distance in time, it seems as if some guardian angel had Magellan's tiny fleet under benevolent invigilation for days and nights too numerous to count. Yet this providence had a less kindly face. Six weeks out of the strait, Magellan's men began to die. In the monotony of a long, landless passage, what proved unbearable was the lack of food aboard the sea-locked ships.

Much of the stores had already gone, carried off on the treacherous *San Antonio*. Such food as the three ships carried began to rot under the soggy tropical airs. The penguins and seals they had killed and salted in Patagonia started to turn putrid; maggots raged through the ships, eating clothes and supplies and rigging; water supplies turned scummy and rank. Men began to develop the classic symptoms of scurvy—their teeth loosened in their gums, their breath began to smell horribly sour, huge boils erupted from their shrunken frames, they sank into inconsolable melancholia.

In January men began to die. One of the Patagonian behemoths whom Magellan had persuaded aboard was, despite his immense physique and power, the first to go; he begged to be made a Christian, was baptized "Paul" and then died. By mid-January a third of the sailors were too sick to stagger along the decks. Their food was limited to scoops of flour stained yellow by the urine of rats, and biscuits riddled with weevils.

The depression and deep anxiety afflicted Magellan too. At one point he flung his charts overboard in a fit of rage. "With the pardon of the cartographers, the Moluccas are not to be found in their appointed place!" he cried. The fleet did, in fact, strike land in late January—a tiny island they called St. Paul's, and which seems to be the minute atoll now known as Pukapuka, in the French Tuamotu group. (Four centuries later, Pukapuka was the first island to be spotted by Thor Heyerdahl aboard the balsa raft *Kon-Tiki* after his long drift westward from Callao in Peru.) They stayed a week, replenishing their water butts and feasting on turtle eggs. They left in an optimistic mood; surely, they surmised, this island must be the first of a vast skein of atolls and lagoons stretching to the now close Moluccas. But it was not to be; the ships had barely traversed a third of their ocean. Soon the hunger pains, the racking thirst and the sense of unshakable misery began anew, and the dying began once more.

AFTER MEALS OF LEATHER—LAND!

More and more terrible the voyage steadily became. By March 4 the flagship had run out of food completely. Men were eating the oxhides and llama skins used to prevent the rigging from chafing (not too bad a diet—so long as the crew's scurvy-ridden teeth hung in). The smell of death, the knowledge that it was both inevitable and impending, gripped Magellan's sailors. And then dawned March 6, when a seaman called Navarro, the only man still fit enough to clamber up the ratlines, spied what everyone was waiting for—land.

A great cheer went up. Cannon were fired. Men fell to their knees in prayer. A squadron of tiny dugouts sped from shore to meet the Spaniards. Magellan had reached the islands he first called Las Islas de las Velas Latinas and later, after much of his cargo had been filched, Las Islas de Ladrones, the Islands of Thieves. He had made his landfall at what we now call Guam. It was March 6, 1521. Magellan had crossed the Pacific. A voyage the Captain-General had supposed might take three or four days had, in fact, occupied three and a half months.

The fleet stayed in Guam for only three days—to rest, make minor repairs and take on food (such as the "figs, more than a palm long," which must have been bananas) and fresh water. Then Magellan set off, still toward the Moluccas, standing down for the southwest and to the Philippines, islands of which all travelers to these parts had often heard, but which no European had ever seen. Though the Spice Islands, it must be recalled, were the armada's prescribed goal, the official mandate and ambition of Magellan was to discover, name and seize in the name of Spain the immense archipelago that lay north of them.

The only Briton on the expedition, Master Andrew of Bristol, died on this last, short passage. He was never to see the islands that, a novelist was later to write, were "as fair as Eden, with gold beaches, graceful palms, exotic fruits and soil so rich that if one snapped off a twig and stuck it into the ground it would start straightway to grow."

Magellan made his landfall on March 16 on an island at the southern end of the large Philippine island of Samar. Two days later, the first contact was made with Filipinos, though the name "Philippines" was not to be given to the place until 1543, when explorer Ruy

López de Villalobos named one after the Infante, later to become King Philip II, the Spanish monarch whose reign made the words "Spanish Armada" infamous. (The name "Philippines" caught on later to mean the entire island group.) The significant moment came two days later still, when the ships sailed down the Gulf of Leyte and the Surigao Strait, where, more than four centuries later in World War II, one of the world's last great naval battles was fought, and Adm. William F. Halsey reduced the Japanese Imperial Navy to vestigial strength.

Once through the strait, Magellan landed at the island that guarded its entrance, Limasawa. Eight inhabitants sailed out to the *Trinidad* in a small boat. On orders from the Captain-General, his Moluccan slave, Enrique, hailed them. In a moment that must have seemed frozen in time, it became clear that the men in the approaching boat understood the words of the Moluccan perfectly.

Their language was being spoken to them by a man on a huge ship that had come to them from the east. The linguistic globe—even if not necessarily the physical globe—had been circumnavigated. A man who had originated in these parts had traveled across Asia and around Africa to Europe as a slave, and had now returned home by the Americas and the Pacific. Enrique de Molucca may well have been, strictly speaking, the first of humankind to circumnavigate the world; he was never to be honored for so doing.

Nor, by the unhappy coincidence of ill-temper and wretched misfortune, was Ferdinand Magellan ever to be able to savor his own triumph. Just six weeks after landing he was dead, cut down on a Philippine island in a skirmish that is as unremembered as the place in which it happened is unsung—a flat and muddy little island called Mactan, where an airport has now been built to serve the city of Cebu.

The circumstances of the Captain-General's end, however, are riven into every Iberian schoolchild's learning, even today. Despite his crew's objections, Magellan insisted on exploring. He was pleased at the relative ease with which the people took to Christianity. (It is perhaps worth remembering that the Catholic faith, which Magellan and his priests brought to Samar and Cebu and northern Mindanao, flourishes there still today. The Philippines, in fact, is the only predominantly Christian country in Asia, and the influence of the church contributed significantly to the recent overthrow of President Ferdinand Marcos.)

But the successful sowing of the seeds of Christianity were to be Magellan's undoing. His horribly inglorious end came in late April. The precise circumstances were chronicled. Magellan had demonstrated what he felt was his superior status to the local raja of Cebu, and had made Christians of him and all his followers. But significantly, the rest of the Philippine nobility did not go along. Many local junior rajas objected, especially the minor raja of Mactan, a man named Cilapulapu and now known to all Filipinos simply as Lapu Lapu. He declared that he was not going to pay fealty to this Christian interloper, come what may. He cared little enough for the raja of Cebu, let along the Cebuano's newfound foreign friends.

The Spaniards soon got wind of this rebellious mood, and on April 27 Magellan and 60 of his men paddled across the narrow strait to Mactan, in an attempt to bring Lapu Lapu to heel. "You will feel the iron of our lances," Lapu Lapu was told by Magellan's interlocutor. "But we have fire-hardened spears and stakes of bamboo," replied a defiant chieftain. "Come across whenever you like."

THE LAST STAND ON MACTAN ISLAND

The waters at the northern end of Mactan are very shallow and degenerate into warm swamps. A selected 48 of the Spaniards, dressed in full armor, had to wade the last few hundred yards to do battle with the Mactan warriors. They fought for an hour, thigh-deep in the water. Then Magellan plunged his lance into the body of an attacker and was unable to withdraw it quickly enough. It was a fatal delay. Another islander slashed Magellan's leg with a scimitar.

He staggered. Scores of others crowded around him as he fell, and as Pigafetta was to write, "thus they killed our mirror, our light, our comfort and our true guide."

It is worth remembering that Fernao de Magalhaes was a native Portuguese—of whom it used to be said, because they were such energetic explorers, "they have a small country to live in, but all the world to die in." There is a monument near the spot where he fell, a tall white obelisk, guarded solicitously for the past 15 years by a man with the splendid name of Jesus Baring. There are two accounts of the event, one engraved on either side of the cross. Señor Baring derives much amusement from showing his occasional visitors—and there are very few, considering how globally important this spot should be—how markedly they differ.

The one on the monument's eastern side—the side that pedant geographers will recognize as marginally nearer to the Spanish Main—records the event as a European tragedy. "Here on 27th April 1521 the great Portuguese navigator Hernando de Magallanes, in the service of the King of Spain, was slain by native Filipinos. . . ." On the other side, by contrast, it is seen as an Oriental triumph—a heroic blow struck for Philippine nationalism. "Here on this spot the great chieftain Lapu Lapu repelled an attack by Ferdinand Magellan, killing him and sending his forces away. . . ." Baring points to the latter and roars with laughter. "This is the real story. This is the one we Filipinos like to hear!"

Lapu Lapu is thus the first, and to many Filipinos the greatest, of Filipino heroes. These days his memory is being revived, his exploits retold, his adventures made the stuff of comic strips, films and popular songs. Each April there is a full-scale reenactment of the Battle of Mactan on the beach, with an improbably handsome Cebuano film star playing the part of the seminaked hero and, when I was last there, the Philippine Air Force officer Mercurion Fernadez playing the role of the armor-clad Magellan. The two sides struggle gamely in the rising surf until that epic moment when Officer Fernandez contrives to collapse into the shallow sea and grunts his last. The assembled thousands then cheer. Such is Filipino pride in the raja of Mactan that there are firebrands—in Manila as well as in Cebu—who believe their country should shed its present name, a reminder that it is a colonial conquest, and be reborn as LapuLapu-Land.

Little more needs to be said of the tiny armada now, save to note what most popular historians choose to forget. The *Concepción* was scuttled; the flagship *Trinidad*, which tried to make for home via the Pacific once more, was blown north as far as Hakodate in Japan, captured by a Portuguese battle group and became a total loss in the Spice Islands, which had been its original goal. But

one of the ships, the doughty little *Victoria*—at 85 tons she was the second smallest of the original five—did make it back to Spain.

The *Victoria* scudded home under the charge of Juan Sebastian d'Elcano, previously the executive officer of the *Concepción*. She made Java. She made it round the top of Africa, through the waters where freak waves sometimes cause modern oil tankers to founder. She made the Cape Verde Islands, where the crew realized that despite meticulous log-keeping, they had lost an entire day from their calendar: the concept of crossing the international date line was unknown—and profoundly unimaginable—to them.

On September 6, 1523, the *Victoria* made the harbor of Sanlucar de Barra-meda, from where she had set off almost exactly three years before. Juan Sebastian d'Elcano had brought just 17 men back with him: 237 had started out. Circumnavigation, it happened, was a most costly business.

But well rewarded. D'Elcano was given an annual pension and a coat of arms as handsome as it was aromatic: a castle, three nutmegs, 12 cloves, two crossed cinnamon sticks, a pair of Malay kings bearing spice sticks, and above all, a globe circled by a ribbon emblazoned with the motto *Primus Circumdedisti me*. "Thou first circumnavigated me."

We encourage you to photocopy and use this page as a tool to assess how the articles in **Annual Editions** expand on the information in your textbook. By reflecting on the articles you will gain enhanced text information. You can also access this useful form on a product's book support Web site at **http://www.dushkin.com/ online/.**

NAME: _____   DATE: _____

TITLE AND NUMBER OF ARTICLE: _____

BRIEFLY STATE THE MAIN IDEA OF THIS ARTICLE: _____

LIST THREE IMPORTANT FACTS THAT THE AUTHOR USES TO SUPPORT THE MAIN IDEA:

WHAT INFORMATION OR IDEAS DISCUSSED IN THIS ARTICLE ARE ALSO DISCUSSED IN YOUR TEXTBOOK OR OTHER READINGS THAT YOU HAVE DONE? LIST THE TEXTBOOK CHAPTERS AND PAGE NUMBERS:

LIST ANY EXAMPLES OF BIAS OR FAULTY REASONING THAT YOU FOUND IN THE ARTICLE:

LIST ANY NEW TERMS/CONCEPTS THAT WERE DISCUSSED IN THE ARTICLE, AND WRITE A SHORT DEFINITION:

ANNUAL EDITIONS revisions depend on two major opinion sources: one is our Advisory Board, listed in the front of this volume, which works with us in scanning the thousands of articles published in the public press each year; the other is you—the person actually using the book. Please help us and the users of the next edition by completing the prepaid article rating form on this page and returning it to us. Thank you for your help!

ANNUAL EDITIONS: World History, Volume 1, Sixth Edition

ARTICLE RATING FORM

Here is an opportunity for you to have direct input into the next revision of this volume. We would like you to rate each of the 41 articles listed below, using the following scale:

1. Excellent: should definitely be retained
2. Above average: should probably be retained
3. Below average: should probably be deleted
4. Poor: should definitely be deleted

Your ratings will play a vital part in the next revision.
So please mail this prepaid form to us just as soon as you complete it.
Thanks for your help!

We Want Your Advice

RATING

ARTICLE

1. The Evolution of Life on the Earth
2. Mapping the Past
3. Japanese Roots
4. Rediscovering America
5. New Clues Show Where People Made the Great Leap to Agriculture
6. New Dig at a 9,000-Year-Old City Is Changing Views on Ancient Life
7. When No One Read, Who Started to Write?
8. A Tale of Two Cultures
9. City of the Gods
10. The Cradle of Cash
11. Indus Valley, Inc.
12. Saving Knossos
13. Five Ways to Conquer a City
14. Empires in the Dust
15. Out of Africa: The Superb Artwork of Ancient Nubia
16. Tiny Sacrifices at 22,000 Feet
17. In Classical Athens, a Market Trading in the Currency of Ideas
18. Old Sports
19. Cleopatra: What Kind of a Woman Was She, Anyway?

RATING

ARTICLE

20. Countdown to the Beginning of Time-Keeping
21. Ancient Jewel
22. Buddha in the Round
23. What Is the Koran?
24. State and Society under Islam
25. The Dome of the Rock: Jerusalem's Epicenter
26. The Reason God Tested Abraham
27. 2000 Years of Jesus
28. Live Longer, Healthier, & Better
29. Confucius
30. Cracking the Maya's Code: New Light on Dark History
31. The Islamic Legacy of Timbuktu
32. The Arab Roots of European Medicine
33. The Viking Longship
34. The Persistence of Byzantium
35. The Making of Magna Carta
36. Clocks: Revolution in Time
37. Images of Earth in the Year 1000
38. Columbus and the Labyrinth of History
39. How Many People Were Here before Columbus?
40. A Taste of Adventure
41. After Dire Straits, an Agonizing Haul across the Pacific

(Continued on next page)

NO POSTAGE
NECESSARY
IF MAILED
IN THE
UNITED STATES

BUSINESS REPLY MAIL
FIRST-CLASS MAIL PERMIT NO. 84 GUILFORD CT

POSTAGE WILL BE PAID BY ADDRESSEE

Dushkin/McGraw-Hill
Sluice Dock
Guilford, CT 06437-9989

Illdillddidillilddiddidldidildl

ABOUT YOU

Name _____   Date _____

Are you a teacher? ☐   A student? ☐

Your school's name _____

Department _____

Address _____ City _____ State ____ Zip ____

School telephone # _____

YOUR COMMENTS ARE IMPORTANT TO US !

Please fill in the following information:
For which course did you use this book?
_____

Did you use a text with this *ANNUAL EDITION*? ☐ yes ☐ no
What was the title of the text?
_____

What are your general reactions to the *Annual Editions* concept?
_____

Have you read any particular articles recently that you think should be included in the next edition?
_____

Are there any articles you feel should be replaced in the next edition? Why?
_____

Are there any World Wide Web sites you feel should be included in the next edition? Please annotate.
_____

May we contact you for editorial input? ☐ yes ☐ no
May we quote your comments? ☐ yes ☐ no